From the
MARGINS TO THE MAINSTREAM

From the MARGINS TO THE MAINSTREAM

Institutionalising Minorities in South Asia

Edited by
Hugo Gorringe, Roger Jeffery and
Suryakant Waghmore

 www.sagepublications.com
Los Angeles • London • New Delhi • Singapore • Washington DC

Copyright © Hugo Gorringe, Roger Jeffery and Suryakant Waghmore, 2016

All rights reserved. No part of this book may be reproduced or utilised in any form or by any means, electronic or mechanical, including photocopying, recording, or by any information storage or retrieval system, without permission in writing from the publisher.

First published in 2016 by

SAGE Publication India Pvt Ltd
B1/I-1 Mohan Cooperative Industrial Area
Mathura Road, New Delhi 110 044, India
www.sagepub.in

SAGE Publications Inc
2455 Teller Road
Thousand Oaks, California 91320, USA

SAGE Publications Ltd
1 Oliver's Yard, 55 City Road
London EC1Y 1SP, United Kingdom

SAGE Publications Asia-Pacific Pte Ltd
3 Church Street
#10-04 Samsung Hub
Singapore 049483

Published by Vivek Mehra for SAGE Publications India Pvt Ltd, typeset in 10/13pt Berkeley by Zaza Eunice, Hosur, India and printed at Chaman Enterprises, New Delhi.

Library of Congress Cataloging-in-Publication Data Available

Gorringe, Hugo, 1975- editor of compilation.
From the margins to the mainstream : institutionalising minorities in
  South Asia / edited by Hugo Gorringe, Roger Jeffery, and Suryakant
  Waghmore.
Thousand Oaks : SAGE Publications India Pvt Ltd, 2016. |
  Includes bibliographical references and index.
LCCN 2015038688| ISBN 9789351506232 (hardback : alk. paper) |
  ISBN 9789351506249 (ebook) | ISBN 9789351506225 (epub)
LCSH: Minorities—Political activity—South Asia. | South
  Asia—Ethnic relations—Political aspects. | South Asia—Politics and
  government.
LCC JQ98.A38 M543 2016 | DDC 323.154--dc23 LC record available at
http://lccn.loc.gov/2015038688

ISBN: 978-93-515-0623-2 (HB)

The SAGE Team: Rudra Nayaran, Guneet Kaur Gulati, and Ritu Chopra

This volume is dedicated to the memory of
Advocate Eknath Awad and all those who
continue to struggle for equality and justice.

Thank you for choosing a SAGE product!
If you have any comment, observation or feedback,
I would like to personally hear from you.
Please write to me at **contactceo@sagepub.in**

Vivek Mehra, Managing Director and CEO, SAGE India.

Bulk Sales

SAGE India offers special discounts
for purchase of books in bulk.
We also make available special imprints
and excerpts from our books on demand.

For orders and enquiries, write to us at

Marketing Department
SAGE Publications India Pvt Ltd
B1/I-1, Mohan Cooperative Industrial Area
Mathura Road, Post Bag 7
New Delhi 110044, India

E-mail us at **marketing@sagepub.in**

Get to know more about SAGE

Be invited to SAGE events, get on our mailing list.
Write today to **marketing@sagepub.in**

This book is also available as an e-book.

Contents

List of Tables	ix
List of Figures	xi
Foreword by James Manor	xiii
Preface	xvii
Acknowledgements	xix
Introduction: Institutionalising Marginal Actors in South Asia—Processes, Policies, Practices and Pitfalls	xxi
Hugo Gorringe, Roger Jeffery and Suryakant Waghmore	

CHAPTER 1
Identity, Citizenship and Hindu–Muslim Conflict in India 1
Abdul Shaban

CHAPTER 2
Political Power and Democratic Enablement: Devaraj Urs and Lower Caste Mobilisation in Karnataka 31
Valerian Rodrigues

CHAPTER 3
'We Are Still Junglis to Them': Institutionalising Marginalities amongst the Adivasis in Dooars 63
Supurna Banerjee

CHAPTER 4
Rise of Adivasi Janajati Movement and Nepal's Political Interregnum 87
Jeevan Raj Sharma

CHAPTER 5
Institutionalising Marginal Actors in Uttar Pradesh and
Tamil Nadu: Insights from Dalit Electoral Data 104
Roger Jeffery and Hugo Gorringe

CHAPTER 6
From the Cheris to Chennai: Dalit Politics in Tamil Nadu 131
Hugo Gorringe

CHAPTER 7
Challenging Normalised Exclusion: Humour and Hopeful
Rationality in Dalit Politics 153
Suryakant Waghmore

CHAPTER 8
Contentious Spaces: Guru Pujas as Public Performances and the
Production of Political Community 178
D. Karthikeyan

CHAPTER 9
Institutionalising Peace? Mohalla Committees in
Contemporary Mumbai 201
Qudsiya Contractor

CHAPTER 10
Institutionalising Informal Socialities: Dalit
Urban Poor in Dharavi 229
Martin Fuchs

CHAPTER 11
India and the Management of Ethnic Diversity: The Unfinished
Business of Accommodation 245
Wilfried Swenden

Glossary and Abbreviations 281
About the Editors and Contributors 285
Index 289

List of Tables

1.1	Ten communally most violent cities (in terms of number of riots) in India during 1900–1946 and 1947–2013	17
1.2	Number of Hindu–Muslim riots, persons injured and killed, 1900–1946	18
1.3	Number of Hindu–Muslim riots, persons injured and killed, 1947–2013	19
1.4	Fake encounter cases registered at the National Human Rights Commission (NHRC), New Delhi, between October 1993 and October 2009	23
1.5	Percentage share of Muslims in jail inmates of respective states/UTs, 2011	26
2.1	Social composition of Mysore Legislative Assembly 1952–1972: Members and percentage	41
2.2	Performance of social groups in Assembly elections, 1978 and 1983	42
2.3	Caste/community background of TDB presidents— 1960, 1968 and 1978	43
2.4	Representation of caste/communities with more than 1 per cent of total population in state services excluding Class IV as on 1918, 1959, 1972, 1984 and 1988	52
5.1	SC population proportions for Tamil Nadu and Uttar Pradesh, urban and rural, 2001 census	109
5.2	Lok Sabha and Legislative Assembly elections: Dalit voting proportions by party/alliance 2001 to 2011, Tamil Nadu	114
5.3	Lok Sabha and Vidhan Sabha elections: Dalit voting proportions by party/alliance 2002 to 2012, Uttar Pradesh	115
5.4	Gender differences in SC voting behaviours, Tamil Nadu, 2001–2011	117

5.5	Educational differences in SC voting behaviour, Tamil Nadu, 2001–2011	118
5.6	Gender differences in SC voting behaviours, UP, 2002–2012	120
5.7	Educational differences in SC voting behaviours, UP, 2002–2012	121
A5.1a	Voting (post-poll survey) Tamil Nadu, 2001, Legislative Assembly elections	125
A5.1b	Voting (post-poll survey) Tamil Nadu, 2004, Lok Sabha elections	125
A5.1c	Voting intentions (pre-poll survey) Tamil Nadu, 2006	126
11.1	The incidence and frequency of the President's Rule (1950–2012)	259

List of Figures

1.1	Trends in the number of reported communal riots in India, 1900–2013	12
1.2	Number of Hindu–Muslim riots and their spatial extent, 1900–1946	13
1.3	Number of Hindu–Muslim riots and their spatial extent, 1947–2013	14
1.4	Number of persons reported killed in Hindu–Muslim communal violence in India, 1900–1946	15
1.5	Number of persons reported to be killed in Hindu–Muslim communal violence in India, 1947–2013	16

Foreword

The contributors to this collection have set themselves an immensely difficult task. They seek to explain the struggles of marginalised groups in India—and in one case Nepal—for inclusion, voice and influence, by challenging long-standing injustices and the potent interests and processes that sustain them.

Not only must they make exotic material intelligible to non-specialists—a problem faced by all analysts of India, even those writing for Indian readers—but they must also tell the stories of disadvantaged groups who have been misrepresented or scarcely visible in most earlier accounts. In doing so, they also demonstrate that this most complex of societies is, and is 'becoming', even more complicated than it has appeared to be.

Previous commentaries on politics and society have acquainted us with the existence and the interplay of heterogeneities within heterogeneities. But the studies in this book show that the groups engaged in that interplay constantly shift their shapes and, then, encounter ironic complications. Groups coalesce, assert themselves and may acquire some influence. But they then find that the reactions of adversaries—and even some of their successes—create new impediments and sometimes trigger disintegration and disempowerment. These complexities are hard to fathom, but if we are to understand the changing South Asia, we must comprehend them. The contributors to this collection carry us a long way towards that goal.

Their task is made even more daunting by their admirable decisions to take two further steps. First, they have embraced ambiguity. They do not merely offer encouraging accounts of society ridding itself of ancient inequities and marching towards a more just future. The authors show that some gains have been made, but they also see that the hard evidence which they have taken great pains to collect belies such rosy conclusions. Nor, on the other hand, do they confine themselves to litanies of outrages suffered by marginalised groups. Some recent studies do just that—and they have their place since there is no shortage of indignities to report. But to focus only on them is to capture only some of India's intricacies. Instead, these analyses assess struggles for inclusion and decency which only partly succeed—and which, when they make some headway, often lead to paradoxical outcomes, fresh dilemmas and disappointments. Marginalised groups that achieve a degree of political inclusion often discover that it amounts to 'adverse incorporation' which is disempowering because it requires them to moderate or abandon key demands. They may achieve a modicum of acceptance and even unprecedented accommodations with more powerful groups. These are often important, but they may also leave the marginalised—for the moment—co-opted, somewhat enfeebled and even demobilised. But only for the moment. Their struggles continue, so the insights that we gain from this volume will serve us well as future events unfold.

The second decision that has made the contributors' task more onerous was unavoidable. They take us beyond and, crucially, 'beneath' the formalities of politics in diverse parts of the subcontinent. Developing an understanding of the distinctive perceptions and modes of action at the margins is a tall order. So is explaining this to readers who have mainly viewed social processes through the eyes of powerful groups, and political processes from all-too-formalised accounts of the democratic process.

The contributors to this volume proceed from the bottom up and from the margins. They begin by acquainting us with unfamiliar things: the views and vulnerabilities of very specific (and diverse) groups long afflicted by unjust hierarchies, hegemonic norms and time honoured rules of a political game which has served them ill but which also provides them with some useful openings. They then explain the efforts of disadvantaged groups, against great odds, to achieve and to sustain collective strength in order to challenge the old injustices. These groups must 'generate local power' by enhancing the capabilities of the marginalised, not least by strengthening their political capacity—that is, their political awareness, their confidence as political actors, their political skills and their connections with others who share their vulnerabilities and with allies amongst the non-poor.

As if that were not enough, the authors then take us through the efforts of these groups to translate those new capabilities into political influence at higher levels—to move, through contestation, from mere recognition and representation to 'agency' and influence in arenas away from the margins and closer to centres of power. Explaining these efforts to mount challenges and to induce change—along with their sometimes ironic consequences as old inequities are reproduced in new forms—requires subtle explanations of complex social and political processes in varied arenas. This is no easy task, but readers will find rich rewards from this superb collection.

James Manor
Emeka Anyaoku Professor Emeritus of Commonwealth Studies
School of Advanced Study
University of London

Preface

Crossing a bridge over the Cooum in Chennai in 2012, one could see the diverse trajectories of South Asian development writ large. Tucked in under the bridge and pressed up against the water's edge was a settlement of mud and coconut matting houses. The compact dwellings were jammed in against each other, and many sought extra protection from the elements by recycling old vinyl banners to reinforce the roofs. The nearly stagnant water of the river was strewn with litter and, together with the cramped conditions, created the ideal conditions for infestations of mosquitoes. Looming over this precarious slum was a concrete edifice sporting a huge banner advertising 'LIC [Life Insurance Corporation of India] Housing Finance Ltd'. The juxtaposition of vulnerable and impoverished people squatting on a river-bank and evidence of a simultaneous housing boom, speaks to the uneven nature of India's development and the continued exclusion and marginalisation of certain groups from its rewards.

It was these themes and complex processes that a UK–India Education and Research Initiative (UKIERI)-funded thematic partnership between the Tata Institute of Social Sciences (TISS) and The University of Edinburgh sought to address. Over two years, the grant enabled an exchange of staff, students and ideas between the two institutions. It coincided with an Economic and Social Research Council (ESRC)-funded project on Dalit politics and the institutionalisation of Dalit parties on which two of the editors were engaged. Both projects were concerned to understand the processes by which the marginalised are incorporated—often on adverse terms—into mainstream institutions, or continue to be frozen out of them. The UKIERI project led by Waghmore and Gorringe enabled us to expand our horizons beyond the Dalit population to include an analysis of Muslims, OBCs and Adivasis.

The chapters in this volume were first presented as papers in Edinburgh in 2013, at a small workshop entitled 'Institutionalising Marginal Actors'.

Papers delivered by Bipin Jojo, Antje Linkenbach, James Manor, Carole Spary and Andrew Wyatt contributed to discussions and added insights even though they could not be included here. Over two days, we discussed the various ways in which marginal groups—Dalits, Muslims, Tribals, women, linguistic minorities and others—seek to get their concerns onto the sociopolitical agenda. Affirmative action programmes have been in existence in South Asia since the early part of the twentieth century and yet enduring structures of poverty, difference and identity continue to affect the life chances of marginal actors. Rather than reading sociopolitical inclusion off from numbers of representatives, cash flows or resources, therefore, the workshop sought more nuanced and detailed analyses of the processes of institutionalisation—whether they were political, social or economic. The papers presented at the Edinburgh workshop have been revised in light of these debates and subsequent comments from reviewers and they constitute the chapters presented in this volume.

Acknowledgements

All volumes are collective enterprises in some sense, edited collections more than most. This book would not have been possible without the help, inspiration and hard work of many people. The editors particularly wish to thank all the participants of the 'Institutionalising Marginal Actors' workshop that took place at The University of Edinburgh in September 2013. Many had travelled long distances to be there and all prepared insightful papers and offered valuable comments on the papers. Contributors to this volume are owed extra thanks for bearing with us, responding to comments and queries and working hard to fit papers into the overarching themes. We are especially grateful to Professor James Manor, who delivered the keynote speech and offered a constructive dissection of the key concepts we were working with as well as penning the Foreword to this volume. We are indebted to the British Council's UKIERI grant (UKUTP201100138) which facilitated greater cooperation between colleagues in TISS and The University of Edinburgh and which funded the event. Aspects of the collaboration and research were also supported by the ESRC (Grant RES-062-23-3348) project on which Gorringe and Jeffery were working, and we'd like to acknowledge their assistance. A special mention must go to Supurna Banerjee who not only presented a paper at the conference, but did many of the painstaking tasks required to organise such an event. We are grateful to Rudra Narayan Sharma at SAGE for encouraging this project and urging us towards completion and to the anonymous reviewer and the editorial team at SAGE for all their work on the manuscript. Needless to say, the volume would not have been possible without invaluable contributions from all of the above, but any remaining errors remain our own.

Introduction: Institutionalising Marginal Actors in South Asia—Processes, Policies, Practices and Pitfalls

Hugo Gorringe, Roger Jeffery and Suryakant Waghmore

The premise of democratic politics is that all citizens are equal and have equal rights to speak up on national politics. This substantive, rather than procedural, definition of democracy, however, is observed far more in the breach than in practice. 'Social exclusions of many kinds' as Bhattacharyya, Sarkar and Kar (2010: 2) put it, 'remain the most solid challenges to Indian democracy and development'. These authors offer rich insights into the persistence of forms of exclusion and marginalisation in India and numerous studies testify to the enduring nature of social inequalities (Gorringe et al. 2009). It is also important to distinguish different kinds of exclusion and marginalisation. Some forms of marginalisation result from geographical location, as rural residents or people living in slums within urban areas may be ignored in policy-making. But marginalisation of some regions within states can become central to identity-making processes, leading (for example) to mobilisations to establish new states or for secession. Cross-cutting these patterns are forms of exclusion that derive from gender, age, disability or sexuality, as well as marginalisation derived from the membership of some castes or religious minority groups. In a wider South Asian context, it is worth remembering that people who may regard themselves as the members of majority religious groups can nonetheless be excluded or marginalised, as with Shias and Ahmediyyas in Pakistan and Bangladesh. All of these elements can play roles in people's exclusion from the good things of life, or capabilities and well-being (Sen 1999).

Economic exclusion—from worthwhile jobs or entrepreneurial opportunities—and social exclusion—from education, health care and other social welfare benefits, for example—may go alongside or be compounded by exclusion from political decision-making processes. There are numerous studies highlighting the nature and scale of marginality and exclusion, but what we focus upon in this volume is the question of what happens when formerly excluded groups are integrated into sociopolitical processes. Our main concern is to chart the processes by which people gain access to institutions—whether these are informal social institutions or the more formal political ones—and unpack the consequences of these processes both for the groups in question and for the institutions that they enter.

Accounts of enduring social inequalities and patterns of exclusion highlight the fact that, as Manor (2004: 6) puts it: 'Democratisation alone is insufficient. Poor people must be more fully included in newly democratised systems.' The intersections of poverty and identity make the democratic politics of 'inclusion' a complex and problematic exercise in the Indian context. The results of the 2014 Lok Sabha elections give these concerns added relevance: the BJP, the party with a track record of working to exclude many marginalised groups (Muslims and Christians in particular) won a parliamentary majority, apparently having gained the support of considerable numbers of Dalits and Other Backward Classes (OBCs; FP Politics 2014). In this volume, therefore, we turn our gaze towards the processes and policies through which hitherto excluded groups and actors are granted—or claim—access to sociopolitical institutions. In doing so, we raise questions about whether and how marginalised populations are accommodated and critically scrutinise the extent and impact of such institutionalisation.

The literature on different means of overcoming marginalisation suggests additional problems. As Gamson reminds us, entry into social institutions is never straightforward. There is no ineluctable link between the presence of marginal actors in institutions and the representation of their interests or an improvement to their material conditions. Speaking of collective action on behalf of socially excluded groups, Gamson notes that:

> Success is an elusive idea. What of the group whose leaders are honoured or rewarded while their supposed beneficiaries linger in the same

cheerless state as before? Is such a group more or less successful than another challenger whose leaders are vilified and imprisoned even as their programme is eagerly implemented by their oppressor? Is a group a failure if it collapses with no legacy save the inspiration to a generation that will soon take up the same cause with more tangible results? And what do we conclude about a group that accomplishes exactly what it set out to achieve and then finds its victory empty of real meaning for its presumed beneficiaries? (Gamson 1990: 28)

Gamson here highlights the complexity of processes of institutionalisation and injects a note of caution into accounts that celebrate the ascension of marginal actors to political institutions as a 'seismic shift' (Lakha and Taneja 2009) or a 'silent revolution' (Jaffrelot 2003). Gaining political recognition and acceptance is important and remains a central goal of disenfranchised groups (Dryzek et al. 2003). To view this as an end in itself rather than a step in a longer process, however, would be to imbue processes of political representation with more significance than they possess. The chapters in this volume, by contrast, set out to interrogate the processes by which marginal actors gain access to institutions and the policies designed to counter exclusion. The emphasis is on deepening our understanding of the complex, contested and sometimes contradictory paths towards a more egalitarian polity, and the impact of such inclusion for the marginalised populations and the wider society.

We begin with a discussion of formal political institutions. In representative democracy, after all, whether one is represented or not serves as a barometer of inclusion and exclusion. How marginalised actors gain access to formal politics, whether representatives reflect the views of their constituents, and what impact participation in democratic institutions have are all vitally important questions. Across South Asia, but particularly in India, there has been a slow accretion of formal political institutions, most obviously through the extension of *panchayati raj* or village and district councils. In each of these arenas—village or urban ward, town or district council, State and National Assemblies—reservations have been used, supposedly to enhance the opportunities for marginalised groups (specifically, women and members of specific castes and tribes, as defined in the Indian Constitution). Crucially, however, we do not confine our analysis to formal politics in these arenas but extend our analysis to encompass social institutions and relations as well.

We supplement some of the political science approaches (Chandra 2004; Jaffrelot 2003; Varshney 2000) in recognising that political institutions are constituted by social relations and need to be understood in the context of wider social relations and structures. Democratisation, we contend, cannot be measured simply through the numbers of voters and elected representatives—important as those undoubtedly are, in any state where personal networks and extended reciprocities of favours are central to political processes, as they are throughout South Asia. Rather, democratisation is a process that alters social relationships and enables marginalised actors to gain the capacity to raise their voices and be heard both in formal institutions and in civil society more generally. Democratisation, thus, affects not just marginalised but dominant groups too. Chapters in this volume see this as fundamental and analyse how the institutionalisation of the excluded can prompt a backlash from dominant groups. This can take the form of repression, co-option or negotiation each of which may shape the impact of institutionalisation. In what follows we chart some of the contours of debates in this field.

Political Institutionalisation

All too often, the expansion of systems of representation to previously excluded groups is seen as addressing the issues of marginalisation. Indeed, scholars like Tarrow (1998) and Jenkins and Klandermans (1995) regard political participation as the aim of protest groups. From this perspective, the process of 'institutionalisation'—whereby marginal groups 'develop internal organisation, become more moderate, adopt a more institutional repertoire of action and integrate into the system of interest representation' (Della Porta and Diani 1999: 148)—is critically important. Coy and Hedeen (2005: 417) highlight the benefits that can accrue from institutionalisation, including material gains, access to influential allies and wider legitimacy. Social or political recognition, however, is a completely inadequate measure of the extent to which marginal actors are actually integrated into processes and institutions of interest and resource mediation.

For instance, in Uttar Pradesh, the Bahujan Samaj Party (BSP; Majority People's Party), a Dalit-led political party, achieved an absolute majority in Assembly elections of 2007, after serving a series of terms in coalition governments in the state. Early analyses of the impact of the BSP at the level of the state government were mixed. Reviewing the party's achievements at the village level, for instance, Pai (2000, 2001) took a more positive view than Jeffery, Jeffrey and Jeffery (2001), demonstrating the complexities involved in evaluating social change. Similarly, some recent research shows how Dalits have been able to benefit from the post-liberalisation economy (Kapur et al. 2010), while other studies point to ways in which casteism has been institutionalised (Thorat and Newman 2010). Given the absence of clear data that institutionalisation serves to benefit the oppressed, the continuance of poverty, discrimination and caste-based violence help explain why many marginal groups have lost faith in the institutions of interest mediation (Chandhoke 2005). Despite these widespread views, however, some data suggests that marginalised groups are more likely to vote than others (Yadav 2001) (though see Jeffery and Gorringe in this volume for more cautious views). Banerjee also argues forcefully for introducing affective elements into understanding how and why people in South Asia vote (Banerjee 2008, 2011). Poor and marginalised people may vote, then, and even vote for parties that offer to represent their interests, and even further, see those parties come to a share of power, without this leading to their integration into what are regarded as mainstream political processes.

Institutionalisation also has costs; movements claiming to represent the marginalised may become 'bureaucratized and technique centred' and their tactics, demands and critiques may be diluted (Coy and Hedeen 2005: 407). In the Indian context, Baviskar (2010) notes how institutionalisation into formal politics has occurred alongside a rise in non-governmental organisations (NGOs) addressing similar goals. The ability to raise financial support from donors rather than members, she notes, has significant implications for decision-making processes and people's participation. Institutionalisation thus, as Piven and Cloward (1971) show, may result in demobilisation or co-optation. As Mosse (2007: 27) puts it: 'Empowerment depends upon political representation, but such a political capacity is gained only at the cost of conceding power to a political system.' Accommodation into a polity driven by majoritarian politics considerably limits the agenda-setting power and the interests of marginal groups. The Indian case is intriguing here, as there are competitive forms of inclusion and institutionalisation, derived by pressures of competing ideologies and deepening democracy. One dominant form is the Congress party, where the marginalised are included but secure limited economic benefits and forfeit their political autonomy. Another is the BJP, where the marginalised groups are accommodated within an identity-based platform that generates negative externalities for other minorities—particularly Muslims and Christians. The competitive inclusive politics and ideology of both Congress and BJP are not, however, at loggerheads with neo-liberalism: they rather create conditions for its consolidation. Away from the two dominant political parties, the Kerala development model has been touted as possibly the best social development model in India, but it too has left Dalits landless and illiterate (Rammohan 2008). The processes and politics of inclusion and institutionalisation, thus, accommodate some groups while perpetuating the exclusion of others. Understanding the process by which radical or marginalised actors are institutionalised is, therefore, vitally important in understanding processes of democratisation and combating social exclusion (Kohli 2001; Tilly 1998).

The significance attached to marginalised people entering the corridors of power arises in large part because of the perceived 'exclusivity of the political field' (Bourdieu 1984). Bourdieu argues that one's position in the field of class relations endows one with enhanced or diminished political competence. A faint echo of this position may be found in Chatterjee's (2004) distinction between civil society—the preserve of the middle class—and political society dominated by subalterns. In the context of British politics, Ray et al. (2003) use network analysis to demonstrate how certain people are integrated into the political field, while others are relegated to the periphery. They argue that there are 'social similarities between members in the cores which allow organisations to share assumptions and values about operating, which in turn produce tendencies towards the creation of a more uniform political field' (Ray et al. 2003: 55). Representatives of marginal groups who enter formal institutions, thus, potentially enter into social networks and practices that dilute their radicalism and channel it in ways that reinforce the existing political system rather than reforming it. The expansion of the franchise to this extent, may result in a more democratic state at the expense of a 'less democratic and vital society' (Dryzek et al. 2003: 106). It was in this sense that Kanshiram (1982) described the Dalit politicians serving the interests of the dominant castes and parties as *chamchas* (stooges). Rather than representing the core concerns of the marginalised, in other words, they were seen as feathering their own nests by toeing the party line. Put another way, processes of political, social and economic inclusion are discontinuous, uneven, lumpy and do not necessarily move at similar speeds or in similar ways.

Adverse Incorporation

While Kanshiram's castigation of political stooges is popular and repeated in some form or the other by activists across India, we argue that political institutionalisation needs to be placed within a wider context. It is important to understand the terms on which marginal actors are able to engage with formal politics. Here, we take our cue from Hickey and du Toit's work on 'adverse incorporation', a term that they:

> explicitly used to 'clear away' some of the problems associated with the term social exclusion—particularly the liberal assertion that 'inclusion' is necessarily a good thing—and to make space for a more explicit focus on power relations, history, social dynamics, and political economy. (Hickey and du Toit 2013: 135).

In a similar vein, rather than assuming that integration into formal institutions is unproblematic or always beneficial, we interrogate the terms on which people or groups are included. Small parties, for instance, may be tied to larger ones due to the resource flows that are increasingly required to fight electoral contests (Suri 2013). More commonly, politicians selected by large parties to contest reserved seats are constrained by the party that put them in power. Challenger groups are also, invariably, constrained by the party system in which they operate (Wyatt 2009). Inclusion, thus, may come at the price of having to abide by the established rules of the political game (Mosse 2007).

The terms on which groups are integrated into institutional arrangements are crucial. Firstly, challenger groups may be incorporated into the peripheries of an institution in ways that serve to reinforce and solidify marginality. The creation of Ministers for Women or Departments for Dalits, thus, relegate aspirant citizens to special categories of people who are marked by their difference as much as their inclusion (Puwar 2004). The perception that certain groups are receiving preferential treatment, furthermore, can generate a backlash by dominant groups which resent any reallocation or distribution of resources and feel threatened by them (Fraser 2003). Heyer and Gopal Jayal (2009), thus, observe that universal schemes targeted at the general population—such as the National Rural Employment Guarantee Act (NREGA)—may be more effective at tackling poverty than more targeted programmes which attract greater opposition.

Universal policies that attempt to move beyond social categories, however, are not immune from the power of societal relations, as seen in well-connected well-to-do families possessing Below Poverty Line (BPL) cards (Ram et al. 2009), and the persistent exclusion of children from low castes, Adivasis and minorities from primary schooling (Human Rights Watch 2014). Finally, marginal groups may be caught in a discursive trap that renders them lesser citizens by virtue of how they are discussed and described in both political and popular parlance.

The concept of adverse incorporation is, thus, useful in shifting our gaze beyond formal political institutions. Analysts such as Phillips (2013), for example, have used the concept to understand the incorporation of workers into markets in ways that are disadvantageous to the labourers. Politics, this reminds us, is merely one social institution amongst others and operates within a wider sociopolitical context. Understanding the incorporation of marginal actors, therefore, requires us to look beyond formal politics. In this volume, chapters examine the incorporation of marginal actors into mohalla committees, social space and public discourses amongst other social institutions. In each case, the focus is on capturing the forms that such inclusion takes and the impact this has. In line with the notion of adverse incorporation, however, analysis also focuses on the terms on which the excluded gain access to, and are able to participate in, particular social institutions.

Empowerment from Above or Below?

The concept of adverse incorporation also raises questions about the processes of institutionalisation. By definition, it implies that elites act to accommodate challenger groups in ways that neuter their impact and mould them into particular ways of doing things. It is akin, in this sense, to the concept of co-option. In analysing institutionalisation, thus, we need to pay due heed both to the processes by which the marginalised enter social institutions and the impact that this has upon them. In her study of the BSP in Uttar Pradesh, for example, Pai (2002) distinguishes between empowerment from above and from below. The former refers to the attempt by political parties to uplift the downtrodden. While such efforts are laudable and can be transformative, those being empowered are often passive players in the process and may not, therefore, reap the full rewards (Jeffrey et al. 2008).

It is also worth remembering that the distinctions between top-down and bottom-up are sometimes drawn too sharply: a party like the BSP is a mix of both, with activism at the grass-roots partial and uneven, leaving many of its supporters waiting passively for action 'from above' before they make any move. Empowerment from below, referring to the mobilisation and assertion of marginal actors which endows them with a sense of their own power to effect social change, is an aspiration rarely achieved in practice. Chatterjee (1997) notes how even the Indian independence struggle—widely portrayed as a mass movement of the colonised—resulted in a 'passive revolution' rather than the wholesale transformation of social structures.

Manor (2004) discusses a range of policies designed to increase local participation and offer citizens a sense of empowerment and their pros and cons. While active states can introduce significant reforms in this area, he argues that empowerment will be most effective and durable where there is agency and autonomous engagement on the part of previously excluded groups. Meaningful inclusion, from this perspective, must mean more than only an entry into pre-existing institutions or participation in particular social networks or relationships. At root, it must entail an increase in the political capacity of marginalised actors. Political capacity, in Manor's (2013: 107) terms, 'implies political awareness, confidence, skills and connections—to be able to operate effectively enough in the public sphere to qualify as a citizen rather than a mere resident or subject'. In exploring forms of institutionalisation, in other words, our analysis must assess the extent to which the inclusion of previously excluded actors has served to enhance their capacity for public action.

This is not to say that after participation, decision-making will inevitably lead to decisions that favour marginalised groups. The process may be a long one, involving what seem to be two steps backwards for every one step taken forward (Ray and Katzenstein 2005). Dalits' incursions into public space, for example, have seen them challenge their residential segregation, but also face a violent backlash from intermediate castes (Pandian 2000). Elsewhere, Wilkinson (2004) points to the widespread use of violence to control or influence elections. Participation, thus, can bear a heavy price. Even policies aimed at reallocating resources such as reservations (affirmative action), can have unintended consequences, as when individual Dalit castes mobilise against each other for a greater share of resources (Chinna Rao 2009). Similarly, Mathews (2003) notes how the reservation of Panchayat seats for Scheduled Tribes (STs) has resulted in violence against them in several places. Elsewhere, in his analysis of the Sachar Committee Report, Wilkinson (2007) notes how Muslims, Scheduled Castes (SCs) and STs are less likely to graduate from college than others once all other variables are controlled for. Access to institutions of higher learning, here, could result in increased spending with little reward. As Mendelsohn and Vicziany (1998: 270) observe in the context of Dalits, it would be scant comfort for the marginalised if social liberation was 'attended by perpetual poverty'. If mobilisation becomes merely a means to political ends, then the aspirations and ambitions of Dalit citizens will continue to be frustrated and the potential for violence will remain. Institutionalisation without transformation, in other words, is a game not worth the candle; but knowing when that transformation will come is hard to predict or to notice when it begins to arrive.

Much of the research on forms of institutionalisation offers a pessimistic reading of its effects. Dryzek et al (2003: 102), for example, argue that the integration of challenger groups 'may adversely affect the quality of democracy because it narrows the available range of positions capable of expression and response in the polity as a whole, thus restricting democracy's scope'. The implication here is that institutionalisation diminishes the capacity of marginal actors to challenge and question power-holders because they too now have a stake in the system. Incorporation of this nature is clearly a possibility and a threat to a vibrant civil society, but it is not, as Manor (2004, 2013) reminds us, an inevitability. The demands and aspirations of activists may not be the best measure of sociopolitical institutions. Political inclusion also has the capacity to enhance people's confidence and connections in ways that make it more likely that they will engage in forms of individual or collective action and perceive local democratic processes as ones that they can participate in and influence.

Amartya Sen's work on policies designed to address chronic hunger encapsulates the issues addressed in this volume. As he notes:

> Many of the underdogs of society face not only traditional problems that have kept them back, but also new adversities arising from public policies that are meant to help the underprivileged but end up doing something rather different.
>
> Given our democratic system, nothing is as important as a clearer understanding of the causes of deprivation and the exact effects of alleged policy remedies that can be used. (Sen 2001)

Rather than accepting the critiques of disillusioned idealists at face value, therefore, we need to offer a detailed analysis of the complex ways in which different forms of institutionalisation affect organisations, leaders and ordinary people. The chapters in this volume seek to chart the complex and contested processes by which the excluded challenge their marginalisation and seek entry into the institutions from which they have been barred. In so doing, they offer rich cases studies and insights that mean we are better placed both to understand and help shape forms of democratisation that are more inclusive and, thereby, more just and legitimate.

Chapters in this Volume

The book begins with Abdul Shaban's discussion of policies of accommodation and inclusion as applied to Muslims in India. The chapter draws on a range of data to highlight the continued marginalisation of India's Muslims and to consider why this is the case. It admirably illustrates the paradoxical nature of inclusion, in demonstrating the growing divide between a wealthy Muslim elite and the continued poverty of the community as a whole. The multiple registers of institutionalisation are also seen here in the way that recent government commissions have served to shift the discursive arena but have yet to significantly alter ground realities. Chapter 2 turns to an analysis of the most important accommodative strategy of the Indian state: the system of reservations. Valerian Rodrigues offers a detailed analysis of Devraj Urs' experiment in extending reservations to the OBC, an experiment that may be seen as a precursor to the subsequent rolling out of such reservations across the country. The early introduction of such reservations in Karnataka enables Rodrigues to analyse the debates surrounding their implementation and the effects of this political strategy in a case study that has much wider relevance.

Chapter 3, by Supurna Banerjee, offers a lucid account of an Adivasi movement that succeeds in getting its demands onto the agenda. The potential perils of political institutionalisation are evident here, though, as movement leaders are seen to succumb to the logic of co-optation. Rather than leaving this as yet another story of movement collapse, however, Banerjee points to the continuing ramifications of the mobilisation and the extra-political impacts that endure beyond the phase of politicisation.

In Chapter 4, Jeevan Raj Sharma shifts the focus of the analysis beyond the nation-state in pointing to the increasing competition for global recognition and acceptance amongst movements for the marginalised. In so doing, his analysis of the Janajati movement in Nepal foregrounds the crucial role played by international organisations and funding agencies. Sharma's nuanced account offers insights into how groups may use external recognition to enhance their claims at the national level on the one hand, while questioning the way in which funding may limit activities and shape rhetoric on the ground. Institutionalisation, Sharma's chapter clearly demonstrates, can no longer be assumed to be confined to the state or nation but is shaped by global flows of knowledge, money and authority.

While Sharma shifts our gaze to the global level, Roger Jeffery and Hugo Gorringe's chapter emphasises the continued importance of comparative analysis in understanding processes of social change. Their chapter on Dalit electoral politics in Uttar Pradesh and Tamil Nadu points towards how different sociopolitical systems can influence the outcomes of similar political movements. Where a Dalit party has been able to gain power in the multi-party contests of Uttar Pradesh, for example, they have struggled to gain a similar foothold in the bipolar political contests in Tamil Nadu. The chapter also raises questions about the data on which much electoral analysis is based, pointing to the limits of mass surveys in understanding complex processes. Hugo Gorringe brings out some of the complexities obscured by the survey data in his chapter on Dalit politics in Tamil Nadu. Returning to the state 12 years after the Viduthalai Chiruthaigal Katchi entered party politics, he charts the various ways in which the party has been institutionalised and considers the impact of Dalit political inclusion in this case.

Shifting its focus away from formal politics, Suryakant Waghmore's chapter analyses the significance of social norms and practices that signal and perform inclusion or exclusion. Waghmore's chapter focuses on humour as a form of social communication and notes how some forms of humour are institutionalised, while others are deployed to pose a challenge to hegemonic forces. The chapter presents upper-caste humour that seeks to humiliate and discredit those beneath them in the caste hierarchy, and counter-poses it to Dalit use of humour that seeks to render power visible and challenge their continued marginalisation. These themes are also central to D. Karthikeyan's richly textured and ethnographic account of contestations over public space in Tamil Nadu. His chapter takes the annual processions which mark the birth anniversaries of community leaders as a point of departure to foreground questions of exclusion in the public sphere. While the dominant caste leader's Guru Puja receives state recognition, that of the Dalit icon continues to be marginalised. In charting the interplay between dominant Thevars and assertive Pallars here, Karthikeyan offers rich insights into processes of caste change and the uneven expansion of the public sphere.

Qudsiya Contractor similarly emphasises the importance of place and space in understanding processes of institutionalisation. Her chapter focuses on local engagement in the form of mohalla (locality) committees instituted after the communal riots in Mumbai, as an associational engagement between the state, NGOs and the city's 'Muslim public'. These committees have been understood as sites of inclusion in the larger interest of maintaining peace and communal harmony, but Contractor's fine-grained ethnographic data offers a more nuanced analysis of this mode of accommodation. In the final empirical chapter, Martin Fuchs addresses the ambivalence of processes of institutionalisation with respect to the overlapping concerns of Dalits and slum dwellers. In this important contribution, he points towards the fragile and provisional nature of processes of institutionalisation and some of the unintended consequences that they can have. He shows that research on institutionalisation needs to be sensitive towards the distinction between processes generated from within and those from without, which indicates the complexity of multiple, often overlapping, processes of inclusion and exclusion.

Finally, in the concluding chapter, Wilfried Swenden offers a theoretically informed account of India's attempts to accommodate and institutionalise diversity since independence. Central to this chapter is the differentiation between integration and accommodation. The key argument is that the Indian state has tended to deploy 'accommodative strategies' more often than 'control' or 'assimilative' strategies. Crucially, 'the shift towards accommodation has provided a better fit for the highly segmented and stratified nature of Indian society than the integrative blueprint at Independence'. The chapter notes how the accommodative emphasis serves to constrain political parties and temper their actions in important ways. Equally, however, Swenden notes how accommodation may itself be limited and end up accommodating marginalised groups into the peripheries of Indian politics. He, therefore, offers thoughts on future directions in institutionalising marginal actors.

In sum, the volume brings together a range of theoretically and empirically informed chapters that—taken together—enhance and advance our understanding of the complex, often contested and contradictory processes by which marginalised or excluded groups are brought into the mainstream. The book, thus, offers nuanced and detailed analyses of the processes of institutionalisation—whether they be political, social or economic—and contextualized analyses of the processes and practices through which marginal actors are excluded, seek to challenge their exclusion, and/or are accommodated into central institutions. Throughout, the authors avoid the simplistic equation of political recognition with 'success' and ask what institutionalisation means and what impact it has for marginalised groups. In so doing, the contributions presented here problematise standard social movement and political science writings on institutionalisation which focus on the state and on formal politics, and ask what we mean by institutionalisation. The chapters also chart processes of inclusion and exclusion that occur in social as well as political institutions. They pose questions such as: 'institutionalisation into what and for whom'? In short, this volume views institutionalisation as a contested *process* rather than a simple transition. In so doing, it will enrich the literature on marginal populations and their engagement with wider sociopolitical institutions. Questions of representation and accommodation lie at the heart of democratic societies. In focusing upon these questions, we hope to contribute to the understanding of and the debates around how democratic societies manage social exclusion and seek to create more democratic and fairer institutions.

References

Banerjee, M. 2008. 'Democracy, Sacred and Everyday: An Ethnographic Case from India', in Julia Paley (ed.), *Democracy: Anthropological Approaches* (pp. 63–96). Santa Fe: School for Advanced Research Press.

———. 2011. 'Elections as Communitas', *Social Research* 78(1): 75–98.

Baviskar, A. 2010. 'Social Movements in India', in N. Gopal Jayal and P. Bhanu Mehta (eds), *The Oxford Companion to Politics in India* (pp. 381–390). New Delhi: Oxford University Press.

Bhattacharyya, H., Sarkar, P. and Kar, A. 2010. 'Introduction: The Politics of Social Exclusion in India', in H. Bhattacharyya, P. Sarkar and A. Kar (eds), *The Politics of Social Exclusion in India* (pp. 1–14). Abingdon: Routledge.

Bourdieu, P. 1984. *Distinction*. London: Routledge.

Chandhoke, N. 2005. 'Revisiting the Crisis of Representation Thesis: The Indian Context', *Democratization* 12(3): 308–330.

Chandra, K. 2004. *Why Ethnic Parties Succeed: Patronage and Ethnic Head Counts in India*. Cambridge: Cambridge University Press.
Chatterjee, P. 1997. *A Possible India*. New Delhi: Oxford University Press.
———. 2004. *The Politics of the Governed*. New York: Columbia University Press.
Chinna Rao, Y. (ed.). 2009. *Dividing Dalits: Anthology on Sub-Categorisation of Scheduled Castes*. Jaipur: Rawat Publications.
Coy, P. and Hedeen, T. 2005. 'A Stage Model of SM Co-optation', *The Sociological Quarterly* 46(4): 405–435.
Della Porta, D. and Diani, M. 1999. *Social Movements*. Oxford: Blackwell.
Dryzek, J., Downes, D., Hunold, C., Schlosberg, D. and Hernes, H. 2003. *Green States and Social Movements: Environmentalism in the United States, United Kingdom, Germany, and Norway*. Oxford: Oxford Scholarship Online.
Fraser, N. 2003. 'Rethinking Recognition: Overcoming Displacement and Reification in Cultural Politics', in B. Hobson (ed.), *Recognition Struggles and Social Movements* (pp. 21–32). Cambridge: Cambridge University Press.
Gamson, W. 1990. *The Strategy of Social Protest*, 2nd ed. Belmont: Wadsworth.
Gorringe, H., Jeffery, R. and Sariola, S. 2009. 'Ethnographic Insights into Enduring Inequalities', *Journal of South Asian Development* 4(1): 1–6.
Heyer, J. and Gopal Jayal, N. 2009. 'The Challenge of Positive Discrimination in India', Centre for Research on Inequality, Human Security and Ethnicity, Working Paper No. 55, Oxford.
Hickey, S. and Du Toit, A. 2013. 'Adverse Incorporation, Social Exclusion and Chronic Poverty', in A. Shepherd and J. Brunt (eds), *Chronic Poverty: Concepts, Causes and Policy* (pp. 134–159). New York: Palgrave.
Human, Rights Watch. 2014. 'They Say We're Dirty: Denying an Education to India's Marginalized', 22 April 2014. https://www.hrw.org/report/2014/04/22/they-say-were-dirty/denying-education-indias-marginalized (accessed 13 July 2015).
Jaffrelot, C. 2003. *India's Silent Revolution : The Rise of Lower Castes in North India*. Delhi: Permanent Black.
———. 2006. 'The Impact of Affirmative Action in India: More Political than Socioeconomic', *India Review* 5(2): 173–189.
Jeffery, R., Jeffrey, C. and Jeffery, P. 2001. 'Social and Political Dominance in Western UP: A Response to Sudha Pai', *Contributions to Indian Sociology* 35(3): 213–235.
Jeffrey, C., Jeffery, P. and Jeffery, R. 2008. 'Dalit Revolution? New Politicians in Uttar Pradesh, India', *The Journal of Asian Studies* 67(4): 1365–1396.
Jenkins, J. and Klandermans, B. (eds). 1995. *The Politics of Social Protest: Comparative Perspectives on States and Social Movements*. London and New York: Routledge.
Kanshiram. 1982. *The Chamcha Age: An Era of Stooges*. New Delhi: Karol Bagh.
Kapur, D., Bhan Prasad, C., Pritchett, L. and Shyam Babu, D. 2010. 'Rethinking Inequality: Dalits in Uttar Pradesh in the Market Reform Era', *Economic and Political Weekly* XLV(35): 39–49.
Kohli, A. (ed.). 2001. *The Success of India's Democracy*. Cambridge: Cambridge University Press.
Lakha, S. and Taneja, P. 2009. 'Introduction: Democracy, Governance and Civil Society: Rethinking the Study of Contemporary India', *South Asia* 32(3): 315–325.
Manor, J. 2004. 'Democratisation with Inclusion: Political Reforms and People's Empowerment at the Grassroots', *Journal of Human Development* 5(1): 5–29.
———. 2013. '"Who Is a Citizen?" A Multi-dimensional Question', in S. Mitra (ed.), *Citizenship as Cultural Flow: Structure Agency and Power* (pp. 107–120). Heidelberg: Springer Berlin.

Mathew, G. 2003. 'Panchayati Raj Institutions and Human Rights in India', *Economic and Political Weekly* 38(2): 155–162.
Mendelsohn, O. and Vicziany, M. 1998. *The Untouchables*. Cambridge: Cambridge University Press.
Mosse, D. 2007. Power and the Durability of Poverty. Chronic Poverty Research Centre, Working Papers No. 107.
Pai, S. 2000. 'New Social and Political Movements of Dalits: A Study of Meerut District', *Contributions to Indian Sociology* 34(2): 189–220.
———. 2001. 'Social Capital, Panchayats and Grass Roots Democracy: Politics of Dalit Assertion in Uttar Pradesh', *Economic and Political Weekly* 36(8): 645–654.
———. 2002. *Dalit Assertion and the Unfinished Democratic Revolution*. New Delhi: SAGE.
Pandian, M. 2000. 'Dalit Assertion in Tamil Nadu: An Explanatory Note', *Journal of Indian School of Political Economy* 12(3 and 4): 501–517.
Phillips, N. 2013. 'Unfree Labour and Adverse Incorporation in the Global Economy: Comparative Perspectives on Brazil and India', *Economy and Society* 42(2): 171–196.
Piven, F. and Cloward, R. 1971. *Poor People's Movements: Why They Succeed, How They Fail*. New York: Vintage.
Puwar, N. 2004. *Space Invaders: Race, Gender and Bodies Out of Place*. Oxford: Berg.
Ram, F., Mohanty, S.K. and Ram, U. 2009. 'Understanding the Distribution of BPL Cards: All-India and Selected States', *Economic and Political Weekly* 44(7): 66–71.
Rammohan, K.T. 2008. 'Caste and Landlessness in Kerala: Signals from Chengara', *Economic and Political Weekly* 43(37): 14–16.
Ray, K., Savage, M., Tampubolon, G., Warde, A., Longhurst, B. and Tomlinson, M. 2003. 'The Exclusiveness of the Political Field: Networks and Political Mobilization', *Social Movement Studies* 2(1): 37–60.
Ray, R. and Katzenstein, M. (eds). 2005. *Social Movements in India: Poverty, Power, and Politics*. Lanham, MD: Rowman & Littlefield.
Sen, A. 2001. 'Hunger: Old Torments and New Blunders', *The Little Magazine* 2(6). http://www.littlemag.com/hunger/aks.html (accessed 23 July 2015).
———. 1999. *Commodities and Capabilities. OUP Catalogue*. Oxford and New York: Oxford University Press.
Suri, K.C. 2013. 'Party System and Party Politics in India', in K.C. Suri and A. Vanaik (eds), *Political Science: Volume 2: Indian Democracy*. Delhi: Oxford Scholarship Online.
Tarrow, S. 1998. Power in Movement: Social Movements and Contentious Politics, 2nd ed. Cambridge: Cambridge University Press.
Thorat, S. and Newman, K. (eds). 2010. *Blocked by Caste*. New Delhi: Oxford University Press.
Tilly, C. 1998. *Durable Inequality*. Berkeley: University of California Press.
Varshney, A. 2000. 'Is India Becoming More Democratic?' *The Journal of Asian Studies* 59(1): 3–25.
Wilkinson, S. 2004. *Votes and Violence*. Cambridge: Cambridge University Press.
———. 2007. 'A Comment on the Analysis in Sachar Report', *Economic and Political Weekly* 42(10): 832–836.
Wyatt, A. 2009. *Party System Change in South India: Political Entrepreneurs, Patterns and Processes*. London: Routledge.
Yadav, Y. 2001. 'Understanding the Second Democratic Upsurge: Trends of Bahujan Participation in Electoral Politics in the 1990s', in Francine Frankel, Zoya Hasan, Rajeev Bhargava and Balvir Arora (eds), *Transforming India: Social and Political Dynamics of Democracy* (pp. 120–145). New Delhi: Oxford University Press.

1
Identity, Citizenship and Hindu–Muslim Conflict in India

Abdul Shaban

Introduction

Modern democratic nations have moved beyond ruler–ruled relationships. There can be different forms of bestowing rights to citizens, and their rights may also differ, but what remains a quintessential element of modern democracy is that governments, theoretically speaking, cannot take away some—or, in principle, any—of their basic rights. A citizen is a member of a political community and should, therefore, enjoy various rights bestowed by the state and should also assume duties of membership (Stanford Encyclopaedia of Philosophy 2011). Although, at the face value, the term 'citizenship' conveys strong meanings of uniform rights enjoyed by the members, in reality the 'citizens' may be characterised with varied state relations and access to state resources, benefits and burdens. The rights and duties of citizens may also differ as per the conception of citizenship such as republican, liberal, non-statist and ethno-nationalist. The processes of making or incorporating people into citizenship determine the nature of citizenship, and its universalistic or particularistic character. In the imagined communities of nations, ethnic minorities face major challenges with regard to their incorporation as fuller citizens. In other words, notwithstanding the formal recognition by state statutes of the membership of all persons of a geographic/political community, at a performative level some groups may be excluded from, or denied, realizing the fuller form of citizenship. In India, the multiple conceptions of citizenship enable the state to manage its diverse social groups and contain many of their underlying conflicts. Given the enormity of socio-economic diversity in the country, the consolidation of independent India had to occur around the notion of 'unity in diversity'.

In India, there has been a shifting balance of discourses amongst the four main notions of citizenship: liberal,[1] republican,[2] ethno-nationalist[3] and non-statist.[4] These have coexisted and have remained in tension with each other since independence. Within a fourfold citizenship regime, groups that were circumscribed by the terms of one citizenship discourse, could employ any one of the three alternatives to argue for inclusion (Shani 2010). Any multiple citizenship regime offers alternatives for diverse group of people to make sense of their social predicament, as well as to define demands for remedies or change. In other words, such a regime—as it played out in India—provides social groups with various ways of being Indian, without necessarily having to relinquish their other social identities. This multiple citizenship regime also provided the Indian State with the effective means of (re)positioning its authority and reclaiming legitimacy from its subjects in the context of contestation and dissent. However, where it has helped in reducing intractable religious antagonisms, it also helped in the survival of the ethno-nationalist claim of citizenship, its recent resurgence and increased violence targeted against religious minorities.

As members of a religious minority, Muslims in India have been at the receiving end of hostility from advocates of ethno-nationalism. Muslim identities have been manipulated and stigmatised and their rights as citizens, bestowed by the Constitution, are often infringed, formally and informally. In this chapter, an attempt has been made to examine (a) the nature of Muslim citizenship in the country and debates around it and (b) how different actors, including the state have played around with the Muslim identity, which has a bearing on (a) the community's access to developmental programmes and other opportunities within everyday life; and (b) violence in the form of communal riots, incarceration and extra-judicial punishment by the police.

The chapter has eight sections. After this introduction, the second section 'Predicament of Muslims and Experience of Citizenship' briefly discusses the nature of Muslim citizenship in India and its incorporation processes in a historical perspective. The problematisation of identity and the resulting marginalisation of the community are discussed in the third section, that is, 'Identity' and Minoritisation, whilst the fourth section—Identity and Exclusion from Development—examines the implication of this identity for inclusion in developmental programmes. Violence against the Muslim community, sustained through communal riots, and illegal custodial and fake encounters by the police, are discussed in the fifth section, that is 'Identity Stereotyping and Communal Violence', and the sixth section, that is, 'Terrorism and Fake Encounters', respectively. The seventh section, that is, 'Incarceration of Muslims', discusses the disproportionate share of Muslims in jails, and the last section concludes the chapter.

Predicament of Muslims and Experience of Citizenship

Muslims face enormous challenges with respect to enjoying the rights of citizenship enshrined in the Constitution. This predicament has arisen out of many historical developments as well as from the nature of the Indian State. The birth of the present Indian State and 'nationalism' is derived from the division of British India into 'India' and Pakistan. Pandey (1999) argues that nations are constructed around a core or a mainstream which is defined in relation to minorities, who are co-constituted in the process. As such, the core uses the power of negativity to define itself, by constructing boundaries, often social and cultural. The core is often expressed and defined in ethnic terms.

Though the Constitution of India provides citizenship to its population in a liberal framework, the tension between ethno-nationalist and other citizenship discourses (liberal, republican) was at play at the time of Independence and has been so since then. Many still ask: Can a Muslim be an Indian? (Pandey 1999). Sardar Patel—the first Home Minister and Deputy Prime Minister of India—posed similar questions about Muslims. He said in a 1948 speech:

> I want to tell them [Muslims] frankly that mere declaration of loyalty to the Indian Union will not help them at this crucial juncture. They must give practical proof of their declaration. (Government of India 1967)

Ethno-nationalist discourses were heard even in the Constituent Assembly in August 1949. For example, P.S. Deshmukh proposed that a citizen of India should be, amongst other things, every person who is a Hindu or a Sikh by religion (Lok Sabha Secretariat 1999). Such were the uncomfortable questions regarding the incorporation of Muslims in India, many of whom were economically backward and had little or no knowledge of what India and Pakistan meant. In fact, the Muslims in India were and still are divided by caste, sect, region, language and race, but they were homogenised in and around 1947 as a religious minority by the ethno-nationalist discourse. This largely stripped Muslims of their specific social identities and belongings, and defined them as 'Muslim' first.

At the time of Independence, two brands of nationalism emerged: (a) 'Hindu nationalism'—the communal or religious variety of nationalism; and (b) secular or constitutional nationalism—'Indian', as conceived by Jawaharlal Nehru and others. As mentioned previously, Muslims in India were asked to show loyalty by opposing the Muslim League, giving up any demand for separatism and separate electorates. Those who stayed in India were accused by ethno-nationalists of being Pakistani spies or members of a Pakistani fifth column (Pandey 1999). As such, Muslims got defined in three ways: (a) as Muslims—connoting membership in a larger religious group not much linked with the Indian nation; (b) as Pakistanis—as anti-nationals and supporters of Pakistan—the term frequently used by the extremist Hindu groups to signify Muslim criminals, terrorists and occasionally the whole Muslim community in the country; and (c) nationalist-Muslims—this term is reserved for those few who have lost their lives in wars with Pakistan or stood against Pakistan in 1947 or thereafter. It is interesting to note that none of these three categories apply to Hindus but only to Muslims. In other words, the nationalist-Muslim category has no equivalent amongst Hindus but instead has a reversed one—Hindu Nationalist—which is another brand of nationalism in which Hinduism has considerable weight (Pandey 1999). These historical legacies and tensions still persist in the country.

> [The] assassination of Mahatma Gandhi in January 1948 at the hands of a Hindu extremist...seems to have brought a good deal of north India back to its senses and marked a turning point in the debate between 'secular nation' and 'Hindu nation'. (Pandey 1999: 614)

This assassination weakened the overtone and aggressive expressions of the ethno-nationalists and provided more space for the expression of constitutional nationalism/citizenship.

The ethno-nationalist discourse was also weakened with the Constitution guaranteeing legal rights to its citizens rooted in liberal discourse and thereafter the centralised planning and conception of socialistic pattern of society promoted the idea of a republican type of citizenship. It provided hope that, irrespective of particularities of individuals and social groups, development would reach equally to everyone. By the end of 1970s, however, it was found that Muslims largely remained deprived, and again the Muslims were not equals amongst others (Shaban 2012). While affirmative programmes were initiated for other deprived communities, Muslims as economically backward castes could not find an appropriate and meaningful place in the schema. For instance, lower caste Muslims were not recognised as Scheduled Castes (SCs) for reservation in government services and educational institutions, nor in other affirmative action by the state.

In general, the failure of centralised planning in bringing about equal and just development led Muslims to assert themselves for their particularities, and their demands became ones that underscored their 'identity', though economic deprivation and access to government services remained major issues. The question of Aligarh Muslim University (declaring it a minority institution), Urdu and Muslim Personal Law took centre stage. The Gopal Singh Committee in 1983 highlighted various demands of the Muslim community with respect to the three aspects just discussed, besides highlighting their economic deprivation and exclusion from the government-run programmes and access to government services. The decade of the 1970s also saw the resurgence of Gandhian thinking, advancing non-statist conceptions of citizenship. This discourse used *Sanskritised* terms to which Muslims could hardly relate, but it kept the ethno-nationalists at bay. The 1970s also saw the reassertion of the republican conception of citizenship, as best reflected in the Minimum Needs Programmes and other development programmes initiated by the government. Its reassertion came to a peak with the imposition of the Emergency by Indira Gandhi in 1975. However, it could not last long and gave way to more liberal and ethno-nationalist claims of citizenship.

By the late 1970s, we also see an upsurge in the assertion of identity by backward castes, tribes and classes in the country. The natural alliances amongst the deprived demographic majority of the country were anticipated to threaten the rule of the dominant minority. To overcome this threat, the ethno-nationalist discourse of citizenship was again highlighted through the Ram Mandir agenda. This kept the poor divided to the benefit of the ruling class. In some places, the poor were used against each other. The secluded and excluded Muslim minority community, left fending for themselves, were further marginalised in political, economic and social spheres. As the Sachar Committee (2006) data reveal, in the first decade of the twenty-first century, Muslims were one of the most underdeveloped communities in the country.

Today, Muslims comprise a substantially higher proportion of jail inmates (Shaban 2010, 2012), beggars, those living in slums (Shaban 2011), landless, those killed in communal riots (Varshney 2002; Wilkinson 2005), and politically excluded groups. The state has failed to meaningfully accommodate Muslims as citizens and empower them. In fact, today, Muslims are more fearful of the state whose role should be to cultivate a sense of safety, security and equality amongst all its citizens. The 'Muslim question' still remains as alive as it was during Partition. Many threaten to 'throw them [Muslims] into the Arabian Sea', while others innovate derogatory phrases for them (Shaban 2010, 2012). The ghettoes where they live are pejoratively called 'mini Pakistan' and they are seen to be constituted by a homogenised Muslim identity, though they are in fact characterised by enormous diversity. Increasingly, democratic and public spaces available to the community are also being constrained by counter-agitation, representation or violence. Although many feel that democracy can provide a way out for Indian Muslims as it allows political bargaining (Akbar 2012), one is also aware of the limitation of democracy with regard to minorities. A democracy can only be as good as its political community. The prospect of Muslims of India as 'citizens' hinges on the nature of this political community.

'Identity' and Minoritisation

The intensification and sharpening of divisions on ethnic lines in recent years has been one of the significant phenomena in the country. This has furthered the minortisation process, which can be defined as the process through which powerlessness is introduced and reinforced in certain sections of population. The perception of being a minority relates to power (social, economic and political), not necessarily to demographic numbers. For example, Muslims hardly constituted 10–15 per cent in India but ruled much of the present-day South Asia from the thirteenth to nineteenth centuries. The real minority of the country, in this sense, have been Dalits. The minoritisation of Muslims starts from 1803 when the forces of Lord Lake entered Delhi and the Mughal King was reduced to a puppet. The leading cleric of the time, Shah Abd-al-Aziz, understood the meaning of the event and declared India as *Dar al-Harb* (a land of war), having previously been a *Dar al-Aman* (a land of peace). This was the first *fatwa* for *jihad*. It was not that the Mughal King became a puppet for the first time as he was earlier subordinate to Marathas in the 1770s, but no fatwa was declared against the Marathas (Akbar 2012) as there was no perception of threat from them regarding discrimination on religious, cultural, political and economic lines.

This shows that the feeling of being a minority is linked with powerlessness, which is what many Indian Muslims had started feeling during British rule and after independence. The persistent cultivation of insecurity by both the Muslim and Hindu right-wing groups led to the partition in 1947. Even after the adoption of a secular constitution based on equality and freedom for all, the feeling of insecurity amongst Muslims was perpetuated through right-wing attacks during communal riots, denial of their share in development programmes, and police or state (in)actions.

'The Muslim' as a religious identity has been manipulated and stereotyped such that it has become larger than national geography (Muslims have been called pan-Islamic sympathisers or Pakistani) and shorter than citizenship. This has threatened the equality and security of the Muslim community guaranteed to them by the Constitution. The characteristics attributed to the stereotyped Muslim identity, amongst others, relate to patriotism (not committed to the nation but to pan-Islamism), anti-nationalism (supporters of Pakistan), demanding appeasement (certain political parties provide Muslims undue favours), terrorism ([all] Muslims are terrorists), foreigners (Muslims have come from outside and plundered the wealth of the nation), suspicion (criminals), over-breeding (their growing population will make the Hindus a minority within their own country), and womanisers (they lure Hindu women through love jihad). All these characteristics are often combined—in varying combinations or altogether—to justify actions that produce marginality and powerlessness amongst Muslims. The category, labelling and practices are invoked not only by a certain section of population but also by public institutions (Sachar Committee 2006).

The increasing religious schism has pervaded Indian society for a long time. In many states, like Maharashtra, Gujarat and Madhya Pradesh, this has resulted in a ghettoisation of the Muslim community in terms of residence, education and employment (Shaban 2008, 2010). There has also emerged a general ignorance about Muslim culture in society, submerged under the pervasive Muslim identities that are assigned to them. To reinforce this process, the media overplays the involvement of individual Muslims in criminal and violent activities, in turn reinforcing the labels.

Identity and Exclusion from Development

As discussed previously, the role of the modern state in the daily life of its citizens should be to establish a sense of security, equality, justice and fair play for all. However, Muslims of India have largely been uncomfortable in dealing with the state, as the organs of the state which need to govern citizens on the previously-mentioned principles have apparently been partisan against Muslims (Shaban 2012: 10). The increased anti-colonial rhetoric and activities in the second half of the nineteenth century by Muslims led the British colonial government to introduce many discriminatory practices against Muslims in recruitment for administrative and military services (Hunter 1871). After independence, the sense of insecurity and discrimination amongst the Muslim community continues as a greater number of state institutions are turning communal and the representation of Muslims in these institutions is dwindling.

The suspicion shown towards Muslims has led to their exclusion from sensitive state services and has it also become difficult for Muslims to get jobs in ordinary state-run institutions. It has been established by the Sachar Committee (2006) that the share of Muslims in government services is nowhere near the proportion of their population to the total population in the country (Basant and Shariff 2010; Ranganath Mishra Commission Report 2007). The representation of Muslims in the Indian Parliament (Lok Sabha and Rajya Sabha) and the state assemblies is also dwindling (Basant and Shariff 2010; Hasan 2007, 2008; Sachar Committee Report 2006). The changing Hindu–Muslim relationship is deterring Hindu voters from supporting Muslim candidates, which adversely affects the chance of Muslims getting elected (Shaban 2012).

Religious identity remains an important factor behind the deprivation of Muslims in India. Though caste and class are important in shaping the destiny of millions in the country, for Muslims these categories are complicated by their religious identity. A lower caste Muslim is more likely to be identified as a Muslim than a Dalit by the majority community and by the state administration. As a result, even Muslim communities that have been included in the OBC list are unable to make any significant impact on the total representation of Muslims in government services. Further, OBC Muslims in India comprise two disparate categories, 'Arzals' and 'Ajlaf'. Arzals are socially equivalent to SCs, and Ajlaf are middle castes, socially equivalent to OBCs amongst Hindus. Unfortunately, the pooling of these two categories to constitute the Muslim OBC category has emerged because of the problematic conception of caste by the Constitutional (Scheduled Caste) Order, 1950, popularly known as Presidential Order, 1950, which restricts the SC status to only Hindu, Sikh and Buddhist communities with unclean hereditary occupations (Shaban 2012). The Sachar Committee Report (2006: 193) notes:

> [The] OBCs among Muslims constitute two broad categories. The halalkhors, helas, lalbegis, or bhangis (scavengers), dhobi (washermen), nais or hajjams (barbers), chiks (butchers), faqirs (beggars) etc belonging to the 'Arzals' are the 'untouchable converts' to Islam that have found their way in the OBC list. The Momins or Julahas (weavers), darzis or Idiris (tailors), rayeen or kunjaras (vegetable sellers) are Ajlafs or converts from clean occupation castes. Thus, one can discern three groups among Muslims: (1) those without any social disabilities, the Ashrafs; (2) those equivalent to Hindu OBCs, the Ajlafs, and (3) those equivalent to Hindu SCs, the Arzals. Those who are referred to as Muslim OBCs combine (2) and (3).

So, in the OBC list, lower caste Muslims are clubbed with middle-caste Hindus, as a result of which Muslims belonging to lower castes find it difficult to compete with those from the Hindu middle castes, who have better class positions and cultural capital. Thus, besides religious discrimination, the unequal footing on which the Muslims have to compete also has a bearing on their representation in state services and educational institutions.

After the Sachar Committee Report (2006), the Government of India led by the Indian National Congress initiated many programmes for the development of minorities. However, most of the programmes were clubbed under the Prime Minister's 15 Point Programme (PM15PP) and Multi-Sectoral Development Programme. A Committee was set up by the Ministry of Minority Affairs for the evaluation of these programmes in 2013 under the chairmanship of Professor Amitabh Kundu. The Committee, also known as the Post-Sachar Evaluation Committee (PSEC), submitted its report in 2014. This showed that in fact these schemes have not been able make any serious dent to the exclusion faced by Muslims in everyday life (Government of India 2014). Despite this, in response to this affirmative action by the government for Muslims, the hostility of a section of the majority community (Hindus) has increased. In fact, communal violence against Muslims has not ended, and the geographical spread of riots has increased. Communal violence in rural areas has also now become more frequent. In recent years, wherever governments have attempted to shield Muslims from everyday exclusion, they have had to face the anger of right-wing organisations. The ruling Samajwadi Party in Uttar Pradesh faced the wrath of right-wing parties on providing protection and living facilities in refugee camps of riot-affected persons after the organisation of *bahu–beti bachao andolan* ('save daughters and honour' from Muslims) resulted in riots in Muzaffarnagar, Uttar Pradesh, in September 2013. Many also attributed the defeat of the Congress Party in the 2014 parliamentary election to the support they had given to Muslims, or as a result of the perceived 'appeasement' of Muslims. From the findings of the PSEC and politics thereafter, it can be concluded that Muslims suffered from more riots and hostility than development in recent years. Schemes designed to benefit them failed mainly due to (a) poor crafting, (b) lack of sufficient resource allocation, (c) lack of zeal amongst government officers to implement the programmes and (d) lack of awareness amongst Muslims to use the programmes.

Identity Stereotyping and Communal Violence

One of the reasons for the deprivation and marginalisation of Muslims in India is the endemic violence against the community. This violence not only destroys the material wealth of the community which they assiduously gather together, but also weakens their resources with which to rebuild their lives, housing and their businesses, and pushes them to look

Identity, Citizenship and Hindu–Muslim Conflict in India 11

backward and adopt conservative attitudes. Communal riots and collective violence against Muslims in the country have increased in frequency and geographical expanse since 1947. From Wilkinson (2005) and from data held by the Centre for the Study of Society and Secularism (CSSS), Mumbai, records of a total of 1,995 riots that have taken place during 1900–2013 have been collated.[5] Over this period, communal violence between the Hindus and the Muslims has risen, but this rise has not been uniform. India has experienced bouts of Hindu–Muslim riots that have been followed by relatively calm periods. The periods of higher communal violence have been 1923–1927 (the period after the Khilafat Movement), 1945–1948 (the years immediately after and before Partition), 1982–1994 (coinciding with the Ram Mandir Movement, the Rath Yatra of the BJP and demolition of Babri Mosque) and 2000 onwards (which peaks with the Gujarat riots in 2002). During most of these periods since 1982, the reported incidence of Hindu–Muslim riots has been, in general, more than 20 per year (Figure 1.1).

In India, urban centres have remained the centres of Hindu–Muslim riots and about 96 per cent of the total deaths in the country between 1950 and 1995 took place in towns (Varshney 2002). The data compiled for 1900–2013 show that communal violence in India has been significantly clustered in the Indo-Gangetic plain and in the western Indian states, where most of the deaths and injuries in communal violence have taken place (Figures 1.2 through 1.5).

Delhi and Kolkata have been the places of significant communal violence in the Gangetic plain, while Vadodara, Ahmedabad, Mumbai and Hyderabad have caught up with these cities mainly due to the rise of communal violence in the post-independence period. Kolkata was the most communally violent city in the pre-independence period, but in the post-independence period it has been Ahmedabad (Table 1.1). However, out of the ten top cities, nine and six cities, respectively, from the first and second periods have been from north India.

The data presented on communal violence in Tables 1.2 and 1.3 and Figures 1.2 through 1.5 show that:

1. The frequency and spatial expanse of communal violence has increased during 1947–2013 in comparison to 1900–1946. Whereas only on an average about nine communal riots took place

Figure 1.1

Trends in the number of reported communal riots in India, 1900–2013

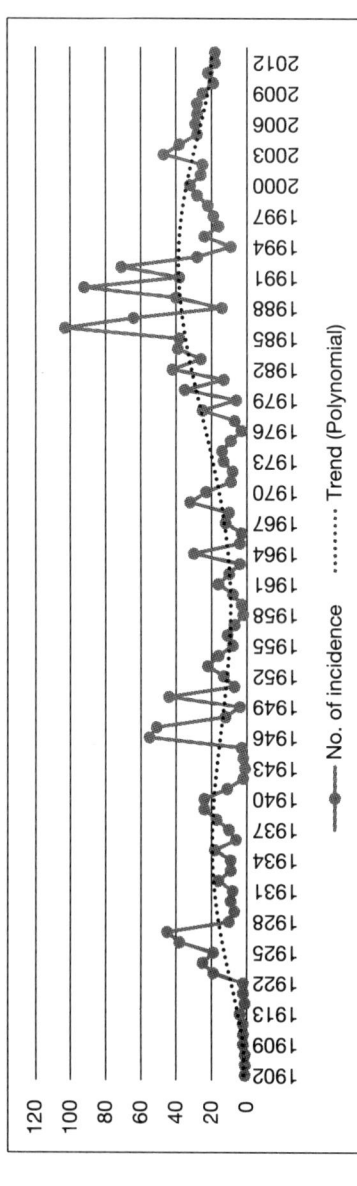

Source: Compiled from data produced in Wilkinson (2005) and the data for the year 1996–2009 are taken from the compilation done by CSSS, Mumbai, from newspaper reports.[5]

Figure 1.2

Number of Hindu–Muslim riots and their spatial extent, 1900–1946

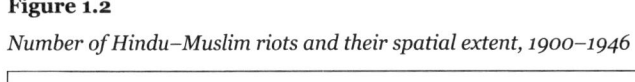

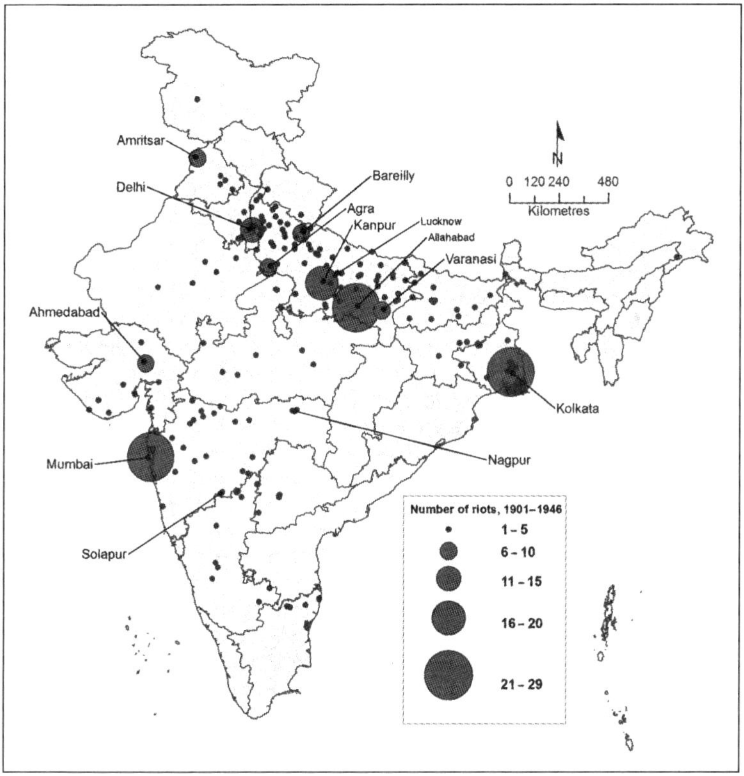

Source: Same as that for Figure 1.1.
Note: This figure is not to scale. It does not represent any authentic national or international boundaries and is used for illustrative purposes only.

every year during the period 1900–1946 in towns in the country, the frequency increased to about 24 per year during the period 1947–2013. Although, the reported death (7.6 deaths per riot) and injured (19.4 persons injured per riot) per communal riot in the post-independence period have been lower than pre-independence period (16.7 death per riot and 65.7 persons injured per riot), the violence has been more organised, institutionalised and politically

Figure 1.3
Number of Hindu–Muslim riots and their spatial extent, 1947–2013

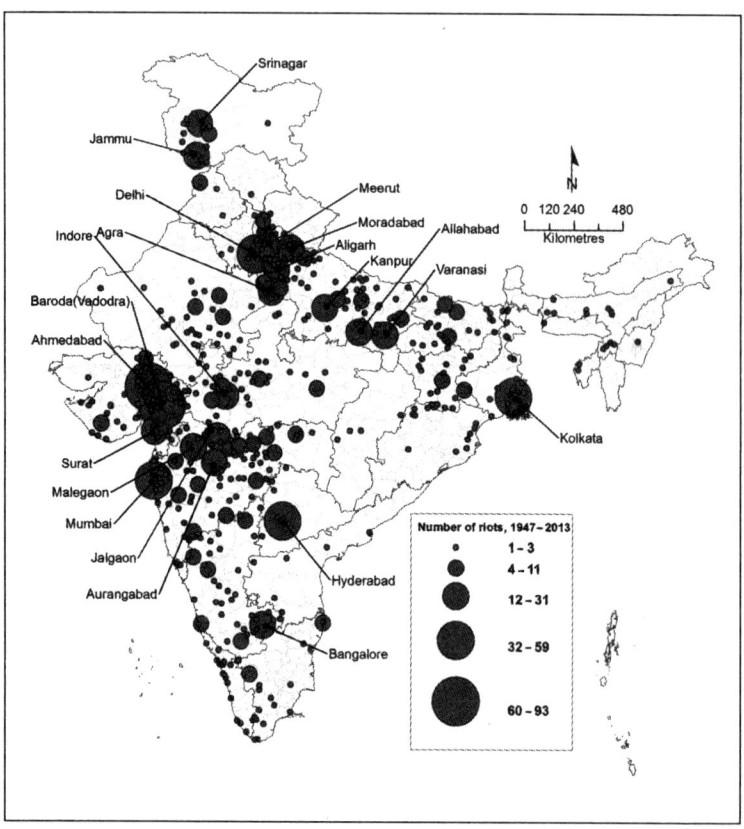

Source: Same as that for Figure 1.1.

Note: This figure is not to scale. It does not represent any authentic national or international boundaries and is used for illustrative purposes only.

calibrated. The geographical extent of the communal violence has also increased and rural areas, as seen in the Gujarat riots in 2002 and in the case of Muzaffarnagar (Uttar Pradesh) in 2013, are also becoming sites of communal violence.
2. There has been a significant geographical shift with respect to the state-wise shares in the total incidence of injuries and deaths in communal violence. Whereas during 1900–1946, most of the riots and

Figure 1.4
Number of persons reported killed in Hindu–Muslim communal violence in India, 1900–1946

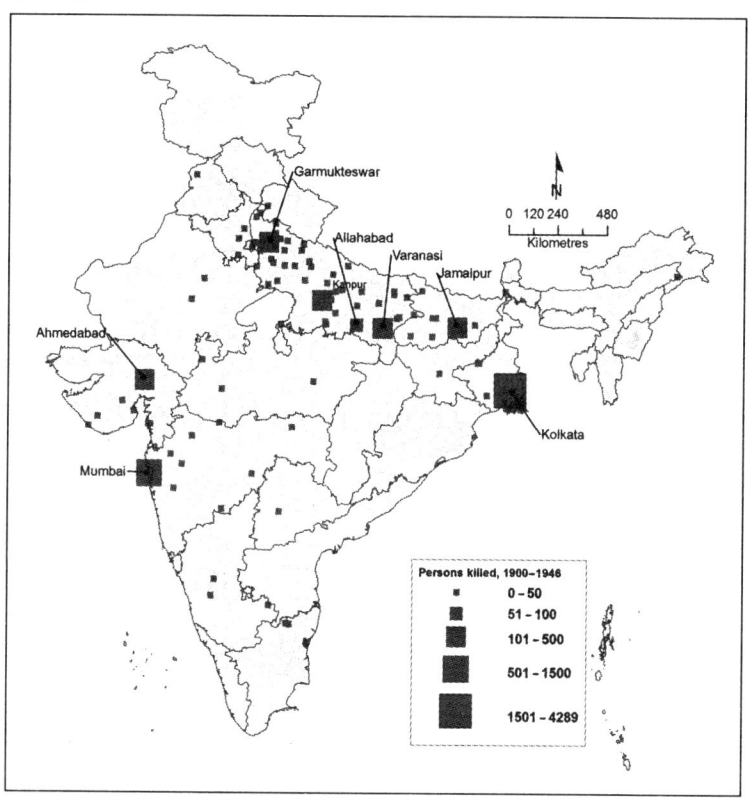

Source: Same as that for Figure 1.1.

Note: This figure is not to scale. It does not represent any authentic national or international boundaries and is used for illustrative purposes only.

deaths took place in towns of Uttar Pradesh (42.5 per cent of the total reported riots and 15.6 per cent of the total deaths), Maharashtra (15.3 per cent of the riots and 13.4 per cent of the deaths), West Bengal (11.6 per cent of the riots and 64.2 per cent of the deaths) and Bihar (6.4 per cent of the riots and 3.6 per cent of the deaths), during 1947–2013, western states like Gujarat and Maharashtra have experienced a significant increase in their share (Gujarat 19.0

Figure 1.5

Number of persons reported to be killed in Hindu–Muslim communal violence in India, 1947–2013

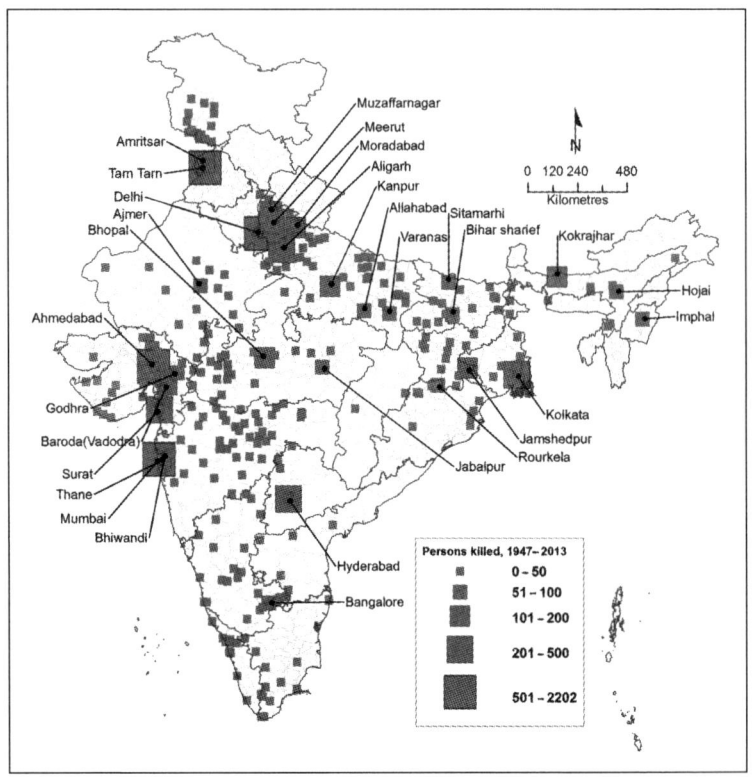

Source: Same as that for Figure 1.1.

Note: This figure is not to scale. It does not represent any authentic national or international boundaries and is used for illustrative purposes only.

per cent and Maharashtra 18.2 per cent of total communal incidents and Gujarat 22.5 per cent and Maharashtra 13.7 per cent of total deaths) while Uttar Pradesh (18.8 per cent of riots and 13.8 per cent of deaths), Delhi (2.6 per cent of riots and 17.5 per cent of deaths) Madhya Pradesh (5.7 per cent of riots and 3.2 per cent of deaths), Telangana (3.8 per cent of riots and 2.9 per cent of deaths) and

Table 1.1

Ten communally most violent cities (in terms of number of riots) in India during 1900–1946 and 1947–2013

Rank	Town/City	Number of incidence	Reported killed	Reported injured
		1900–1946		
1	Mumbai	29	844	5,761
2	Kolkata	26	4,290	12,415
3	Allahabad	22	61	456
4	Kanpur	19	428	962
5	Delhi	13	43	500
6	Agra	10	24	285
7	Ahmedabad	9	112	704
8	Amritsar	6	2	167
9	Bareilly	6	26	349
10	Varanasi	6	117	624
		1947–2013		
1	Ahmedabad	93	2,202	4,872
2	Vadodara	66	125	809
3	Mumbai	59	1,025	2,627
4	Hyderabad	52	338	1,204
5	Delhi	41	2,111	673
6	Kolkata	40	431	2,929
7	Aligarh	31	346	570
8	Meerut	26	267	526
9	Moradabad	19	167	331
10	Srinagar	17	30	788

Source: Same as that for Figure 1.1.

Karnataka (6.0 per cent of riots and 1.7 per cent of deaths) remain other states with a significant share of the total communal incidents and deaths in the country. In sum, during the post-independence period, communal violence has significantly risen in Gujarat, Madhya Pradesh, Telangana, Delhi and Karnataka.

Table 1.2

Number of Hindu–Muslim riots, persons injured and killed, 1900–1946

State/UT	No. of incidence			Percentage to the total		
	Incidence	Reported killed	Reported injured	Incidence	Reported killed	Reported injured
Uttar Pradesh	172	1,056	4,778	42.5	15.6	18.0
Maharashtra	62	902	6,615	15.3	13.4	24.9
West Bengal	47	4,334	12,744	11.6	64.2	47.9
Bihar	26	243	442	6.4	3.6	1.7
Gujarat	20	129	806	4.9	1.9	3.0
Madhya Pradesh	14	8	173	3.5	0.1	0.7
Delhi	13	43	500	3.2	0.6	1.9
Karnataka	13	11	109	3.2	0.2	0.4
Punjab	12	4	188	3.0	0.1	0.7
Others	26	25	254	6.3	0.3	0.9
Total	405	6,755	26,609	100	100	100

Source: Same as that for Figure 1.1.

Note: The figures are indicative as they are based on newspaper reports as compiled by various studies. There are possibilities of riot cases not recorded and the undercounting of the number of persons injured and killed as the studies have often not taken into account the subsequent revised figures which become available after several months of riots. In fact in many cases, the exact figures of persons injured and killed remains unknown. The data is organised as per the current state boundaries. Also see the appendix note in Wilkinson (2005: 405–444).

These acts of mass violence, violating all established human and citizenship rights, have continued without any significant deterrence and punishment for over a century. In order to garner votes, political parties act in strategic rather than in legally and constitutionally correct ways (Varshney 2002). No significant legislation has been passed to stop communal violence; rather, the state institutions like the police, judiciary, intelligence agencies and development department have become communalised. Common Muslims now not only feel discriminated against by many state institutions but also fear for their lives.

Table 1.3

Number of Hindu–Muslim riots, persons injured and killed, 1947–2013

States/UTs	No. of incidence			Percentage to the total		
	Number of incidence	Reported killed	Reported injured	Incidence	Reported killed	Reported injured
Gujarat	302	2,722	7,006	19.0	22.5	22.7
Uttar Pradesh	299	1,666	3,578	18.8	13.8	11.6
Maharashtra	289	1,655	6,915	18.2	13.7	22.4
Karnataka	95	202	1,368	6.0	1.7	4.4
Madhya Pradesh	91	383	1,896	5.7	3.2	6.2
West Bengal	86	601	3,370	5.4	5.0	10.9
Bihar	69	433	794	4.3	3.6	2.6
Rajasthan	62	188	644	3.9	1.6	2.1
Telangana	60	355	1,400	3.8	2.9	4.5
Jammu & Kashmir	57	49	1,477	3.6	0.4	4.8
Delhi	41	2,111	673	2.6	17.5	2.2
Others	139	1,713	1,685	8.9	14.2	5.4
Total	1,590	12,078	30,806	100	100	100

Source: Same as that for Figure 1.1.

Terrorism and Fake Encounters

The rise in religious fanaticism at the global level has implicated Islam and Muslims such that it has become a common perception—globally and in India—that terrorism is a monopoly of Muslims. This perception can be found amongst India's police and politicians. However, it has also been argued that Indian Muslims have not been *much* involved in cases of terrorism but are often falsely implicated by the police. Many also argue that, like any religious community, Muslims have criminal elements within their community. These criminals and their acts are often projected by the media and the police as evidence of Indian Muslims' association with Islamic jihad and terrorism.

In India, many bomb blasts have taken place, killing a number of citizens. The police have claimed that many of these bomb blasts were carried out by Indian Islamic terrorist outfits. However, later investigations have revealed that in a number of high-profile instances, the police falsely fabricated cases against the Muslim youth though the real culprits were associated with right-wing Hindu organisations. Ram Puniyani, a scholar on Hindu–Muslim communalism, says:

> In most of these cases, the police operated with the perception that 'all terrorists are Muslims' and arrested Muslim youths indiscriminately without any reliable evidence. Many of these youths had to be released after the courts ruled that there is no evidence whatsoever against these youths. (Government of Maharashtra 2013: 210)

Puniyani also discusses the role of right-wing Hindu outfits in terror attacks. On 6 April 2006, two Bajrang Dal (Hindu right-wing organisation) workers died making bombs in Nanded, Maharashtra. The place where they died belonged to a Rashtriya Swayamsevak Sangh (RSS) worker and a saffron flag was hoisted atop the house. There was also a board of Bajrang Dal Nanded Branch on the wall of the house. The police recovered bomb-making materials, a diary, a fake beard and moustache, and pyjama-kurta (the attire of Muslim clerics). The Anti-Terrorist Squad of the Police established that the place was used for making bombs. After this, the Maharashtra Inspector General (IG) of Police conceded that it was a bomb blast and that those involved in the blast were members of Bajrang Dal. Local newspapers reported that a diary found from the spot had the details of bomb-making techniques and other relevant information. On 11 April 2006, the Special IG of Police, Surya Prakash Gupta, declared that it was not an isolated event; rather a bomb-manufacturing centre (Bomb *Nirmiti Kendra*) was functioning at the house and had been working for a long time. He also added that one of the injured, Rahul Pande, had categorically confessed to having made many such bombs earlier (Government of Maharashtra 2013). In Kanpur, Uttar Pradesh, on 25 August 2008, two persons were killed while manufacturing bombs. It was found that one of the deceased belonged to the Bajrang Dal. Muslim organisations argued that this Kanpur blast was also a part of the series of blasts by the communal Hindu organisations to spread terrorism in the country for which 'Muslims are blamed' (Ali 2008).

Identity, Citizenship and Hindu–Muslim Conflict in India 21

Bomb blasts were witnessed in many places around that time, Mecca Masjid in Hyderabad, Samjhauta Express in Haryana, Ajmer, Delhi, and Parbhani, Malegaon, Jalna, and Aurangabad in Maharashtra. In most of these cases, Muslims were killed and the police claimed the perpetrators were members of Islamic outfits. The Nanded investigation 'leads' were not pursued by the police. The attitude of the police in this investigation has been criticised by social activists, who complained about this to the Human Rights Commission. The Superintendent of Police (SP) failed to turn up even for the hearing (Government of Maharashtra 2013).

Again in Nanded on 10 February 2007, a 28 year-old Shiv Sena *Shakha Pramukh*, Pandurang Bhagwan Amilkanthwar, died on the spot due to a bomb blast. 'Amol Biscuits', a bakery shop, was run by the deceased, at Shastrinagar, Nanded. At the time of blast, the shop was closed. Later in Thane, Maharashtra, on 4 June 2008, two Hindu Jagran Samiti workers were arrested for planting bombs at the basement of Gadkari Rangayatan Auditorium, due to which seven people got injured. The same group was also involved in the blasts in Vashi and Panvel in Navi Mumbai. This group idolises Savarkar and Hedgewar and indoctrinates its members into hating Christians and Muslims (Government of Maharashtra 2013).

As per the police version, in an alleged attack on the RSS office in Nagpur on 1 June 2006, three Fidayins (suicide bombers) were killed in a police encounter. The Citizens Inquiry Report, headed by Justice Kolse Patil, seriously doubted the police version but the authorities did not provide any clarifications for the inconsistencies in their reports. In one of the major breakthroughs in the investigation of various incidents of bomb blast, Maharashtra ATS chief Hemant Karkare found the involvement of Sadhvi Pragya Singh Thakur, Swami Dayanand Pandey, retired Major Upadhya and serving Lt Col Prasad Shrikant Purohit. Many of them were the members of different Hindu right-wing organisations. This shows that in India, the theory that blames Indian Muslims as terrorists involved in blasts needs to be seriously questioned. However, in all these cases, the first targets of the Police were Muslims. They were rounded up at odd hours and arrested. This needs to be understood as attempts by sectarian elements to further marginalise Muslims from the public sphere and to deny their claims to citizenship and belonging in Indian society.

There has been a significant encroachment of Muslims' citizenship rights in recent years. In earlier cases, right-wing Hindu groups were generally involved in the killing of Muslims in riots. In recent years, however, the coercive force of the state—the police—has killed many Muslims in fake encounters. The national intelligence agencies have been equal partners in these crimes. The case of the Ishrat Jahan 'encounter' is being opened up layer by layer by the Central Bureau of Investigation (CBI). They have shown that Intelligence Bureau (IB) officials and Gujarat Police personnel together conspired to kill the Muslim youths on the pretext that they were planning to kill the State Chief Minister (*Times of India* 2013). Similarly, the case of Sadiq Jamal shows the culpability of conspiracy by the State Police and IB.

Data available for the states as produced in Table 1.4 shows that there were a total of 1,220 fake encounters in the country during October 1993 to October 2009 and the share of Muslims in that was 17.4 per cent as against their share of 13.4 per cent of the national population. Although there has been substantially higher proportion of fake encounters of Muslims (as against their share in total state population) in majority of the states in India, the proportion is significantly higher in Gujarat, Karnataka, Madhya Pradesh, Maharashtra, Delhi, Jharkhand, Chhattisgarh and Uttrakhand. In 2010–2011, 2011–2012 and 2012–2013 (till 15 February 2013) a total of 129, 197 and 126 fake encounters have been reported, but the share of Muslims in these are not known (Government of India 2013).

It is worth summarising a number of such cases to flesh out what the term 'fake encounter' means and how officers have been acting with impunity in many cases:

1. Sadiq Jamal, 23 years old, a resident of Bhavnagar city of Gujarat, was killed by a team of Gujarat's Crime Branch in an encounter near Galaxy Cinema on the outskirts of Ahmedabad on 13 January 2003. It was claimed by the police that Sadiq Jamal was a member of the Dawood Ibrahim gang and that he had arrived to kill BJP leaders to avenge the 2002 post-Godhra riots in Gujarat. However, evidence suggests that Sadiq Jamal was already in Gujarat Police and IB Custody and was a petty criminal (*Times of India* 2013a).

Table 1.4

Fake encounter cases registered at the National Human Rights Commission (NHRC), New Delhi, between October 1993 and October 2009

State/Union Territory	No. of fake encounters	No. of Muslims victims of fake encounter	Percentage of Muslims as victims	Share of Muslim population (%) to the total population of the respective state, 2001
Gujarat	20	12	60.0	9.1
Jammu & Kashmir	18	9	50.0	66.8
Delhi	22	8	36.4	11.7
Uttarakhand	29	9	31.0	11.9
Karnataka	10	3	30.0	12.2
Maharashtra	61	16	26.2	10.6
Jharkhand	21	5	23.8	13.9
Uttar Pradesh	716	131	18.3	18.5
Haryana	18	3	16.7	5.8
Manipur	18	3	16.7	8.8
Chhattisgarh	6	1	16.7	2.0
Madhya Pradesh	36	5	13.9	6.4
Rajasthan	11	1	9.1	8.5
Bihar	79	4	5.1	16.5
Andhra Pradesh	73	2	2.7	9.2
Others	82	0	0	–
Total (of the above)	1,220	212	17.4	13.4

Sources: The data for encounters are taken from NHRC, http://twocircles.net/2010mar26/uttar_pradesh_top_fake_encounter_specialist_india.html (accessed 3 August 2013) and http://www.ndtvmi.com/b4/dopesheets/aastha.pdf (accessed 3 August 2013); 2. The data related to the share of Muslims in state population are taken from Census of India (2001).

2. Ishrat Jahan Sheikh along with Javed Sheikh, Amjad Rana and Zeeshan Johar were gunned down by the Gujarat police on 15 June 2004 on the pretext that they were going to kill the Gujarat State Chief Minister. Later, it was found that these youths were already in police custody and the police and IB were involved in their cold-blooded murder (*Times of India* 2013b).

3. Sohrabuddin Anwarhussain Sheikh was killed by the State Police on 26 November 2005, while he was in the police custody. Sheikh was claimed to be an agent of Lashkar-e-Taiba and Pakistan's Inter-Services Intelligence. It was said that he was planning to kill 'an important political leader' (*Outlook* 2005) in Gujarat.
4. Kauser Bi, wife of Sohrabuddin Anwarhussain Sheikh, was raped, poisoned, killed and burnt by the officers of the Gujarat Police because she threatened to expose the policeman involved in her husband's killing (Bunsha 2007; Dabhi 2010). Her ashes were thrown into Narmada River, near Bharuch, by the police (PTI 2010).
5. Sayyed Khwaja Yunus, a 27-year-old software engineer, was murdered by the Mumbai Police's encounter specialists. He was arrested in a false case for his role in the Ghatkopar, Mumbai, bomb blast in January 2003. Yunus was killed and his 'body was burnt at a farm in Asangaon in Raigad district and a cemented platform was constructed at the place so that no one could find the bones and the ashes' (Tare 2012).

Incarceration of Muslims

The police have become overzealous in putting Muslims in jails or shooting them down in fake encounters. The 'national security' arguments are the cover used to justify the violation of human and citizenship rights. It is not surprising, therefore, that the share of Muslims in jail has remained very high in India, more than twice or thrice the share of their population (Shaban 2010). The latest Prison Statistics from 2013 show that, as against their population of 14.2 per cent at all India level, the share of Muslim convicts was 17.1 per cent (22, 145 convicts). Amongst the major states, the share of Muslim convicts was almost double to the Muslim population in West Bengal, Maharashtra, and Rajasthan. Out of the total under-trials of 2,78,503in 2013 in the country, 20.8 per cent belonged to Muslim community, while 19.7 per cent (613 persons) of the detenues belong to the Muslim community. About 51 per cent (392 out of 768) of Muslims constituted the category of 'other' prisoners in the country's jails (NCRB 2013). The share of Muslims is significantly higher (in comparison to their share in respective state populations) in these categories of jail inmates in Gujarat, Maharashtra, Rajasthan, Madhya Pradesh, Uttar Pradesh, West Bengal and Delhi. In some of these states, the ratio between the share of Muslim convicts, under-trials, detenues and other prisoners, and the share of total population is more than three times (see Table 1.5), though this discussion might lead us to question the reasons for this.

Conclusion

Notwithstanding the fact that citizenship issues with regard to diverse ethnic communities of India have been resolved by the Constitution bestowing equal rights and protection to all, the question of Muslim citizenship and incorporation remains alive. Historical events and Muslim identity are manipulated in such a way that hinders effective assertion of citizenship rights and/or human rights by Muslims. The share of Muslims in state employment remains negligible and their political representation is dwindling. The cover of the global Islamic terrorism has been used to incarcerate and kill Muslim youth in fake encounters by the state security agencies. This has occasionally been done in order to gather rewards from political bosses, many of whom clandestinely or openly favour a heavy hand in dealing with the marginalised Muslim community. The manipulation of Muslim identity has become very productive in the country for certain political parties. That also incites communal riots and mass crime against the community. In general, any attempt to overcome the deprivation of Muslims and promote their culture is met with increased hostility. The limited efforts by the Congress party in post-Sachar years to create affirmative action for development of Muslims have been met with increased hostility from right-wing Hindu groups and political parties. The consequence of this has been that where policies by the Congress party failed to make any mentionable impact on the welfare of the Muslim community, Muslims faced continuing communal stereotyping and violence. The institutionalisation of marginal actors, in other words, needs to be understood in a wider historical and social context that can reveal the obstacles impeding inclusion and explain the sometimes contradictory outcomes of attempts to enter the mainstream.

Table 1.5
Percentage share of Muslims (per cent) in jail inmates of respective states/UTs, 2011

S.N.	States/UTs	Population (2011)	Percentage of Muslims in				Total jail inmates
			Convicts	Undertrials	Detenues	Other prisoners	
1	Andhra Pradesh	9.6	13.9	14.5	0.0	0.0	14.3
2	Arunachal Pradesh	2.0	9.1	12.3	–	–	12.0
3	Assam	34.2	29.1	37.7	60.0	0.0	34.5
4	Bihar	16.9	16.1	16.9	19.2	4.2	16.7
5	Chhattisgarh	2.0	4.3	6.0	0.0	0.0	5.3
6	Goa	8.3	13.4	16.7	–	–	15.9
7	Gujarat	9.7	23.3	23.6	35.1	–	24.1
8	Haryana	7.0	7.2	10.7	–	0.0	9.3
9	Himachal Pradesh	2.2	3.0	3.6	–	–	3.3
10	Jammu & Kashmir	68.3	43.7	60.5	84.7	–	58.5
11	Jharkhand	14.5	23.0	22.4	10.0	–	22.5
12	Karnataka	12.9	23.3	13.2	16.0	14.3	16.4
13	Kerala	26.6	25.0	25.0	–	0.0	25.0
14	Madhya Pradesh	6.6	9.9	13.0	29.8	12.9	11.5
15	Maharashtra	11.5	29.0	32.0	42.9	–	31.1
16	Manipur	8.4	49.4	15.4	14.0	–	19.4

17	Meghalaya	4.4	18.1	12.1	0.0	–	12.1
18	Mizoram	1.4	1.7	5.2	–	–	3.6
19	Nagaland	2.5	21.1	11.1	4.0	100.0	12.5
20	Odisha	2.2	2.1	6.9	–	–	5.7
21	Punjab	1.9	2.9	1.2	75.0	0.0	1.8
22	Rajasthan	9.1	18.5	16.6	–	0.0	17.2
23	Sikkim	1.6	2.9	4.0	–	–	3.5
24	Tamil Nadu	5.9	21.3	19.9	11.2	–	19.3
25	Tripura	8.6	8.6	20.6	–	–	13.9
26	Uttar Pradesh	19.3	19.8	26.6	25.6	38.9	24.6
27	Uttarakhand	13.9	28.6	35.0	–	–	31.8
28	West Bengal	27	42.0	46.9	–	85.9	46.4
29	A & N Islands	8.5	3.3	15.0	–	–	5.3
30	Chandigarh	4.9	11.1	11.0	–	–	11.0
31	Delhi	12.9	19.0	21.7	50.0	0.0	21.0
	All-India	14.2	17.1	20.8	19.7	51.0	19.7
	Total (Muslims)	172,245,158	22,145	57,936	613	392	81,086

Source: Computed using data from NCRB (2013).
Note: The states with below 9 per cent of Muslims in total jail inmates (in the respective states) are not shown in this table.

Notes

1. The liberal conception assumes individuals as the bearers of a package of rights and the state's duty remains to protect their rights and personal liberties. It is the most inclusive and universalistic form of citizenship.
2. The republican conception contains the notion of a common good that is prior to the individual citizen and their choices. Rights are granted in accordance with the contribution of citizens to the common good. The collectivist nature of the republican discourse engenders and creates the scope for a strong sense of solidarity, a sense of belonging and security, which can contribute to the individual's self-fulfilment. The republican citizenship discourse can also divide and stratify the social body as it favours those who are perceived to be important for the common good and discriminates against those who are not ranked highly in such terms. It is less tolerant towards group grievances (Shani 2010).
3. The ethno-nationalist conception anchors membership by descent group like common blood ties, kinship, belief, and so on. This is the most exclusionary form of citizenship.
4. The non-statist conception has an ideological and institutional basis that can be inferred most prominently from Gandhi. In this conception, a citizen has an 'inherent right' to civil disobedience, and in some circumstances, it is the citizen's 'sacred duty'. It proposes minimal interaction with the state to protect individuals or group. It propagates a conception of village republics—people in villages having full power and managing their affairs, villages as autonomous as possible from the state—that will lead to *survodya* (uplift of all). However, it uses Sanskritised and Vedic terminologies that did not appeal to non-Hindu groups (Shani 2010).
5. The data for 1900–1949 has been compiled by Wilkinson (2002). The data for the period 1950–1995 was compiled by Ashutosh Varshney and Wilkinson as reported in *The Times of India* during the period. The data related to the period 1996–2013 has been compiled from various newspapers by the CSSS, Mumbai. Data related to Hindu–Muslim riots available from these three sources have been used in this chapter. It is possible that more number of riots are being reported in recent years as media coverage of geographical areas and accessibility to information have increased.

References

Akbar, M.J. 2012. 'Minority and Minorityism: Challenge before Indian Muslims', in Abdul Shaban (ed.), *Lives of Muslims in India: Politics, Exclusion and Violence* (pp. 25–34). New Delhi and London: Routledge.

Ali, Mohammad. 2008. 'Muslim Organisations Demand High Level Enquiry into Kanpur Blast', 26 August. www.twocircles.net/nod/100294 (accessed 12 August 2013).

Basant, Rakesh and Shariff, Abusaleh. 2010. *Handbook of Muslims in India*. New Delhi: Oxford University Press.

Bunsha, D. 2007. 'Fake Encounter', *Frontline*, 24(9). http://www.hindu.com/fline/fl2409/stories/20070518002303400.htm (accessed 3 August 2013).

Census of India. 2001. *Population Census 2001, C-15*. Data on CD. Office of the Registrar General and Census Commissioner, Ministry of Home Affairs, Government of India, New Delhi.
Dabhi, P. 2010. 'Kausar Bi was Raped before Killing: Ex-ATS Officer to CBI', *Indian Express*, 29 October. http://www.indianexpress.com/news/kausar-bi-was-raped-before-killing-exats-officer-to-cbi/704260/ (accessed 3 August 2013).
Government of India. 1967. *For a United India: Speeches of Sardar Patel 1947–1950*. New Delhi: Publication Division, Ministry of Information and Broadcasting.
———. 2013. 'Reply to the Loksabha Unstarred Question No.1368', Ministry of Home Affairs, New Delhi.
———. 2014. Post-Sachar Evaluation Committee Report. Ministry of Minorty Affairs, New Delhi.
Government of Maharashtra. 2013. 'Socio-economic and Educational Backwardness among the Muslims in Maharashtra', the Mahmoodur Rahman Study Group's Interim Report, Office of the Chief Minister, Mumbai.
Hasan, Zoya. 2007. *Democracy in Muslim Societies: The Asian Experience*. New Delhi: SAGE Publications.
———. 2008. *Politics of Inclusion: Caste, Minority, and Representation in India*. New Delhi: Oxford University Press.
Hunter, W.W. 1871. *The Indian Mussalmans* (Reprinted in 2002 with Introduction by Bimal Prasad). New Delhi: Rupa and Co. Ltd.
Lok Sabha Secretariat. 1999. *Constituent Assembly Debate (CAD), IX, 30 July 1949 to 18 September 1949, (third print) page 352*, Government of India, New Delhi.
NCRB (2013). *Prison Statistics 2011*, Ministry of Home Affairs, Government of India, New Delhi.
Outlook. 2005. 'Criminal sent by LeT, ISI to Kill Gujarat Leader Shot Dead', http://news.outlookindia.com/items.aspx?artid=337770 (accessed 3 August 2013).
Pandey, Gyan. 1999. 'Can A Muslim be an India?', *Comparative Studies in Society and History* 41(4): 608–629.
PTI (Press Trust of India). 2010. 'Kausar Bi Killing: Farmhouse Owner Arrested', 27 July. http://www.ndtv.com/article/india/kausar-bi-killing-farmhouse-owner-arrested-40107 (accessed 3 August 2013).
Ranganath Mishra Commission Report. 2007. 'Report of the National Commission for Religious and Linguistic Minorities', Ministry of Minority Affairs, Government of India, New Delhi.
Sachar Committee Report (Government of India). 2006. 'Social, Economic and Educational Status of the Muslim Community of India', Prime Minister's High Level Committee, Cabinet Secretariat, Government of India, New Delhi, November.
Shaban, Abdul. 2008. 'Ghettoization, Crime and Punishment in Mumbai', *Economic and Political Weekly* 42(23): 68–73.
———. 2010. 'Introduction', in Abdul Shaban (ed.), *Lives of Muslims in India: Politics, Exclusion and Violence* (pp. 1–24). New Delhi/London: Routledge.
———. 2010. *Mumbai: Political Economy of Crime and Space*. Orient Blackswan: Hyderabad.
———. 2011. 'Socio-economic and Educational Status of Muslims in Maharashtra—A State Report', submitted to Maharashtra State Minorities Commission, Government of Maharashtra, Mumbai.
———. 2012. *Live of Muslims in India: Politics, Exclusion and Violence*. Routledge: New Delhi/London.

Shani, Ornit. 2010. 'Conceptions of Citizenship in India and the "Muslim Question"', *Modern Asian Studies* 44(1): 145–173.

Stanford Encyclopedia of Philosophy. 2011. *Citizenship*. http://plato.stanford.edu/entries/citizenship/ (accessed 12 August 2013).

Tare, Kiran. 2012. 'Ghatkopar Blast Case: Khwaja Yunus Died of Cold Water, Reveals Encounter Specialist'. *India Today*, 1 March. http://indiatoday.intoday.in/story/2002-ghatkopar-bomb-blast-khwaja-yunus-encounter-custodial-death/1/176011.html (accessed 3 August 2013).

Times of India. 2013a. 'CBI to Quiz IB Officer in Sadiq Jamal Encounter Case', Mumbai, 29 July. http://articles.timesofindia.indiatimes.com/2013-07-29/india/40871089_1_sadiq-jamal-encounter-case-j-g-parmar (accessed 3 August 2013).

———. 2013b. 'Killing Street of Kotapur: The CBI's Summary Report on the Ishrat Encounter Gives a Chilling Account of Murders most Foul', Mumbai, 5 July, p. 14.

Varshney, Ashutosh. 2002. *Ethnic Conflict and Civic Life: Hindus and Muslims in India*. Yale University Press.

Wilkinson, Steven I. 2002. *Votes and Violence: Electoral Competition and Ethnic Riots in India*. New York: Cambridge University Press.

———. 2005. *Religious Politics and Communal Violence*. New Delhi: Oxford University Press.

2

Political Power and Democratic Enablement: Devaraj Urs and Lower Caste Mobilisation in Karnataka[1]

Valerian Rodrigues

Introduction

Lower caste mobilisation and organisation continues to inspire much political imagination in India as integral to processes of enablement and democratic inclusion. The non-Brahmin and anti-caste movements in southern and western India, and the low caste and Backward Class assertions in northern and eastern India, however, had charted their distinct social and political trajectories from early on, throwing up different democratic possibilities. These legacies inform the processes of enablement and inclusion and find diverse expressions although they share certain sympathies and concerns in common. These movements and assertions have redrawn the fault lines of social cleavages extending to castes and communities' differential access to political power, resources and opportunities. Dalits, as low castes, however, came to assert their autonomy from Backward Class movement from the early 1920s, distinguishing themselves by a set of specific demands, although they too had common demands with the backward castes and communities. The overlaps and conflicts that this entire churning with caste as matrix has bequeathed have led to several political initiatives with regard to enablement and inclusion in different parts of India. Much of it remained at the sub-federal level till the Mandal agitation for reservation to Other Backward Classes, in the late 1980s and the early 1990s, made it an all-India concern. This chapter is a critical exploration into one such initiative, pursued by Devaraj Urs, the Chief Minister of the State from 1972 to 1980, by deploying the resources of the government, and the institutions and instrumentalities of law for the purpose. It sought inclusion with redistribution of resources and strove to undermine caste dominance by enhancing the political presence of low castes. It demonstrates the limits and possibilities such initiatives hold for the pursuit of social justice under a functioning parliamentary democracy.

It is widely accepted that Devaraj Urs employed resources of the state—law, bureaucracy, finances and intellectual and cultural apparatuses closely aligned with the state—in support of organising lower and backward castes and communities, and encouraged them to register their own voices in devising public policy. It has been argued that such support and encouragement enabled these groups to redefine their terms of social association with other castes and communities afresh.[2] Those who applaud Urs' initiative suggest that without such support, these castes and communities would have continued to live under the tutelage of the existing modes of dominance. However, such an initiative, then and even now, has been charged as having institutionalised caste, in favour of its elite stratum, its eventual beneficiaries being the large and dominant castes. It has been argued that at the social level, this initiative enabled the dominant castes to co-opt the elites of the castes and communities in question, thereby limiting demands that might have arisen from members of the latter castes as a whole. It has also been suggested that this policy has led to the fragmentation of social relations making the social and political arena a market place for competitive bidders of caste-ware. In spite of such criticisms, Urs continues to enjoy enormous popularity amongst backward castes and communities, even a generation later. Besides, there are many intellectuals and social activists in the state straddling across caste and ideological divides, who subscribe to the argument that the Urs' initiative on the caste-front not merely enabled the backward castes and communities but also strove to forge a cohesive public across the deeply fragmented state.

Assumptions and Prior Claims

Two broad caveats right at the start: First, the articulation of caste in Indian politics cannot be simply read through an all-India lens. It takes specific overtones in the regional contexts.[3] Second, the relation between the dominant castes[4] and the backward castes is not merely a matter of unequal distribution of power. The dominant castes tend to think that they constitute the public; that they have a natural claim to power; that they are the norm and standard. Often the apparatuses of the state act as if they are the institutional expressions of the dominant castes. Public policy is deeply marked by such dominance. Backward castes have, generally, low presence in these institutions and if they do, it remains highly muted. They have to constantly prove that they are up to the mark set for them by others. Backward castes at first have to lay down their claims to power, if they have to make significant advances in other domains.[5] For such an outcome, the bases of power themselves have to be altered, and the legitimacy of such relocation has to be established afresh. Mere ethnic, linguistic and equal rights considerations are not adequate for the purpose, although they might be useful to register some advance, particularly of an incremental kind. Undoubtedly, such an assertion goes against the dominant approach, different shades of political perspectives, be it from the right or the far left, have proposed to social and economic development in India: the former restricts itself to incremental changes, while the latter rejects the present dispensation lock, stock and barrel in the name of a utopia!

Caste as an Axis of Power

Urs was deeply aware of the second caveat. He drew attention to it early, that is, to the proclivity of dominant castes to claim themselves as the public. In the former Princely State of Mysore, along with Laksmi Devi Ramanna, Urs was one of the first to draw attention to the sandwiching of other castes between the two dominant castes, the Okkaligas and Lingayats, which had laid claim to the whole of the public (Nair 2011: 265). He thought that such social cleavages that mark a public domain cannot be simply dressed up by an appeal to linguistic bonds as the Karnataka Unification Movement had attempted to do. In other words, merely demanding a separate state on the plea of a shared linguistic bond did not hold appealing prospects for groups and communities likely to be excluded from the public domain. In Mysore State Legislative Assembly in 1953, during the discussion on the Andhra State Bill, Urs was to say:

> Linguistic province is not an issue that concerns most people, and therefore there is not much interest in it. Only intelligent merchant class is enthusiastic about this... For the people of the country and the workers if the linguistic province is not formed, their lives will not become worse. From this economic point of view, it is difficult to say that their lives will improve. (Nair 2011: 264)[6]

While the linguistic issue was not unimportant, at this stage, Urs diagnosed the central concern of politics as enhancing the life prospects of 'most people'. He conceived the 'people' as primarily made up of castes and communities. Enablement of people meant enablement of the discrete castes and communities that people were composed of. In its basics, this approach was in tune with the one that Mysore Princely State had earlier come to embrace, according to many commentators, for instrumental reasons. The Mysore rulers did not wish to see public power as the monopoly of any single caste/community. The Urs caste itself was a miniscule minority. Urs, however, redefined caste relations in a much more radical fashion, but this radicalism was not premised on anything like a pronounced egalitarianism or the class approach.[7] It resonated a common sense which felt that the public constituted under the nationalist and democratic impulse was largely defined by a set of dominant castes. At the same time, it is important to note the hiatus that existed between Urs' perception of the nature of this dominance and those of other political strands who did not wish to see the public as caste dominance. Many amongst the latter in Karnataka approached the question through elements of socialist ideology culled from the ideas of Ram Manohar Lohia,[8] and the practices of the Gandhians that emphasised non-state initiatives, village and small-scale industry, land to the tiller and bringing caste abuse to an end.[9] Communists who had a weak, and mainly localised, presence in the state spoke of class mobilisation, and little probed the relation between caste and power. Urs sought a resolution of the issue by redesigning the architecture of power through the representational and policy route.

In this context, it is also important not to establish a direct correlation between the position of a member of a caste in the social hierarchy and his or her political stances. Urs was deeply aware of it. The complex cultural articulation, in which social agents were located in Karnataka, as elsewhere in India, could make some people belonging to a caste assume different social positions, or argue social values. For instance, Rachappa Mallapa Desai of Bijapur District, himself a Lingayat, whose family possessed over 6,000 acres of land spread over 14 villages, stood to lose a lot through the reforms undertaken by Urs, but remained faithful to him throughout (Shetty 2000: 36). Asceticism was an important cultural value in India, and Gandhi in popular culture came to be a reassertion of this value. Further, there was the solidarity engendered by the national movement, asserting a shared bond across Indians, particularly Kannadigas, and it was to become an important input in the public domain along with other partisan values. Eventually, some of these cultural elements came to deeply mark the political experiment of Urs, in one way or another. At the same time, it is important to note that some of the civil society institutions which seemed united in shared beliefs as the guardians of probity were prone to differential social responses. It could be seen clearly in instrumentalities such as the media.[10] Urs, however, was not cautious enough to negotiate across this messy terrain particularly on the issue of caste locations that invariably have a pronounced tilt to specific political preferences.

For the institutionalisation of caste in Karnataka after independence, we need to look into the conjuncture of unification of Karnataka, rather than merely construct it on the basis of the dynamics of castes in the princely state of Mysore at the time of independence. In the Southern part of the state, made of the erstwhile Mysore state, Okkaligas had emerged as the predominant caste, and till the time of unification in 1956 political power revolved around this caste. The unification of the Kannada-speaking region brought the more populous Lingayat areas within a single state, making it the most numerous caste in the state.[11] While the Mysore princes were friendly with a section of the national Congress leadership, there was a tension between the mass character of the national movement, and the mutual deference expressed by the former to each other. Given the conciliatory approach of the leadership of the national movement to

Mysore rulers (Manor 1977: 13), and the resistance the latter offered to an autonomous growth of the national movement in the state, the legacy of the movement largely came to be claimed by the Karnataka Pradesh Congress that had a stronger mass base outside the princely domain in the rest of the Kannada-speaking region. In much of this region, Lingayats were the largest popular bloc. They, therefore, came to closely associate themselves with the national movement, probably next only to Brahmins. Besides, by the first three decades of the twentieth century, *Veerashaivism* came to be constructed as a socially progressive ideology in tune with the larger aspirations of the masses (Boratti 2012). It boosted the moral stature of Lingayats, the adherents of Veerashaivism. In fact the Congress regime in the state led by Nijalingappa from the time of unification till the late 1960s appropriated to itself all this social capital. The assertion of other castes had to take into account not merely the demographic weight of this community but this stock of social capital as well, and rearticulate power differently.

Caste Relations in the Regional Context of Karnataka

It is important to note the specific form caste relations assumed in Karnataka. In Mysore, demand for a share in government jobs, hitherto monopolised by different sub-sections of Brahmins, came to be made by the dominant non-Brahmin castes from the beginning of the twentieth century. Caste and community associations played a major role in this regard: The Lingayat Education Fund Association was started in 1905; the Okkaliga Sangha (Okkaliga Association) in 1906 and the Central Mohammedan Association in 1909. When C.R. Reddy, a pioneer of the non-Brahmin movement in Madras Province came to Mysore, the emphasis of the movement shifted to representational demands and not merely access to education. In 1917, Reddy formed a forum called *Praja Mitra Mandali* (Association of People's Friends) which made a representation to the Maharaja demanding better access to employment and other opportunities. In 1918, the Maharaja who was sympathetic to the non-Brahmin plea appointed the (Sir Leslie) Miller Committee to enquire into the representation of non-Brahmins in the state administration. This Committee, in its report of August 1919, recommended special provisions for non-Brahmins in scholarships and in educational facilities, and in appointments to state services. Sir M. Visweshwarayya, the then Dewan, resigned when the Maharaja appointed the Committee, arguing for the principles of merit and efficiency in public services, an argument that has remained with the upper castes in the state ever since. The Miller Committee however felt that efficiency could be furthered by a fairer distribution of offices and positions amongst different communities. In its report, it stated:

> Efficiency, however, is not to be measured solely or even mainly by academic qualifications and it will not be denied that there are many important branches of administration in which other qualities such as sympathy, honesty of purpose, energy and common sense go as far to make an efficient officer as literary superiority. (Miller 1919: 12)

It further said,

> For the fact cannot be ignored that an officer in the exercise of his duty, making appointments and promotions, finds it easier to see the virtues of his own community than those of others. (Miller 1919: 12)

When Mirza Ismail was the Dewan (1926–1941) of the state,[12] widespread communal riots broke out in Bangalore and other cities of the Mysore state in 1928 that made the reservation policy in the state the target.[13] The communal riots succeeded in breaking up the non-Brahmin movement and sought to wield a political bloc by appeals to equality of treatment and merit. This nebulous bloc was to assume umpteen forms, but essentially served the interests of privilege in the name of merit and equality. The region did not go through an ideological churning that Non-Brahmin and Self-Respect Movements wrought in the Madras province, or the Satyasodak Samaj precipitated in the Bombay province.[14] By 1930, a new generation of grass-roots leaders educated in modern schools had come up and they formed the *Praja Paksha* (People's Party) breaking away from *Praja Mitra Mandali*, but this new elite with their roots in the mofussil were primarily connecting the Mysore model of development from the elite to the wider masses drawn into the public arena during this period. Therefore, it did not take them much to unite with Praja Mitra Mandali again in 1934 calling themselves as *Praja Samyukta Mandali* (People's United Association) which became the base for starting the party,

People's Federation, with its membership open to one and all. In 1937, the Federation joined the Indian National Congress widening the base of the latter. In a process of such political co-option, caste and community as socially embedded identities and power relations were little interrogated in the state leave alone challenged. In fact, they unproblematically informed the emerging public in the state. It is interesting to note that the term 'praja' (with a set of elastic connotations both substantial and relational, meaning 'masses', 'peoples', 'subjects', etc.) came to be fused with the Congress idea of the 'nation'. Cleavages of this kind continued to persist within the Congress Party in the state, taking on a new hue with the unification of the state.

It is important to point out that the Miller Committee Report of 1919 extended reservation to 'non-Brahmins' or 'Backward Castes', but there were no special provisions for Dalits until they were granted political reservation in 1940. It has been suggested that there was strong opposition amongst the non-Brahmins on granting any reservation to Dalits on the specious rationale that, 'If special preference is given to the Depressed Classes (DCs) then there would be only two dominant groups in the civil services—the Brahmins and the DCs' (Omvedt 1994: 269).[15] Therefore, when in 1937, the non-Brahmin Party came to merge with the Congress and the Congress came under the control of non-Brahmin leaders, Dalits in Mysore remained aloof from the national movement and questioned the demands for a responsible government. The Government of Mysore Act, 1940, set aside 60 of 310 seats in the Mysore Representative Assembly for minorities and of these, 30 were for DCs. Dalits feared that if a responsible government was introduced, it would not be sympathetically disposed towards them, with power concentrated in the hands of communities which had kept them down so far. It is not that such a stance led to an alternate imagination of the future. On the contrary, it made them cling to a benevolent autocracy. As a consequence, a negative alliance between Brahmins on one hand and DCs on the other remained at work. A number of Brahmin leaders had also reinforced this axis through their reformist interventions in Mysore and peripheral regions.[16]

In the other regions that eventually merged into Mysore state, caste dynamics were significantly different. In the Bombay region of Karnataka, Lingayat dominance held sway, reinforced by invoking the egalitarian and radical anti-caste legacy of the sect. In the Hyderabad region, the Arya

Samaj attempted to provide a strong communal cleavage to the movement directed against the autocracy of the Nizam of Hyderabad. The muted presence of caste in this region helped the Arya Samaj to pitchfork a common identity by 'othering' Muslims, and associating them with the Nizam's rule. Gandhian influence in the region of Karnataka as a whole reinforced a paternalistic attitude towards Dalits particularly through such organisations as the Harijan Sevak Sangh and Hindustan Seva Dal.[17] A 'Lingayat public', and not an unmarked public, took shape in both these regions which came to relate itself to Gandhian ideas of self-help by drawing deep parallels with its supposed heritage. This complex sociopolitical formation was unified with the Mysore state, through the route of state reorganisation in 1956. The relatively minor regions of southern coastal Karnataka and Coorg (Kodagu) were far too insignificant to affect caste dynamics in the state, and if they did, it was done in association with their counterparts in the rest of the state. There were three markers that stood out as the attributes of the new unified state: a crisscrossing Lingayat affinity; an invocation of a shared linguistic identity; and a stronger association with Indian nationalism, as an encompassing identity.

Karnataka became one of the test cases to challenge affirmative action measures towards *Backward Classes* through recourse to the judiciary, where the conflict between equal rights of citizens and group-rights was played out.[18] The government order of July 1958 treating all non-Brahmins, except Christians and Muslims, as backward and specifying 57 per cent reservation was disapproved by the Court as violating the principle of non-discrimination. In fact the Court invoked a constitutional principle much at variance with the government order, which was in tune with the policy prevailing in Mysore state for long. In the wake of the court order, the government constituted a Backward Classes Committee to specify the Backward Classes in the state and recommend policy measures for them. The Committee, in its Interim Report in 1960, identified those castes and communities as Backward Classes which according to it were unfavourably placed in terms of literacy and public employment. The Court too endorsed the list recommended by the Committee. But when, under political pressure, the Lingayats were included within the list by the government, the Court disapproved the order, since it had made caste the sole or primary criterion for the purpose. However, when the government issued an order solely on the ground of economic criteria, the High Court overruled it in *Vishwanath vs. Government of Mysore* on the ground that backwardness cannot be defined solely on economic criteria and invoked the Supreme Court verdict in the Balaji Case, where it was decided that caste could be a relevant consideration to decide backwardness. But the Supreme Court eventually overruled this judgement arguing that the kind of interpretation that the High Court had given to Balaji was not legitimate. While caste could be a relevant consideration, it is not necessary that it be so in every case. The outcome of such legal wrangles led to the reinforcement of the dominance of the dominant castes in the political and public employment arena. Determination of backwardness sans caste tended to benefit the poorer sections of the dominant castes, reinforcing the existing caste dominance further. It strengthened the cohesiveness within dominant castes. Legal wrangles that came in the way of policy sustained the status quo, which was generally in favour of the dominant castes.

Urs Intervention

Devraj Urs attempted to alter the configuration of caste relations that we have outlined previously by challenging the correlation of social dominance with political power. His intervention was on several fronts, and he himself conceived its impact as cumulative rather than discrete. In 1972, and again in the 1978, state legislative elections, he succeeded in allotting more electoral tickets to the non-dominant castes whereby their representation in the legislative bodies registered a proportionally higher share.[19] He also nurtured and carefully built up political leaders hailing from backward castes, Scheduled Castes (SCs), Scheduled Tribes (STs) and religious minority groups (Hegde 2013: 138). He made way for Backward Classes in public employment and higher education by evolving formal administrative categories for the purpose through duly constituted commissions. The land reform measures that he proposed led to the denting of power that landlords wielded in the countryside. Urs also instituted several welfare measures for the weaker sections although many of them went under the banner of the 20 Point Programme announced during the Emergency by the Indira regime at the centre. These measures included the Minimum Wages Act, Abolition of Bonded Labour, Debt Relief Act, People's Housing Scheme, Old Age Pension, bank finance to artisans, free legal aid, restructuring of co-operative societies, etc. It is important to note that Urs strove to reach out to the poorer sections of dominant communities as well by making a place for them in the schemes mentioned previously. Although some of the commentators have read these interventions as political expediency, they could very well be construed as integral to the conception of social justice that Urs was trying to advance.

Shift in Political Power

Prior to the unification of Karnataka in 1956, Okkaligas constituted the largest caste group in Mysore state. As per the 1930 census, the last census based on caste-wise enumeration, they formed 20.4 per cent of the population, whilst Brahmins, Lingayats and Muslims were 3.8, 12.0 and 5.8 per cent, respectively (Manor 1977: 64). In 1961, following unification, the proportion of the Lingayat Community rose to 15.57 per cent, pushing the Okkaligas to the third position with 12.98 per cent, after the SCs (Government of Mysore 1961: 41).[20] However, as Table 2.1 demonstrates, over one-third of the members of the Assembly from 1957

Table 2.1

Social composition of Mysore Legislative Assembly 1952–1972: Members and percentage

Caste/Community	1952	1957	1962	1967	1972
Lingayat	18 (18.55)	73 (36.13)	69 (34.5)	70 (38.65)	58 (27.35)
Vokkaliga	42 (43.29)	46 (22.77)	57 (28.5)	47 (23.26)	47 (22.16)
Brahmins	6 (6.18)	18 (8.91)	12 (6.0)	18 (8.91)	14 (6.60)
Marathas	–	9 (4.45)	8 (4.0)	9 (4.45)	9 (4.24)
SCs/ STs	19 (19.59)	29 (14.35)	29 (14.5)	29 (14.35)	32 (15.09)
Muslims	–	9 (4.45)	7 (3.5)	8 (3.96)	13 (6.13)
Christians	–	2 (0.99)	1 (0.5)	3 (1.49)	3 (1.41)
Other Backward classes	12 (12.37)	16 (7.92)	17 (8.5)	18 (8.91)	36 (16.98)
Total	97	202	200	202	212 (100)

Source: J.S. Sadananda (1994: 52).

Note: Figures in the bracket indicate percentage.

to 1967 belonged to the Lingayat community, and Okkaligas commanded twice the number of seats in the Assembly relative to their population size. The same was the case with Brahmins as well. These three caste groupings with a share of one-third of the population had over two-thirds of the seats in the Assembly from 1952–1967.

According to Shetty, the 1972 election was a war to break the hold of the Lingayats on political power in Karnataka. Following unification, they had regarded the state as their *Jagir* (estate) (Shetty 2000: 84). Urs' intervention made a remarkable shift in the proportion of representation of different castes and communities in 1972 as indicated in Table 2.1. The representation of Backward Castes and Muslims registered a dramatic change. While the Cabinet did retain important members of the dominant castes, many were inducted into it from the lower castes such as D.K. Naicker of Hubli (*kuruba*, shepherd); Devendrappa Ghalappa of Gulbarga (*ambiga* or boatman) and R.D. Kittoor of Belgaum (*chamar*, leather-work). In fact Devendrappa Ghalappa was to publicly state, 'The era of Veerendra (Patil) is gone and that of Devendra (Ghalappa) has begun' (Shetty 2000: 87).[21] This trend continued in 1978, till it was reversed in 1983, when Urs was no longer on the scene (see Table 2.2).

Table 2.2

Performance of social groups in Assembly elections, 1978 and 1983

Caste/Community	1978	1983
Lingayats	53 (23.55)	66 (29.33)
Vokaligas and Bunts	47 (20.88)	54 (24.00)
Brahmins	16 (7.11)	16 (7.11)
Marathas	7 (3.11)	11 (4.88)
SCs and STs	39 (17.33)	38 (16.88)
Muslims	17 (7.55)	2 (0.88)
Christians	3 (1.33)	3 (1.33)
Backward classes and other minor groups	43 (19.11)	35 (15.55)
Total	225 (100)	225 (100)

Source: Government of Karnataka (1986: 71).

Note: Figures in the brackets indicate percentage.

Table 2.3

Caste/community background of TDB presidents—1960, 1968 and 1978

Caste/Community	1960	1968	1978
Lingayat	43.55	47.20	30.85
Vokkaliga	27.60	27.95	30.85
Brahmin	6.16	8.07	7.42
Non-dominant Backward Classes	14.11	10.55	19.42
Kodava	1.22	1.24	1.14
Bunt	4.90	2.48	0.57
SCs	–	–	2.28
STs	–	–	1.14
Jain	1.22	1.86	1.71
Muslims	1.22	0.62	4.00
Christians	–	–	0.57

Source: Amal Ray and Jayalakshmi Kumptla (1987: 1827).

Note: All figures are in percentage.

This shift in representation occurred not merely at the level of the State Legislative Assembly but at local levels as well. Table 2.3 demonstrates it at the taluk, or sub-divisional level. It shows the precipitous decline in Lingayat representation at this level and the upsurge in that of lower castes and Muslims. This shift in power affected Lingayat representation much more than that of Okkaligas.[22]

We can appreciate the gains the Backward Classes and Muslims had made during the Urs regime by comparing the results of 1978 and 1983 Assembly elections. The 1972 and 1978 elections were fought under Urs' leadership. With the setback to the social engineering experiment undertaken by him, the dominant communities regrouped themselves afresh in 1983 (see Table 2.2.) The significance of Urs' reforms can be seen by contrasting them with the approach of the regimes after 1983. The ministries that came to be formed in 1983 and again in 1985 in Karnataka had a much stronger presence of the dominant castes (Hegde 2013: 148–149). In fact in the 1985 elections, the Janata Party that came to power allotted 65 per cent of tickets to candidates belonging to dominant communities.

Even in the Panchayat Raj institutions that were radically revamped, and a measure that the Janata regime trumpeted as progressive, Okkaligas and Lingayats captured 51 per cent of the total seats in Mandal Panchayats and Zilla Parishads (Hegde 2013: 149).

If we consider the composition of the Cabinet as a register of the distribution of power, the intervention of Urs clearly stands out. One of the perceptive analysts of the political scene in Karnataka describes it as follows:

> In the years after the reorganisation of the then Mysore State, the Council of Ministers formed by the first three Chief Ministers—Nijalingappa, Jatti and Veerendra Patil (1957 to 1971)—saw more than half the ministers belonging to the dominant castes. In the ministries formed under the chief ministership of Devraj Urs, the dominant castes accounted for only 37 per cent of the ministers....On the other hand, the OBCs accounted for 28 per cent of the Urs ministry. The percentage of the dominant castes in the ministry once again registered an increase with the Janata Party coming to power....It is also interesting to note that in the Council of Ministers formed by Nijalingappa, Jatti and Veerendra Patil, the dominant castes accounted for at least three of the five senior most ministers. In the first phase of the chief ministership of Devraj Urs (1972–77), at least two of the five senior-most ministers were from the dominant castes. In his second term as Chief Minister (1972–1980), not even one of the five senior-most ministers hailed from the dominant castes. (Shastri 2009: 273)

Reservation to Backward Castes

After assuming power, one of the first major policy interventions of Urs was the constitution of a Backward Class Commission[23] in 1972, under the chairmanship of L.G. Havanoor, an advocate who hailed from the backward *Beda* (hunter) community. The Commission was expected to determine the criteria to be employed to determine backwardness of those groups that the Indian Constitution describes as Socially and Educationally Backward Classes, identify the groups and the special benefits they were entitled to, and recommend policy measures for the purpose. The Constitution of India had not laid down any criteria to determine backwardness, and there was no agreement on the issue in the recommendations of the First All India Backward Classes Commission, popularly called the Kaka Kalekar Commission (1953–1955).[24] The press initially threw scorn at the Havanoor Commission and gave an impression that a person of no consequence was made the Chairman of the Commission. The bureaucracy too was non-cooperative and refused to supply official data. Eventually the Commission had to be vested with the powers of a Court to issue formal summons, to an official, if need be, if he or she refused to cooperate with the Commission (Shetty 2000: 96). After conducting extensive investigation into the social fact of backwardness, the Commission identified a set of backward castes/communities by applying multiple tests—economic, residential and occupational. The primary units that the Commission chose to determine backwardness were castes/communities with considerations such as income, literacy levels, residential locations, etc. as remedial qualifiers. The remedial qualifiers were also employed to further classify the Backward Classes and the weightages of preferential considerations to be extended to them. Under Article 15(4) of the Constitution, the Commission classified Backward Classes into three categories:

1. Category 1, consisting of 15 *backward communities*
2. Category 2, consisting of 128 *backward castes*
3. Category 3, consisting of 62 *backward tribes*

It excluded six communities from category 1 and 13 communities from category 2, but retained the rest of the mentioned threefold categories intact for entitlements under Article 16(4).[25] It recommended an overall reservation of 32 per cent for educational and employment benefits—16 per cent to backward communities, 10 per cent to backward castes and 6 per cent to backward tribes. From amongst the populous castes, it included the Okkaligas as backward. The recommendations of the Commission stoked strong protest and resistance.[26] The Commission had identified caste or sub-caste as the unit entitled to determine backwardness and did not go with the prevailing sociological tendency of recognising caste clusters. Thereby, it had made the target group more focused, and closer to groups experiencing backwardness rather than to an encompassing caste cluster with a common name, such as Lingayats. Apart from recommending groups for employment and educational purposes, the Commission also recommended the Constitution of an Advisory Board for the Backward Classes, sought the institution of scholarships, provision of hostel facilities, a separate Directorate for Backward Classes and setting up a separate financial corporation for them. The government, however, issued orders for the implementation of these recommendations by making some modifications. It included Muslims in category 1 and Scheduled Caste converts to Christianity up to second generation in category 2 above.[27] A new category called the *Backward Special Group* was created to accommodate poorer sections of Brahmins, Lingayats, Catholics, etc. with 5 per cent reservation to the group. These concessions went some way towards blunting the edge of resistance although they were susceptible to the charge of political expediency. The Commission's identification of Backward Classes and recommendation of policy measures came to be challenged in the High Court of Karnataka. The Court upheld the categorisation of Backward Classes and the inclusion of most of the castes and communities in them, whilst excluding a few, including the Urs caste to which Devaraj Urs himself belonged. Incidentally, it is worth mentioning, that the Court also agreed to the inclusion of Muslims and Scheduled Caste converts to Christianity amongst Backward Classes arguing that a religious community ipso facto need not be excluded from the ambit of Backward Classes.

The Havanoor Commission Report and a favourable response to its recommendations led to a concerted attack on Urs by dominant communities, and votaries of perspectives who wanted to employ other economic parameters to measure backwardness. Urs himself adopted certain tactics in retaliation. He supported the organisation of minor castes such as the *kumbar, kuruba, madivalla, lambani,* etc. and addressed their meetings. In fact, they were drawn to the public domain in their identities as backward castes or communities, forcing the others to confront, and if need be challenge, such claims. Urs also channelled money and resources, both party funds and governmental patronage to caste-based associations, encouraging them to hold public rallies. Thereby the public arena became a site for contestation of equality claims amongst deeply unequal groups. Urs tried to revamp the social base of his own party through such interventions. One perceptive observer of Karnataka politics, and an opponent of Urs, had this to say in this regard:

> Urs was instrumental in establishing caste associations for groups, usually rather depressed and/or numerically weak and/or widely scattered, which had not previously possessed any such organization. Of course, when he

revived or founded such associations, he naturally saw to it that his own allies from those social groups were inserted as very prominent figures in them. (Hegde 2013: 139)[28]

At the same time, Urs tried to reign in radicalism and reinforcement of opposition to his initiatives at one pole of the divide. For instance, Basavalingappa, the Revenue Minister, who belonged to a Dalit community and was a bitter critic of Brahmanism, demanded that 'trade in dharma' be stopped in the Hindu temples, and if the existing practices continued, they would be brought under the *mujrai* control (Shetty 2000: 100).[29] Urs did not extend overt support to such stances, as he thought that they would have consolidated political opposition too hot to handle.

Shift in Categories of Enumeration

One of the remarkable achievements of Urs' classification of castes and communities is its significance not merely for policy, but also for its bearing on the classification criteria employed by subsequent commissions in the State, in other states of India, and particularly the Second Backward Class Commission under the Janata Government in the 1970s at the Union level. The inclusion and exclusion of castes and their location within specified categories also begot much endorsement and disapproval, channelling political processes in certain determinate directions, not merely in Karnataka but in other parts of India as well. The relation of hierarchy came to be defined very differently in the process. It also resulted in a specific brand of politics into which castes and communities consciously inserted themselves, rather than hide themselves under the cloak of equal rights and liberties. Subsequently those who upheld abstract citizen equality had to invent strategies to defend the same by appealing to group-based caste/community claims to water down or even to undermine such claims. This was clearly the case with the Janata Party government that came to power in the state in 1985. The exclusion of both Lingayats and Okkaligas from Backward Classes by the Venkataswamy Commission Report (1983–1986) precipitated militant agitation by these two dominant castes. It led the then Janata Party government, not very well disposed towards the Backward Classes, to reject the recommendations of the Commission. At the same time, this government created a hold-all category of Backward Classes that included both these dominant castes. In the process, whilst all substantial enablement to deserving Backward Classes was reduced drastically, the regime thought it necessary to accommodate group-based representation, claiming to uphold equality.

Urs' initiative in the classification of backwardness that factored in status and development threw up a new perspective that linked backwardness to the existing articulation of social relations rather than merely as something transmitted from the past. It was to have a major impact on subsequent discourse on backwardness in the state and elsewhere. For instance, Justice Chinnappa Reddy, Chairperson of the Third Backward Classes Commission (1988–1990) in the state, examined the relative position of different castes and communities with reference to their political power, land ownership, economic prosperity, poverty, landlessness, literacy, education and employment. He further factored in relative rankings of these castes and communities with traditional social status, gradation and hierarchy and prepared two lists of backwards and forwards. He further subjected his assessment of the castes/communities in these lists to economic criteria (Hegde 2013: 153.) Such correlations enabled Justice Chinnappa Reddy to propose 38 per cent reservation for Backward Classes, dividing them into three categories. The government of the day, however, did not warm to such an initiative. In contrast, Urs recognised the adverse political responses that Backward Class categorisation invoked, and resorted to prudential but principled political action. The political responses of the governments subsequently, by contrast, can be described as modus Vivendi, accommodation to dominance wherein their primary effort was to placate the Lingayats and Okkaligas and relatively developed castes and communities such as Devangas, Ganigas, Padmashalis and Catholic Christians. In the process, adjustment and compromise came to be traded-off for a principled stand on this politically explosive issue. There is a world of difference between prudence that foregrounds principles, and which seeks retention of power at any cost.

While formally caste/community became the point of departure to identify backwardness and often such groups were further demarcated in terms of sub-units, which groups are entitled to be considered as backward became a matter of intense debate in Karnataka. The Urs intervention played a quite significant role in fueling and channelling this debate during his political helmsmanship of the state and subsequently as well. Such public debate led to the fine-tuning of some of the criteria employed by the Havanoor Commission by subsequent commissions. This legacy is exemplified by the deliberative process employed by the Second Backward Class Commission in Karnataka. In the public discussions that were held initially through seminars and conferences, factors like occupational pattern, rural- or urban-based living status as determined by occupation, the prevalent social taboos, sanitary conditions, primitive ways of worship, primitive techniques adopted in their traits, addiction to vices, literacy of parents, representation in service, environmental factors, political weight or importance attained were suggested as issues for consideration. Eventually, the Commission employed multiple tests using 17 indicators for the purpose. It is important to stress that a deliberative process characterised by relatively open-ended contestation led to the choice of these indicators.

The Urs' intervention on the issue also led to an intense discussion with regard to domain-specific backwardness. One could be disadvantaged in certain domains but need not be so in others. For instance, the Third Backward Class Commission or the Justice Chinnappa Reddy Commission, clearly stated that 'Economic and cultural impoverishment together with social deprivation are what constitute social and educational backwardness and such group impoverishment and group deprivation is what determines who socially and educationally backward classes are' (Government of Karnataka 1990: 38). This Commission further argued that economic impoverishment may be judged by levels of poverty, cultural impoverishment by low level of literacy and education, and social deprivation through inferior status and treatment. According to it: 'It is not economic impoverishment alone, nor cultural impoverishment only, nor social deprivation by itself, that makes for social and educational backwardness, but the combination of a right brew of these factors' (Government of Karnataka 1990: 38). One can see that in these formulations, the markers of backwardness were strongly correlated to development rather than cultural practices associated with modes of worship, beliefs or related practices.

It is also important to note that without acknowledging the internal differentiation within Backward Classes, benefits of backwardness would have been cornered by social strata whose experiences were truly distant from those of the vast majority of the disadvantaged. The relatively advanced castes and communities within the Backward Classes would have garnered most of the benefits. At the same time it was important to ensure that a caste or community did not aggrandise multiple benefits for the same disadvantage. For instance, the Havanoor Commission excluded prominent communities like Lingayats, Muslims and Catholic Christians alongside some other minor communities from the ambit of special consideration. The Lingayats were excluded on the ground that they were above the state-average in education and had adequate representation in public employment. Muslims and Christians were excluded on the ground that they were being treated as religious minorities, entitled to separate constitutional protection. Urs, sensitive to the limitations of the reach of equal rights and minority claims enshrined in the Constitution, argued that disadvantaged groups within religious groupings and minorities needed to be brought within the net of affirmative action. As a result, Lingayats performing low status occupations were retained in the Backward Class category, qualifying class with caste. Similarly, Brahmins, Jains and Christians below an income ceiling were included in the Backward Special Group, and some Christian converts from SCs were included in Group II. Urs was also deeply sensitive to the internal cleavages within the Muslim community and the low indices of development of the community as a whole following unification. This sensitivity made him include Muslims in Group I. In fact, Urs' differentiated understanding of this community subsequently came to shape the approach of the Second Backward Class Commission in the state, the Venkataswamy Commission. According to the latter, many castes and sub-groups were found amongst Muslims during its 1984 survey of the state, which were reflected in their addresses/surnames such as *Bhagawan, Chapparband, Darvesu, Fakura, Hanafi, Jatagera, Kallal, Katukaru/Kasai, Labbe, Laddaf/Nadaf, Madari, Mapillay/Moplah, Kaka/Biyari, Mohamadiyan, Momin, Pathan, Pendar, Phoolmali, Pinjar/Doodekula, Qureshi, Saiyed, Shafi, Shaik, Shia* and *Sunni* (Government of Karnataka 1986). The Third Backward Class Commission, or the Justice Chinnappa Reddy Commission, further reported that 56.5 per cent Muslims were living below the poverty line and their state of living was just above that of the SCs and STs in the state (Government of Karnataka 1990: 142).[30] In other words, these reports endorsed the deep inequalities amongst Muslims, embedded in their social stratification, which Urs had noted much earlier.

Some of the issues highlighted to determine backwardness were highly contested. For instance inclusion and exclusion; the need to separate creamy layer; levels of backwardness and usefulness of compartmentalisation; and backward class benefits (Hegde 2013: 234–317). It is to the credit of Devaraj Urs that he adopted a stand with regard to all these issues, although the stand itself did not find universal endorsement in the concerned constituency. It is also important to note that sometimes the association of castes and communities as akin and placing them within the same category lacked necessary empirical evidence.[31] The policy intervention, thus, created an affirmative action regime by unpacking social and economic backwardness in specific policy markers, such as:

1. The socially and educationally backward are not necessarily co-related with the poor. People may be poor but not socially and educationally backward.
2. If economic criteria were to be the sole test to determine backwardness, then the constitution would have used the term economically backward rather than the expression 'socially and educationally backward'. In other words, the constitution itself was read by the protagonists of Backward Classes as upholding 'group-based claims'.
3. Further, these protagonists argued that Article 15 (4) is not a poverty eradication programme, although programmes aimed at removal of backwardness may impact poverty reduction.
4. The partisans of caste/community-based criteria of backwardness argued that the economic criterion itself is not free from arbitrariness or confusion, particularly if income is co-related with that of the family. Further, economic criteria would invariably help the upper castes.

Impact of the Policy on Backwardness

Urs' intervention on the reservation issue had a multi-pronged impact which cannot be pursued in detail in this chapter. In the 1970s, a job in public services commanded great prestige, vastly more than the salary and benefits it offered. Urs' initiative led to several members of small

Table 2.4
Representation of caste/communities with more than 1 per cent of total population in state services excluding Class IV as on 1918, 1959, 1972, 1984 and 1988 (percentage)

S. No.	Caste/Community	Population percentage	1918	1959	1972	1984	1988
1	Agasa	1.00	–	0.51	0.70	0.75	0.75
2	Balija	1.33	–	–	1.93	1.50	1.57
3	Beda	2.75	–	0.79	1.68	1.11	1.61
4	Bestha	2.80	–	0.37	1.20	1.79	1.30
5	Brahmin	3.81	69.64	23.93	18.30	15.54	13.96
6	Golla	1.46	0.1	–	0.48	0.76	0.82
7	Idiga	2.54	–	0.52	1.25	1.18	1.69
8	Kuruba	6.92	0.3	2.80	2.62	2.81	3.28
9	Lingayat	16.92	3.61	14.83	19.90	19.68	18.56
10	Maratha	3.20	0.6	2.70	3.15	3.26	2.09
11	SC	15.86	0.48	4.73	8.31	8.53	12.96
12	ST	2.82	–	0.03	0.24	0.83	0.55
13	Uppar	1.31	–	0.3	0.39	0.83	0.55
14	Vishwakarma	1.96	0.06	1.51	1.93	2.24	2.02
15	Vokkaliga	11.68	2.42	8.95	9.69	11.74	11.57
16	Christian	1.89	2.83	4.81	4.04	3.98	2.9
17	Muslim	10.97	7.72	13.56	12.47	9.45	8.01

Source: Dinesh Hegde (2013: 310) (The information adduced in the table has been culled from the Reports of various Backward Class Commissions and Committees).

Note: All figures are in percentages.

castes/communities finding a presence in these services. Sometimes, Urs succeeded in arresting the process of representational decline as was happening, for instance, for Muslims. Table 2.4, highlights this trend.

The impact of a policy on public employment cannot be ascertained immediately, and needs to be monitored over years. Table 2.4 shows that Brahmins had a near monopoly in state services till 1918, which declined over the time, but continued to remain high relative to their population. Okkaligas and Lingayats, the two dominant castes, registered a steady increase in state services and, at the most, Urs succeeded in arresting this growth rather than reversing it. But generally, the small castes with moderate population found a favourable growth prospect in public employment due to the Urs intervention. The minorities, particularly Muslims, had reached their peak in state services in 1959[32] that started declining in subsequent years. Urs' intervention contained this decline within limits, although there was a precipitous decline of Muslim representation in state services by the late 1980s.[33]

Land Reforms

The Indian state and different provinces within the state have adopted diverse strategies to intervene on the land question. Urs' intervention traversed a specific route, which was connected to his idea of the linkage between dominant castes and political power in the state. In this understanding, the apparatuses of the state, particularly the revenue administration, were seen as deeply entwined with the dominant castes. Therefore, he set up a parallel administration for land reforms by constituting land tribunals where designated local representatives with a senior government official specifically appointed for the purpose judged on the issue of entitlements to land as per the law enacted for the purpose. The decisions of such tribunals could be challenged only at the High Court and beyond. The landlord on one hand and the tenant/landless labourer on the other appeared before the tribunal as equals and the former had to prove against the claims of the latter that the entitlements were his or hers. In the case of a perceived adverse judgement, a tenant/landless labourer could approach the High Court, and a provision was made for free legal support to such appellants. This structure of arbitration removed, or at least minimised, the element of power and dominance that hitherto clouded the choices of tenants/landless labourers. It also minimised the significance of coercion that mobilisation of dominant castes could bring to bear on such situations to thwart the choices of the lower rungs of the peasantry. It kept at bay revenue administration which was generally seen as pro-dominant castes and pro-landlords. However, there was a caveat in these measures, that is, the desire to claim entitlements as one's own rather than that of the landlord. In several parts of the state, a claim to land by the tenants/landless labourers was undercut precisely because those to whom the land was due as per the legal provisions, did not lay a claim to the same. The success of land reforms had a close correlation to the earlier mobilisation of the peasantry which made such claims legitimate and those of the erstwhile title-holders illegitimate.[34] Behind the simple act of submitting a declaration to a piece of land, there was a subtle shift in the principles of legitimacy of entitlement.

Urs' intervention on agrarian relations and the employment of political power for the purpose transferred significant productive assets primarily to lower castes, resources they were skilled to tap. Although specific information with regard to the extent of accrual of land to backward castes and communities is still to be sorted out, some of them such as the Billavas, Kurubas, Bedas, etc. stood to gain enormously from this intervention. Besides, there is no doubt, with regard to who lost land in the process. Invariably, most of them were landlords, who belonged to the upper castes or institutions at their behest. Moreover, the provision of homestead land under the Land Reforms Act benefitted a large number of lower castes, SCs and STs. There is ample evidence to suggest that the proliferation of schools and colleges in the regions that experienced extensive impact of Land Reforms from the later part of the 1970s cannot be explained without the success of this measure which freed children of vast layers of the peasantry from their effective bondedness to land in one form or the other. The provision with regard to the distribution of surplus land in the Act stipulated that 50 per cent of the same should be distributed to SCs and STs. This measure benefitted a large number of households belonging to SCs and STs. An estimated impact of the measure is as follows:

> Out of 3,551,230 agricultural holdings in Karnataka in 1971 as identified by the Agricultural Census, 485,446 tenant-holdings succeeded in acquiring rights over their land under the Land Reforms Act, 1974, i.e. 13.7 percent of the total agricultural holdings... If we add to this proportion another 1.5 percent of the rural households who came to benefit from surplus and homestead land distribution, up to 15 percent of the rural households came to benefit from this Act in one way or another.[35] (Rodrigues 1994: 48)

Urs displayed a keen interest in certain other measures such as the abolition of bonded labour, debt mortgage, abolition of manual scavenging and welfare schemes like the stipendiary project directed at unemployed educated youth. Their benefit accrued primarily to the members of specific lower castes/communities, mainly based in rural areas.

Limits and Limitations of Urs' Political Imagination

Urs' attempts undoubtedly brought castes and communities hitherto marginalised to the political sphere to be reckoned as equal claimants to the promise of democracy in political space. He also enabled such presence by deploying the resources that he could garner and strove to remove what he thought were the hurdles blocking the path of disadvantaged groups/communities to be equal claimants. Further, by foisting group identity as central to most of his interventions, he ensured that contexts of recognition and belonging were not eroded, and democracy did not get overburdened with atomistic claims. Lastly, his attempt to package multiple entitlements did not confine political action to a single pursuit.

At the same time, Urs' intervention was a snapshot. At the most, his complex legacy was seen by his successors as organising the Backward Classes for effective political action within the framework of India's electoral democracy. There was little attempt made to tease out an alternative imagination of the political by interrogating Urs' political practices. His strong political association with the troubled legacy of Indira Gandhi as Prime Minister and Opposition Leader, often made people reduce his legacy to the populism and authoritarianism that became integral to her political agenda. Further, groups and community identities as foundational to the constitution of the political and for developmental strategy were not seriously interrogated to craft an alternative imagination for organising public life in India.

We cannot, however, ignore the great flaws in Urs' political approach: He missed the wood for the trees. He did not rework the categories that he employed to devise public policy and pursue political action to rework the architecture of politics afresh. His focus on a few concerns as public goods left other concerns to fend for themselves and he often deployed the resources of the polity for the partisanship that he fostered. He sometimes portrayed the polity, whose resources he tapped, as morally deficient because it did not serve the common man or the poor as it was controlled by dominant partisan interests. In this political language of partisanship, taking away resources from the dominant interests or from the polity as a whole in favour of the partisanship that he fostered became quite legitimate. In the process, he paid little interest to the rule of law, institutional sobriety and robustness, and downplayed the deleterious significance of corruption as a means of fostering political partisanship. Eventually, it made the political system revolve around his personal charisma rather than accord with constitutional norms and regulations. Group-based considerations need not necessarily lend themselves to personalisation of power, but Urs did not attempt to shift the logic of group-based enablement to constitutional modes of functioning.

Urs' intervention was not based on a contestation of ideas, but appeared as merely seeking a shift in political power. This shift in political power was projected as an exercise in undercutting the role that dominant castes had played hitherto, an act of political strategy. Placing his political practice in the domain of contestation of ideas would have led Urs to make a public case regarding the complicity of political power with the dominant castes/communities and the need to revisit such power through the markers of group identities based on caste/community. While the dominant castes can dominate by invoking an unmarked political domain, the marginal castes/communities necessarily have to invoke their markers to make their presence felt. Urs did not problematise this issue and thereby converted what was necessarily a domain of ideas and the contestations they are caught in, into a matter of political practice. Engagement with the issue as a political contention would have probably led to the idea of democratic enablement as foundational to the contemporary Indian polity.

Eventually Urs' interventions resulted in fragmenting the public domain into umpteen spaces with few bridgeheads across them except the overarching state and its agencies. There could have been a new imagination of the public around which the discrete group identities fostered by Urs could have converged. In fact, they need not have pitched the dominant castes in frontal opposition, either. It was quite possible to re-imagine the radical legacy of Veerashaivism or the inclusive traditions of a peasant ethos to undercut cruder claims of caste dominance. Urs did not show an imagination in this direction. In its absence, what stood out were fragmented caste publics with little interface across them. Many of these caste publics eventually and even during Urs' lifetime proved ruthless, creating within them an internal paternalism and prepared to go to any extent to inflict repression on communities and castes they considered as the 'other'. Thereby, a specific form of instrumentalism came to characterise politics.

There is no doubt that Urs' intervention created a critical stratum in a number of castes and communities and their members came to regard their belonging to these categories as an asset to be tapped. Consequently, they also thought that some amount of investment had to be made in these assets. But it was also in the interest of this stratum to assert their separateness from others. Such a pursuit left few bridgeheads across gated public entities that came to be paraded in the name of caste and community. The politics it precipitated severed the link between state power and a shared conception of the public.

There was also a majority in every caste and community that Urs' reforms did not reach. He could have followed a two-pronged strategy in this regard: (a) Mobilise communities as self-help units to build up their own enabling institutions, such as schools. The elite of these groups could have been asked to invest in this endeavour. There were already models for such a moral mobilisation available in the state in the initiatives of the Lingayats, the Christians and even the Dalits. (b) There could have been investment in capacity-building for such sections through education, health facilities, etc. While the pedantic efforts underway in this regard during Urs' time continued, there was no imaginative redeployment of public power in this direction.

Urs' interventions did not benefit some relatively deprived castes/communities as much as they did their other counterparts. Several service castes did not stand to gain much from his interventions and thereby became easy targets for the appeal of communal bigotry. While Urs attempted to reverse the trend with regard to the Muslims, there were few opportunities that his interventions opened up for them. In fact, a very different imagination in the economic domain was called for, particularly in sectors such as small-scale industry and traditional crafts, to make a place for them within the economy. The public sector industry that came to loom large in Karnataka had made little place for the presence of Muslims. Similarly, Urs' intervention left a very ambivalent legacy for Dalits. Some of his initiatives on the land front created hopes which, together with the contestation that they bred against dominance, marked a space for protest.

But, beyond it, these protests found themselves at a crossroads, eventually to be splintered into umpteen expressions. Probably, social groups like Muslims and Dalits called for a radical recognition of difference that Urs' narrowly construed political imagination could not grapple with.

The intervention that Urs made in a context of caste dominance by deploying state power and patronage eventually led to the reconstitution of dominance in new-found ways. But it also opened up new democratic possibilities to wield an alternative political bloc. Political developments of the early 1980s, however, by giving a different spin to Indian politics, and to that of Karnataka in particular, reconfigured political power in new ways, and there were not many takers for Urs' strategy of inclusion with redistribution.

Notes

1. An earlier and shorter version of this chapter was published in *Economic and Political Weekly*, Vol. XLIX(25), 21 June 2014.
2. Much of this work is in Kannada. Some of the important writings in English in this regard are: Dushkin (1985), James Manor (1977, 1980, 1989), Nataraj and Nataraj (1982) and Thimmaiah (1993), Thimmaiah and Azeez (1984). An important recent works that has its focus on Karnataka in the larger context of India is Hegde (2013).
3. One of the early work drawing attention to this issue is Kothari (1986).
4. The term dominant caste is employed here to refer to a caste which wields economic or political power and by occupying a fairly high position in the social hierarchy acts as the cultural norm-setter. Such a caste claims high status and position in all the fields of social life, although such a claim does not remain uncontested.
5. This does not mean that lower castes taking over the reins of power employ it to this end. Indian politics has demonstrated time and again that when lower caste representatives come to power, they tend to subserve sectional and partisan ends.
6. Urs, Mysore Legislative Assembly Debates, 9, No. 37 (1953): 2708, Quoted in Nair (2011: 264).
7. All evidence suggests that Urs was quite well-read, and kept himself abreast with broad trends and issues till he was thrown into the vortex of electoral politics. In his own words:

> I was deeply interested in philosophy. I had read closely several good and useful books in the field. Without such study and reflection how does one find mental strength and stability? I had a basic acquaintance with the ideas of Russell, Kant, Hegel, Marx, Gandhi, Periyar, Ambedkar, Lohia etc. I had read closely the Ramayana and Mahabharata… I had read too the novels of Bankimchandra, Galaganath, Venkatacharya… Besides, I was familiar with the works of contemporary litterateurs B.M. Venkannayya, Kuvempu, and Bendre. (Gowda 1984: 12–13)

Political Power and Democratic Enablement 59

However, whatever evidence that we have suggests, that for Urs, these assorted readings formed a personal accomplishment sharpening his sensitivities, and intellectual and emotive reach. They did not constitute an ideology, in the sense of political action, made of a set of values, beliefs, understanding and diagnosis of social situations, calling upon its adherents for collective and concerted action.

8. Ram Manohar Lohia was an important socialist leader in India at the time of Indian independence, who laid much stress on democracy, agrarian reforms, Indian languages, anti-casteism and Gandhian ideas like decentralization of power, village industries and labour-intensive enterprises. His influence was widespread in Karnataka.
9. For long, the latter harboured strong suspicions of Urs, given his closeness to Indira Gandhi and the Emergency rule. Urs, however, saw many of them closer to his beliefs as Delhi politics came to take its toll, during the latter years of his chief ministership.
10. For instance, the news media which displayed much support to Indira Gandhi at the national level did not display the same ardour towards Urs in Karnataka. At the same time, some of his interventions, while they engendered widespread opposition, also elicited crucial support from other quarters, not very well disposed to the Indira Regime in Delhi.
11. Janaki Nair has argued that the contestation between the two dominant castes was central to the apprehensions the unification of Mysore Princely State with the rest of Karnataka engendered, following independence. See, Chapter 8, Nair (2011: 245–267).
12. Under the Mysore rulers, *Dewan* was the de facto head of the Government. Mirza Ismail took over the executive responsibility of government when the non-Brahmins were pressing for greater say in public employment. One of the ways in which resentment of the upper castes was expressed towards the policy of reservation was by fomenting the communal riots in Bangalore in 1928, see Manor (1977: 62–72).
13. See S. Chandrashekar (1985).
14. For the Non-Brahmin and Self-respect movement in the Madras province, a useful guide is Geetha and Rajadurai (1998); and for the Satyasodak Movement, Omvedt (1976).
15. V.K. Nataraj, cited in Omvedt (1994: 269). This reluctance to accord special consideration to Dalits may have much more to it than merely the opposition of non-Brahmin leaders, given the response of Mysore to untouchability. In the official parlance, the term DCs was employed to denote untouchable and akin castes till 1935. Under the India Act, 1935, the untouchable castes were brought under the category SCs.
16. Noteworthy amongst them were Gopalswamy Iyer in Mysore, and Kudmul Ranga Rao in Mangalore.
17. The Harijan Sevak Sangh was set up by M.K. Gandhi in 1933, following the Poona Pact, for the upliftment of the untouchables, whom he called 'Harijans', people of God. The paternalism of the Harijan Sevak Sangh is aptly captured in Ambedkar (1945). The Hindustan Seva Dal was set up as a non-violent militia of volunteers in support of the Indian National Congress in 1923 under the leadership of Dr N.S. Hardikar.
18. Some of these legal suits are discussed in the seminal work, Galanter (1983).
19. In the 1972 Karnataka Assembly elections, the Indira Congress list consisted of 133 candidates drawn from SCs, STs, socially low castes and religious minorities. The rest 90 seats went to Lingayats, Okkaligas and Brahmins. Out of them, it won 163 seats, and amongst the winning candidates, 92 belonged to the SCs and STs, socially low castes and the religious minorities, see Shetty (2000: 87). Congress Party MLAs belonging to dominant castes declined from 59.5 per cent to 49.1 per cent from 1967 to 1972. See Shastri (2009: 256).

20. The Venkataswamy Commission which conducted a demographic survey of nearly 92 per cent of the households in the state estimated the Lingayat population as 16.92 per cent and Okkaliga population as 11.68 per cent.
21. Virendra Patil, a Lingayat, was the Chief Minister of Karnataka, whom Urs replaced as Chief Minister in 1972.
22. The Urs administration did not exclude the Okkaligas, as much as it did the Lingayats. The Lingayat resentment against such exclusion persisted for years, eventually to converge in the extensive support the community extended to BJP in 1990s and beyond.
23. Urs however, did not initially suggest that this was a radical move, but projected it as a requirement for the pursuit of laid-down policy. Announcing the constitution of the Commission in the Mysore Legislative Assembly, he said,

> 1. In reply to the debate for grants for general administration department and various other departments, I had indicated that the government was actively considering the constitution of a Backward Classes commission. 2. The Supreme court and several High Courts have observed that for the purpose of determination of the backward classes, for the purpose of Article 15 (4) and 16 (4) of the constitution, definite criteria should be applied. It is desirable that any criteria fixed and any list of backward classes prepared should be periodically reviewed. In Mysore state, the criteria applied since 1963, have been income cum occupation and this has not been reviewed so far. 3. In order to evolve proper criteria and prepare a list of backward classes, a detailed inquiry is necessary. Government has therefore decided to constitute a backward classes commission. (Government of Karnataka 1972: 678)

24. The Kalekar Commission named 2,399 communities across India as backward and recommended 25 per cent reservation in Class I employment, 33.33 per cent in Class II employment, and 40 per cent in Class III and IV employment. It also recommended 70 per cent of the seats to such Backward Classes in professional and technical institutions. Besides, it suggested several programmes for their socio-economic development (See Government of India 1955). Eventually, the Commission Chairperson himself retracted from the categories employed to determine backwardness and consequently from his own Commission's recommendations. The Government of India too did not think that it is advisable to lay down a set of criteria for backwardness at the all-India level, and left the task to the state governments. Prime Minister Nehru and other important Nationalist leaders belonging to the Congress Party preferred economic criteria and discrete citizen as a unit rather than social criteria and group-based identities. See Galanter (1983) and Government of India (1980: 120).
25. Art. 15(4) speaks of 'special provisions for the advancement of any socially and educationally backward classes of citizens', and Art 16(4) speaks of 'provision for the reservation of appointments or posts in favour of backward class of citizens'.
26. For an account of the resistance, see Hegde (2013: 193).
27. The Commission had excluded these two religious minorities from its purview on the plea that there were other constitutional provisions to attend to their needs.
28. Also see, Manor (1990: 353).
29. The Muzrai Department of Government of Karnataka handles matters related to religious structures and Hindu temples.
30. After a few years, the Rehman Khan Committee report was to highlight the stark picture of inequality of Muslims in the state vis-à-vis other communities. See R. Khan (1995).

31. For instance, it has been pointed out,

> That of the 205 castes listed as Other Backward Classes by the (Havanoor) Commission, only 68 had any relevant statistical information. Moreover, of the 205 castes presented by the Commission Report, the SSLC-pass particulars had been furnished in respect of only 33 castes. Particulars regarding representation in services have been furnished in respect of 30 castes only. (Hegde 2013: 266)

32. The probable reasons for the high representation of Muslims in state services in 1959 are twofold: first, a favourable presence of the community in the services of Mysore Princely State at the time of independence; second, the unification of Kannada-speaking region into a single state in 1956, brought into it large territories from the erstwhile Hyderabad state, where under the rule of the Nizam, Muslims had a better presence in state services.
33. The Karnataka Minority Commission Report, 1995 draws attention to the pathetic condition of Muslim representation in public services in the state, see, K. Rahman Khan, *Report of High Power Committee on Socio-economic and Educational Survey*, 1994.
34. The Urs-inspired land reforms in Karnataka succeeded to a great extent in the Coastal and Malnad regions of the state and to an extent in the Bombay Karnataka region, i.e. in Belgaum, Dharwad, Bijapur and North Karnataka districts. The peasantry in these regions was mobilized by communists and socialists for over a generation demanding entitlements over land. In the other regions of the state, the prevalence of caste dominance allowed little space for a major exercise of re-distribution of land to seize the imagination of the tenants and sharecroppers. See for instance, Rajan (1986) and Rodrigues (1994).
35. The estimate of the extent of the benefit from the homestead plot provisions varies. One estimate states, 'Starting from 1974, within two years over a million succeeded in obtaining homestead land' (Shetty 2000: 103).

References

Ambedkar, B.R. 1945. *What Congress and Gandhi have done to the Untouchables*. Bombay: Thacker and Co.
Boratti, V.M. 2012. *The Discovery of the Vachanas: Halakatti and the Medieval Kannada Literature in Colonial Karnataka*. Hampi: Kannada University—Prasaranga.
Chandrashekar, S. 1985. *Dimensions of Socio-Political Change in Mysore, 1918–1940*. New Delhi: Ashish.
Dushkin, Lelah. 1985. 'Backwards and Forwards', in Robert E. Frykenberg and Pauline Kolenda (eds), *Studies of South India—An Anthology of Recent Research and Scholarship*. New Delhi: New Era Publications.
Galanter, Marc. 1983. *Competing Equalities: Law and Backward Classes in India*. New Delhi: Oxford University Press.
Geetha, V. and Rajadurai, S. 1998. *Towards a Non-Brahmin Millennium: From Iyothee thass to Periyar*. Calcutta: Samya.
Government of India. 1955. *Report of the Backward Classes Commission*. New Delhi: Publications Division.
———. 1980. *Report of the Second Backward Classes Commission*, Vol. 2. New Delhi: Publications Division.

Government of Karnataka. 1972. *Mysore Legislative Assembly Debates (MLAD)*, Vol. 1. Bangalore: Government Press.

———. 1986. *Report of the Karnataka Second Backward Class Commission*, Vol. 1–3. Bangalore: Government Press.

———. 1990. *Report of the Karnataka Third Backward Class Commission*, Vol. 1–3. Bangalore: Government Press.

Government of Mysore. 1961. *Mysore Backward Classes Committee, Final Report*, Vol. 1–3. Bangalore: Government Press.

Gowda, K.V. 1984. *Sri D. Devaraj Urs*. Bangalore: Yashaswi Prakashan (Kannada).

Hegde, Dinseh M. 2013. *Backward Class Movement in India*. New Delhi: Jawahar Publishers.

Khan, Rehman (ed). 1995. *Report of the High Power Committee on Socio-economic and Educational Survey of Religious Minorities in Karnataka*. Bangalore: Karnataka Minority Commission.

Kothari, R. 1986. 'Masses, Classes and the State', *Economic and Political Weekly* 21(5): 210–216.

Manor, James. 1977. *Political Change in an Indian State: Mysore 1917–1955*. New Delhi: Manohar.

———. 1980. 'Pragmatic Progressives in Regional Politics—The Case of Devaraj Urs', *Economic and Political Weekly* 15(5–6–7): 201–213.

———. 1989. 'Karnataka: Caste, Class, Dominance and Politics in a Cohesive Society', in M.S.A. Rao and Francine Frankel (eds), *Dominance and State Power in Modern India: Decline of a Social Order*, Vol. 1 (pp. 322–361). New Delhi: Oxford University Press.

Miller, Leslie. A. 1919: *Report on the Committee Appointed to Consider Steps for the Adequate Representation of Communities in Public Service*. Bangalore: Government of Mysore.

Nair, Janaki. 2011. *Mysore Modern*. New Delhi: Orient Blackswan.

Nataraj, V. 1994. *Dalits and Democratic Revolution: Dr. Ambedkar and the Dalit Movement in Colonial India*. New Delhi: SAGE.

Nataraj, V. and Nataraj, L. 1982. 'Limits of Populism: Devraj Urs and Karnataka Politics', *Economic and Political Weekly* 17(3): 1503–1506.

Omvedt, Gail. 1976. *Cultural Revolt in a Colonial Society: The Non-Brahmin Movement in Western India: 1873–1930*. Bombay: Scientific Socialist Education Trust.

——— 1994. *Dalits and the Democratic Revolution*. New Delhi: SAGE.

Rajan, M.A.S. 1986. *Land Reforms in Karnataka*. New Delhi: Hindustan Publishing Corporation.

Ray, A. and Kumptla, Kayalakshmi. 1987. 'Zilla Parishad Presidents in Karnataka—Their Social Background and Implications for Development', *Economic and Political Weekly* XXII: 42–43: 1825–1830.

Rodrigues, Valerian. 1994. 'The Politics of Land Reform in Karnataka', *Guru Nanak Journal of Sociology* 15(1): 27–51.

Sadananda, J. 1994. 'Sri Devaraja Arasu: Hindulida Vargagala Sangathan Mattu Havanuru Varad', *Arivu Baraha* No. 7 (in Kannada): 41–67.

Shastri, S. 2009. 'Legislators in Karnataka: Well-entrenched Dominant Castes', in C. Jaffrelot and Sanjay Kumar (eds), *Rise of the Plebians? The Changing Face of Indian Assemblies* (pp. 244–276). New Delhi: Routledge.

Shetty, V. 2000. *Bahuroopi Urs*. Bangalore: Sapna (in Kannada).

Thimmaiah, G and Azeez, A. 1984. *The Political Economy of Land Reforms*. New Delhi: Ashish Publishing House.

Thimmaiah, G. 1993. *Power, Politics and Social Justice: Backward Castes in Karnataka*. New Delhi: SAGE.

3
'We Are Still Junglis to Them': Institutionalising Marginalities amongst the Adivasis in Dooars

Supurna Banerjee

Long live the movement
Our struggle will go on
We fight for our rights
Remembering those who have struggled before us we promise to keep alive the fight
Those who have given their lives for our liberation
We have taken an oath to avenge their debt of blood and dedication
Remembering those who have struggled before us we promise to fight on'
(song from the Language Movement).

The given extract is a loosely translated song from the Bhasha Andolan (Language Movement) which occurred in the Dooars region in the early 1990s demanding that Sadri be recognised as a language in educational institutions in North Bengal.

Introduction

The tea plantation workers of North Bengal consisted of the Adivasi and Nepali workers. The former were the tribal groups of Chotanagpur Plateau recruited by the colonial planters since the 1860s (Bhowmik

1981; Chatterjee 2003). Though there might have been a constant flow of Nepali workers for a long time, it was in 1950 with the signing of the India Nepal Peace and Friendship Treaty that the recruitment of Nepali workers picked up (Meena and Bhattacharjee 2008: 16). The tea plantation workers have, however, been portrayed in the plantation literature primarily as workers. Being top-down studies, the labour force remains locked in a class analysis, a nameless, faceless, passive mass that forms the backbone of the plantation system, yet remains deprived of their personhood (Beckford 1972; Daniel et al. 1998; Graham 1984). While class analysis is undoubtedly important in understanding the history of tea plantations, the plantation workers do not just have a class position, they also have ethnic, religious, caste and gender identities. While there has been a mention of tribal identities amongst the workers of North Bengal and Assam (Bhadra 1997; Chatterjee 2003; Das Gupta 1994; Jain 1998), there has been little sustained analysis of the intersections of these identities in determining the position and condition of the workers. Their multiple, usually subordinate, identities have remained subsumed under the class identity rendering invisible the multiple strands through which marginalisation takes place and is legitimised.

Working in the tea plantations through generations, subsumed under the class narrative and rendered almost invisible within the dominant culture of West Bengal—carving out a space for their distinctive identity has not been easy for the Adivasi (tribal) workers. Through their customs, rituals and culture, they have maintained their distinct identity in their everyday life, but in the sociocultural narrative of the mainstream they have remained on the margins. In spite of this, they have organised themselves time and again to carve out a space for recognition of their identity, culture and distinctiveness within the mainstream Bengali culture of North Bengal. This chapter draws on recent fieldwork to explore the trajectory and impact of the movement for linguistic recognition which took place in the early 1990s called the Bhasha Andolan (Language Movement) in some parts of the Dooars region of North Bengal. The fate of the movement raises important questions about the role that institutionalisation plays in giving shape to the final destiny of such indigenous movements of a peripheral population.

Methodology

The chapter is based on the data from my PhD fieldwork conducted in 2010–2011 in Kaalka, a tea plantation in Dooars. The method of data collection consisted of participant observation for a period of 15 months in the plantation. Towards the later stage of the fieldwork, I also did semi-structured interviews and oral histories. Alongside these, a very useful source of information was the informal group and individual conversations that I had with my research participants. The main research participants were women, and it is mostly their perception and voices through which I have captured the language rights movement. I did speak to some of the men too who were active in this movement and to a couple of the second tier leaders. Since the movement had occurred years before my fieldwork, the narrative of the movement is constructed through the accounts of the people. The intention here is not only to provide a description of the movement, but to map the participants' perceptions of how an indigenous movement arising as a response to their marginalisation went on to embed these very marginalities. Since there is not much archival data available on this movement, accounts, perceptions and narratives form the backbone of this chapter as they bring out the contradiction between the rhetoric of the movement and the politics of its organisation. The focus here is less on the workings of the movement itself so much as the longer term impact of its actions. The lengthy gap between the movement's active phase and my interviews, from this perspective, is less of an issue since the aim is to capture a sense of change over time.

'Because If You Do Not Make Noise, Nobody Listens to You': Language and Identity

> It was not just about language, it was about our identity, it was about us; all that we were made of. We have been in North Bengal for generations now, much before the Nepalis. But we are still junglis (wild) to them. Why? We have our culture, our language and we fought for it. (Bandini 2011)

During the establishment of the tea plantations in North Bengal in the colonial period, tribal communities from Jharkhand were brought there as a labour force (Das Gupta 1994). Settled in the plantations for generations, this community was identified as the Adivasis and formed a significant section of the population of North Bengal. The Adivasis were naturally not a single homogenous group but made of multiple caste groups. Oraons constitute roughly half of the population and the rest comprised the Munda, Kharia, Kujur, Santhal, Lohar and Baraik (Das and Banerjee 1964; Sarkar and Bhowmik 1998: 50). In addition to the distinctive culture of the caste groups, there had also emerged a more homogenous Adivasi culture. Alongside this, they developed a common dialect; Sadri. Sadri grew out of the Sadani Hindi of Jharkhand combined with the different dialects of the various tribal groups (Nandy 2013). This was the common language of communication not only across but also within the caste groups. Sadri, however, had no recognition within the state's official languages. English, Bengali, Hindi and Nepali were the languages used for official communication with any of the state bodies like the post office, the Block Development Office and also as medium of instruction in the educational institutions. Nandy (2013) argues that without this basic educational right, the workers would remain ignorant about the laws, about the obligation of the state organs, about their rights. They would also be deprived employment opportunities and chances of social mobility as Mohni points out in the extract below.

> Imagine how much our children suffered. They could not understand what was taught in the schools. So right from the beginning they were lagging behind. The Bengalis, Marwaris and Nepalis got all the jobs. They had the facilities while we were ignored for years and years. (Mohni 2011)

This difficulty was compounded by the fact that Sadri had no script. Thus, every time a deputation was given or an agitation organised, the local government cited this lacuna and negated their demands.

Mitchell (2009), amongst others, points out how language can become a powerful force through which shared identity and context are projected. The language of a group hardly ever remains limited to being a medium of communication but often transcends into becoming the marker for their history, culture, identity and very personhood. Thus, the denial of the recognition of their language signified a refutation of their very identity. This was encapsulated in their widespread identification as 'junglis'. 'Junglis' are constructed as wild and uncultured as against the Bengali 'bhadrolok'—the cultured, educated Bengalis. Such discursive tropes effectively negated the Adivasi culture. The demand for recognition of their language, thus, was directed against this othering and the negation of their identity.

The discontent with this discriminatory treatment was building up and sporadic protests occurred against it in different parts of North Bengal but particularly in the Kaalka[1] region. While this continued for a few years, the movement gathered momentum with the formation of the Jharkhandi Adhikar Mancha (JAM: Platform for the Rights of Jharkhandis) in the early 1990s, which became the organising body for the protests. JAM was a loosely formed social movement organisation created by the more active members of the Adivasi community with the help of some professional activists. The latter were ultra-leftist activists (many of whom later became affiliated to the CPI [ML]) mostly from West Bengal and some from Jharkhand. This group of activists had been active in this area of Dooars for many years working towards the workers' welfare and rights. They acted as the leadership of the movement, though in course of time some of the indigenous Adivasi workers also became a part of this leadership. Based on their history of activism for labour welfare in tea plantations and support for such activism in coal mines in erstwhile Bihar (presently Jharkhand[2]), sections of these activists also had contacts with poets, song writers and dancers from Jharkhand who were sympathetic to their cause. Many such performers came to train the participants in the cultural forms of self-expression and organised programmes in solidarity where they themselves performed to showcase the glory of their culture and language. When the movement was at its height, the organisation also enjoyed support of the intelligentsia, especially in North Bengal and Jharkhand. Though the movement was limited in its geography to certain parts of the Dooars, it enjoyed a popular support in the region, especially within the Adivasi community.

> I had been actively involved in the movement for the rights of our culture. We had this organization called Jharkhandi Adhikar Mancha and we fought a great deal for the right to have our language recognized. We were amongst the first to come to West Bengal but we did not have a single school in our own language. Other communities came up and established schools of their own language but we had nothing. So we fought a lot for this. Many of us were active and we sacrificed a great deal for it. (Nabhitha 21 September 2011)

The movement proceeded along two streams—cultural and political. In the initial stages, these two streams were entwined. Blockades and rallies were accompanied by both slogans and songs. The opening quote is a loosely translated version of one such song. In their analysis of social movements, Della Porta and Diani (2006) point out that one of the important questions for social movements is the process through which values, emotions and ideas are converted into collective actions. How can they be used to explain the start and persistence of collective actions and how can organisations maximise the strength of such collective challenges?

> The movement was unpredictable, volatile and spontaneous. Imagine a whole group of 300–350 people, men, women and children blockading schools and singing songs eulogizing their culture, recounting its glorious history. The officials, the police all were clueless as to how to deal with this. There were street corner plays but there were also political demonstrations. The cultural aspect of the movement was the backbone of its politics. There was violence too. Because if you do not make noise nobody listens to you.
> (Tarak Chatterjee 10 October 2011)

Chatterjee, one of the second-tier leaders of the movement, in the extract just discussed illustrates how the movement, in addition to using the usual political repertoires of a protest like demonstrations and street corners, also had its unique elements. At the initial stage, the participants enjoyed a centre stage. Their emotions fuelled the course of the protest and the leadership seemed to be in tune with these emotions channelling them whether through cultural programmes or through violence in order to make an impact. This, however, started changing as the movement gained more force and attention. Della Porta and Diani (2006: 6) ask whether the traits of a political system and its attitudes towards citizens' demands influence the impact of the movement in the political arena. In line with this, I turn my attention to the ways in which the movement changed its character which can help in understanding how protest tactics and strategies change over time and why?

'The Leaders Betrayed Us and Our Movement': Institutionalising Marginalities?

Gamson (1990) identifies securing advantages for the participants and acceptance as political players as the two fundamental aims of social movements. The chronicle of this movement suggests that these two outcomes can be contradictory to each other. Coy and Hedeen (2005) have shown how social movements are often co-opted within the political system in such a way that they become institutionalised within the very structure and system that they set out to challenge in the first place. The social movement organisation grows in strength as it mobilises a grievance through developing shared consciousness and collective identities by which they translate a perceived injustice to a social movement (Piven and Cloward 1977) as was seen in the case of the JAM. Following this inception a process of negotiation with the political system, and in many cases co-option within it, begins.

Coy and Hedeen (2005: 413) argue that the process of co-option is marked by appropriation of rhetoric and style of the challenging movement and by appropriating the movement actors by invitation to participate in policy making. Though they claim the former usually precedes the latter, in the case of this movement, the co-option of the leaders preceded the institutionalisation of the movement's performance. As the movement gained in force, the state government began to take more notice of it and then began the process of co-option. Committees were formed to look into the demands of the JAM and its supporters. Leaders of the movement were invited to join the committee.

> The invitation was a major victory for us. The government which had ignored us for so many decades was now being forced to recognise us and in fact beg us to join them. We were given the right to play a role in deciding on our future. (Shiva 2011)

To many, leaders and supporters alike the formation of the committee with members from the movement was, thus, perceived to be acceptance as political players. Research (Gamson 1990; Katzenstein 1998; Kriesberg 2003; Stagenborg 1988) has shown that integration can bring about positive policy changes or enable the protesters to carve out a space within the decision-making structure of the political system. While these are no doubt important and did result in some gains for the Adivasis, the implications of the process of co-option were much more uncertain in this case.

The decision to accept the invitation was certainly not uncontested.

> Many of us were opposed to this. The government has ignored us for so long. Our culture, our history has never been recognised. Today because

of our movement they are giving us importance but why should we be bought by them? Some of us and even some of the leaders said that we will join the committee only after the government has acceded to our demand, not before that. (Nabhitha 21 September 2011)

Nabhitha's opinion was an expression of generations of distrust in a government which had ignored their needs. Many (Melucci 1989) have defined social movements and their organisation to be incompatible, by their very nature, with institutionalisation. Rucht (1990) also makes a distinction between public dissent through protests and conventional forms of political participation such as voting or lobbying, holding these to be distinctly separate forms. Social movements through their willingness to use unconventional and even illegal actions engage in disruptive performance rather than working with existing institutional frameworks (Aminzade 1995: 40). By pushing the conflict to the limits beyond compatibility with the system, movements question the legitimacy of power and the very system (Melucci 1989: 176). A similar emphasis on the oppositional basis of social movements is found in the quote just discussed. To Nabhitha and others like her, the movement had to proceed through a confrontational relation with the political system through which the government and its agencies would be *forced* to accede to their demands. Thus, this acceptance to work with the state and its institutions, to them, went against the foundational principle of their movement.

The two shades of opinion show that what one group supported as the government's cooperation was perceived by the other group as *being bought* or co-opted. Movements are often split over such issues of institutionalisation. Offe (1990), amongst others, has illustrated a very similar split in the German Greens when one group did not want any dealings with the government (*fundis*) and the pragmatists who were not averse to working within the system (*realos*). In this case, however, the movement did not split in spite of this lack of unanimity amongst the protestors about the decision to accept the invitation. Rather the majority view amongst the leadership prevailed and the invited leaders acceded to the government's request and joined the committee. Through this act, one stream of the movement gained prominence over the other. Many of the leaders who opposed this move resigned from the organisation and began to concentrate on grass-roots organisation and providing training, while others reluctantly made their peace with the decision. Through the committee formation and its deliberations, the leadership was given responsibility within the very system they were protesting against and the movement rapidly started getting more institutionalised. The committee made a decision to appoint a commission to look into the demand of inclusion of Sadri as a medium of instruction in the schools. This commission was to have two members from JAM as the community representatives.

While the incorporation into the government-formed committee gave the leaders a voice in the policy decisions, this did not come without a cost. There was a compromise on relative autonomy. JAM's leadership decision to hold off the more radical aspects of the protest till the commission's report, was a case in point. Mediated by the boundaries of the existing policies and embedded structures of power, the movement's ability to launch a fierce and unrestrained critique of the status quo was significantly neutralised, and the role of the mass of participants was reduced. Coy and Hedeen (2005: 417) point out that emotional commitment of the leadership gets siphoned off in this manner, leaving a large section of the protestors clueless and disillusioned.

The commission, however, kept delaying its reports and some of its members, including two of the JAM leaders, resigned in the protest. The resignation was met with the decision to re-launch the protest in its full force. But as the movement played out, it became apparent that it had changed from an 'alternative to an integrative movement' (Coy and Hedeen 2005: 418). Its performance brought to fore the disjuncture which had started appearing between the rhetoric of the movement and its organisation.

> Being in the government the leaders had also matured. Earlier the movement was wild (jungli jaisa). There was not much planning involved. There would be one or two meetings and the volunteers from each plantation would tell the others. Then in the blockades we would sing songs. There was also 'fighting, regular fighting'. We often in rage went and wreaked havoc in school buildings and other places. But now they explained to us that this was not the way to proceed. Violence would make us *unacceptable* to the others (mainstream). Everything was well planned and the volunteers were made responsible for their units. They told us we cannot behave like junglis if we want them to take us seriously, we have to show discipline like an army. (Durga 23 July 2011, emphasis mine)

Gorringe (2011) illustrates how spontaneous movements get subsumed into institutionalised politics and its expression. He notes how, in moving from a radical mass movement challenging the very basis of the existing political institutions to becoming a political player within that system, the Viduthalai Chiruthaigal Katchi (Liberation Panther Party) came to resemble the very institutions which it set out against (Gorringe 2011). Palishkar (2013) points out a further dilemma which faces a party or organisation and its supporters. This is the contradiction between sticking to its support base and, hence, limiting its aims, or extending the aims and losing that support base and/or letting the supporters down. In the previous extract, it can be seen that gaining acceptance within the mainstream had attained a top priority in the movement now. The movement was now politicised in a formal sense and this entailed a loss of, or at least an erosion of, direct activism. It was now more closely aligned to the hegemonic structure within which protests could gain legitimacy. This was met by disappointment from a section of the supporters as will be seen below.

The leadership now rejected the two main planks through which the movement had come to the attention of the government in the first place, that is, violence through destruction of public property and its unpredictable volatile nature. Rather the emphasis now was on planning and execution. The political and cultural strands of the movement were separated out with organising cultural programmes and street corner plays on the one hand and on the other having blockades and demonstrations where slogans were shouted and speeches were given. Delivering speeches by the leaders and invited speakers, in fact, was a completely new addition in the second edition of the movement. These speeches, once again, were designed to speak to an outside audience.

Aminzade (1995) claims that there is nothing inevitable about a movement becoming institutionalised as its internal organisation becomes more formalised. But as the previous extract shows, in this case the movement had begun diverting its energies from organising mass defiance to accommodating the status quo (Piven and Cloward 1977). Being more formally organised rather than being loosely knit as it used to be, JAM also had suppressed or toned down their ability for disruption and was now looking to extract concessions. Burstein, Einwohner and Hollander (1995) argue that it is the outsider status that defines a social movement as different from the mainstream organisations. But as the changing tactics and politics of JAM demonstrated, once it began to succeed at some level, especially through collaborations with institutional agencies, it tended to abandon its outsider status and looked to be a part of the mainstream. Della Porta and Diani (2006) illustrate the trade-off between radical actions and losing the confidence of general public. The radical actions through which rank and file support can be maintained and solidarity within the movement preserved, might be the very acts which alienate the potential target groups within the public (Della Porta and Diani 2006: 179). These create exclusive identities and in reaching out to potential allies, the leaders are often compelled to alter this. The way the political system is structured tends to generate certain forms and modalities of expression (Gorringe 2011: 8). The change in tactics was designed to enable the movement to reach out to an outside population rather than isolate them. At the same time, by adhering to the established template of political protest, the movement isolated a large section of its own members, in a way pushing them to the margins of a movement aimed at protesting against their marginalisation.

> In the meetings the leaders would always ask us to reign in our rage. Always 'control your anger', 'listen to your group coordinator'. Arrey (exclamation of incredulity), we are protesting from our anger, how can we let that go? Suddenly it did not seem like our own anymore. (Lachmani 27 August 2011)

Thus, by recreating the form, structure and rhetoric of the politics against which they were protesting, and from which they were excluded, the movement in its present form further embedded the marginalisation of the participants. As the movement became more organised, the sense of ownership of the ordinary participant started dissipating. With emphasis placed on the following procedures, the role of mass defiance became secondary. In this almost professional method of protests, the role of hierarchy and the following orders had to be subscribed to. While there are many practical advantages of a social movement becoming institutionalised, it often results in a sense of loss and betrayal amongst many of the participants (Offe 1990). This was heightened at the next stage of the movement.

A period of protest followed, but it was apparent that the movement was losing its steam.

> We were now playing more of a waiting game. The intensity of the movement was determined by the way the government committee functioned. I have had enough and decided to formally resign though I had mentally moved away from the movement when its first death knell was struck by its leaders. (Chatterjee 2011)

Coy and Hedeen (2005: 422) argue that co-option is often followed by rationalisation where, for the sake of greater efficiency, 'broader goals of community empowerment, relationship building and democratization of justice' are set aside. Both the previous extract and Chatterjee's words seem to point at this changing role of the protests. Thus, the established path of how to do institutional politics which had already been set up acted as both an opportunity and a constraint for the protesting body (Gorringe 2011: 3). Jenkins (1985) amongst others have shown how formalisation of movement and rational leadership are not incompatible with grass-roots' protest as often long-term survival becomes possible through the employment of strategies which already enjoy a certain amount of legitimacy within the system. Working within the system gives the movement access to crucial resources like decision-making procedures (Kriesi 1996: 155–156). Thus, the professionalisation of the movement might be a price worth paying for securing these advantages. Piven and Cloward (1977) have, however, remained sceptical of this phenomenon. Besides viewing this as wastage of scarce resources, they also argue that this tends to temper mass defiance which is the only resource available to the marginalised population. By taming the protests, it alienates crucial sections of its support base and in the long run loses its sustained momentum as was seen in the next stage of this movement.

After almost a year of deliberations, the government committees announced that due to lack of infrastructure like trained teachers in Sadri and the lack of a script, it was not possible to immediately introduce Sadri as an official language. But assurance was given that efforts will be made towards this direction and commissions will be elected periodically to look into this. These commissions will have members of the Adivasi community on board. Also, schools will be encouraged to have cultural programmes showcasing Adivasi culture alongside Nepali and Bengali. Finally, they announced a grant to be given to the JAM to work towards the betterment and development of the indigenous population of the region. Some of my respondents reported that some younger educated men were also given jobs in government institutions.

This announcement also yielded mixed response. Though all accepted this as disappointing, there was no unanimity about the way forward.

> We had lost the movement but they were not willing to accept it. They (the leaders) said this is victory for us. Not all were like that, some opposed like Kalan but they were few. Some withdrew completely, others were bought

in and most of us in the rank and file, we stupid people (buddhu) they explained to us that this is not over. We had to bide our time and make preparations. Using the grant they said was the first step to this preparation *of being recognized as a part of the system*. You tell me, if our own people, our own organisation does not take our side, why should we expect it from the Bengalis (humara apna jati, apna party agar humarai saath na de, toh un Bengaliose kyon umeed rakkhe hum). (Nabhitha 2011, emphasis mine)

NGO Formation: A Full Circle?

The final shock, however, came a few months later when JAM decided to disband itself and reform as an NGO called *Shakti*. Further, this NGO was to work towards the welfare and empowerment of tea plantation workers rather than limiting its activities only to the Adivasis.

> It was important for us to realise that this movement can only be strengthened from within and that will not come through protests but through development. But this development will not be meaningful if it is of just one community. In this tea plantation belt, as you have seen, the entire labour force is deprived. Thus as a social service organisation it is our responsibility to work for not only the Adivasis but also the Nepalis and Biharis who toil in this plantation alongside our community. (Bhavani 15 October 2011)

Snow et al. (2004) argue that as social movements develop over time to become more institutionalised, they often go on to evolve into interest groups or even political parties. JAM's decision to form an NGO also seemed to proceed along this same trajectory of institutionalisation. But this decision completely negated the fundamental identity through which the movement had unfolded and reached this point. The question now was not of self-expression or identity but of development, the people were no longer Adivasis, they were once again subsumed into being tea plantation workers. It was ironical that a movement which had emerged in order to assert the identity of the Adivasis and protest against subsuming their culture, language and personhood in the indistinguishable category of workers, finally ended in a body which drew its existence by negation of these very particularities. This final step signified a successful and complete co-option into the political system and also most effectively put an end to a movement which had begun from the demand for self-expression of marginalised people.

After the formation of Shakti, there was nothing to say. I completely became aloof from the movement. Our leaders betrayed us. There is nothing more to say. (Lachmani 2011)

Added to these, there were also charges of corruption. Whilst none of these accounts could be validated, they were still important as they pointed to a larger problem of accountability and trust.

In the middle of the movement when it was gathering momentum they started saying that this movement is petering out and instead reorganized as an NGO. Many of the earlier active members having already understood their intentions had withdrawn from the movement. By forming an NGO they automatically became eligible for government money which they used for some of the work and maybe also took for themselves. They became the agents of the government. We had invested our faith in the JAM when they had said come with us but the leaders betrayed the movement midway. (Pushpita 12 July 2011)

The JAM, thus, in some ways, came to reflect 'the hegemonic organisational structures, priorities and discourses of the institutions from which it was excluded' (Gorringe 2011: 9). While its assimilation into the political system of West Bengal was greeted by a section of the supporters with anger and disappointment, its further reorganisation into an NGO eroded its legitimacy in their eyes, while conversely making them a more legitimate player in West Bengal politics and society. Through inspiring commitment, mobilizing resources, creating and recognising opportunities, devising strategies and demands, the leaders of a social movement prove to be critical to the movement (Morris and Staggenborg 2004: 172). The followers invest their faith in the leaders to articulate and act on their behalf. However, they also point out that often in the course of the movement (as in the case of this one), the leaders become a part of the political elites, more concerned with organisational maintenance than with the original goals of the movement (Morris and Staggenborg 2004: 173). Meyer and Tarrow (in Gorringe, this volume) have demonstrated how social movements have commonly been a medium for the advancement of its leaders. This, then, brings them into conflict or at least in opposition with the ordinary participants of the movement and can drive a wedge between the leaders and the led. In this context, Gorringe (2011) illustrates how allegations of links with political parties, businesses and charges of corruption are important indicators of how an organisation is perceived by those it is supposed to represent.

'What We Fought For, They will Achieve': Agency at the Margins

While the process of institutionalisation usually proceeds through stages, these are neither linear nor are they inevitable (Coy and Hedeen 2005: 426). Melucci (1989) argues that accepting the inevitability of co-option and institutionalisation of marginalities forecloses the possibility of recognising the potential of social movement organisations to challenge the status quo, fight for deeply held values and sometimes give rise to new movements with new demands. Snow et al. (2004) point out that while looking at social movement organisations and their ability to effect change, there is often a tendency to disregard changes at the individual and personal level. While the social movement itself might get institutionalised and its organising body co-opted, often these movements create spaces of agency—spaces which refuse to be appropriated, spaces where the distinctiveness of identity is protected and played out. While formal institutionalisation of the movement was perceived by the participants to be a let-down, there were other aspects of the struggle which did result in some gains, as will be seen here.

As mentioned previously, some of the participants in the movement did land up with government jobs in educational institutions and administrative offices. Though limited in nature and in number, this also had its spill-over effects. For instance, Bipin who was working as a primary teacher in one of the government schools in Kaalka, used to give tuition in Sadri to students as a way of supplementing their studies. While he was a teenager at the time of the movement, his father had been an active member of the JAM.

> As I walk into the courtyard I stumbled into a makeshift classroom. 15–20 students were sitting on the ground in front of a big board while Bipin sat on a stool in front of them explaining to them the complexities of the 2nd World War in Sadri. I saw his father sitting on a chair nearby watching with pride. As I approach him he explains to me, 'We fought so much for the right to be taught in our own language. Nothing came of it. Our children did not get jobs as they could not do well in the exams. How will you do well if you don't understand properly? But now all that will slowly change. Many young men and women like my son are teaching the children in classroom and outside. One day we will reap benefits of this. What we fought for, they will achieve.' (fieldnotes, Kaalka 23 May 2011)

By providing the extra support to overcome the language barrier, Bipin and others like him sowed hope in the minds of many, a hope that maybe gradually a change will be possible. The act reflected the intention to take an active role in shaping his community's own destiny rather than being dependent on others for assistance. Here were instances which showed that while the institutionalisation of the movement as a whole caused it to lose its way, other aspects of the movement, such as these tuition centres were institutionalised, in less formal ways. Recognising the obstacles, the classes were meant to prepare the new generation to manage them better. This illustrated how institutionalisation can take different forms. Such instances of institutionalisation, in fact, endeavoured to meet the everyday needs of the people and also invest them with greater confidence to take on, even if in minute ways, the institutional barriers that they face.

Della Porta and Diani (2006: 91) speak of the intersection between 'collective involvement and personal engagement which characterizes so much of collective action'. These collective experiences provide a sense of continuity and a sense of community. This sense of collective belonging was institutionalised almost invisibly and very gradually by handing it down through the generations, thus keeping the sense of community and culture alive.

Bandini, one of the women active in the movement, along with some of her other neighbours teach the children of the villages in the plantation songs, dances and poetry.

> We learnt many songs at the time of the movement. I had a good voice and we would often sing in the protests...I don't want our children to be deprived of their culture. Hence we used to teach these songs to our daughters and their friends. Now they have grown up but their children come. Every year on Birsa Munda Day we have a big performance. Earlier this used to be small, only within Kaalka. But now slowly children from other plantations come too. It is now like class. Last year a woman came, she was like you. She had come from Bombay and we did a performance for her. She enjoyed it, video (record)ed it. Last month she sent us a cd with all the recordings. (Bandhain 12 October 2011)

Measuring these acts by their revolutionary potential to cause immediate impact will fail to capture their importance. While their effort to teach the future generations the idioms of their culture will probably not amount to a social movement, it gives them a space of recognition. Moreover, as the children go to school and perform these songs, it also provides a network through which they connect with others who in turn then join these classes. The classes then are not just about teaching performing arts, they denote something more fundamental, a passing on of a heritage to a future generation, of ensuring that even if in small ways these are protected and also of developing a connection based on that common heritage.

Through such practices, a space of autonomy was created, a space in which the distinctiveness of a culture was recognised and valued. While it could be argued that these spaces still remained isolated in many ways from the mainstream, these acts referred to what Kabeer (1999) terms transformative agency. They do not only aim towards immediate inequalities but look to initiate longer-term processes of change in the structures of domination as Bipin's father hoped that the fruits of their sacrifice through the movement will be reaped by a future generation. Both these extracts and other instances like this illustrate that social movements and effects of their institutionalisation have to be understood at multiple levels and often outside the binaries of gain and loss. People make use of aspects of movements in their own ways.

Taylor (1989: 761) speaks of abeyance structures through which movements sustain themselves in non-receptive environments and provide continuity from one stage of mobilization to the other. The upsurge of the Akhil Bharatiya Adivasi Bikash Parishad (All India Committee for Development of Adivasis—ABAVP), a political party clamouring for greater recognition of the rights of the Adivasis might have gained from such abeyance structures. In a movement in abeyance, the activists most intimately connected with the movement create and find a niche for themselves in which the values, identities and political vision can be sustained when the movement peters out (Sawyers and Meyer 2009). This provides for movement continuity and may sow future mobilisation opportunities. Taylor (1989: 762–770) argues that even if such groups have limited impact during their life time and might actually even contribute to the status quo, they are often the sources of protest and change by providing crucial resources like pre-existing activist networks, repertoires of goals and tactics and a collective identity. The rise of the ABAVP cannot be seen as a resurgence of the movement making use of those activist networks. Some of the members of the ABAVP in the region, however, had family members who had been actively involved in the fight for the recognition of Sadri. The sense of collective belonging, pride in the indigenous culture and even some of the songs found their way into the political rhetoric of the ABAVP at the local level in North Bengal. This was because some of the grass-roots cadres of the party had imbibed these aspects of the movement from the previous generation. In some sense, it seemed that the institutionalisation of the core ideals and values of the movement had continued in abeyance to once again emerge on the political canvas of the ABAVP to influence some aspects of its politics and rhetoric.

The social movement literature has argued that the potential of social movements cannot be measured only through the success of their end results. Research on social movement outcomes (Giguni 1998; Wagner and Cohen 1991) show that different outcomes can be understood relationally and often outside the binary of success and failure. In their study of labour strikes in Grunwick and Gate Gourmet, Anitha, Pearson and McDowell (2012) quote one of the strike participants who says that even if the strike has failed in its objective, she can tell her daughter when she grows up, how she fought for her rights. The strike in itself did not achieve much but by focussing on this aspect of the strike can its transformative potential be rejected? This right to self-respect remained latent in the lives of the participants in the Language Movement and also finds expression as rationale for many of their involvement with the ABAVP. Della Porta and Diani (2006: 91) illustrate that narratives of social movements are often about identities—the relationship between individual and collective identity. It is a process through which meanings are attributed to systems of social relations within which they are embedded and a sense of collective affinity and belonging develops.

Giugini (1998) argues that the notion of success can be problematic as it assumes uniform perception, homogeneity of the participants and focuses on a particular end result. Rather than measuring in terms of impact on government policy or legislation, multiple outcomes could be possible such as cultural impact, spill-over effect from one movement to the other. Further, they could have unintended consequences often even in contradiction to their original goals (Giguni 1998: 385–387).

Wagner and Cohen (1991) make the important distinction between a social movement *for* and social movement *of* the target group. One of the outcomes of the latter protests is the transformation of challengers into members of the polity (Gamson 1993) as has been seen with the participants of this movement. Wagner and Cohen (1991: 553) point out that such non-material gains sometimes translate into material resources for the deprived who otherwise might lack access to social networks and institutions as was evidenced by the limited number of jobs that were given to a section of participants. Structuring the protests around the idioms of rights, honour or respect the participants claimed something more than mere survival, claiming their space not only as humans but also as political citizens. Drawing on and adapting a repertoire of available strategies for protest, they made a powerful claim to be considered as conscious political agents.

While most elements of the movement get co-opted, some small remnants often endure. In small often invisible ways, it created a counter-discourse latent within the mainstream, a discourse which refused to be institutionalised. This was not just about language rights or even identity; it was also about their struggle. The sense of pride in having fought for one's rights, for one's identity persisted and passed on through generations. The movement might have lost out to institutionalisation, but it made cultural identity a site for struggle for one's personhood and the story of the struggle endured through generations and expressed itself in small ways as seen previously.

Conclusion

The Language Movement, though limited in scale and impact, was a significant event in the history of the Adivasi community of the North Bengal tea plantation belt. The movement raises some complex questions about issues of ownership and institutionalisation of movements, the role of social movement organisations in challenging or embedding peripheries and finally whether there is an alternative way in which ideas of marginalisation can be challenged. Through this, the chapter speaks to some of the key issues that this volume as a whole tries to highlight. It illustrates the complex and multi-layered ways in which institutionalisation takes place spelling different gains and losses for the participants—organisation, leaders and ordinary participants. The ethnography grapples with some of the central questions of the volume—does institutionalisation of social movements lead itself to adverse incorporation or to empowerment? What is the nature of this empowerment—top-down or bottom-up? Can it be understood with the yardstick of success and failure only? The three key arguments of this chapter address some of these issues.

As a social movement organisation (SMO), JAM was initially successful in gaining acceptance in the political process. While there were some gains secured at individual levels like jobs, money and, finally, NGO funding, this did not translate into gain for the community as a whole. Thus, incorporation might not translate into any real advantage for the social movement itself. The movement gained recognition but almost no gain and was, thus, co-opted. The co-option seemed so complete that the existence of the organisation seemed redundant at which point it was reformed into an NGO. The issue was not institutionalisation per se. In the previous section, some gains of less formal means of institutionalisation have been highlighted. Also having Sadri taught in schools, which was the demand of the movement, would have meant a greater formal recognition and institutionalisation of the Adivasis and their culture within the political-administrative system. The crucial element in this regard was the timing of institutionalisation. JAM acceded to the process of institutionalisation and incorporation into the political system too hastily, before it could establish itself as a mass organisation even in North Bengal. This led to a loss of momentum as an SMO while at the same time not giving it enough bargaining power as a significant political player.

The movement and its fate also provide an insight into the complex process through which marginalisation gets institutionalised. JAM became a platform on which the Adivasi identity was institutionalised as a force to reckon with. This institutionalisation of identity challenged the homogenous worker identity within which it was trapped and which rendered the distinct needs of the community invisible. As the movement gained force, the stakes of the organisation as a political player became higher. This necessitated certain modalities of political expression demanded by the political system in order to gain legitimacy within it (Gorringe 2011: 8). Through the appropriation of the voice of the movement, inevitable contradictions started emerging within the goals and organisation of the movement. As JAM became more institutionalised within the political structure, a large section of its support base became more marginalised within the movement. Finally, in abandoning the Adivasi identity and donning the 'worker' and 'development' rhetoric the movement came full circle in once again making ethnic identity invisible or trivial and, thus, institutionalising the marginalities within which the Adivasi community has been living for generations.

The trajectory of the movement points to the complex and multiple ways in which institutionalisation occurs. Institutionalisation does not proceed in a linear pattern and can be understood only as a process of gradual adaptation to the prevalent political culture. While in managing the process of institutionalisation, in this instance, JAM largely reinforced the marginalisation of the very group it sought to fight for, there is still a need to reconceive a social movement beyond the binaries of getting institutionalised and failing to achieve its end on one hand and remaining disruptive and outside the mainstream sociopolitical space. It illustrates that institutionalisation is not a binary between adverse incorporation, and empowerment and aspects of both can co-exist. By looking beyond this yardstick, we will be able to map the potential of individual acts of agency and the less formal ways some aspects of the movement endured to negate, even if in minor ways, the larger failures of the movement.

No process of institutionalisation is ever absolute. The movement failed to achieve its demand, but people continued to work towards these goals in their own individual, unspectacular ways. While there was disappointment, betrayal, anger; conversations, songs, aspiration, hope and determination became tools through which the fight for recognition endured even if in minute ways. It was through this endurance of everyday life, the unspectacular tools through which people make the movement or some aspects of it survive. Even in an institutionalised, largely co-opted movement, empowerment did not then necessarily depend on acts just discussed, it can be wrested by the ordinary marginalised participants in invisible ways through the practices of their everyday life. The song sung annually on the Birsa Munda day, which actively reconstructs a history which is indigenous, is testimony to this endurance which cannot be co-opted.

Come back to us Birsa Munda
Oh come back Sidhu Kanu
Come back our leaders
Tilka Majhi oh! Return to our midst
See how your blood gushes through our fists

> Oh the glorious story of our community
> You became martyrs for us rather than to accept a life of slavery
> You continued a life long struggle for your race
> Uncaring about the life of difficulties you had to face...

Notes

1. To maintain anonymity, the region, the names of the plantation, the organisation and the participants have been anonymised.
2. The support for coal mine agitations were the cause for the Jharkhandi activists to get involved in the tea plantations. Some had shifted their area of work primarily to the tea plantations.

References

Aminzade, R. 1995. 'Between Movement and Party', in J. Jenkins and B. Klandermans (eds), *The Politics of Social Protest* (pp. 39–62). Berkeley: University of California Press.

Anitha, S., Pearson, R. and McDowell, L. 2012. 'Striking Lives: Multiple Narratives of South Asian Women's Employment, Identity and Protest in UK', *Ethnicities* 12(6): 754–775.

Beckford, G.L. 1972. *Persistent Poverty: Underdevelopment in Plantation Economies of the Third World*. London: Oxford University Press.

Bhadra, M. 1992. *Women Workers of Tea Plantations in India*. New Delhi: Heritage Publishers.

Bhowmik, S.K. 1981. *Class Formation in the Plantation System*. Kolkata: People's Publishing House.

Burnstein, P., Einwohner, R.L. and Hollander, J.A. 1995. 'The Success of Political Movements: A Bargaining Perspective', in J. Jenkins and B. Klandermans (eds), *The Politics of Social Protest* (pp. 275–295). Berkeley: University of California Press.

Chatterjee, P. 2003. *A Time for Tea: Women's Labour and Post-colonial Politics on an Indian Plantation*. New Delhi: Zubaan.

Clemens, E. and Minkoff, D. 2004. 'Beyond the Iron Law: Rethinking the Place of Organisations in Social Movement Research', in D. Snow, S. Soule and H. Kriesi (eds), *The Blackwell Companion to Social Movements* (pp. 155–170). Oxford: Blackwell.

Coy, P. and Hedeen, T. 2005. 'A Stage Model of Social Movement Co-optation: Community Mediation in the United States', *The Sociological Quarterly* 46(3): 405–435.

Daniel, E.V., Bernstein, H. and Brass, T. 1992. *Plantations, Proletarians and Peasants in Colonial Asia*. London: Frank Cass & Co Ltd.

Das, A.K. and Banerjee, H.N. 1964. *Impact of Tea Industry on the Life of the Tribals of West Bengal*. Kolkata: Tribal Welfare Department, Government of West Bengal.

Das Gupta, R. 1994. *Labour and Working Class in Eastern India: Studies in Colonial History*. Kolkata: K.P. Bagchi.

Della Porta, D. and Diani, M. 2006. *Social Movements: An Introduction*. Malden: Blackwell Publishing.

Gamson, William A. 1990. *The Strategy of Social Protest*. Belmont, CA: Wadsworth Publishing.
Giugni, M.G. 1998. 'Was It Worth the Effort? The Outcomes and Consequences of Social Movements', *Annual Review of Sociology* 24: 371–393.
Graham, E. and Floering, I. 1984. *The Modern Plantation in the Third World*. Sydney: Croom Helm Ltd.
Gorringe, H. 2011. 'Party Political Panthers: Hegemonic Tamil Politics and the Dalit Challenge', *South Asia Multidisciplinary Academic Journal* [Online]: 1–19, http://samaj.revues.org/3224 (accessed 28 August 2015).
———. 2013. 'From the Margins to the "Mainstream": Dalit Politics in Tamil Nadu'. Paper presented at UKEIRI workshop on *Institutionalising Marginal Actors in South Asia: Processes, Policies, Practices and Pitfalls*, University of Edinburgh, 18–19 September.
Jain, S. 1998. 'Gender Relations and the Plantation System in Assam, India', in S. Jain and R. Reddock (eds), *Women Plantation Workers: International Experiences* (pp. 107–128). Oxford: Berg.
Kabeer, N. 1999. 'Resources, Agency, Achievements: Reflections on the Measurement of Women's Empowerment', *Development and Change* 30(3), 435–464.
Katzenstein, Mary. 1998. 'Stepsisters: Feminist Movement Activism in Different Institutional Spaces', in David S. Meyer and Sidney Tarrow (eds), *The Social Movement Society: Contentious Politics for a New Century*, pp. 195–216. Lanham, MD: Rowman & Littlefield.
Kriesi, H. 1989. The Organizational Structure of New Social Movements in a Political Context in D. McAdam, J. McCarthy and M.N. Zald (eds), *Comparative Perspective on Social Movements: Political Opportunities, Mobilizing Structures, and Cultural Framing* (pp. 152–84). Cambridge and New York: Cambridge University Press.
Kriesberg, Louis. 2003. *Constructive Conflicts: From Escalation to Resolution*. Lanham, MD: Rowman & Littlefield.
Meena, R.K. and Bhattacharjee, D. 2008. 'Siliguri in Gorkhaland: A Political Nightmare for West Bengal', *Economic and Political Weekly* 43(25): 15–16.
Melucci, A. 1989. *Nomads of the Present Social Movements and Individual Needs in Contemporary Society*. Philadelphia: Temple University Press.
Mitchell, L. 2009. *Language, Emotions and Politics in India: The Making of a Mother Tongue*. Indiana University Press: Bloomington.
Morris, A.D. and Staggenborg, S. 2004. 'Leadership in Social Movements', in D. Snow, S. Soule and H. Kriesi (eds), *The Blackwell Companion to Social Movements* (pp. 172–196). Oxford: Blackwell.
Nandy, V. 2013. 'Tea Garden Struggles', *Frontier* 46(13–16).
Offe, C. 1990. 'Reflections on the Institutional Self-Transformation of Movement Politics', in R. Dalton and M. Kuechler (eds), *Challenging the Political Order* (pp. 232–250). Cambridge: Polity.
Palishkar, S. 2013. 'Of Radical Democracy and Anti-Partyism', *Economic and Political Weekly* XLVIII(10): 10–13.
Piven, F.F. and R.A. Cloward. 1977. *Poor People's Movements: How They Succeed How They Fail?* New York: Pantheon Books.
Rucht, D. 1990. 'The Strategies and Action Repertoire of New Movements', in R.J. Dalton and M. Kuechler (eds), *Challenging the Political Order: New Social Movements in Western Democracies* (pp. 156–175). Cambridge: Polity Press.
Sarkar, K. and Bhowmik, S. 1999. 'Trade Unions and Women Workers in Tea Plantations', *Economic and Political Weekly*, 33(52): L50–52.

Sawyers, T.M. and Meyer, D.S. 1999. 'Missed Opportunities: Social Movement Abeyance and Public Policy', *Social Problems*, 46(2): 187–206.

Snow, D.A., Soule, S.A. and Kriesi, H. 2004. 'Mapping the Terrain', in D. Snow, S. Soule and H. Kriesi (eds), *The Blackwell Companion to Social Movements* (pp. 3–16). Oxford: Blackwell.

Staggenborg, S. 1988. 'The Consequences of Professionalization and Formalization in the Pro Choice Movement'. *American Sociological Review* 53(4): 585–606.

Subramanian, T. 2001. 'The Caste of Character', *Frontline*, 18(4): 46–48.

Taylor. V. 1989. 'Social Movement Continuity: The Women's Movement in Abeyance', *American Sociological Review*, 54(5): 761–775.

Wagner, D. and Cohen, M. 1991. 'The Power of the People', *Social Problems* 38(4): 543–561.

Walker, R. 2010. '"My Older Brother's Tree": Everyday Violence and the Question of the Ordinary in Batticaloa, Eastern Sri Lanka'. Unpublished PhD dissertation, University of Edinburgh.

4
Rise of Adivasi Janajati Movement and Nepal's Political Interregnum

Jeevan Raj Sharma

Introduction

A social movement is generally understood as a collective public action that operates operates outside formal political institutions, engages in contentious politics and maintains a loose and less bureaucratic structure. Tilly defines it as:

> ...[A] sustained series of interactions between power holders and persons successfully claiming to speak on behalf of a constituency lacking formal representation, in the course of which those persons make publicly visible demands for changes in the distribution or exercise of power, and back those demands with public demonstrations of support. (Tilly 1984: 306)

Based on the shared beliefs and solidarity, the social movements mobilise resources and support, and work to bring about political transformation through various forms of protests (Della Porta and Diani 1999). As social movements develop in local and national contexts, they move beyond their initial aim and get involved in wider political movements, leading to the processes of state restructuring, building cooperative links with institutional actors which includes seeking support from international partners and donors and joining formal party politics. However, it would be simplistic to assume that such a process is unproblematic.

The inclusive politics of a social movement can lead to the exclusion of other marginal groups, thus, presenting a significant challenge to broader projects of democratisation. Ethnicity-based social movements presents challenges to inclusion and broader projects of democratisation. Why and how do social movements join institutional politics, garner international support and enter wider political movements? What are the consequences of institutional politics for the wider project of democratisation and equality?

After the restoration of parliamentary democracy in 1990, Nepal has seen an explosion of contentious politics that ranged from the ethnic, regional and Dalit movements, to the violent Maoist insurgency amongst others (Lawoti and Hagen 2013). What started as social movements to claim rights and recognition that were guaranteed by the democratic constitution of 1990, gradually shifted their demands to include representation in the state structures through reservation and quota systems since the early 2000s. Since the onset of election to the CA in 2008, these demands have further shifted to radical restructuring of the state through ethnicity and identity-based federalism (Hagen 2010; Lawoti and Hagen 2013; Shneiderman and Tillin 2015). This chapter discusses the institutional politics of the Adivasi Janajati ('indigenous peoples') movement, a major social movement based around ethnic identity as well as the broader processes of democratisation and state-restructuring that have unfolded across Nepal since the early 1990s. It engages with the following questions: What does the process of institutionalisation of Adivasi Janajati movement mean for democratisation and state restructuring in Nepal? How has the Adivasi Janajati movement transformed the ideas of equality, ethnicity, belonging and nationalism in Nepal that has graduated from recognition, to representation and then to 'ethnicity and identity based federalism'? What has been the role of international donors like the UK Department of International Development and other European donors, who have funded a NEFIN (Nepal Federation of Indigenous Nationalities), a federation of different Adivasi Janajati organisations? What are the consequences of Adivasi Janajati politics of ethnic federalism for the wider project of democratisation in Nepali society and the inclusion of most marginalised groups such as Dalits and other economically and politically marginalised groups within and outside Janajati groups that are dispersed throughout the country?

This chapter begins with a brief discussion of the dominant context against which the Adivasi Janajati movement was launched. It is followed by a discussion on history and the rapid growth of the movement that emerged as a major player in shaping the political processes in the country, especially since the 1990s. The movement entered institutional politics with the passing of the National Foundation for Development of Indigenous Nationalities Act (NFDIN) in 2002 and a significant boost to the movement also came with funding from international donors such as the UK's Department for International Development (DFID). Further, it discusses how the Adivasi Janajati movement played a major role in pushing for their demands to obtain representation in the state structures through reservation, including the proportionate electoral system, which resulted in Nepal adopting a mixed electoral system, thereby making Nepal's first Constituent Assembly (CA) most diverse. Building on this strength, the Adivasi Janajati movement played a critical role in forming a caucus of Janajati members of parliaments in the CA to push for ethnic federalism, which polarised Nepali politics and ultimately led to the dissolution of the first CA in 2012. Following which, the Adivasi Janajati movement has faced a dilemma on how to combine the politics of engagement with the politics of contention that led to divisions and split within the movement. The decision of some of the leaders from the Adivasi Janajati movement to form a new political party met with several challenges including its ideology, constituency as well as the constraints of party politics for an ethnicity-based movement in a multicultural society. Despite its rhetoric of inclusion and democratisation, the tendency within the Adivasi Janajati movement's fight for ethnic or identity-based federalism, while offering opportunities for dominant sections of a few communities produces disempowerment and exclusion of Dalits and other economically marginal groups both within and outside Janajati groups.

Exclusionary State

In the post-1990 era, anthropologists and other social scientists, both 'foreign' and 'Nepali' have consistently highlighted the ethnic dimension of the Nepali state. Much has been written about the exclusionary and extractive nature of the Nepali state, dominated by what some social scientists have categorised as 'Parbatiyas', that is members of the hill caste groups that have always been Nepali speaking (Gellner et al. 1997; Hagen 2010; Lawoti 2005). Starting with King Prithvi Narayan Shah, the Nepali state has defined itself against external threats, especially the rising British Empire, while trying to be a pure Hindu land at home. Prior to 1769, Nepal was divided into many principalities. Prithvi Narayan Shah and his successors started integrating Nepal into a single nation with an ambition to establish 'asal Hindustan' or true Hindu land (Whelpton 2005). Although the dominant Nepali nationalists continue to feel proud of the moves of King Prithvi Narayan Shah and his successors towards creating a greater Nepal and strategically resisting the external threat, his critics see his aim to create asal Hindusthan as a way of marginalising the non-Hindu ethnic groups (Gellner et al. 1997).

Under the absolute control of the King, Nepal functioned as a socially hierarchical Hindu polity with no legal or constitutional recognition of ideas related to the concept of equality until the mid-nineteenth century when Hindu-ritual-based hierarchy and inequality was legally recognised as the basis of the state (Whelpton 2005). The political ideology of the pre-1990 Nepali polity revolved around some specific themes including state-backed Hinduism and the Nepali language.

Nepal came under the Rana regime for 104 years (1846–1950) through a coup called *kot parba* (courtyard massacre). In the Rana period, Nepal allowed itself to be the semi-colony of the British Empire (Blaikie et al. 2001). The Ranas got exposure to the Western ideas and institutions by coming in contact with the British Empire. One of the outcomes was the *Muluki Ain* (National Code), which was enforced in 1854, legitimising the caste system, gender hierarchy and superiority of the Hindu religion (Whelpton 2005). The original Muluki Ain of 1854 contained a five-tier national caste hierarchy in which the people of Nepal were divided into the following categories according to the ascribed ritual purity: wearers of holy cord; non-enslavable alcohol-drinkers; enslavable alcohol-drinkers; impure but touchable castes; and impure and untouchable castes. The high caste hill Hindus (bahun, thakuri and chetri) were placed at the top. Below them were the traditionally non-Hindu groups under the rubric of *matwli* (alcohol-drinker). Hindu castes that were said to be impure but touchable along with Muslims and Christians were ranked one above the bottom and Hindu castes deemed as impure and untouchable were placed at the bottom. Overall, the pre-1951 rulers put Nepal under a Hindu ritual framework. Pfaff-Czarnecka offers the following analysis:

> From the point of view of rulers, the plurality of Nepali society was conceived of within the uniform socio-political framework. Rather than seeking to establish national unity through a vision of a culturally homogenous population, the rulers sought to define a national identity which allowed for cultural variation but which had Hinduism as its major pillar. (Pfaff-Czarnecka 1997: 425)

When India became independent from the British rule, and the Rana regime subsequently ended, the Shah rulers attempted to promote one nation sharing a common culture in the post-1951 era. Its nationalism based on cultural unity mobilised the concept of development (*bikas*): physical infrastructure such as road and air transport, radio, education system and administrative system privileging Nepali language amongst others. In the post-1951 period, the schooling system and the state-owned mass media with Nepali as the official medium language contributed to its widespread use. A polity in which the Nepali language was a tool of administration and governance was beneficial to the high caste Hindus who were accustomed to the language and its intricacies at the expense of other languages spoken by Janajatis and other linguistic groups in Terai.

To summarise, Janajatis as a group have faced multiple exclusions and disparities in the Nepali society within the Hindu state though the level of exclusion and inequalities suffered by each Janajati groups varies, and there are inequalities within each Janajati group. These deprivations are thought to be the result of their political and sociocultural marginalisation within the framework of a unitary Hindu state. Mainly, the Adivasi Janajati movement is a response to this complex set of exclusion and inequalities rooted in Nepal's history and state structure, and the movement has worked through various of evolving strategies to correct these.

Rise of *Adivasi Janajati* movement

Although the Janajati movement has a long history (Fisher 1993), in the post-1990 era, Nepal has been experiencing a surge in Janajati movements more recently leading up to contentious demands for ethnic federalism that challenged the unitary image of Nepal. The Adivasi Janajati movement, united under the leadership of the Nepal Janajati Mahasangh (Nepal Federation of Ethnic Nationalities, NEFEN), which was later renamed NEFIN as a way to align their struggle with the international language on indigineity and cultural rights aims to challenge the exclusionary and extractive nature of the Nepali state, dominated by Nepali speaking high caste Hindus and by creating a vision of Nepal as a multiethnic, multi-linguistic and multi-religious state and build an inclusive Nepal in which 'discrimination against ethnic groups does not exist' (Hagen 2010; Onta 2006).

Fundamental rights embedded in Nepal's new constitution in 1990 enabled the formation and mobilisation of organisations representing regional, caste, linguistic and ethnic identities, which was not possible in the previous Panchayat regime in the country. In addition, compared to the earlier constitution, the constitution of 1990 was progressive in its recognition of the multiethnic and multi-lingual nature of Nepali society. By using the term Janajati explicitly in Article 26(10), the Constitution acknowledged their presence and their relative deprivation in social and economic terms. Although the new constitution asserted Nepal as a Hindu kingdom and declared the Nepali language as the 'language of the nation' and Nepal's 'official language' and calling all other mother tongues spoken within Nepal 'national languages', the fundamental rights guaranteed by the 1990 Constitution played a critical role in creating necessary preconditions for the Janajati movement to mobilise and grow. By exercising their right to association within the democratic framework guaranteed by the Constitution of 1990, many Janajatis formed new organisations and strengthened and expanded the existing organisations that continued to work in cultural, social, religious, educational, service-delivery and human rights fronts (Hagen 2010). While the government during the Panchayat era monopolised radio in Nepal, there was a media boom in the years after 1990, as newspapers and FM stations multiplied, offering varieties of perspectives from across the political spectrum (Onta, 2002). This coupled with the growth and proliferation of a different civil society, Maoist insurgency, and the ethnic and non-governmental organisations (NGOs) in the following years have transformed the character of Nepal's public sphere, creating a conducive environment for the movement to flourish (Onta, 2002). Since the issues raised by the movement have resonated ideas of equality, rights, justice, democracy, participation and development (*bikas*), the movement was able to draw the attention and participation beyond Janajati actors and institutions from across academia, intellectuals, media, political parties, professional associations and development NGOs which were receiving financial, technical and political support from international donors. Janajati activists associated with various political parties either individually or through Janajati wings in their respective parties also played a key role in the movement. The UN declaration of 1993 as the International Year for the World's Indigenous People and the decade 1995–2004 as the International Decade of the World's Indigenous People provided further impetus for the use of the term indigenous (or Adivasi) peoples and align the movement to international languages, movements and ideas. As the demands of the Janajatis gained strength during the 1990s and the early 2000s, the Nepal government responded with the various initiatives in an effort to address those demands by creating institutional entities within the government bureaucracy to implement some of its responses and programmes (Onta 2006: 303).

Institutionalisation of Adivasi Janajati Movement

The process of institutionalisation of Adivasi Janajati movement began with the process of creating a list of Janajati groups because Nepal had no such schedule unlike neighbouring India. In 1996, the Nepal government responded to the Adivasi Janajati movement's claim to recognise its constructed pan-identity by accepting a Task Force Report that recommended a list of 61 Janajati groups in the country and the formation of a national foundation for Nepal's ethnic groups. Consequently, a National Committee for the Development of Nationalities was founded, and Nepal got its first government institution concerned with Adivasi Janajati issues with the passing of the National Foundation for Development of Indigenous Nationalities Act (NFDIN) in 2002. For the first time, Adivasi Janajati got recognition as a legal category. It defined Adivasi Janajati as those ethnic groups or communities that 'have their own mother tongue and traditional customs, distinct cultural identity, distinct social structure and written or oral history of their own'. On 10 February 2002, the Ministry of Law, Social Justice and Parliamentary Affairs confirmed a final list of 59

Adivasi Janajatis of Nepal. This step constituted an important element in the history of the Adivasi Janajati movement. Further, it also enabled the Adivasi Janajati groups to access funds from the government, and international donors for their development and empowerment. Unlike in the past where Janajati mobilisation was mainly supported by the voluntary contributions and time from its members, Adivasi Janajati mobilisation began to receive funding to support its work and expand its network.

> The increasing visibility and legitimacy of this organization and its new sources of funding are reflected in the change in its official quarters: although it originally occupied a couple of rooms in a building by the dusty central bus station, it is now located in an elegant new multi-story house on the south side of the capital city. (Hagen 2010: 39)

Not only were the activists, academics and intellectuals working in Janajati organisations paid as salaried workers and consultants, they were drawn within the global circulation of networks, ideas and rhetoric flowing within the field of international development and rights discourse. With this, Janajati movements' cultural claims for recognition and inclusion encountered donor funding that were aimed at the development and empowerment of marginal and excluded groups in Nepal.

Alongside the Adivasi Janajati movement was Nepal's Maoist insurgency (1996–2005), which was built around an agenda, which at its core attacked the feudal nature of Nepali society and the structural inequalities inherent in it (Hutt 2004). Many of the ideas were drawn from Mao's 'Red Book'. Whether this agenda was instrumental—a tool for overthrowing the monarchy and capturing power—or represented the aspiration for a profound social revolution is difficult to assess, but the Maoist insurgency had a significant impact in the Adivasi Janajati movement. One of the demands in the list of 40 points submitted by the Maoists to the Prime Minister of Nepal on 4 February 1996 included ending all kinds of exploitation and prejudice based on caste and providing autonomy to groups who have a majority. During the insurgency, the Maoists did carve out the state in ethnic terms by splitting Nepal into several ethnic states and organising their party organisation accordingly. Grievances based on ethnicity was one of the key organising rhetoric of the Maoists, and with Maoists emerging as an important political actor after the 2000s, issues of ethnic identity received growing attention in Nepali politics. The direct engagement of Adivasi Janajati groups in political change began with NEFIN, taking part in street demonstrations against the King in 2002 and 2005 alongside political parties. With the establishment of democratic institutions in 1990, Nepal became a 'pet country' of international donors: aid inflows increased, most notably from European countries. Unlike in the past, there was a growing emphasis on funding NGOs and civil society organisations not only as agents of service delivery but also as promoters of good governance, rule of law, human rights, women's empowerment, child welfare and people's participation in development. Like many other civil society organisations, Adivasi Janajati organisations and NEFIN were not immune to opportunities for financial and technical support from international partners. NEFIN began to run projects and its leaders and activists began to take salaried positions and consultancies. Particularly noteworthy in this has been support from the British, Danish and Norwegian governments, as well as the European Union donors. The former, through DFID, has probably offered the largest single allotment to NEFIN, apportioning NPR195 million (£1.52 million) over four years for what is known as the Janajati Empowerment Project (JEP) that attracted quite a lot of attention from commentators. Using the fund from JEP, NEFIN categorised 56 Adivasi Janajati groups in a five-tiered categorisation as 'endangered', 'highly marginalised', 'marginalised', 'disadvantaged' and 'advantaged', which has since formed the basis for 'targeting of much of the development projects from European donors'. With funding from DFID, the World Bank undertook a major assessment called Gender and Social Exclusion Assessment (GSEA), which stressed on overcoming the legacy of caste, ethnic and gender-based social exclusion in Nepal by influencing policy and supporting its implementation. The EU has contributed NPR150 million for two projects that target highly marginalised Janajatis; while in 2005, the Norwegian government set aside NPR170 million to establish a Social Inclusion Fund, aimed at supporting research on social inclusion and helping to build the research capacity of students and scholars from excluded communities.

However, donor support to Adivasi Janajati groups has met with the nationalist- and sovereignty-based sentiments that are reflected in the media reporting as well as perception and everyday resistance of Nepali bureaucracy that sees DFID's engagement as promoting ethnic divisions in

Nepali society as well as political instability. The visit of the UK Minister for International Development in July 2012 was met with some stiff questioning by journalists on DFID's role in stirring ethnic conflict in Nepal. There is a strong narrative, especially amongst the high-caste elite, that donors are undermining the unitary nature of the Nepali state and are considered responsible for radicalising ethnicity, creating divisions and fuelling hatred in Nepal. The work of donors who began to support more inclusive development by funding targeted programmes for ethnic groups has come under criticism that aid agencies have helped re-affirm ethnic identity through the process of categorisations and classifications. More recently, the issue became much more complex with a major feud between DFID and NEFIN on JEP. On 11 May 2011, DFID announced that it would no longer continue its financial support to NEFIN and withdrew a support of NPR110 million from the Janajati Empowerment Project II (JEP II) citing violation of the terms of funding between DFID and NEFIN because the latter had been continuously involved in organising 'bandas' (shutdowns or general strike) as a part of NEFIN's struggle for ethnic federalism in the country. Since September 2004, DFID had provided over £2 million to NEFIN for different projects. The Head of DFID–Nepal wrote to NEFIN President stating:

> [D]ue to NEFIN's recent continued involvement in supporting the 27 April "banda" and based on information verified with you that NEFIN is part of a wider front to call a 'banda' on May 13 (Friday) to protest for constitutional rights of Janajati and wider people from the marginalized communities, I am sorry to inform you that DFID will not be able to provide any further funding as a result.'

The letter further mentioned, '…we cannot continue our support to [an] organisation that is organising "banda", which is totally against Human Rights'. In response NEFIN president wrote, '…we are quite surprised from your immature and childish decision to discontinue support to Janajatis'. The NEFIN president accused DFID advisors for the decision to withdraw support and went on to warn DFID that:

> All Janajatis are demanding convincing answer from DFID for its decision. I want to aware (warn) you that situation may be critical if DFID is failed to satisfy Janajatis and justify its decision. In such situation, DFID will be responsible for creating communal tension and anarchy in Nepal.

The president of NEFIN accused DFID of practicing 'double standards' and 'promoting corruption' in the name of providing assistance for transparency and good governance. The president added that they won't stop organising 'banda' due to anyone's pressure: 'We won't be slaves of the donors to receive funds. Donors can support us if they want, but we will never stop fighting for our rights.' He further added, 'We cannot put our future on stake for a few 'crore'. We will only accept support if there are no conditions attached to it, but we won't stop our strike.' This particular incident helps understand challenges faced by movements in institutionalisation and donor support. Although donor support was very important to further the Adivasi Janajati movement as it played a key role in the classification of Adivasi Janajati groups, taking the movement across Nepal and expanding its networks and membership, it came with some significant challenges.

Following 10 years of the Maoist insurgency as well as the coup by King Gyanendra on 1 Febuary 2005, the Maoists and the alliance of seven democratic parties forced world's only Hindu King to give up power and a Comprehensive Peace Agreement (CPA) was signed in 2006. Reflecting the sentiments of ethnic minorities and those who fought against the Hindu monarchy, the new government declared Nepal a secular state. Overthrowing the monarchy in 2006, the declaration of Nepal as a secular state and removal of Hindu monarchy replaced by a Federal Democratic Republic in 2008 is seen by a few critics as the work of donor agencies. Critics who rejected the regime change in 2006 claim that it was not the result of the 'people's movement' but because of the work of some European donors who supported Janajati movement as a way to get rid of Hindu monarchy. Critics argue that as the monarchy represented the protector and symbol of the dominant social and religious order, for those interested in the transformation of Nepali society, it was an obvious move to dismantle the institution that was seen as a major obstacle (Shah 2008). A Wikileaks cable sent from New Delhi on 1 April 2005 is cited as evidence by critics to support their claim that some donors including Denmark had agreed in March 2005 (one month after the royal takeover of 1 February) to regime change in Nepal. Further, the declaration of Nepal as a secular state, given that Hinduism was an important source of power for the monarchy and the dominant nationalism, is seen as a result of the work of Christian evangelists supported by donors. Citing the activities of the evangelical lobbyists and the Western embassies based in Kathmandu at the time of declaration of Nepal as secular state, Shah (2008: 17) writes, 'Although, the formal rationale has been to separate the state from Hindu religion, the unstated consideration has been to weaken the king by removing the symbolic ties between the Hindu crown and the state'. These narratives clearly show that donor support to Adivasi Janajati movement and Nepal's transformation into a secular federal state were seen by critics as a part of larger geopolitics and donor's complicit intervention.

Furthermore, the Nepalese government signalled its obligation towards the special support of ethnic groups by defining specific targets for the development of Adivasi Janajati in the Three Year Interim Plan 2008–2010. By ratifying the ILO No. 169 Convention on Indigenous and Tribal People, the only legally binding international instrument concerned with the rights of indigenous people and the adoption of the UN Declaration on the Rights of Indigenous People in 2007, Nepal joined the worldwide discourse on indignity at the legal level and promised its commitment to international standards. Role of international actors and global circulation of ideas and rhetoric has certainly influenced Adivasi Janajati movement in a significant way.

With the declaration of Nepal as a secular state and abolition of monarchy following the end of the Maoist insurgency where the Adivasi Janajati movement played an important role, Adivasi Janajati activists demanded the introduction of reservations to guarantee proportional representation of marginalised groups in state apparatus, provinces to be named after ethnic and regional groups, and boundaries drawn to make them dominant minorities. The government signed a series of agreements with the Adivasi Janajati and other groups reiterating the commitment to federalism, proportionate representation in the CA election, quota system in government, police and army. Consequently, the CA election of April 2008 that deployed a mixed electoral system including proportional system resulted in the most diverse and inclusive parliament in Nepal's history and was a major boost to Adivasi Janajati movement.

In the CA election of 2008, unlike Madhesi political leaders, Adivasi Janajati leaders did not leave their political parties to form a separate political party. Except for a few small Adivasi Janajati parties, most of the indigenous leadership contested the election from within the established political structures. There are two reasons for this. *First*, many still hoped that the mainstream political parties would become inclusive enough to address their concerns. *Second*, these leaders really had no other option but to join the existing parties—they were either too diverse to be organised into a single party, or they did not have the capacity to organise such a front.

Immediately after the elections, on 28 May 2008, the new parliament declared Nepal a 'Federal Democratic Republic'. Nepal's CA parliament was tasked to write a new constitution by 28 May 2010, which was extended until 27 May 2012, representing the perceived grievances and wishes of one of the world's most diverse and complex societies. Nepal's first CA was dissolved dramatically on 27 May 2012 following stark differences between those supporting ethnicity-based federalism pushed by Janajati members and the Maoist party versus those who did not support such a state structure.

Joining Formal Politics?

From its start, NEFIN has refrained from joining formal politics and defined itself as a social movement, different from that of a political party or NGOs receiving foreign fund. However, the context changed drastically when an agreement between different political parties in Nepal's parliament could not be reached on the nature of federalism in the new constitution in the post-monarchy era. With Adivasi Janajati politicians from different parties coming together as a caucus to lobby for an ethnicity-based federalism during the tenure of Nepal's first CA, the polarisation between those members who fought for ethnicity-based federalism, also supported by the Maoist party and those who fought against it intensified, which ultimately led to the dissolution of the CA on 27 May 2012. This caucus was one of the biggest political forces along with the four major political parties in the final days of the CA. Following their inability to convince their leadership in the respective parties, several CA members belonging to Janajati groups defected from their main party.

As the party leaders did not listen to the demand for ethnic federalism, so in the days approaching the deadline for the constitutional assembly, the leader of the Janajati caucus put his dilemma as: 'I have been in CPN-UML party for 40 years. Should I continue to struggle within the party and force it to accept issues concerned with the oppressed peoples? Or should I quit since even after 40 years, the party has not internalized these issues?' He said, 'We will continue to wage inner-party struggle. If the party refuses to consider our concerns on federalism and proportional representation, we will have to think of an alternative.' As several Janajati members from CPN-UML (Communist Party of Nepal [Unified Marxist–Leninist]) and other parties openly lobbied against their party's policy on federalism, the party leadership divested these proactive ethnic leaders of any responsibility on grounds of indiscipline.

A task force set up by NEFIN concluded that the existing parties in Nepal were 'Brahmanical, patriarchal, and controlled by upper Caste supremacists', and it was a 'historic necessity' to set up an inclusive party based on principles of 'human rights, social justice, equality and equity, and ethnicity theory'. A committee of intellectuals and activists was mandated to engage in consultations to discuss the feasibility of starting a political party. It met intellectuals, professionals, retired bureaucrats and army personnel from ethnic communities in Kathmandu, and then visited seven districts in western Nepal. The committee was tasked with a set of questions—Whether there should be a new party?; Should it only include ethnic groups or all oppressed communities?; What should its philosophy, ideology, objectives and policies be?; What will its structure be?; Will it give space to leaders presently in the big parties?; How will be resources generated?; What will its foreign policy orientation be? The committee found that there was a widespread feeling that the big parties, led by hill upper castes, have failed. It concluded that the CA did not deliver a constitution precisely because these bigger parties wanted to prevent a constitution that guaranteed rights to Adivasi Janajati. However, the debate raged on in Janajati circles. A senior and an experienced Janajati politician cautioned that setting up a party cannot be based on an impulse and needs careful homework especially in a 'multi-ethnic society like Nepal'. But a political scientist, whose work dealt with exclusion in Nepal, commented that it was the right moment to set up a new party. 'I think the cadres are ready. Sociocultural ethnic organisations say they need a political front. The ground is ready; the big question seems to be who will take the initiative and lead it.' With deliberations over weeks and months, the dispute over ideology led to the formation of two different parties. A major section formed a political party named Federal Socialist Party (FSP), which kept Marxism as a guiding principle. The party includes those who left all major and fringe parties because of their conviction that there should be single ethnic identity-based federalism. To disprove that the party is solely an ethnic party, at least 10 leaders were selected from bahun and chettri communities and many leaders from Madhesh-based communities, besides Dalits. The other Janajati faction refused to join FSP over an ideology row and formed their own party named Social Democratic Pluri-national Party (SDP) that says it is committed to social democracy against the FSP's guiding principle of federal socialism and Marxism. Leaders of SDP claimed that unlike other Janajati parties, theirs will lay more emphasis on the agenda of inclusion, federalism, identity and proportional representation. Although the initial attempt of NEFIN together with Janajati intellectuals was to urge leaders to focus more on issues of inclusion, federalism and proportional representation by keeping their ideological differences intact, this aspiration was short-lived.

A new election for CA took place on 19 November 2013 that resulted in Nepali Congress and Communist Party of Nepal–United Marxist Leninist re-emerging as the leading political party with significant loss to the Maoists, Madhesi regional parties and other parties fighting for ethnicity- and identity-based federalism. More recently, the word ethnic federalism is increasingly being used synonymously or replaced with identity-based federalism, which perhaps shows a strategic move on the part of activists seeking to expand their political platform to include those who do not identify themselves as belonging to particular ethnic groups (Shneiderman and Tillin 2015). The Adivasi Janajati politics has since become much more fluid with its activists and leaders aligned to two political divides, that is those who support the idea of ethnicity-based federalism have aligned themselves to the Maoists and the Madhesi regional parties and joined street protests, and the other groups have aligned more closely to the ruling coalition and have taken a more soft approach to federalism that is based on recognition of multiple identities beyond a singular ethnic identity.

Conclusion: Exclusive Inclusion?

Over the years, the Adivasi Janajati movement has graduated from recognition, to representation, and then to ethnicity- and identity-based federalism. This became possible due to several factors including the democratic constitution of 1990 that guaranteed fundamental rights and allowed the

Adivasi Janajati to form associations and articulate their grievances. In addition, the state put forward a number of policies and provisions based on the demand of the movement by creating a list of Adivasi Janajati groups, putting forward reservations and launching the targeting programmes for their upliftment and empowerment. The role of international agencies such as the United Nations (UN) as well as ILO on 'indigenous people' were extremely important for the Janajati movement to articulate itself as an Adivasi Janajati movement, and these institutions were instrumental in urging its members to ratify and pursue international instruments. The financial support from DFID and other European donors provided a significant boost to the movement, primarily by allowing it to engage in the process of categorisation as well as through the various activities aimed at empowering the groups. Over the years, the Adivasi Janajati movement has combined the politics of contention with the politics of engagement, took foreign aid from donors and of late has decided to engage directly with formal politics. While it is too early to draw any conclusive statements on the Adivasi Janajati movement and institutionalisation, the process involved has already highlighted some of the challenges. In particular, the politics of inclusion through ethnic federalism and associated ideas of prior rights has been met with politics of exclusion with particular adverse impact for Dalits and other economically marginal groups both within and outside Janajati groups. The Adivasi Janajati movement has also refrained from the questions of class hierarchy where the upper class dominates the lower classes of the same Janajati group.

This chapter looked at the institutional politics of the Adivasi Janajati movement that marks a significant aspect of Nepali politics. While the movement gained tremendously, in terms of recognition, representation and political strength, two major issues emerged: (a) a social movement draws on international partners and discourses that are important for mobilisation and institutionalisation of social movement, but it also risks losing support when it graduates to institutional politics and garners political strength and (b) a social movement that speaks only on the issue of Adivasi Janajati rights in a multiethnic society where ethnicity is an important indicator of structural violence and inequality in Nepal but is not the only one throws significant challenges to the projects of democratisation. The politics of Adivasi Janajati while promising inclusion to its own Janajati groups seems to exclude Dalits—who remain the most marginal group in Nepal—as well as other economically and politically marginalised groups within and outside of Janajati groups. Thus, it is difficult to understand how ethnic politics on its own will be able to address the concerns of horizontal inequality and exclusion in one of the most complex multicultural societies in South Asia where demands for ethnic federalism and its project of categorisation has excluded the most marginalised populations.

References

Blaikie, Piers M., Cameron, J. and Seddon, D. 2001. *Nepal in Crisis: Growth and Stagnation at the Periphery*. Rev. and enlarged ed. New Delhi: Adroit Publishers.
Della Porta, D. and Diani, M. *Social Movements: An Introduction*. Oxford. Blackwell.
Fisher. W. 1993. Nationalism and Janajati. *Himal* 6(2): 11–14.
Gellner, David N., Pfaff-Czarnecka, J. and Whelpton, J. 1997. *Nationalism and Ethnicity in a Hindu Kingdom: The Politics of Culture in Contemporary Nepal, Studies in Anthropology and History*. Amsterdam: Harwood Academic.
Gellner, David. 2007. Caste, Ethnicity and Inequality in Nepal. *Economic and Political Weekly* 42(20): 1823–1828.
Hagen, Susan. 2010. *The Rise of Ethnic Politics in Nepal: Democracy in the Margins, Routledge Contemporary South Asia series*. London: New York: Routledge.
Hutt, M. 2004. *Himalayan People's War: Nepal's Maoist Rebellion*. London. Hurst & Company.
Lawoti, Mahendra. 2005. *Towards a Democratic Nepal: Inclusive Political Institutions for a Multicultural Society*. New Delhi, London and Thousand Oaks: SAGE Publications.
Lawoti, M. and Hagen, S. (eds). 2013. *Nationalism and Ethnic Conflict in Nepal: Identities and Mobilization after 1990*. London, New York: Routledge.
Onta, Pratyoush. 2002. 'Critiquing the Media Boom', in Kanak Mani Dixit and Shastri Ramachandran (eds), *State of Nepal* (pp. 253–269). Kathmandu: Himal Books.
———. 2006. 'The Growth of the *Adivasi Janajati* Movement in Nepal after 1990: The Non-political Institutional Agents', *Studies in Nepali History and Society* 11(2): 303–354.
Pfaff-Czarnecka, Joana. 1997. 'Vestiges and Visions: Cultural Change in the Process of Nation-Building in Nepal', in D.N. Geller, Joana Pfaff-Czarnecka and J. Whelpton (eds), *Nationalism and Ethnicity in a Hindu Kingdom: The Politics of Culture in Contemporary Nepal* (pp. 417–470). Amsterdam: Harwood Academic.
Shneiderman, S. and Tillin, L. 2015. Restructuring States, Restructuring Ethnicity: Looking across Disciplinary Boundaries at Federal Futures in India and Nepal. *Modern Asian Studies* 49(1): 1–39.
Shah, Saubhagya. 2008. *Civil Society in Uncivil Places: Soft State & Regime Change in Nepal*. Washington DC: East West Center.
Tilly, C. 1984. 'Social Movements and National Politics', in C. Bright and S. Harding (eds), *Statemaking and Social Movements* (pp. 297–317). Ann Arbor, Michigan: University of Michigan Press.
Whelpton, J. 2005. *A History of Nepal*. Cambridge: Cambridge University Press.

5

Institutionalising Marginal Actors in Uttar Pradesh and Tamil Nadu: Insights from Dalit Electoral Data

Roger Jeffery and Hugo Gorringe*

Introduction

> People often use elections effectively to choose their representative and the government but rarely can they use elections to choose policies about issues that matter most to them. (Yadav 1999: 2399)
>
> [Dalits] need a state which can intervene for welfare purposes and to ensure the base of education and health; they also need a well-functioning market. Assertive electoral participation for a long-term project of reformulating the path towards a society of social justice is their challenge ahead. (Omvedt, n.d.)

Voting in national or state elections, as Yadav and Omvedt agree, is only part—and not necessarily a very substantial one—in making much difference to the everyday lives of Dalits. Even having a government led by, or which has substantial numbers of members who are, Dalits, is no guarantee that the lot of the ordinary Dalit will improve.[1] Since

---

* We are indebted to Jens Lerche and John Harriss for detailed and constructive comments on the chapter. While they are to thank for much of the coherence of the chapter, any lingering errors are our own. The data presented here was collected thanks to ESRC Grant RES-062-23-3348. Finally, we are grateful to Lokniti for permission to use their electoral data.

independence, a prominent strategy to overcome the marginalisation of disadvantaged groups such as women, Dalits and Adivasis—in relation to elections—has been to create 'reserved constituencies', in which all the candidates must come from the marginalised category. This measure was introduced for several reasons—partly because Congress ruled out the idea of separate electorates, on the basis of the experience under British rule—but in essence the measure was expected to protect the interest of disadvantaged castes by ensuring a minimum representation in all levels of India's representative democracy.[2]

Political scientists who have looked at the impact of caste reservations on panchayat behaviour differ in their conclusions. Duflo argues that:

> Reservation significantly increases the access of disadvantaged groups to political decision making.... There is also a significant reallocation of the goods toward the preferred allocation of the group in power, [and] reservation clearly emerges as a powerful redistribution tool. (Duflo 2005: 677)

Reserved constituencies, district council positions or panchayat positions were designed to increase the representation of, and ensure some leadership positions for the marginalised groups. How this might link to reductions in inequalities that disadvantaged such groups was less clearly spelt out. Chandra (2004) argues that such reductions happen where 'identity politics' is strong, as in Uttar Pradesh (UP). If different caste groups have different class or other interests, it may be possible to identify policies that differentially reward them. Does SC caste origin lead members of the Lok Sabha, Legislative Assemblies or panchayats to introduce policies that tend to benefit more of the poor, for example (Bardhan et al. 2010; Besley et al. 2007; Pande 2003)? By contrast, after taking account of the possibility that the constituencies that have been selected to be 'reserved', already show some evidence of more power and influence for Dalits, a detailed analysis of panchayats in Karnataka finds 'at most weak effects of quotas on the targeting of material benefits' (Dunning and Nilekani 2013: 52). These accounts are, of course, ones that focus on material indicators of inclusion: the targeting of public policies, for example. But the existing evidence suggests at least considerable room for doubt over whether reservations of this kind work—or work well—to overcome marginalisation and exclusion.

Similarly, there is no necessity that the creation of political parties in the name of a marginalised group will lead to identifiable changes in social inclusion, even if voting patterns change. Indeed, rather than institutionalising marginal actors and bringing them into decision-making bodies, the creation of dependent Dalit parties can result in the institutionalisation of marginalisation through processes of adverse incorporation. Nonetheless, Lakha and Taneja (2009: 317) recently argued that the upsurge of lower caste (Dalit and 'Other Backward Caste') groups has engendered 'a seismic shift in patterns of political participation and structures of power'. Other authors spoke of a 'Dalit revolution' (Jaffrelot 2003) and noted that Dalit parties may mobilise hitherto passive citizens to vote for them (Gorringe 2005) or attract significant number of votes away from the established parties (Roberts 2010). Many of these studies are confined to one state and/or are qualitative in nature—analysing perceptions and attitudes rather than more general voting patterns or trends. In this chapter, however, we offer an analysis of Dalit voting patterns in two significant states—UP and Tamil Nadu (TN)—since 2001. We take account both of the available quantitative electoral data as well as qualitative studies that provide insights into the processes that underlie how and why Dalits vote.

Whilst choosing two states allows for more in-depth analysis—and prevents us from making too many false generalisations on the basis of a single case study—TN and UP are not 'typical'. Nonetheless, with Maharashtra, they have regularly been treated as bellwethers for more national-level trends. They also have the benefit of appearing, on the face of it, to exemplify two different approaches to Dalit parliamentary political assertion. UP is famous for the fact that the Bahujan Samaj Party (BSP)—an avowedly Dalit party, at least in its origins—managed to be the dominant party in three of that state's coalition governments in 1995, 1997 and 2002–2003, before winning an outright majority in the Vidhan Sabha in 2007. The BSP was heavily defeated—dropping from 206 to 80 in terms of seats—in the 2012 elections, but still gained nearly 26 per cent of the votes polled (compared to about 30 per cent in 2007). In TN, by contrast, Dalit-led parties have only appeared since 1996 (Gorringe 2007) and they have not managed to establish a viable presence, being reduced largely to negotiating to join groups led by either the Dravida Munnetra Kazhagham (DMK), the All India Anna Dravida Munnetra Kazhagham (AIADMK) or a 'Third Front' in elections since then.

Despite this appearance of Dalit assertion in UP, Mehrotra's (2006) research concluded that Dalits in TN fare better in terms of social indicators than their UP counterparts, suggesting that Dalit power is no panacea. Similarly, although Harriss (2006: 236) highlights the importance of political participation amongst the lower castes and classes for the implementation of welfare programmes, he points to the negative impact of upper caste domination. Dalit well-being, this implies, may rest less on their support for a 'Dalit party' but much more on their political participation per se and on the absence of an organised and obstructive dominant caste. An analysis of Dalit voting patterns in both states, thus, could help shed light on what strategies 'work' for Dalit citizens as an outcome of the interaction between their own activism and that of upper-caste opponents.

Despite these caveats, in this chapter, we will start from the premise that voting patterns can tell us something about how far electoral politics can lead to processes of overcoming marginalisation, even if we remain unable to comment directly on local contexts of upper caste opposition. If Dalits consistently vote for parties with high involvement of Dalits as leaders, it is at least plausible that this can lead to the institutionalisation of Dalit influence in policy-making, through the ability of these politicians to influence appointments, to limit the involvement of officials (like the police) in the harassment of low-caste political groups, and in shaping policies and legislation. Such interventions may be strengthened if those parties gain power, whether on their own or as members of coalitions. That is certainly what politicians argue and is the basis on which they often ask for votes.

That said, it is important to pause here and stress that for all the political rhetoric about 'Dalit politics' and Dalit unity, 'Dalits', even within a state, are not a homogeneous category. Different Dalit castes have different interests, sometimes occupying very different social and economic positions, and are differentially distributed throughout the state. They face different conjunctions of other castes in these different settings. Thus, for example, Chamars/Jatavs (Mayawati's caste) are more prominent in western UP than elsewhere in the state, and in western UP they face Jats and Muslims as major competitors for political influence. In the south-west of UP, Yadavs play a more dominant political role, and in the east, centre and south, different social fissures are significant. Unfortunately, the data we use later in the chapter rarely differentiates within the category of SC or

Dalit, and where (as in TN, see Table A5.1a–c) it does so, the categories that are reported are not consistent through time.

In a series of papers in 1999–2001, Yogendra Yadav described a second democratic upsurge in a third political system for India (Yadav 1999, 2001). In many respects, his analyses have set a framework for discussions of caste and politics in the decade since he wrote. The standard model of the second democratic upsurge is that Dalits' increasing involvement in politics has been characterised by more of them voting, and more of them voting for candidates from their own caste (or at least, for other Dalits—Jaffrelot 2013), whether as a sign of political identity or in the expectation of personal or collective rewards (Chandra 2004). Dalit parties are, thus, portrayed as vehicles for caste assertion or mobilisation rather than 'proper political parties'. As Verma puts it:

> In the post-Bhimrao Ambedkar era, the narrative on Dalit politics in the country is more often confined into the binaries of 'identity assertion' or 'opportunistic politics'. The scholarship that has attempted to explain participation in electoral politics among Dalits has often treated the community as a homogeneous category without dissecting the demographic details and inter-state variations. (Verma 2009: 95)

But voting patterns—for all sections of the electorate—seem to be increasingly unstable. Not only are there sometimes considerable swings from one general or state election to the next, but voters also behave quite differently in Lok Sabha and in state elections. At the national level, a slow attrition of Dalit voters from Congress and towards the BSP can be identified in the Lok Sabha elections from 1971 to 2009 (Verma 2009: 96), but the 2014 Lok Sabha election seems to have resulted in a considerable migration of Dalit voters to the BJP (Verma 2014). One explanation is the success in UP of the 'communal' card (Pai 2014)—with the BJP leader Amit Shah, for example, stressing that 'our community' is in danger (Varadarajan 2014). Other factors seem to have been the ability of Narendra Modi to appeal across caste barriers, and the precipitous decline in the popularity of Mayawati in UP. The BSP could not win even one seat and its vote share dropped from about 27 per cent in 2009 to 20 per cent in 2014. In TN, for the first time since 1999, there were multiple coalitions in the fray. Any thoughts that this fragmentation of votes might aid the Dalit parties, however, came to nought as the AIADMK swept the board winning 37 out

Institutionalising Marginal Actors in Uttar Pradesh and Tamil Nadu

of 39 seats. The party succeeded in garnering a significant number of Dalit votes (Verma 2014), but the implosion of the DMK means that it is hard to read too much into the results. Certainly the Viduthalai Chiruthaigal Katchi (VCK—Liberation Panther Party) and Puthiya Tamizhagam (PT—New Tamil Nadu)—the two largest Dalit parties in the state—secured nearly 30 per cent of the vote in the three constituencies they contested even though they failed to win a seat (Elections.in 2014).

In this chapter, we consider the prehistory of the 2014 election patterns and use data from the sample surveys, pre-election and post-election, carried out by Lokniti at the Centre for the Study of Developing Societies (CSDS), to investigate how Dalits and others have voted in UP and TN Lok Sabha and Assembly elections since 2001. We address the following questions:

1. How have Dalits in UP and TN voted, and how have these patterns changed through time?
2. What seems to account for the voting patterns by social characteristics such as gender and education?
3. Are there differences in voting patterns between the Lok Sabha and Assembly elections?
4. What is the relationship between elections—as illustrated by these data—and the institutionalisation of marginalised groups, in this case, Dalits?

Comparing TN and UP is not implausible: both states have similar proportions of Dalits (see Table 5.1) and similar distributions. For example, in both states, Dalits are more likely to live in rural areas, where they

Table 5.1

SC population proportions for Tamil Nadu and Uttar Pradesh, urban and rural, 2001 census

	Rural	Urban	All
Tamil Nadu	23.8%	13.9%	19.0%
Uttar Pradesh	23.1%	12.7%	21.2%
India	17.9%	11.8%	16.2%

Source: Census data online (accessed 31 August 2013).

constitute between 20 and 25 per cent of the population, than in the towns, where they constitute 12–14 per cent of the population (see Table 5.1).

In understanding the similarities and differences, and patterns of change over time, we need to keep several confounding factors in mind. The first is the role of voting in Dalit politics and identity: Do Dalits vote, and if so, why? The second concern is whether similar factors are at work in all states; and the third, whether there are variations within the population of Dalits as to their voting patterns.

Voting and Non-voting by Dalits

Early assumptions that the poor and non-literate in general, and Dalits in particular, might be less likely to vote, were overthrown by CSDS data that seemed to show very high levels of voting by Dalits. Since Yogendra Yadav's ground-breaking article (Yadav 2001), it has been taken as axiomatic that the poor, and Dalits in particular, are more likely to vote than the 'middle class' or other castes. But evidence on non-voting by caste is much more problematic than might be thought. Pushpendra (1999) notes, with respect to the 1996 and 1998 Lok Sabha elections:

> In the 1996 general election, the percentage of SC voter turnout has been 89.2 per cent as against the national average of 87.3 per cent and a corresponding figure of 85.6 per cent in the case of upper castes. This trend continued in the 1998 elections where the voter turnout figures for the SCs and the upper castes were 93 per cent and 91.9 per cent respectively…. (CSDS Data Unit, CSDS, Delhi). (Pushpendra 1999: 2611)

However, in a footnote, he describes the complexity of establishing the validity of this claim, since the national turnout figure according to the Election Commission was much lower (57.9 per cent). Three reasons are adduced for the large difference: (a) a tendency to report about having voted to the CSDS researchers even though one has not done so; (b) a very strong bias in the sample towards those present in the locality on the day of the vote, or within 30 hours afterwards—who are more likely to have voted than those who were absent because of migration, work obligations, and so on; and (c) since the voters' list includes many—perhaps 12–13 per cent—of 'ghost' names, actual turnout—even using the Election Commission's figures—should be inflated to about 66 per cent. Unfortunately, each of these three factors—differential reporting, likelihood of being around to report having voted or not, and the presence of additional names on the register—is likely to be influenced by caste, class and occupation, so we cannot apply these figures across the board (Pushpendra 1999: 2618, note 1). The reported differences between upper caste and lower caste turnout are also really very small, and unlikely to be either statistically or socially significant. Taking these considerations into account would mean that no claim about differences in turnout can be supported on the basis of this evidence. Furthermore, there has been change on all these fronts through time: willingness to admit to not voting, levels of migration (which can be seasonal); and voter registration drives, including efforts to rid voter lists of non-residents. We conclude that the case for higher levels of Dalit voting remains 'not proven' for the period from 2001 with which we are concerned here.

There is also some uncertainty about the significance of voting for the poor, and for Dalits in particular. Mukulika Banerjee, for example, accepts the argument that the poor are more likely to vote than middle or upper class electors, but she argues that voting has a strong affective dimension. Not only do many poor or lower caste people see voting as a civic duty, they do so despite a general cynicism about the likely effects of their voting on the—generally agreed—corruption of politicians in India. Furthermore:

> ...[T]here exists a third realm of politics that [is] available to everyone: the politics of participation and citizenship. The very act of voting, for a large proportion of the electorate, is performative of *uber* democratic ideals: political equality (when each person is genuinely equal to another), popular sovereignty (a moment when each individual matters—*ek din ka sultan* is how people put it in Hindi), and citizenship (when people have a chance to perform their rights and duties). By turning up to vote, queuing patiently [at] polling stations, exercising their choice, and wearing their blackened fingers as a badge of honour, they demonstrate their belief and participation in the most demotic acts of democracy, which continues to flourish despite the demonic politicians. (Banerjee 2011: 82–83)

Similarly, Ahuja and Chhibber suggest that

> ...[T]he poor mostly report that the state mistreats or ignores them yet makes every effort on Election Day to ensure they are treated equally. The recognition the state grants to the poor on Election Day leads them to view

voting as a valued right, one that gives them a rare chance to associate with those who govern as equals. (Ahuja and Chhibber 2012: 389)

In considering whether—and if so, how much—these factors differ from one state to the next, or amongst different subsets of Dalits, we have to acknowledge that the data are sparse, though Carswell and De Neve's (2014) recent study found similar sentiments amongst Tamil Dalit voters. Ahuja and Chhibber (2012: 407) also report that Dalits were more likely to use the language of 'rights' in TN than were members of Other Backward Classes or members of other castes, but the differences are small. The numbers of respondents in the surveys we report here seem to be huge to start with; but by the time one is starting to look for variations amongst Dalits, by state and by social factors like education, gender or *jati*, cell sizes rapidly become very small. Nonetheless, they do shed some light on these broader patterns, and we consider in turn the questions of how voting patterns in TN and UP vary; and then the evidence of variations by social indicator. In both cases, we look to see what evidence there is of stability or of change through time. The data come from the pre- and post-poll surveys carried out in the National Elections Surveys (NES) conducted by teams coordinated by the Lokniti section of the CSDS, Delhi. For UP, the elections we consider are the post-poll surveys for the Vidhan Sabha (Legislative Assembly) elections of 2002, 2007 and 2012 and the Lok Sabha elections of 2004 and 2009; for TN, the data relate to the legislative assembly elections of 2001, 2006 and 2011, and the Lok Sabha elections of 2004 and 2009. For the 2006 legislative assembly elections, only a pre-poll survey is available. Unfortunately for the possibility of making comparisons through time or across states, the NES data is not presented on the same basis in each election. Numbers surveyed also vary considerably from election to election. We have not carried out statistical tests to assess the significance of the differences displayed here: they remain merely suggestive of possible larger patterns.

State-level Variations in Dalit Voting

It is clear that the political systems in each state have been increasingly disjoined from one another, especially since the establishment of a third political system around 1990. Whereas in the first and second political systems, Yadav argues, national politics influenced state elections, in the third system:

There is an unmistakable fore-grounding of the state in the political horizon of an ordinary citizen. Political loyalties, opinions and even social identities are now chosen at the level of the state. Now people vote in the parliamentary elections as if they are choosing a state government. (Yadav 1999: 2399)

While Yadav's assertion has become part of the 'common-sense' of political analysis, it has rarely been subject to empirical scrutiny. Qualitative research from TN (Wyatt 2010), however, suggests that national considerations continue to play a part in voting for Lok Sabha elections in the state. While opinions and identities may be formed at the state level, therefore, people are not ignorant of, or isolated from, wider politics.

The ordinary voter would seem, on the face of it, to experience very different political scenarios in the different states. In TN, at least since Kamaraj and the decline of Congress, state-level politics has been dominated by the AIADMK and the DMK. National parties join as the members of alliances and coalitions that shift from one election to another, but rarely make an impact on their own. As a result, in any constituency, it is often a two-horse race and the winner needs at least 40 per cent to be sure of victory. In UP, by contrast, the national parties—especially Congress and the BJP—have retained an interest and an ability to influence elections. About one-quarter of the winning candidates in UP in the 2012 Vidhan Sabha elections were elected on one-third of the votes or fewer (NES data). The BSP model of Dalit politics cannot be easily 'exported' to other states, amongst other reasons because of the differences in party systems across India.

Changes in Voting Patterns, 2001–2012

Because voting is affected by alliances, and these shift through time (and are very different in UP and TN), we treat changes through time separately, before drawing out some comparisons between the two states:

1. **Tamil Nadu**
   A complicating factor here is that the DMK and AIADMK are part of broad alliances and often Dalit parties join both, as in 2011, sometimes fielding candidates on the symbol of the dominant party, making it doubly hard to disentangle voter preferences. Table 5.2

Table 5.2

Lok Sabha and Legislative Assembly elections: Dalit voting proportions by party/alliance 2001 to 2011, Tamil Nadu

Tamil Nadu	2001 LA	2004 LS	2006 LA	2009 LS	2011 LA
AIADMK	36.8%	36.6%	46.8%	31.0%	50.4%
DMK	43.4%	21.6%	39.4%	45.6%	40.5%
Others	19.8%	41.8%	13.8%	23.4%	9.2%
	N=419	N=134	N=1053	N=171	N=917

Source: NES, data supplied by CSDS Data Unit.

Note: 2006 data is pre-poll survey, and the percentages are calculated on only those planning to vote.

provides an overview of Dalit voting preferences in the 2001, 2006 and 2011 legislative assembly elections, and in the 2004 and 2009 Lok Sabha elections. The year 2004 is interesting as both VCK and PT were in a Third Front, so one would expect Dalit votes for 'others' to increase, which indeed they did. Other parties also did better in the 2009 Lok Sabha elections—when the film actor Vijayakanth launched an alternative party—than in the legislative assembly election of 2006, and their vote shares dropped again in the legislative assembly election 2011.

The votes for the DMK and the AIADMK and their allies overall in 2011 were much the same as their vote shares amongst Dalits—39.4 per cent for the DMK+ and 51.7 per cent for the AIADMK+, suggesting that Dalit voters are not necessarily as distinct as identity-based parties would have us suppose. One effect of reservations for SCs, of course, is that Dalits are present in each party. The fact that autonomous Dalit parties did not really emerge in the state till the late 1990s, means that Tamil Dalits have historic ties and attachments to the Dravidian parties that can be hard to shake off (Carswell and De Neve 2014).

2. **Uttar Pradesh**

Table 5.3 sets out the voting patterns of Dalits in UP in the 2002, 2007 and 2012 Vidhan Sabha elections, and the 2004 and 2009 Lok Sabha elections. Some aspects of the picture are to be expected—the

Table 5.3

Lok Sabha and Vidhan Sabha elections: Dalit voting proportions by party/alliance 2002 to 2012, Uttar Pradesh

Uttar Pradesh	2002 VS	2004 LS	2007 VS	2009 LS	2012 VS
Congress	4.2%	7.6%	7.4%	8.7%	8.6%
BJP	6.5%	4.3%	5.0%	6.1%	5.9%
BSP	72.2%	72.0%	52.0%	77.1%	57.7%
SP	7.6%	12.8%	27.6%	6.1%	14.3%
Others	9.5%	3.3%	8.0%	2.0%	13.5%
	N = 263	N = 329	N = 3,352	N = 446	N = 1,301

Source: NES, data supplied by CSDS Data Unit.

very low levels of support by Dalits for the BJP in all the elections (save for the most recent polls), and the evidence of slowly increasing support for Congress. Less expected, perhaps, is that the BSP dropped by 20 percentage points (or about 30 per cent) from 2002 and 2004 levels (when over 70 per cent of Dalits supported the BSP) in the Vidhan Sabha elections of 2007 and 2012 (when under 60 per cent voted for the BSP). These figures suggest a steady core level of support for the BSP amongst Dalit voters, though of course the overall percentage can hide substantial individual shifts into and out of 'non-voting' and between parties. There is, though, some evidence here of Dalits supporting the BSP more when it was not extending its appeal beyond its core voters. These voters seem to have shifted to the (Samajwadi Party) SP in 2007 but only about half of this support carried over into the 2012 Vidhan Sabha elections, so Dalits are marginalised in the SP government formed after that election. According to the NES post-poll survey, Dalits probably provided only about 10 per cent of those who voted for the SP in 2012. Such data also tell us, of course, nothing about local conditions of voting: was the increased support for SP in 2007 the result of local power holders exerting their dominance—perhaps in reaction to past electoral reversals—or was it a reflection of unhappiness with the *sarvajan* approach?

Patterns of Voting within SC Populations

In 2009, Verma argued (as we have seen earlier) that there was a need to unpack voting by Dalits with reference to a historical analysis of politics, informed by spatial patterns and demographic variables (Verma 2009: 95). In our approach to understanding Dalit voting in the two states of TN and UP, we have been concerned to address several possible issues:

1. To what extent do Dalits vote as a bloc, that is, in the sense of there being very little variation by major social categories, such as caste or gender?
2. Is there any evidence of the 'creamy layer'—here represented by those with more education than the rest—voting differently from the rest of the Dalit population?

Tamil Nadu

Caste

The NES data have been collected with different purposes in view from one election to the next, and the changing classifications and total of those interviewed by caste reflect this (see Table A5.1a–c). The caste classification for 2001 is not very useful: AdiDravida and Paraiyar are often used coterminously (Gorringe 2005) but are differentiated here. Pallars and Paraiyars might be expected to vote differently (a point that shows up clearly in the 2006 figures), but are run together under a heading that demonstrates a disregard for local sensitivities: the suffix—on the end of Paraiyar is seen as demeaning but is used here in an unproblematic way. The two main Dalit parties referred to previously, the VCK and PT, predominantly appeal to the Paraiyars and Pallars, respectively, though significant numbers of both remain affiliated to Dravidian parties. Arunthathiyars, the third most populous Dalit caste cluster in the state, have yet to launch an equivalent party and were mobilised much later than the other two castes. Arunthathiyars are currently being assiduously wooed by different parties in part because they are not seen to be

Institutionalising Marginal Actors in Uttar Pradesh and Tamil Nadu

committed to any particular political group. Even where parties are not in competition, however, status competition and rivalry between Dalit castes saw VCK activists voting against their coalition partners in some places, in order to support a Paraiyar candidate at the expense of a Pallar one (Gorringe 2012). To assume a 'Dalit' vote bank, in other words, would be misguided. Because the categories change, furthermore, it is not possible to look at changes through time in caste-wise voting patterns. While the analysts eagerly anticipate reports based on NES data following each election, we would suggest the need for some caution in this regard and highlight the need for such data to be supplemented by detailed empirical data from each state.

Gender

Previous research suggests that women tend to be a bit more favourable to the AIADMK than the DMK and this finding is more or less visible in Table 5.4, though whether any of the numbers are statistically significant or not is unclear. The figures for the 2009 Lok Sabha election show a reversed pattern amongst Dalit women, though the AIADMK retained a slight gender gap overall (Deshpande 2009). The requirement for more

Table 5.4

Gender differences in SC voting behaviours, Tamil Nadu, 2001–2011

Tamil Nadu		2001 LA	2004 LS	2006 LA	2009 LS	2011 LA
AIADMK+	M	31.3%	31.0%	43.8%	34.8%	46.6%
	F	41.7%	46.0%	50.1%	26.8%	54.2%
DMK+	M	49.8%	22.6%	42.5%	38.2%	42.7%
	F	37.6%	20.0%	36.0%	53.7%	38.2%
Others	M	19.0%	41.8%	13.7%	27.0%	10.6%
	F	20.6%	34.0%	13.9%	19.5%	7.6%
		N=419	N=134	N=1,053	N=171	N=917

Source: NES, data supplied by CSDS Data Unit.

Note: 2006 data is pre-poll survey, and the percentages are calculated on only those planning to vote.

detailed local data is clear here; while this blip could reflect the fact that the VCK were prominent members of the DMK coalition, it could also reflect concerns over the violence in Sri Lanka which was at a height in 2009 (see Carswell and De Neve 2009).

Education

As with all the TN data for the 2004 and 2009 Lok Sabha elections (see Tables 5.2 and 5.4, as well as Appendix Table 5.1b), sample sizes are small. But if we take voting differences for Dalits by educational status (Table 5.5) at face value, there are some surprising patterns. Thus, in 2001, 2004 and 2006, better educated Dalits were more likely to vote for the DMK or its allies than less educated Dalit voters; but in 2009, they were less likely to do so; and in 2011, their voting pattern was indistinguishable from that of the less educated voters. Another interesting finding is that the middle group (those with Upper Primary schooling) were far more likely than those less or more educated than them to support other parties in

Table 5.5
Educational differences in SC voting behaviour, Tamil Nadu, 2001–2011

Tamil Nadu		2001 LA	2004 LS	2006 LA	2009 LS	2011 LA
AIADMK+	Non-literate	34.1%	43.4%	52.3%	26.5%	52.6%
	Upper Primary	45.5%	29.7%	51.6%	25.4%	51.1%
	Upper Primary+	31.5%	35.6%	41.6%	35.4%	49.1%
DMK+	Non-literate	49.6%	20.8%	30.9%	44.4%	38.5%
	Upper Primary	29.1%	13.5%	34.4%	44.7%	41.7%
	Upper Primary +	50.0%	31.1%	46.3%	36.7%	40.8%
Others	Non-literate	16.3%	35.9%	16.7%	22.2%	8.9%
	Upper Primary	25.4%	56.7%	14.0%	13.1%	7.3%
	Upper Primary +	18.5%	33.4%	12.1%	10.0%	10.1%
		N=419	N=134	N=1,053	N=171	N=917

Source: NES, data supplied by CSDS Data Unit.

Note: 2006 data is pre-poll survey, and the percentages are calculated on only those planning to vote.

2004, the year when the VCK and PT were part of a Third Front having failed to gain entry to either of the main alliances. Whilst more research is clearly required here, this would be in keeping with findings that Dalit parties appeal mostly to the upwardly mobile SCs rather than the most impoverished or already established Dalits who may well owe allegiances to more established parties.

Uttar Pradesh

Caste

The NES does not seem to have broken down voting amongst SCs in UP by caste. Some authors have attempted to understand Dalit voting in UP by looking at voting patterns in reserved constituencies, but this is clearly fallacious. Similarly, looking at SC proportions in particular constituencies, or in regions of UP, is a very poor predictor of voting by Dalits within those constituencies. Verma provides an analysis of caste and class in voting patterns for BSP by different castes in the 'Hindi belt' and suggests that Jatavs (with which he includes Charmakars and Madigas) were much more likely to vote for BSP in 2009 Lok Sabha elections amongst the urban and rural lower class (Verma 2009: 95). It is generally said that Kathiks and Balmikis are more likely to support the BJP. The lack of clearly comparable data, however, frustrates a comparative or temporal analysis.

Gender

Until the 2012 elections, the voting figures by gender for Dalits in UP, presented in Table 5.6, show very small differences, none of them socially significant. One change that does emerge in 2012 is that women seem to have been more disillusioned than were the men with the Mayawati BSP government, with the men's vote rising from the 2007 level to 60 per cent, whereas the women's BSP vote share stayed around 54 per cent. Further research is required to probe the reasons for this, given Govinda's (2008) finding that Dalit women felt politically represented by the BSP. Pai's (2013) argument that there has been a shift from identity-based assertion to a demand for improved governance and inclusive development may

Table 5.6

Gender differences in SC voting behaviours, UP, 2002–2012

Uttar Pradesh		2002 VS	2004 LS	2007 VS	2009 LS	2012 VS
Congress	M	4.6%	8.9%	7.5%	7.2%	6.9%
	F	3.8%	6.2%	7.2%	11.0%	10.9%
BJP+	M	5.4%	4.1%	4.9%	6.4%	6.5%
	F	7.5%	4.4%	5.0%	5.5%	5.1%
SP+	M	7.7%	13.0%	27.7%	6.8%	14.4%
	F	7.5%	12.5%	27.4%	4.9%	14.2%
BSP	M	73.8%	69.2%	51.9%	76.9%	60.5%
	F	70.7%	75.0%	52.3%	77.5%	54.1%
Other	M	8.5%	4.7%	7.9%	2.7%	11.6%
	F	10.5%	1.9%	8.1%	1.1%	15.7%
		N = 263	N = 329	N = 3,352	N = 446	N = 1,301

Source: NES, data supplied by CSDS Data Unit.

be relevant here given that the concerns for everyday 'bread and butter' issues tend to be highly gendered.

Education

In 1999, Pushpendra concluded that 'the BSP is primarily a party of the rural poor' (Pushpendra 1999: 2616). For this chapter we have only analysed educational achievement as an indicator of social class, and it is clear from Table 5.7 (ignoring issues of sample size and statistical significance for the moment) that the less educated have been more likely to vote for BSP throughout the period 2002–2012. In the early elections, whilst very few Dalits supported the BJP and its allies, the middle and upper educational groups were more likely to do so. This pattern seems to have reversed by 2012. In contrast to TN, this perhaps suggests that the BSP had managed to use their political power to dispense patronage to the 'creamy layer' and that this might have worked in terms of attracting and cementing their support in the following elections. Given the BSP's emergence from BAMCEF (Backward and Minority Communities Employees' Federation)—the organisation of government employees founded by Kanshiram—this is credible. This history, however, also means that 'creamy layer' Dalits

Table 5.7

Educational differences in SC voting behaviours, UP, 2002–2012

Uttar Pradesh		2002 VS	2004 LS	2007 VS	2009 LS	2012 VS
Congress	Non-literate	4.4%	8.5%	6.2%	10.2%	6.9%
	Upper Primary	1.8%	5.1%	8.1%	10.3%	10.9%
	Above	8.0%	6.8%	8.5%	6.5%	8.6%
BJP+	Non-literate	5.0%	3.5%	4.6%	4.9%	6.5%
	Upper Primary	10.5%	5.1%	6.3%	6.4%	5.1%
	Above	8.0%	6.8%	4.7%	7.8%	5.9%
SP+	Non-literate	6.1%	10.0%	24.1%	6.3%	14.4%
	Upper Primary	12.3%	20.5%	29.9%	2.6%	14.2%
	Above	4.0%	14.8%	30.6%	7.8%	14.3%
BSP	Non-literate	74.0%	75.5%	55.9%	78.5%	60.5%
	Upper Primary	66.7%	68.2%	49.4%	74.4%	54.1%
	Above	76.0%	64.8%	48.7%	74.5%	57.8%
Other	Non-literate	10.5%	2.5%	9.1%	0.0%	11.6%
	Upper Primary	8.8%	0.0%	6.3%	6.4%	15.7%
	Above	4.0%	14.8%	7.6%	3.3%	13.4%
		$N=263$	$N=329$	$N=3,352$	$N=446$	$N=1,301$

Source: NES, data supplied by CSDS Data Unit.

in particular have a sense of ownership and an emotive link that could explain their shift in voting patterns.

Relationships between Voting and Institutionalisation of Marginalisation

Although castes and parties are often closely identified with each other (as in the BSP and the Jatavs in UP), this does not mean that all members of the caste 'vote their caste' by supporting that party. As Jaffrelot points out, intra-caste factionalism might lead to a split vote because more than one party nominates a candidate from that caste; and voters may reject the party that claims to stand for their interests for a variety of reasons (Jaffrelot 2013:

114) including the caste of the candidate (Gorringe 2012). Furthermore, there is the issue of 'ethnic identifiability': in a recent study, 'nearly one-third (29.2 per cent, to be exact) of voters we surveyed across Bihar misidentified the jati of the candidate they had voted for in the election literally just days before' (Vaishnav 2013). It is, therefore, hazardous in the extreme to make assumptions about issues of identity and interests from voting patterns. In trying to understand changes through time, it is also crucial to keep in mind that people move from voting to non-voting and back again; and apparent overall stability may mask the fact that individuals or groups may shift in opposite directions so that the net changes might be made up of far more substantial shifts than finally appear. It is also worth noting that voting is not always straightforward, as Carswell and De Neve (2014: 1047) note in their reflections on why people do not vote: the lack of a valid voter card, migration for work, and illness may all prevent people from voting. These issues, furthermore, may be gendered, as when women who migrate for marriage are not registered to vote in their new locations (Carswell and De Neve 2014: 1047). Nonetheless, some simple conclusions might be in order:

1. In both states, over time, Dalit votes have shifted quite considerably from one party or alliance to another. This is most obvious in TN, where (as with the electorate as a whole), the fortunes of the DMK and the AIADMK go up and down from one election to the next. The dominance of these two organisations means that Dalit parties also tend to move from one coalition to the other rather than standing alone. This makes gauging support for Dalit parties themselves rather difficult. The efforts to support 'third parties' in TN seem to have worn themselves out after only two elections (1999 and 2004) perhaps because, despite gaining many votes, they won no seats in the bi-polar electoral contests that characterise the state. But even in UP, where the BSP has been the overwhelmingly dominant party of choice for Dalits, their support has waxed and waned to a considerable extent, from a low of 52 per cent in 2007 to a high of 77 per cent in 2009. The almost complete failure of the BSP in the 2014 Lok Sabha elections in UP is a case in point. Though the party retained a sizeable number of Dalit votes, the frequent references to a 'Dalit vote-bank' for particular parties, therefore, need to be treated with caution.

2. Caste within the Dalit population is important—perhaps especially in UP, where Jatavs and Balmikis (for example) have often differed markedly in their voting patterns. The NES data for TN (see Tables A5.1a–c) also suggests considerable variability in voting by caste but the lack of consistent data by caste over time means that it is hard to draw firm conclusions. The further complicating factor in TN is that Dalit parties—which might be expected to polarise the intra-Dalit vote more—have rarely stood alone.
3. Voting patterns by gender or by education—whilst interesting—do not seem to be stable.

The picture derived from voting patterns, then, is not an unchanging or consistent one. Over time, or by sub-group of Dalits, the picture changes in somewhat baffling ways. One way of interpreting this might be to suggest that Dalits are not a meaningful electoral category. Another might be that as marginalised groups, they do not have as fixed electoral commitments as some commentators have assumed, either because there is no party (neither local nor national) that can be relied upon to further their interests or because—in an increasingly populist political system—parties learn new ways of inducing social groups or categories to vote for them, but then fail to deliver and are so rejected at the next election or are outbid in the next election (as often happens in TN). Devoid of ideological champions, thus, Dalit voters may adopt pragmatic means to further their own individual interests.

Conclusion

The main features of the picture we have been able to draw are twofold. On the one hand, even the relatively simple level of analysis that has been possible shows that the evidence for some received views—such as the higher turnout of marginalised electors in national and state elections—need to be reconsidered, though it is clear that Dalits continue to vote in large numbers. The second conclusion is that voting patterns amongst Dalits are more fluid than the literature suggests, even in UP, once the possibilities of moving between voting and non-voting, as well as bidirectional flows between parties, have been taken into account. We have not set ourselves the task of comparing this fluidity with that amongst other groups in the

UP and TN electorate, but we suspect that it would be hard to find reliable indicators of 'fluidity' for which there is sufficient evidence to carry out a valid test to show whether or not Dalits are unusual in this respect. More problematically, perhaps, we have found little in the voting patterns and views that would shed light on how far Dalit electoral behaviour either reflects degrees or kinds of political institutionalisation, or acts as a powerful tool for achieving this. Our two case studies provide different conclusions that are equally depressing from the standpoint of Dalit politics. In TN, the transformation of a Dalit social and political movement into a political party seems to have ended up with Dalits as a whole little better off. While the castes identified with the VCK may have strengthened their political clout for a while, by 2011, it would seem that the pull of the large electoral fronts, one behind the DMK and the other behind the AIADMK, had returned to being the norm in legislative assembly elections. In UP, the impressive successes of the BSP in the 2007 elections, and its effort at being taken seriously in the 2009 Lok Sabha elections, increasingly look like being a flash-in-the-pan effect, here today and gone tomorrow. The flip-side of this argument, of course, is that Dalit voters are becoming increasingly canny in their political choices and are prepared to vote beyond their caste if they perceive it to be in their interests to do so. For years, Dalit movements castigated established parties for treating Dalits as little more than 'coolie labourers'. They may now be discovering that increasingly conscious Dalit voters are not prepared to take directions from Dalit parties either.

Notes

1. See Jeffery, Jeffrey and Jeffery (2001) for an ethnographic approach to this issue for UP.
2. The experience of Muslims, denied such protection, is instructive: Muslim representatives have always been well below what their demographic position would predict.

Appendix

Voting Patterns by Caste, Tamil Nadu

Table A5.1a

Voting (post-poll survey) Tamil Nadu, 2001, Legislative Assembly elections

Tamil Nadu, 2001		AIADMK+	DMK+	MDMK	Other	N/A	Total	N
Adidravida	M	22.1%	57.5%	6.2%	8.0%	6.2%	100.0%	113
	F	39.3%	42.9%	0.0%	2.9%	15.0%	100.0%	140
	All	31.6%	49.4%	2.8%	5.1%	11.1%	100.0%	253
Pallar/Paraiyan	M	44.9%	39.1%	4.3%	10.1%	1.4%	100.0%	69
	F	43.6%	25.5%	18.2%	9.1%	3.6%	100.0%	55
	All	44.4%	33.1%	10.5%	9.7%	2.4%	100.0%	124
Other Dalit	M	36.8%	42.1%	0.0%	5.3%	15.8%	100.0%	19
	F	52.2%	34.8%	8.7%	0.0%	4.3%	100.0%	23
	All	45.2%	38.1%	4.8%	2.4%	9.5%	100.0%	42
All SC	M	31.3%	49.8%	5.0%	8.5%	5.5%	100.0%	201
	F	41.7%	37.6%	5.5%	4.1%	11.0%	100.0%	218
	All	36.8%	43.4%	5.3%	6.2%	8.4%	100.0%	419

Table A5.1b

Voting (post-poll survey) Tamil Nadu, 2004, Lok Sabha elections

Tamil Nadu, 2004		AIADMK+	DMK+	Congress	Other	Total	N
Chakkiliyars and Pallars	M	29.6%	22.5%	2.8%	40.8%	100.0%	71
	F	48.5%	18.2%	9.1%	24.2%	100.0%	33
	All	35.6%	21.2%	4.8%	38.5%	100.0%	104
Other SCs	M	38.5%	23.1%	23.1%	15.4%	100.0%	13
	F	41.2%	23.5%	11.8%	23.5%	100.0%	17
	All	40.0%	23.3%	16.7%	20.0%	100.0%	30
All SC	M	31.0%	22.6%	6.0%	35.7%	100.0%	84
	F	46.0%	20.0%	10.0%	24.0%	100.0%	50
	All	36.6%	21.6%	7.5%	31.3%	100.0%	134

Table A5.1c

Voting intentions (pre-poll survey) Tamil Nadu, 2006

Tamil Nadu, 2006		AIADMK+	DMK+	BJP	DMDK	Others	NA	All	N
Pallar	M	23.1%	55.4%	0.0%	5.4%	11.5%	4.6%	100.0%	130
	F	28.2%	43.5%	0.0%	4.0%	16.1%	8.1%	100.0%	124
	All	25.6%	49.6%	0.0%	4.7%	13.8%	6.3%	100.0%	254
Paraiyar	M	46.5%	34.4%	0.5%	7.2%	2.6%	8.8%	100.0%	387
	F	47.3%	29.9%	0.0%	6.1%	2.9%	13.6%	100.0%	374
	All	46.9%	32.2%	0.3%	6.7%	2.8%	11.2%	100.0%	761
Chakkiliyar	M	41.7%	31.2%	2.1%	14.6%	4.2%	6.2%	100.0%	48
	F	52.5%	20.3%	1.7%	8.5%	3.4%	13.6%	100.0%	59
	All	47.7%	25.2%	1.9%	11.2%	3.7%	10.3%	100.0%	107
Other SC	M	35.7%	46.4%	0.0%	0.0%	10.7%	7.1%	100.0%	28
	F	47.6%	19.0%	4.8%	0.0%	9.5%	19.0%	100.0%	21
	All	40.8%	34.7%	2.0%	0.0%	10.2%	12.2%	100.0%	49
All SC	M	40.5%	39.3%	0.5%	7.1%	5.1%	7.6%	100.0%	593
	F	43.8%	31.5%	0.3%	5.7%	6.1%	12.6%	100.0%	578
	All	42.1%	35.4%	0.4%	6.4%	5.6%	10.1%	100.0%	1,171

References

Ahuja, Amit and Chhibber, Pradeep. 2012. 'Why the Poor Vote in India: "If I Don't Vote, I Am Dead to the State"', *Studies in Comparative International Development* 47(4): 389–410.

Banerjee, Mukulika. 2011. 'Elections as Communitas', *Social Research* 78(1): 75–98.

Bardhan, Pranab, Mookherjee, Dilip and Torrado, Monica Parra. 2010. 'Impact of Political Reservations in West Bengal's local government on Anti-Poverty Targeting', *Journal of Globalization and Development* 1(1): 1–38.

Besley, Timothy, Pande, Rohini and Rao, Vijayendra. 2007. 'The Political Economy of Gram Panchayats in South India', *Economic and Political Weekly* 42(8): 661–666.

Carswell, Grace and De Neve, Geert. 2009. *Tamil Nadu Election Report, India, 2009*. http://sro.sussex.ac.uk/50465/ (accessed 29 April 2015).

———. 2014. 'Why Indians Vote: Reflections on Rights, Citizenship, and Democracy from a Tamil Nadu Village', *Antipode* 46(4): 1032–1053.

Chandra, Kanchan. 2004. *Why Ethnic Parties Succeed: Patronage and Ethnic Head Counts in India*. New York: Cambridge University Press.

Chhibber, Pradeep, Jensenius, Francesca Refsum and Suryanarayan, Pavithra. 2012. 'Party Organization and Party Proliferation in India', *Party Politics*. Online first: DOI: 10.1177/1354068811436059: 1–27.

Ciotti, Manuela. 2011. 'Remaking Traditional Sociality, Ephemeral Friendships and Enduring Political Alliances: "State-made" Dalit Youth in Rural North India', *Focaal* 2011(59): 19–32.

Darapuri, S.R. 2009. 'Why Dalits have Slammed Mayawati's Sarvjan Rule?' *Countercurrents*. http://www.countercurrents.org/darapuri210509.htm (accessed 29 April 2015).

Deshpande, Rajeshwari. 2009. 'How did Women Vote in the Lok Sabha Elections 2009?' *Economic and Political Weekly* 44(39): 83–87.

Devika, J. 2013. 'Contemporary Dalit Assertions in Kerala: Governmental Categories vs Identity Politics?' *History and Sociology of South Asia* 7(1): 1–17.

Duflo, Esther. 2005. 'Why Political Reservations?' *Journal of the European Economic Association* 3(2–3): 668–678.

Duncan, Ian. 1997. 'Agricultural Innovation and Political Change in North India: The Lok Dal in Uttar Pradesh', *The Journal of Peasant Studies* 24(4): 246–268.

———. 1997. 'New Political Equations in North India: Mayawati, Mulayam, and Government Instability in Uttar Pradesh', *Asian Survey* 37(10): 979–996.

———. 1999. 'Dalits and Politics in Rural North India: The Bahujan Samaj Party in Uttar Pradesh', *The Journal of Peasant Studies* 27(1): 35–60.

Dunning, Thad and Nilekani, Janhavi. 2013. 'Ethnic Quotas and Political Mobilization: Caste, Parties, and Distribution in Indian Village Councils', *American Political Science Review* 107(1): 35–56.

Elections.in. 2014. 'Elections in Tamil Nadu: 2014 Results', *Elections.in*. http://www.elections.in/tamil-nadu/#info_id1 (accessed 2 September 2014).

Gorringe, Hugo. 2005. *Untouchable Citizens: Dalit Movements and Democratization in Tamil Nadu*. New Delhi: SAGE.

———. 2007. 'Taming the Dalit Panthers Dalit Politics in Tamil Nadu', *Journal of South Asian Development* 2(1): 51–73.

———. 2008. 'The Caste of the Nation Untouchability and Citizenship in South India', *Contributions to Indian Sociology* 42(1): 123–149.

———. 2010. 'Shifting the "Grindstone of Caste"? Decreasing Dependency among Dalit Labourers in Tamil Nadu', in Barbara Harriss-White and Judith Heyer (eds), *The Comparative Political Economy of Development: Africa and South Asia* (pp. 248–266). London, Routledge.

———. 2010. 'Beyond "Dull and Sterile Routines"?: Dalits Organizing for Social Change in Tamil Nadu', *Cultural Dynamics* 22(2): 105–119.

———. 2010. 'The New Caste Headmen? Dalit Movement Leadership in Tamil Nadu', in Pamela Price and Arild E. Ruud (eds), *Power and Influence in India: Bosses, Lords and Captain* (pp. 119–143). London: Routledge.

———. 2012. 'Caste and Politics in Tamil Nadu', *Seminar* 633(May 2012): 38–42. http://www.india-seminar.com/2012/633/633_hugo_gorringe.htm (accessed 18 August 2015).

Govinda, Radhika. 2008. 'Re-inventing Dalit Women's Identity? Dynamics of Social Activism and Electoral Politics in Rural North India', *Contemporary South Asia* 16(4): 427–440.

Gupta, Dipankar. 2005. 'Caste and Politics: Identity over System', *Annual Review of Anthropology* 34: 409–427.

Harriss, John. 2002. 'Whatever Happened to Cultural Nationalism in Tamil Nadu? A Reading of Current Events and the Recent Literature on Tamil Politics', *Commonwealth and Comparative Politics* 40(3): 97–117.

———. 2006. *Power Matters*. Delhi: Oxford University Press.

Harriss, John, Jeyaranjan, J. and Nagaraj, K. 2010. 'Land, Labour and Caste Politics in Rural Tamil Nadu in the 20th Century: Iruvelpattu (1916–2008)', *Economic and Political Weekly* 45(31): 47–61.

Heath, Oliver. 2005. 'Party Systems, Political Cleavages and Electoral Volatility in India: A State-wise Analysis, 1998–1999', *Electoral Studies* 24(2): 177–199.

Huber, John D. and Suryanarayan, Pavithra. 2013. 'Ethnic Inequality and the Ethnification of Political Parties: Evidence from India', 4 April 2014. http://polisci.columbia.edu/files/polisci/u86/huber_suryanarayon.pdf (accessed 20 July 2015).

Jaffrelot, Christophe. 2003. *India's Silent Revolution: The Rise of the Low Castes in North Indian Politics*. Delhi: Permanent Black.

———. 2013. 'Do Indians Vote Their Caste—While Casting Their Vote?' in Atul Kohli and Prema Singh (eds), *Routledge Handbook of Indian Politics* (pp. 107–118). Abingdon and New York: Routledge.

Jaoul, Nicolas. 2006. 'Learning the Use of Symbolic Means: Dalits, Ambedkar Statues and the State in Uttar Pradesh', *Contributions to Indian Sociology* 40(2): 175–207.

———. 2007. 'Political and "Non-political" Means in the Dalit Movement', in Sudha Pai (ed.), *Political Process in Uttar Pradesh: Identity, Economic Reform and Governance* (pp. 142–168). New Delhi: Pearsons.

Jeffery, Roger, Jeffery, Craig and Jeffery, Patricia. 2001. 'Social and Political Dominance in Western UP: A Response to Sudha Pai', *Contributions to Indian Sociology* 35(3): 213–235.

Jeffrey, Craig, Jeffery, Patricia and Jeffery, Roger. 2008. 'Dalit revolution? New Politicians in Uttar Pradesh, India', *Journal of Asian Studies* 67(4): 1365–1396.

———. 2008. *Degrees without Freedom? Education, Masculinities, and Unemployment in North India*. Stanford, CA: Stanford University Press.

Jeffrey, Craig, Jeffery, Roger and Jeffery, Patricia. 2005. 'Reproducing Difference? Schooling, Jobs and Empowerment in Uttar Pradesh, India', in Radhika Chopra and Patricia Jeffery (eds), *Educational Regimes in Contemporary India* (pp. 256–275). New Delhi, Thousand Oaks and London: SAGE Publications.

Kohli, Atul and Singh, Prerna. 2013. *Routledge Handbook of Indian Politics*. New York: Routledge.

Kumar, Vivek. 2002. *Dalit Leadership in India*. Delhi: Kalpaz Publications.

———. 2006. *India's Roaring Revolution: Dalit Assertion and New Horizons*. Delhi: Gagandeep Publications.

Lakha, S. and Taneja, P. 2009. 'Introduction: Democracy, Governance and Civil Society: Rethinking the Study of Contemporary India', *South Asia* 32(3): 315–325.

Lerche, Jens. 1999. 'Politics of the Poor: Agricultural Labourers and Political Transformations in Uttar Pradesh', *The Journal of Peasant Studies* 26(2–3): 182–241.

Mehra, Ajay K. 2013. *Emerging Trends in Indian Politics: The Fifteenth General Election*. London: Routledge.

Mehrotra, Santosh. 2006. 'Well-being and Caste in Uttar Pradesh: Why UP is not like Tamil Nadu', *Economic and Political Weekly* 41(40): 4261–4271.

Murali, Geetha Kamalakshi. 2007. *Tracing the Signs: Voter Mobilization and the Functionality of Ideas in Tamil Nadu*. Ann Arbor: ProQuest.

Nooruddin, Irfan and Chhibber, Pradeep. 2008. 'Unstable Politics Fiscal Space and Electoral Volatility in the Indian States', *Comparative Political Studies* 41(8): 1069–1091.

Omvedt, Gail. n.d. 'Dalits and Elections', in *ambedkar.org*: dalit e-forum. http://www.ambedkar.org/gail/Dalitsand.htm (accessed 2 September 2014).

———. 2000. 'Dalit Elections, I and II', *The Hindu*, 5 and 6 November 2000.

Pai, Sudha. 2001. 'Social Capital, Panchayats and Grass Roots Democracy: Politics of Dalit Assertion in Uttar Pradesh', *Economic and Political Weekly* 36(8): 645–654.

———. 2013. 'Uttar Pradesh: New Patterns of Mobilization in the 1990s and Beyond', in Atul Kohli and Prerna Singh (eds), *Routledge Handbook of Indian Politics* (pp. 261–269). New York: Routledge.

———. 2014. 'Uttar Pradesh: Competitive Communalism once Again', *Economic and Political Weekly* 49(15). http://www.epw.in/election-specials/uttar-pradesh-competitive-communalism-once-again.html (accessed 18 August 2015).

Pande, Rohini. 2003. 'Can Mandated Political Representation Increase Policy Influence for Disadvantaged Minorities? Theory and Evidence from India', *American Economic Review* 93(4): 1132–1151.

Pandian, M.S.S. 2000. 'Dalit Assertion in Tamil Nadu: An Explanatory Note', *Journal of Indian School of Political Economy* 12(3 and 4): 501–517.

Phadnis, Aditi. 2012. 'Dynamics of UP's Dalit Vote', *Business Standard*, 13 February 2012. http://www.business-standard.com/article/economy-policy/dynamics-of-up-s-dalit-vote-112021300027_1.html (accessed 20 July 2015).

Pushpendra. 1999. 'Dalit Assertion through Electoral Politics', *Economic and Political Weekly* 34(36): 2609–2618.

Rawat, Ramnarayan S. 2003. 'Making Claims for Power: A New Agenda in Dalit Politics of Uttar Pradesh, 1946–48', *Modern Asian Studies* 37(3): 585–612.

Roberts, Nathaniel. 2010. 'Language, Violence, and the State: Writing Tamil Dalits', *South Asia Multidisciplinary Academic Journal*, since 31 January 2010. http://samaj.revues.org/index2952.html (accessed 18 August 2015).

Shastri, Sanjal. 2013. 'Going Beyond Identity Politics: Evidence from Uttar Pradesh and Punjab', in *Lokniti Newsletter*. New Delhi: CSDS.

Simha, Sunṃta. 2002. *Caste Re-configurations and UP Elections*. New Delhi: Kanishka Publishers.

Singh, Jagpal. 1998. 'Ambedkarisation and Assertion of Dalit Identity: Socio-cultural Protest in Meerut District of Western Uttar Pradesh', *Economic and Political Weekly* 33(40): 2611–2618.

Subramanian, Narendra. 2002. 'Identity Politics and Social Pluralism: Political Sociology and Political Change in Tamil Nadu', *Commonwealth and Comparative Politics* 40(3): 125–139.

Taagepera, Rein. 2007. 'Predictive versus Postdictive Models', *European Political Science* 6(2): 114–123.

Vaishnav, Milan. 2013. 'Elections in India: Errors Voters Make', in *India in Transition Blog*. Philadelphia: Centre for Advanced Study of India. https://casi.sas.upenn.edu/iit/milanvaishnav (accessed 30 April 2015).

Varadarajan, Siddharth. 2014. 'Votes and Vengeance', in *Indian Express* 8 April 2014. http://indianexpress.com/article/opinion/columns/votes-and-vengeance/ (accessed 18 August 2015).

Verma, Rahul. 2009. 'Dalit Voting Patterns', *Economic and Political Weekly* 44(39): 95–98.

———. 2014. 'The Story of Dalit Vote: Between the BJP and the BSP', *The Hindu*. Chennai, http://www.thehindu.com/opinion/op-ed/the-story-of-dalit-vote-between-the-bjp-and-the-bsp/article6090744.ece (accessed 20 July 2015).

Viswanathan, S. 2005. *Dalits in Dravidian Land: Frontline Reports on Anti-Dalit Violence in Tamil Nadu, 1995–2004.* New Delhi: Navayana.

Wyatt, A.K.J. 2002. 'New Alignments in South Indian Politics: The 2001 Assembly Elections in Tamil Nadu', *Asian Survey* 42(5): 733–753.

Wyatt, Andrew. 2010. *Party System Change in South India: Political Entrepreneurs, Patterns, and Processes.* London: Routledge.

Yadav, Yogendra. 1999. 'Electoral Politics in the Time of Change: India's Third Electoral System, 1989–99', *Economic and Political Weekly* 34(34–35): 2393–2399.

———. 2001. 'Understanding the Second Democratic Upsurge: Trends of Bahujan Participation in Electoral Politics in the 1990s', in Francine Frankel, Zoya Hasan, Rajeev Bhargava and Balvir Arora (eds), *Transforming India: Social and Political Dynamics of Democracy* (pp. 120–145). New Delhi: Oxford University Press.

6

From the Cheris to Chennai: Dalit Politics in Tamil Nadu

Hugo Gorringe

Introduction

> Insurgency is always short-lived. Once it subsides and the people leave the streets, most of the organisations which it temporarily threw up and which elites helped to nurture simply fade away. As for the few organisations that survive, it is because they become more useful to those who control the resources on which they depend than to the lower class groups which the organisations claim to represent. (Piven and Cloward 1979: xxi)

In 1999, after a decade of sociopolitical mobilisation, grassroots activism and widespread consciousness-raising, the largest Dalit party in Tamil Nadu—the Viduthalai Chiruthaigal Katchi (VCK—Liberation Panther Party) decided to enter the political process and contest elections. The ideological clarity of the new party and the close ties between leaders and followers invited optimism amongst a range of commentators. Writing in *Frontline,* noted political analyst Viswanathan (1999) saw the development 'as having the potential to bring about substantial changes not only of electoral politics in the state, but in the nature of political activism in general and the approach of mainstream political parties to organisations that represent Dalits' aspirations'. They were portrayed as 'redrawing the political map of Tamil Nadu' (Gorringe 2005: 301).

The rise of Dalit parties in the state seemed to offer another instance of caste-based mobilisation expanding the political mainstream and democratising Indian democracy. While India's democratic system has struggled to accommodate oppositional movements, according to Lakha and Taneja (2009: 316), the recent upsurge of lower caste (Dalit and 'Other Backward Caste') groups is reshaping political institutions. Indeed, these authors describe the political accommodation and electoral successes of such movements as 'a seismic shift in patterns of political participation and structures of power' (Lakha and Taneja 2009: 317). Certainly, autonomous Dalit parties have kept caste discrimination on the agenda, held authorities to account and gained impressive electoral victories. The Bahujan Samaj Party's (BSP—Majority People's Party) formation of several governments at the state-level in India's most populous state of Uttar Pradesh (Pai 2002), led some commentators to identify a 'Dalit revolution' in northern India (Jaffrelot 2003) even before it won an unparalleled assembly majority in 2007.

Carried away on a tide of radical rhetoric and the emergence of novel actors, it was easy to envision social change. Even at the zenith of movement activism, however, there were indications that the transition to political participation would be neither smooth nor rapid for the representatives of the lowest castes and classes. Internal opposition to the VCK's political ambitions was abundant and vociferous. As one party stalwart put it:

> If you rear a calf with pigs, then the calf too will eat shit. That is why we reject politics. We can protest and gain from that—we can fight the governments from the outside. If the calf joins the piglets then the two become one and you cannot distinguish between them—both fall into the gutter. (Subramani Interview, April 1999)

Captured here are both the radical activists' perception of politics as tainted, and recognition of the influence that the prevalent political culture can have on emergent organisations. Optimistic accounts of the Dalit parties arguably downplayed these deep-seated institutional impediments to change. Returning to Tamil Nadu a decade on from the entry into politics this chapter draws on ethnographic data to offer an analysis of the VCK's ongoing process of institutionalisation[1]. The chapter charts the VCKs gradual inclusion into and participation within political institutions before analysing the impact that this has had on how they organise and what they are able to demand in the political sphere. We conclude by questioning whether institutionalisation has shorn the Panthers of their radicalism or whether they retain the capacity for autonomous action. We begin, however, with an overview of the theoretical work on institutionalisation and social movements that places this case within a wider context.

Institutionalising Contentious Politics

Institutionalisation here refers to the process by which movements move from extra-institutional action to more formal engagement with, and action within, formal politics and the institutions of interest mediation. A range of social movement theorists regard institutionalisation as an almost inevitable stage within a 'protest cycle', but there is disagreement as to whether it represents the 'success' of a movement and the sociopolitical recognition of its concerns and influence, or whether it signals a movement's demise as a radical group due to an increasing preoccupation with bureaucratic processes, resource mobilisation and self-preservation (Hensby 2012). Some see integration into political institutions as the end-goal of extra-institutional mobilisation (Gamson 1990, Offe 1990), while others see it as a form of demobilisation and de-radicalisation (Coy and Hedeen 2005). The two perspectives, of course, may co-exist within any group. As Offe (1990) notes, movements are usually divided into pragmatists and idealists. The former perceive the formation of formal organisations with due-paying members and clear structures of leadership as a means of sustaining activist concerns. By contrast, the idealists—*'fundis'* in Offe's terms—'refuse to join the institutional learning process' and bemoan the loss of autonomy, spontaneity and specificity that accompanies increasing formalisation (1990: 249–250).

Political theorists such as Meyer and Tarrow (1998) argue that activism can become a vocation for cadre. Given the inevitable ebbs and flows of mobilisation, therefore, such activists seek to professionalise and advocate for their concerns on a more stable footing. Indeed, a range of studies illustrate the benefits of institutionalisation in terms of obtaining vital resources (McCarthy and Zald 1977), influencing policy changes (Kriesi 2004), or creating further opportunities for mobilisation (Pettinicchio 2012). Large organisations, however, operate according to a different logic to social movements. They require members, infrastructure, a division of labour and resources. In their study of Social Movement Organisations, therefore, Jordan and Maloney (1997) argue that the quest for bureaucratic stability and efficiency sees the focus on radical action and change give way to recruitment drives and campaigns to raise money.

A corollary process witnesses a decline of mass activism in favour of professional activists who organise events or engage in mediated stunts on behalf of the more passive membership. While Jordan and Maloney focus on 'protest businesses', the focus here is on what we might call 'protest parties'. Such parties, however, experience similar compulsions to businesses: they need to expand beyond the core constituency to have an impact, they need to secure resources to wage electoral campaigns and they need to attract the votes of significant numbers of people to stand any chance of winning (Poguntke 1993). This latter objective may entail the dilution or neglect of key movement demands in favour of broader or more general appeals, or it may result in pragmatic electoral alliances with other parties with all the negotiations, compromises and possible decline in mobilisation entailed (Maguire 1995).

Drawing on their work in Latin America, Petras and Veltmeyer (2006: 91) describe 'electoral politics as a trap'. They argue that entry into the party system invariably results in de-radicalisation. This finding is echoed in much of the social movement literature in which, as Pettinicchio (2012: 501) notes, institutionalisation generally has a 'negative connotation'. Tarrow (1998: 208) argues that movements which adopt 'institutional routines, can become imbued with their logic and values'. Others, however, maintain that institutionalisation need not lead to goal displacement or de-radicalisation and that formal movement organisations can secure gains and concessions from the political system (Clemens and Minkoff 2004; Staggenborg 1988).

As regards processes of institutionalisation in Tamil politics, the dominant political parties in the state have established a template for both how political challengers enter political institutions, and what it means to 'do politics' (Gorringe 2011). Successful movements in the recent past have legitimised both extra-institutional action and caste-based politics. This template is widely recognised. As Thirumavalavan, leader of the VCK, told cadres at a party meeting:

> If we look at the political history of Tamil Nadu, most of the parties that emerged in the past twenty years or so perceive politics as a tool to get political power—to get power you need caste support, to get caste support

you need caste feelings, if you provoke caste feelings you will get caste support, and if you get caste support you will get power. This is the perspective of political parties, of most of the political parties that emerged in the past twenty years in Tamil Nadu. They form, first, caste-based organisations, then, convert them into political parties. (Speech, April 2012)

Racine (2009) similarly notes how caste dominates political calculations surrounding which candidates to field and which constituencies to address. This is one reason why the proportion of reserved jobs for 'Backward' and 'Scheduled' Castes is so high in the state—exceeding the Supreme Court ceiling of 50 per cent by a considerable margin at 69 per cent (Racine 2009; Ziegfeld 2013). The political mobilisation of lower castes in Tamil Nadu has, to this extent, succeeded. This benchmark, however, means that there is limited scope for emerging parties to lobby for further concessions. There is, as Racine (2009: 470) puts it, 'a gap between successful agitations by a caste association and their political dividends'. In part this is because of the absolute dominance of the two Dravidian parties who have not gained less than 67 per cent of seats in the legislative assembly in the ten elections since 1971 (Racine 2009: 454).

The emergence of non-Dravidian challengers, as Wyatt (2009) notes, has not displaced the Dravidian duopoly but forced these parties into a range of alliances. Political recognition in Tamil Nadu, therefore, takes the form of an alliance with one or other of the main parties rather than an ability to stand alone. Roberts (2010) argues that the Dalit parties have successfully weaned Dalit votes away from the main parties, but given that they have done so by forging alliances with those same parties, the gains are marginal (Gorringe 2011). Most critiques—or celebrations—of the party have focused on their performance in politics but, as Jaoul (2007) notes, Dalit politics has an impact in the social as well as political spheres.

Institutionalisation—this suggests—occurs on multiple levels and in various registers. There is a need, therefore, to analyse the broader processes of sociopolitical institutionalisation in which radical groups are inducted into a particular political culture replete with its own norms, attitudes and ways of doing things. In what follows, therefore, this chapter focuses on the wider processes through which the party has been institutionalised into Tamil ways of *doing* politics. Institutionalisation—it is argued—is not a clear cut event. Entering electoral politics, as Aminzade (1995) observes, can co-exist with an informal and decentralised organisational structure and need not (initially at least) lead to formalisation and professionalisation. Electoral contestation, similarly, does not necessarily mark the end of extra-institutional agitation. Institutionalisation, thus, must be understood as a process. It is to this process of change amongst the Panthers that we now turn.

Institutionalising Rebellion

The VCK entered politics for multiple reasons. There were the 'push' factors of repression, marginalisation and alienation from the masses (Gorringe 2005). During its radical mobilisation phase, the Panthers were portrayed as an extremist organisation and faced political repression. Launching a party, therefore, was about establishing their democratic credentials as much as anything else. Alongside this, however, there are also 'pull' factors. First, as Palshikar (2013: 10) notes, any new party also 'thinks it can break the monopoly of the "established" parties and gatecrash into the system'. True to this goal, the VCK first competed as part of a Third Front led by the Tamil Maanila Congress (Tamil State Congress) in a bid to contest Dravidian hegemony. Wyatt (2009: 127) notes, however, that political structures in the state conspire against emergent and poorly resourced parties. In a first-past-the-post electoral system, the candidate receiving the highest percentage of the vote wins the contest and all other votes are disregarded. This, combined with the bi-polar nature of Tamil politics, means that parties require a significant vote-share to win. The VCK has not been able to do this independently (Gorringe 2005; Wyatt 2009). Shortly after its initial foray into electoral politics, therefore, the VCK allied with one of the main Dravidian parties and—barring a coalition with the Janata Dal (United) in 2004—has contested elections in one or the other of the main fronts since 2001. Their autonomy has been constrained both by a lack of resources and through the strategies of the dominant. In an echo of Petras and Veltmeyer (2006), Punitha Pandian—editor of the long-running *Dalit Murasu* (Dalit Drum)—saw politics as a trap. He recounted an instance in the late 1990s—at the height of VCK mobilisation—when the Deputy General of Police called Thirumavalavan into a meeting:

> It is a conspiracy. If any revolutionary type figure—any element who seems like they might destroy the *varnashrama*, brahminic order—emerges, then they try and inveigle them into politics. That is what the DGP himself said:

'Why don't you start a party Thirumavalavan?...Come and speak in the Assembly, it will be in the papers. Now no one pays attention. In the house, Karunanidhi will have to respond. Why do you remain outside, speaking like a naxalite? Come to the system.' This did not happen over one or two days, but was a long process of brain-washing. He said: 'Why do you come and complain to me that he was arrested or he was beaten? Become an MLA and then give me a call. I'll come to your house.' (Pandian Interview, April 2012)

VCK activists and leaders in Madurai recounted instances in which Thirumavalavan was arrested and intimidated (fieldnotes, 2012). They recalled the cases filed against them and the sea of police at any demonstration, as opposed to the respect they now receive.[2] The carrot and stick approach forecloses the options available to protestors. This contributes to what Pandian sees as a more fundamental form of institutionalisation. The Dalit parties, he argues, have bought into the idea that institutional politics is key:

> Since the 1990s Dalits have started their own parties. That was the main set back. Everyone sees 1990 as the time of great uprising. Of course there was an uprising, but no huge change in consciousness. You are realising this now. With the uprising there was a flaw. Post 1990s what the Dalit intellectuals said was that Dalit politics alone would rule India. What they meant by Dalit politics was electoral politics. (Pandian Interview, April 2012)

In this regard, the victory of Mayawati in UP, he insists, has further limited the Dalit political imagination to party politics and political power. Dalit parties, in other words, have been institutionalised into particular ways of doing politics that neglect the wider sociocultural and economic contexts within which discrimination persists. 'The time worn response to dissent', Nandy (1998: 51) asserts, 'is to neutralise it by absorbing it into the mainstream'. This neutralisation, it seems, extends to the political imaginaries of political challengers.

Acceptable Allies?

The compulsions to enter politics, then, are powerful, but what of the VCK's performance as a party? Many critics argued that the VCK should have kept away from established parties. Indeed, the BSP's state secretary, Armstrong, insisted that a vote for the VCK was wasted because the Dalits who had been attracted away from the Dravidian parties by the promise of an alternative were shoring up those same parties through alliance politics (Personal Communication, September 2012). Others were even more cynical, arguing that the VCK now acted as the 'SC/ST Wing of the DMK'. Just as Kanshiram—founder of the BSP—portrayed Dalit politicians as *chamchas* (stooges), so these critics argued that the VCK had done little more than getting some of their people fielded as candidates. VCK supporters, themselves, were upset by their leader's obsequious behaviour towards allies. I asked Thirumavalavan about this:

> H: Do you need to go and stand before politicians with your hands bowed?
> T: No. No compulsion at all. It is up to us. We can refuse to go and see them and maintain a party that is 500 or so strong.
> H: But if you want to be a meaningful party?
> T: Then we need to observe certain protocols. Go and see Kalaignar Karunanidhi on his birthday and my birthday for instance. We also need to watch our language to some extent, things like that. (Personal Exchange, August 2012)

To insist that the VCK should stand independently, furthermore, is to apply different standards to them than to others. The infinitely better resourced and established Communist parties, for instance, similarly ally with the regional power-holders. The common view is that the only way of making electoral gains is to piggy-back on the major parties. As Thirumavalavan (2009: 266) wrote: 'Contesting alone was considered, but it would be like clapping with one hand'. Working for the masses, he notes, may mean having to join hands with others even though no party in Tamil Nadu can be seen as a 'true friend of the Dalits' (Thirumavalavan 2009: 28).

In electoral terms, as Wyatt (2009: 129) notes, the results of these alliances are 'very modest'. The VCK have won three seats in the legislative assembly and one Lok Sabha seat since 1999. The most they have won in any election is two seats at state level. Of their representatives, Thirumavalavan (2009)—the first VCK candidate to be elected—resigned his MLA seat on a point of principle. Of the two elected in 2006, one defected to another party. Only one of their three MLAs, therefore, has lasted a full term in office—Ravikumar represented Kattumannarkovil constituency from 2006 until his defeat in the 2011 elections. In 2013, Thirumavalavan, MP for Chidambaram, remained the sole elected representative of the VCK, and he too lost his seat in the 2014 general election.

While the VCK has now been in alliance with both major parties: 'we have not received full acceptance or recognition from either party. They totally see us as "just a Dalit party" and it could take some time before that perception changes' (Sannah Interview, September 2012). In an interview for the party magazine *Tamil Mann* (Tamil Land), Thirumavalavan expanded on this:

> Whenever non-Dalits start a party they can open branches wherever they like. They can campaign with independence. They can express their opinions without fear or favour. It is a huge struggle for the VCK to simply go to a place and raise a flag there. If we take up general issues then that is a problem too. We took out car rally from Batlagundu to Cumbam on the Mullaperiyar issue [The dam located in Kerala that is a source of constant disputes], but as soon as we entered Cumbam, dominant castes surrounded our vehicles and threw stones at us. We said that we were protesting on their behalf too, but their view is: 'Who are you to speak up on this problem'. (Thirumavalavan 2011: 40–43)

Similarly, numerous party members pointed out how often their leader had called for a Third Front. In 2009, at the height of the crisis in Sri Lanka, for instance, he sought to forge a Tamil Nationalist Front and even invited others to lead it, but none accepted his invitation. There are pragmatic reasons to reject a Third Front, but the rejection was couched in caste terms. Institutionalisation here, therefore, is not simply the creation of a party and engagement with elections; it entails a radical change of political culture: educating both the Dalit masses and the other parties about political engagement. Indeed, respondents in an urban housing estate in Madurai maintained that one of the main achievements of the VCK had been to politicise and educate the Dalit masses.

Most accounts, however, focus on elections and, on this score, unfavourable comparisons have been drawn between the Vanniyar-based Paatali Makkal Katchi's (Toiling Peoples' Party) electoral returns and those of the VCK (Wyatt 2009: 130), such accounts do not tell the whole story. It is true that Paraiyars and Vanniyars have similar populations in the state, but we need to understand their respective performances in context. First, the PMK was most successful *before* the VCK became an established party and eroded their vote-base. Since that point, the PMK's electoral fortunes have declined. In 2011, the PMK managed to win only 3 of 30 seats it contested despite standing in alliance with the VCK. Caste arithmetic suggested that this was an unassailable combination, but such calculations neglect wider sociopolitical considerations. Most respondents noted that this was a loss for the DMK alliance as a whole rather than anything. Corruption scandals, accusations of nepotism and power cuts conspired to fuel an anti-incumbency wave. Within that broader framework, however, local contests saw a different logic at play:

> Dalit votes fell for non-Dalit candidates, but the votes of the non-Dalits were not cast for Dalit candidates. This is the backdrop and underlying reason for the VCK's loss in 10 seats. (Sannah Interview, September 2012)

I was repeatedly told that caste played a factor in the elections. From this perspective, a purely political analysis of the VCK's electoral performance is flawed since it neglects the social discrimination that Dalits continue to face, which can mean that non-Dalits refuse to vote for a Dalit party (Gorringe 2005).

This is not to suggest that people automatically or necessarily vote for their caste. Indeed, Sannah noted that both Dalit and Vanniyar votes were divided. While the PMK has been able to mobilise around 50 per cent of the Vanniyar vote, Wyatt suggests that the VCK has not been able to emulate this success with regards to Paraiyar votes (Wyatt 2009: 130). Following Hickey and Du Toit (2007), however, we need to analyse the terms on which groups are included into institutions. The Dalit upsurge did not mobilise a previously excluded category so much as one lacking in political consciousness. Their core constituents were *already* integrated into the political system albeit on the margins. Dalit parties, furthermore, emerged after those of other caste parties and—partly as a consequence—found key political positions and the status of most-favoured ally already occupied. Third, Dalit parties lack the resources that other political challengers can muster. Fourth, Dalits entered political institutions but were not able to shed their social identities and faced discrimination as a result: in 1999 cow-dung was smeared on the posters of Dalit parties, in numerous elections non-Dalits refused to vote for them, and in 2012 party flagpoles were uprooted from village squares and posters defaced.

Three key differences between the PMK and VCK stand out: first, the VCK has never mobilised Paraiyars on a caste basis—preferring to use the language of Dalits or Tamils instead. The PMK, by contrast, has been most successful when mobilising Vanniyars. Sure enough, following its electoral reversals, the PMK reverted to a politics of caste assertion in 2012 in a bid to boost its fortunes. Second, that Dalit voters have long been integrated into political institutions, thanks to the reservations for SC candidates. Dalits not only stand for all parties, therefore, but have long-standing ties and relations to particular parties that are hard to break. Consequently, as one social scientist noted: 'After the PMK agitation then suddenly there were Vanniyars in both Dravidian parties in great numbers, but the same has not happened in this case' (Bala, Personal Communication, April 2012). Finally, the lack of resources means that the VCK are unable to cherry-pick constituencies or contest from the same number of seats as the PMK. As Thirumavalavan noted: 'we do not have resources to bankroll candidates and so we are very much at a disadvantage in negotiations' (Personal Communication, September 2012).

Reshaping Politics? Rebels in Power

Given the structural inequalities and asymmetries of power that emergent challengers are confronted with, it would be unrealistic to expect wholesale alterations to the political system. Shifting our focus from seats won to agenda setting, however, shows how Dalit concerns have been institutionalised to some degree. One 'spill-over' (Whittier 2004)—or consequence—of Dalit parties has been a focus on caste by Communist Parties. Samuel Raj, a leader of the CPI(M)-affiliated Tamil Nadu Untouchability Eradication Front conceded that the Dalit parties were instrumental in forcing his party to rethink its strategy. Their focus was on the economic exploitation of the working class, but the Dalit parties forced them to consider whether Dalits should 'have to live in social oppression till they get economic liberty' (Samuel Raj Interview, April 2012). While none of the other parties have so explicitly addressed Dalit demands, they have arguably been more receptive to them and have certainly paid more attention to Dalit icons like Ambedkar than they did in the past.

If the police firing that killed six Dalits in Paramkudi in 2011 indicated the entrenched casteism of police forces in an area characterised by Backward (but dominant) Caste Thevar clashes with Dalit Pallars, subsequent events suggest shifts in caste power. In 2012, several attacks on Thevars generated a feeling of insecurity amongst them as reflected by the formation of the *Thevar Inam Paadukarpu Peravai* (Thevar Caste Protection Front) (Dhanraj, Personal Communication, October 2012). Later that year, the Thevar leader 'Prabakaran was arrested… on charges of creating animosity between two groups in Kamuthi and Mudukulathur by making provocative speeches, distributing pamphlets and by posting write ups in his website 'marathamizhar.blog.com', denigrating Dalit leaders' (*The Hindu* 2012). Subsequently, in early 2013, the AIADMK government responded to caste violence by Vanniyars against Dalits by clamping down on the PMK and even placing its leader under arrest (*The Hindu* 2013). While it would be misleading to suggest that Dalit parties and voters are shaping the institutions they joined in the late 1990s, they can no longer be disregarded.

If political institutions are shifting in response to Dalit participation, how have Dalit parties and politicians themselves changed? We have seen how the Dalit parties are imperfectly integrated into Tamil politics, but given that new parties seek new gains in politics, we should ask what they have achieved through their electoral engagement. The most obvious way in which parties can affect change is through interventions in the elected chambers. It is not, however, straightforward for a single MP or MLA to gain time and space in Parliament. Respondents mentioned Ravikumar MLA speaking on a range of issues from housing, to debt, pornography, prohibition, the rights of transgenders and food for prisoners (Tamizh Murasu and Tamizh Kanni, Personal Communication, March 2012).[3] Others noted Thirumavalavan's fasts and speeches on Tamil issues—relating to the violence in Sri Lanka or the allocation of water for Tamil Nadu. In 2012, however, his most vociferous intervention came on the subject of a cartoon in an NCERT (National Council of Educational Research and Training) textbook that was said to denigrate Dr Ambedkar—first law minister of India and pre-eminent Dalit leader. In Parliament, Thirumavalavan launched a tirade against the publishers and a demand for the withdrawal of the cartoon and an apology in speech that sparked a national debate.

That one intervention, a speaker at a VCK memorial in June argued, justified his five-year term (fieldnotes, June 2012). Others, however, castigated Dalit leaders for their focus on issues of identity (Teltumbde 2012), or for their silence on other matters:

> Six minutes he spoke on that [Ambedkar cartoon]. Six minutes. After that—again the Eelam [Tamil nation in Sri Lanka] problem and the UN

resolution. That is all. After that he never opened his mouth. For that matter no one opened their mouths—we have 110 stooges there [referring to reserved MPs]. (Anon Interview April 2012)

In the eyes of such critics, Dalit politicians merely prop up the established parties or enrich themselves. Perhaps, though, the expectations of those who were mobilised by Thirumavalavan's fiery speeches in the 1990s are over-optimistic. As one more tempered interviewee noted, when asked what he expected from the party:

Not much—they are a small outfit with just one MP. What do you expect them to do? They need to give us a voice and raise our issues and try and get political power—this is what they are doing. (Ambedkar Interview, June 2012)

An otherwise critical union worker said that no other politician had spoken up on behalf of conservancy workers:

Even those who are government employees did not have a set wage—they were paid different amounts at the panchayat level, the regional level and state level and in different institutions. The village workers would have to work for left-overs or face caste wrath. After years of campaigning to highlight their plight, including conferences and protests and a huge rally in Chennai under the auspices of the communist parties, I finally approached Thirumavalavan who listened to the issues and raised them in the media and then Ravikumar raised them in the Legislative Assembly with the result that an order was passed to give the workers a minimum standard wage of ₹3000 a month. (Kondavelai Interview, April 2012)

While this interviewee was sympathetic towards the VCK and offered a rosier picture of this event than others, it should come as no surprise that he approached the VCK, nor that they raised the issue (see Ravikumar 2011). As one Dalit academic, who was a fierce critic of VCK politics, conceded; 'if I needed to speak to an MLA or MP then the VCK are the only ones I have any sort of access to, so yes I guess I would turn to them'. 'Political entrepreneurs', as Wyatt (2009: 87) puts it, 'function as mediators' or brokers. Such brokerage often has negative connotations. As activist and writer Raj Gowthaman remarked: 'Once they enter electoral politics they [movements] become mere vehicles for distributing goods to members' (Personal Communication, April 2012).[4]

From a different perspective, however, one can argue that Dalits now have their own brokers. During 2012, I encountered many Dalits who credited the VCK with obtaining jobs, transfers or land deeds for them, but as the quote from Kondavelai previously indicates, mediation may be on behalf of groups as well as individuals. Such mediation, significantly, is expected of all parties. 'Tamil politics', as academic and activist Lakhsmanan argues, 'de-politicises the masses' through hand outs and patron–client relations (Personal Communication, March 2012). What the entry of Dalit politicians has done, is widen the reach of such patronage networks to include those who were previously excluded from the rewards of office. To gain benefits and concessions of this nature, however, requires the VCK to negotiate or bargain with officials and other parties.

Getting things done, in other words, requires institutionalisation into the informal politics of the state. Early in 2012, I attended a Party wedding.

> My attention was drawn towards the veshti's (traditional waistcloths) that the men were wearing. Several sported red, white and blue lines printed down the edges thus identifying them as VCK supporters. Others wore their affiliations literally on their sleeves as well. One attendee sported the black shirt and veshti with black border of the Dravida Kazhagham, others had DMK colours.... One late comer was ushered in to sit pride of place on the stage behind Thirumavalavan. When he got up to talk, I was told that he was a bigshot in the AIADMK. (fieldnotes, February 2012)

The VCK, thus, had institutional attire and had also forged ties with the members of other parties. While reservations mean that there are Dalits in every party, the VCK had gone beyond kin networks. The Madurai District secretary, for instance, not only invited DMK strong-man and Karunanidhi's son Azhagiri to her housewarming, she was in turn invited to his son's wedding. My host at the wedding just discussed explained that:

> The VCK have gone beyond the stage of being purely oppositional and become a proper party now with recognition from all the others. They all have to work together to get things done and so they make such visits and shows of respect. (fieldnotes, February 2012)

Dhanapal, a building contractor who has been a member of the VCK for a decade now spoke of how the movements' characterisation as extremist used to sideline their concerns. Now, he insisted, they have the authority to make themselves heard:

> Now that we are a party, if we want to hold a protest we get a response from officials, our voices are heard, we have the opportunity to interact with alliance partners. We've been in the DMK Front and the ADMK Front and so can speak to District Convenors and officials in each district or area. Now the VCK District Convenor and the DMK District Convenor and ADMK convenor have links. So what happens with these connections is that we can deploy them in the interests of the people. If someone comes to us, we can contact the district convenor by phone and they say 'Right, I'll look into it' and they facilitate things. (Interview, March 2012)

The informal and mediated nature of how things work in Tamil politics is captured here. While Dhanapal, who had a post in the party, put this in a positive light others were more critical. Placing Dalit actions in a wider context, Raj Gowthaman observed:

> You know what Tamil politics is like—you need connections to get things done. The Dalit parties do not have much clout on their own, which is why they need coalition partners. Now the DMK [the VCK's coalition partner at the time] is in opposition—they will have to sit quiet for five years. That is what it is like. (Personal Communication April 2012)

At a seminar on Raj Gowthaman's work, the discussion turned to Dalit politics. The frustrations of disillusioned intellectuals as well as their recognition of the wider political culture within which Dalit parties must operate were captured in a humorous exchange:

> M: The start [for Dalit Parties] was good, but since joining politics they have stagnated and started to mimic all the other parties. Yesterday there was a shooting [of Dalits] in Paramakudi which the leaders condemned, but today there is an election and so they join an alliance. What do the leaders think of the people? What are they talking?
> In response to this rhetorical question one wag shouted out 'politics' and the room erupted into laughter. (fieldnotes, April 2012)

The Cost of Connections?

Institutionalisation into backroom politics has enabled the VCK to secure land deeds and jobs and ensure that party officials now get respect from police officials. The problems for Dalit critics of the VCK come when the ties forged to other party leaders and groups lead the party into the murkier aspects of politics. As one leading lawyer in Madurai observed:

> Now that they are a party they are in contact with other party leaders. Many of the accused [in Prevention of Atrocity cases] will have party connections and so pressure is put on this lot to drop cases or come to some agreement. (Vakil Interview, July 2012)

The term used to describe this is the English word 'compromise'. The alliances and links with other parties, I was repeatedly told, mean that it is harder for the VCK to stand firm against caste discrimination or violence. They are put under pressure by officials, allies and dominant castes to affect a compromise between perpetrator and victim. VCK leaders insist that they would never sell out, 'especially not for serious cases', but concede that some 'miscreants' in the party might do so. Given the lack of a salary for party workers, the temptation certainly exists. Others justified informal settlements in relatively minor cases pointing out that such deals secured rapid compensation and saved lengthy and uncertain legal procedures and fees and avoided animosity between groups. As the party propaganda secretary, Gautham Sannah, argued:

> In some villages there are minor or petty confrontations and we also have the responsibility to ensure that we engage in dialogue to prevent these small problems from escalating into major caste clashes. You see the Panthers can make a fuss and then leave the village, but the villagers there need to live in peace. We cannot allow the problems caused by a few to adversely affect the entire village. In such situations we have to resolve matters through dialogue as there is no other option. One or two frustrated people might come in these circumstances and accuse us of compromise. (Interview, September 2012)

Having repeatedly encountered rural Dalits' distress over long-drawn out and expensive (both in terms of travel and lost earnings) legal proceedings and heard fearful Dalits voice their trepidation about Dalit activists stirring up a hornets' nest before leaving, Sannah's argument is persuasive. To many, however, any settlement is an anathema. VCK cadres in Periya Oorcheri near Madurai printed sports shirts bearing the motto 'no compromise' to celebrate the village temple festival. Activists nurtured on the slogan 'hit back', are appalled by any suggestion of shady deals letting culprits off the hook.

From the Cheris to Chennai: Dalit Politics in Tamil Nadu 147

Increasingly, these critics argue, members of the party are using their new-found power to better themselves rather than the community. Social movements everywhere have been seen as vehicles for the advancement of activists (Meyer and Tarrow 1998), and the VCK is said to be no exception. Such tales are hard to verify and very few concrete cases were mentioned. While the VCK is now routinely said to be engaged in *katta panchayats* (kangaroo courts) that resolve issues informally with money changing hands, Thirumavalavan contested such rumours:

> I have heard that, but is there any proof? Also, all parties do this. Why are we the ones who are singled out? This is the result of jealousy and an attempt to break the party. Give me details of one instance where we have compromised. (Personal Communication, September 2012)

When I mentioned one party member who told me he was elected as Panchayat president having promised to resolve any caste issues *without recourse to* the Prevention of Atrocities Act, Thirumavalavan insisted that the party cadre would not countenance this and asserted that 'we can never compromise on atrocities'. He did not, however, promise to take action against the president.

Many of the rumours and misinformation are prompted by jealousy. While other parties are clearly more involved in kangaroo courts and real-estate, the fact that many VCK officials are now relatively well-off, grates with those left behind and with other castes.[5] Profiting from politics is not confined to Tamil Nadu. The Karnataka Election Watch (Manor 2013: 52) found that 'the average MLA is worth 23.54 crore' in Karnataka, reinforcing people's conviction that politics was a business. 'All these forms of brokerage' as activist and intellectual Paari Chezhian observed, 'are very lucrative' (Personal Communication, February 2012). He pointed to kangaroo courts, land estate deals and other forms of mediation as means to make money. The widespread practice of spending money in elections follows the belief that such investment could be recouped through taking a cut of any contract or deal requiring official approval. VCK candidates for local body elections spoke of spending several hundred thousand (lakh) rupees on their campaigns: on posters, food for volunteers, leaflets and money for voters.

Pavalar Talaiyari (a pen name), writing for the VCK's *Tamil Mann*, recognised that money could not buy elections but that it was widely used:

> It is not just money that determines victory or success. Coalition strength, party strength, individual authority all determine victory. Only in fourth place is money. Despite all this the shameful practice of giving money for votes has been established. (Talaiyari 2011: 44)

He called for major electoral reform, but pending that, many VCK candidates appear to have adapted to the existing practices. The VCK, as one Dalit publisher noted, has become a mirror image of the Dravidian parties (Ezhuthallar, Personal Communication, March 2012). Contesting the worst accusations, a legal advocate insisted that one cannot make vast sums of money from Dalit constituents and suggested that real-estate was a more likely source of income (Jawahar Interview, March 2012). Underpinning the rumours was the fact that the need to amass wealth like the other parties had become important for the VCK and helped fuel attempts to take the party 'into the mainstream'. As the VCK branches out and incorporates even more non-Dalits it increasingly protests on more general issues, which is a sore point for some:

> Now Dalit leaders are protesting about price hikes and so on. That is fine. They can hold a general meeting and condemn Congress, but they should remember that they are a community party. When they hold a 'general meeting' who turns up? Dalits only! So these parties should address their problems first and foremost. (Manickam, Interview, June 2012)

Thirumavalavan rightly insisted that the VCK, unlike established parties, protested on both these *and* Dalit issues, but the perception of a party growing away from its core constituents persists at the grassroots.

Conclusion: Just Another Party?

> When insurgency wells up, apparently uncontrollable, elites respond. And one of their responses is to cultivate those lower-class organisations which begin to emerge in such periods, for they have little to fear from organisations, especially from organisations which come to depend on them for support. Thus, however unwittingly, leaders and organisers of the lower classes act in the end to facilitate the efforts of elites to channel the insurgent masses into normal politics, believing all the while that they are taking the long and arduous but certain path to power. (Piven and Cloward 1979: xxii)

The VCK, as the quote from Piven and Cloward reminds us, are not alone in managing the fraught process of institutionalisation. Like many before them, they have experienced both the benefits and costs of the process. While members have signed up in droves, many core activists have become increasingly disillusioned. Having entered politics, the VCK have found that they cannot stand independently. For all their emphasis on maintaining autonomy and respect, therefore, some compromises have been made. One of the main changes to the party has been the decision in 2007 to admit non-Dalits to leadership posts and the related emphasis on Tamil nationalism as a unifying force. As with political participation more generally, this move has both costs and benefits. Non-Dalit members have given the VCK a toe-hold in villages that they could not think of entering in the past, but the rapid promotion of newcomers results in growing unease amongst Dalit supporters. As one academic commentator concluded:

> At one stage there were hopes that the VCK would be different—they did create great awareness and introduce some ideas, but that has now come to nothing. They have become another party—another middle man.
> (Perarsareer, Personal Communication, March 2012)

Institutionalisation, we have seen, must be understood as more than mere entry to political institutions. It is not a one-off, once-and-for-all process, but a gradual adaptation to a prevalent political culture. Despite over a decade in politics, the VCK have yet to formalise structures of leadership or membership and remain, in this sense, very much 'a political movement trying to become a political party' (Ravikumar, Personal Communication, August 2013). This was perhaps best illustrated when the VCK decided to emulate all other Tamil parties by launching its own TV channel. Lacking resources, the VCK hit on the idea of celebrating Thirumavalavan's 50th birthday by collecting gold from members. Rarely can the funding for a channel have been collected so transparently. For all the criticisms of the direction taken by the party and, more specifically, some of its functionaries, supporters responded to the call with enthusiasm and purpose. There was a real sense of ownership both of the party and the prospective (still prospective in 2015) channel that belie suggestions of the party's demise. It is no small matter that Dalits now have people in authority to whom they can turn to, relate to and interact with. Tamil politics in that sense *has* been democratised by the institutionalisation of the Panthers.

Notes

1. Data was collected over 10 months in 2012 during ESRC (Grant RES-062-23-3348) funded fieldwork in and around Madurai District, central Tamil Nadu.
2. A politics of principle may have its own reward, but it is a costly and precarious process as the anti-nuclear protestors in Kudankulam found to their cost in 2012 when boys as young as 15 were charged with sedition for their part in a peaceful protest against the commissioning of a nuclear reactor: http://www.thehindu.com/news/cities/Madurai/article3898050.ece
3. In 2011, Ravikumar published a book of his Assembly Speeches to counter the frequent charges that the VCK did not speak up on issues. They include speeches on *panchami* land, Sri Lanka, water-tank workers and employment opportunities—many of which gained no coverage at all.
4. For an example of how patronage networks operate, see: http://www.thehindu.com/news/cities/Madurai/watchmen-sweepers-hired-on-political-recommendation-school-department/article5090201.ece (accessed 23 July 2015).
5. *Empowering India*, for instance, notes that Ravikumar—VCK General Secretary and MLA from 2006 to 2011—registered assets worth ₹401,155 in 2006. In 2011, this figure had risen to ₹1,844,496. There is no suggestion of wrongdoing or that he is doing anything that other leaders do not, but such figures feed the discontent of cadres. http://www.empoweringindia.org/new/preview.aspx?candid=462374&p=&cid=159 (accessed 2 April 2015). It should be stressed that this is chickenfeed compared to the amounts detailed by Manor, and also that a petition asking authorities to investigate Ravikumar 'for allegedly acquiring assets disproportionate to his known sources of income' was dismissed by the High Court in 2014. http://www.business-standard.com/article/pti-stories/hc-dismisses-plea-against-vck-candidate-114042301370_1.html (accessed 13 April 2015).

References

Aminzade, R. 1995. 'Between Movement and Party', in J. Jenkins and B. Klandermans (eds), *The Politics of Social Protest* (pp. 39–62). Berkeley: University of California Press.

Clemens, E. and Minkoff, D. 2004. 'Beyond the Iron Law: Rethinking the Place of Organisations in Social Movement Research', in D. Snow, S. Soule and H. Kriesi (eds), *The Blackwell Companion to Social Movements* (pp. 155–170). Oxford: Blackwell.

Coy, P. and Hedeen, T. 2005. 'A Stage Model of SM Co-optation', *The Sociological Quarterly* 46(4): 405–435.

Hensby, A., Sibthorpe, J. and Driver, S. 2012. 'Resisting the "Protest Business": Bureaucracy, Post-bureaucracy and Active Membership in Social Movement Organisations', *Organization* 19(6): 809–823.

Hickey, S. and Du Toit, A. 2007. 'Adverse Incorporation, Social Exclusion and Chronic Poverty', Working Paper 81, *Chronic Poverty Research Centre*.

Gamson, W. 1990. *The Strategy of Social Protest*. 2nd ed. Belmont, California: Wadsworth Publishing.

Gorringe, H. 2005. *Untouchable Citizens*. New Delhi: SAGE.

Gorringe, H. 2011. 'Party Political Panthers: Hegemonic Tamil Politics and the Dalit Challenge', *SAMAJ (South Asia Multi-disciplinary Academic Journal)*, http://samaj.revues.org/3224 (accessed 23 July 2015).
Jaffrelot, C. 2003. *India's Silent Revolution: The Rise of the Low Castes in North Indian Politics*. Delhi: Permanent Black.
Jaoul, N. 2007. 'Political and "Non-political" Means in the Dalit Movement', in S. Pai (ed.), *Political Process in Uttar Pradesh: Identity, Economic Reform and Governance* (pp. 142–168). New Delhi: Pearsons.
Jordan, A. and Maloney, W. 1997. *The Protest Business? Mobilizing Campaign Groups*. Manchester: Manchester University Press.
Kriesi, H. 2004. 'Political Context and Opportunity', in D. Snow, S. Soule and H. Kriesi (eds), *The Blackwell Companion to Social Movements* (pp. 67–90). Oxford: Blackwell.
Lakha, S. and Taneja, P. 2009. 'Introduction: Democracy, Governance and Civil Society: Rethinking the Study of Contemporary India', *South Asia* 32(3): 315–325.
Manor, J. 2013. 'Lucky in its Adversaries', *Economic and Political Weekly* XLVIII(47): 51–59.
Maguire, D. 1995. 'Opposition Movements and Opposition Parties', in J. Jenkins and B. Klandermans (eds), *The Politics of Social Protest* (pp. 199–228). Berkeley: University of California Press.
McCarthy, J. and Zald, M. 1977. 'Resource Mobilisation and Social Movements',*American Journal of Sociology* 82(6): 1212–1241.
Meyer, D. and Tarrow, S. (eds). 1998. *The Social Movement Society*. Lanham: Rowman and Littlefield.
Nandy, A. 1998. *Exiled at Home*. Delhi: Oxford University Press.
Offe, C. 1990. 'Reflections on the Institutional Self-transformation of Movement Politics', in R. Dalton and M. Kuechler (eds), *Challenging the Political Order* (pp. 232–250). Cambridge: Polity.
Pai, S. 2002. *Dalit Assertion and the Unfinished Democratic Revolution*. New Delhi: SAGE.
Palshikar, S. 2013. 'Of Radical Democracy and Anti-Pertyism', *Economic and Political Weekly* 48(10): 10–13.
Petras, J. and Veltmeyer, H. 2006. 'Social Movements and the State: Political Power Dynamics in Latin America', *Critical Sociology* 32(1): 83–104.
Pettinicchio, D. 2012. 'Institutional Activism: Reconsidering the Insider/Outsider Dichotomy', *Sociology Compass* 6(6): 499–510.
Piven, F. and Cloward, R. 1979. *Poor People's Movements: Why They Succeed, How They Fail*. New York: Vintage.
Poguntke, T. 1993. *Alternative Politics*. Edinburgh: Edinburgh University Press.
Racine, J-L. 2009. 'Caste and Beyond in Tamil Politics', in C. Jaffrelot and S. Kumar (eds). *Rise of the Plebeians? The Changing Face of Indian Legislative Assemblies* (pp. 439–489). London: Routledge.
Ravikumar, D. 2011. *Sollum Seyal (Speeches and Actions): Assembly Speeches*. Pondicherry: Manarkeni Publications.
Roberts, N. 2010. 'Language, Violence, and the State: Writing Tamil Dalits', *South Asia Multidisciplinary Academic Journal* 3, http://samaj.revues.org/index2952.html (accessed 23 July 2015).
Staggenborg, S. 1988. 'The Consequences of Professionalization and Formalization in the Pro-Choice Movement', *American Sociological Review* 53(4): 585–605.
Talaiyari, Pavalar E. 2011. 'What is Needed is a Major Electoral Reform', *Tamil Mann* 6(62): 44–48.

Tarrow, S. 1998. *Power in Movement*. 2nd ed. Cambridge: Cambridge University Press.
Teltumbde, A. 2012. 'Bathani Tola and The Cartoon Controversy', *Economic and Political Weekly* 47(22): 10–11.
The Hindu. 2012. 'One More Caste Outfit Leader Held under NSA', *The Hindu* 16 December 2012. http://www.thehindu.com/news/national/tamil-nadu/one-more-caste-outfit-leader-held-under-nsa/article4204204.ece (accessed 19 August 2013).
The Hindu. 2013. 'Sporadic Violence Continues in Parts of Tamil Nadu', *The Hindu* 3 May 2013, http://www.thehindu.com/news/national/tamil-nadu/sporadic-violence-continues-in-parts-of-tamil-nadu/article4677495.ece?homepage=true (accessed 19 August 2013).
Thirumavalavan, T. 2009. *Thai Sol (Mother Says)*. Chennai: ThaiMann Publications.
———. 2011. 'Dravidian Parties are just Using the Dalit People as a Vote Bank: Questions and Answers with Thirumavalavan', *Tamil Mann* 6(62): 40–43.
Viswanathan, S. 1999. 'A Consolidation of Forces', *Frontline* 16(17): 24–27 August.
Whittier, N. 2004. 'The Consequences of Social Movements for Each Other', in D. Snow, S. Soule and H. Kriesi (eds), *The Blackwell Companion to Social Movements* (pp. 531–551). Oxford: Blackwell.
Wyatt, A. 2009. *Party System Change in South India: Political Entrepreneurs, Patterns and Processes*. London: Routledge.
Ziegfeld, A. 2013. 'Tamil Nadu', in A. Kohli and P. Singh (eds), *The Routledge Handbook of Indian Politics* (pp. 282–290). London: Routledge.

7
Challenging Normalised Exclusion: Humour and Hopeful Rationality in Dalit Politics[1]

Suryakant Waghmore*

In August 2014, Ram Gopal Verma, a Bollywood movie director faced legal action and the wrath of Hindus spanning all political affiliations. This was for poking fun at God Ganesha and for questioning the relevance of Ganesh Chaturthi (a festival in honour of the God Ganesha). Mr Verma wrote in one of his tweets, 'I have an innocent question…can someone please tell me how a Lord who couldn't save his own head will save others' heads?' This created a furore against him. His short tweets poking fun at Ganesha were indeed humorous, but failed to seem so for most of the modern Hindus who occupy the virtual world. A joke on the incongruence of God Ganesha was not to be considered humour, cases were filed against him and Ram Gopal Verma soon issued an apology.[2]

One robust theory of humour—the one that best fits my ethnographic study—is that humour is generated by 'the humour mental experience of *discovering* and *appreciating* ludicrous and absurdly incongruous ideas, events or situations' (McGhee 1979: 6, emphasis added). Humour is, thus, conceptualised as 'the *enjoyment of incongruity*': 'based on the violation of

---

* I am thankful to Joel Lee for insightful comments on an earlier version. Discussion with colleagues at CeMIS, Göttingen helped in consolidating some arguments. All shortcomings are however my own.

something that is expected or considered normal in given circumstances, humour emerges from two overlapping but opposed scripts' (Tsakona and Popa 2011: 4). Thus, for humour to be transacted and performed, it is central for participants to comprehend its incongruence and inconsistence. The *doxa* (Bourdieu 1977)—taken-for-granted aspects of everyday life— will further construct what is tolerable humour and what could be considered heresy. Humour therefore, may not always generate its expected outcome in all contexts, and may also lead to fear, agony, anxiety, panic, indignation, curiosity, disgust, etc., as a result of deviating from the norms and disrupting the social order (Tsakona and Popa 2011). Such relativity in meanings and outcome of humour are explored here through elite humour on Dalits and the oppositional humour in Dalit movements that counters caste privilege and purity. As I will argue in the following pages, there indeed is a distinction between humour of elite castes and of Dalits, while the former is standard, the latter besides being oppositional is not always a hidden transcript. Deriving from Freud's (1959 [1911]) emphasis on social relations in study of humour, I suggest that normalised caste exclusion can be better explored by including humour at the centre of analysing social relations in modern India. Such an analysis can also help us interrogate the accommodative policies and politics targeting Dalits. Social relations and associated power processes actively construct the norms of (tolerable) humour.

That Ram Gopal Verma failed to have visible supporters on twitter, offers an insight into the caste *doxa* and practice of vernacular modernity in India. A contrary statement from Prime Minister Narendra Modi better explains *congruence* (and science) under vernacular modernity. Narendra Modi recently emphasised scientific advances in the ancient Hindu times through Ganesha's head-replacement surgery:

> We worship Lord Ganesha. There must have been some plastic surgeon at that time who got an elephant's head on the body of a human being and began the practice of plastic surgery.[3]

In making the previous statement, Mr. Modi was not making a joke about the Hindu god Ganesha. Rather he was reiterating the scientific advances in the glorious Hindu past and the need to relive it in the present. His statement evoked no laughter, but applause in agreement.[4] The Indian History Congress did not consider this as either scientific or as humorous, and were quick to understand this as a 'distortion' of history.[5] Contrary to this elite intellectual view, however, Narendra Modi is increasingly considered an epitome of Hindu power, kindness and modernity in the present neo-liberal times, so much so that People for the Ethical Treatment of Animals (PETA) enthusiasts in India chose him as the hottest vegetarian[6] celebrity.

Critical voices within deliberative democratic theory have sought either radical reform of the liberal state, to make it more authentically deliberative, or the specification of alternative venues where deliberation might be sought (Dryzek 2000: 27). Going beyond those deliberative democrats who traffic in 'public reason' and impose narrow limits on what constitutes authentic deliberation, Dryzek (2000) favours those who would allow argument, rhetoric, humour, emotion, testimony or storytelling and gossip. Indian popular culture and politics has an excess of rhetoric, humour, emotion, storytelling and gossip—these, though, are hardly based on reason. The recent murder of Narendra Dabholkar—the well-known and respected rationalist campaigner—in Maharashtra exemplifies the intolerance of popular Hinduism to scientific and rational misadventures.

Poking fun at Hindu Gods and rituals is, however, not an abnormal practice for those relegated to the margins of society. The response of *unlaughter*[7] to Ram Gopal Verma's tweets would have seemed odd to several Dalit movement participants of Maharashtra. The disjunction between the *unlaughter* for Ram Gopal Verma and applause for Narendra Modi's scientificity helps us to better understand the vernacular nature of Hindu modernity and the limits to Dalit accommodation. The rise of Narendra Modi coupled with accommodative politics of BJP[8] is in many ways a continuation of Congress politics of Dalit inclusion. Culturally, it represents the rush of Hindu modernity in neoliberal times—where ritual and economy do not contradict but reinforce each other. My concern in this chapter is with the social meanings of such accommodation and modernity for Dalits—something that I explore through the study of the caste dimensions of humour.

As vernacular modernity under neo-liberalism turns both hyper-consumerist and simultaneously hyper-Hindu; any public anti-Hindu sentiment (humour included) has to be either withdrawn or apologised for. Elst (2011), while providing a historical overview of humour in Hinduism, sees the present Hindu intolerance of humour as opposed to its age-old tolerance of criticism and satire. Humour that is understood as anti-Hindu in nature is increasingly a matter of *unlaughter* for the mainstream. As opposed to this *unlaughter*, Dalit political humour challenges predominant forms of vernacular modernity and constitutes a critical counter public.

This chapter, thus, explores normalised prejudice against Dalits through a study of humour. Drawing from ethnography on Dalit movements in Marathwada, it engages with the meanings of laughter and *unlaughter* for Dalits. Exploring caste and anti-caste dimensions of humour helps decipher how anti-Dalit sentiments are increasingly voiced in polite and non-violent forms. Dalit protest humour, however, continues to challenge the modernised irrationalities and exclusions of caste. The public performance and private practice of anti-caste humour in Dalit movements contribute to a kind of 'hopeful' rationality in Dalit politics. Such rationality is also engaged in altering the popular notions of tolerance and touch and stretching the Hindu-modern boundaries of laughter and self-critique, thus making a critical contribution to civilising India's popular democracy and deepening the processes of inclusion that are ongoing in the political sphere.

Accommodating Dalits or Modernising Disgust?

One of the significant outcomes of Ambedkar's politics for Dalit liberation was his evoking of anti-caste sentiment as a moral sentiment necessary for the success of democracy. This moral sentiment was forced upon the society through the Constitution of 1950. The Constitution did not necessarily curb the freedom of caste or its inner realm, but 'untouchability' as a socio-religious practice was banned in the public sphere and considered illegal. The Constitution, while imposing such a sentiment through laws like the Untouchability Offences Act, also enhanced the autonomy of caste through other constitutional provisions (Galanter 1963). Caste, thus, far from being abolished is also enhanced through constitutional provisions and democracy. This was a problem that Galanter (1963) observed long back, and referred to as the Westernisation of the notions of caste. What Galanter (1963) viewed as westernisation, however, can also be understood as indigenising of modernity and nationhood in India.

Challenging Normalised Exclusion 157

State policies aimed at accommodating Dalits were a product of Ambedkar's struggle and negotiations with the nationalist leaders and the colonial government. Mendelsohn and Vicziany (1998) categorise the policies aimed at the accommodation of Dalits into compensatory discrimination and action against adverse discrimination. They suggest that:

> ...the first grew out of Ambedkar's approach, and consists in guarantees of seats in legislatures, positions in public employment, and education benefits. The second closely reflected Gandhi's position, and has been concerned to bring about a cessation of discriminatory behaviour on the part of caste Hindus. (Mendelsohn and Vicziani 1998: 118)

Accommodative politics and policies targeting Dalits have had a much more complex cultural past however. During the Poona Pact face-off and the resulting compromise, Gandhi emphasised to Ambedkar that: 'In accepting the Poona pact you accept that you are Hindus' (Jaffrelot 2005: 67). Ambedkar was wary of the cultural basis of Dalit accommodation emphasised by Gandhi, however, and felt that there was no equality possible for Dalits within Hinduism. Despite this, even during the constituent assembly debates on reservations for Dalits, the Hindu logic of expiation for the past sins of caste Hindus was evoked by Congress Constituent Assembly Members (Bajpai 2000). In prohibiting untouchability too, the Hindu majoritarians were most concerned with establishing the 'Hindu' identity of untouchables (Chiriyankandath 2000) and insisted on framing the Scheduled Castes (SCs) as Hindus and not as a non-Hindu minority. It is policies of these kinds (cow protection, no reservations for Dalit Muslims and Christians) within the constitution that give secularism and modernity a Hindu form (Chiriyankandath 2000; Singh 2005). Swenden (this volume) suggests that accommodative and integrative policies can complement each other.[9] Accommodative policies targeting Dalits, however, seem more to fit in the logics or Hindu politics of (limited) integration. Pandey (2013), thus, rightly suggests that the success of Hindu nationhood and modernity is also a triumph of Hindu prejudice over Dalit aspirations of dignity.

The imposition of anti-caste sentiment in a Hindu-secular mode has had complex postcolonial outcomes; neither caste nor untouchability has been abolished as the power of Hindu modernity/nationhood thrives in India's popular democracy. There is a strongly articulated criticism of the postcolonial state for being isolated from the logic of the social order

(Kaviraj 1984), and for its secular aspirations that were not in touch with the cultural practices of ordinary citizens (Madan 1997). An interrogation of caste prejudices and Dalit exclusion, on the other hand, suggests far more proximity between state and caste morals (Waghmore 2013). This explains why the secular aspirations and impositions of the state on society have had limited impact in erasing caste prejudice and more particularly untouchability.

The persistence of Dalit exclusion despite the procedural power of anti-caste sentiments points rather to the impossibilities of justice, tolerance and civility in India's popular democracy. Under the ongoing postcolonial surge of Hindu modernity, the practice of untouchability is fast modernising, and humour serves as a means to practice the political (in)correctness of caste. There are hardly any studies available on caste dimensions of humour in India, which may be the symptom of a larger sociological apathy towards the study of humour which is not considered as a serious and scientific subject. More importantly, it is not considered a sociological subject (Davis 1995). There is, however, a need to take humour seriously as humour is integral to social relationships and social interaction (Lockyer and Pickering 2008). A study of humour in relation to caste can help us engage in the critical questions of laughter and unlaughter and more particularly the challenges for shared laughter on questions of caste and untouchability. This, in turn, throws light on the normalisation of caste exclusion despite the institutionalisation of anti-caste sentiments as a modern Hindu sentiment.

Untouchables in Mainstream Humour: From Caste Slang to Disparagement

If humour as enjoyment of incongruence is central to making humour work, what form of incongruence and ludicrousness is appreciated and enjoyed as humour under the vernacular modernity and the modern caste *doxa*? The modern Hindu *unlaughter* towards humour that is incongruent with caste *doxa* and the Hindu religion, should not make us assume that the ever-dynamic modern Hindus lack a sense of humour. Their preference, however, is for standard humour and not spontaneity. Spontaneous instead of standard humour is considered critical in societies witnessing rapid social and cultural change, as this fractures the common frames of reference into old and new variants (Mulkay 1988). Much accepted or standard humour in India involves making fun of women, homosexuals, fat and dark people.[10] Standard humour, thus, recycles and reinforces the dominant Hindu views and values. How is the question of caste and untouchability addressed in the mainstream humour? How are the outcaste subjects treated?

In Marathwada, social distance based on ideas of caste and purity innovatively puts humour, anger and disgust together to use. It is sometimes difficult to distinguish between the crass abuses of caste and the humour attached to it. What Dalits may experience as humiliation, may seem like humour for the dominants. For instance, there is a general saying that 'where there is a village, there is a Mahar locality' (*Gaav tithe Maharuda*). While not an example of humour, it captures the everyday nature of caste-based exclusion. The 'village' here refers to cleanliness and purity, whereas the Mahar colony connotes everything bad and polluting. If a reference has to be made to something dirty/bad/impure and its inevitability, non-Dalits would use this saying, '*Gaav tithe Maharuda*'. Further, there are common and casual forms of abuse in Marathwada which involve Mahars and Mangs. People are denigrated by being told: '*tujhya aaila mahar lavala*' (your mother was fucked by a Mahar[11]) or *Mang jhavichya* (born to a woman who had sex with Mang), *Chamarachya devala chappal cha maar* (The god of Chambars needs beating with Chappals—used to justify violence). Previously, such normalised anti-Dalit slang entertained the elite castes as they were routinely used to humiliate Dalits in public. Now, these phrases are mostly used by non-Dalits to humour and insult each other. The anti-Dalit sentiments and the laughter around Dalit disparagement are not always grounded in incongruity. The caste-hate proverbs like the ones discussed earlier problematise the dependence of humour on incongruence, as disparagement of Dalits in itself may seem humorous to non-Dalits—irrespective of the logic of incongruity. This further complicates the relationship between laughter and humour. Laughter devoid of incongruity and ludicrousness against Dalits is a form of normalised anti-Dalit sentiment. Thus, Dalits at times can generate laughter for the privileged without any pre-requisites of incongruity and anti-Dalit sentiment could suffice to comprehend such humour of caste-hate.

However not all anti-Dalit humour lacks incongruence and caste abuses are increasingly restricted to personal conversation within privileged castes. Such abuses rarely figure overtly in their communication with Dalits. More so in Maharashtra as politicised Dalits could resort to the use of SC/ST (Prevention of Atrocity Act—PoA) Act (Waghmore 2013). Such widespread suppression of previously banal caste behaviour is coupled with increasing anti-Dalit humour based on incongruence and disparagement.

Marathas, as a dominant caste, have resorted to a newer vocabulary of disparagement humour that mocks the incongruence of Dalit ideology and politics. For instance, reacting to Dalit demands to rename Marathwada University after Ambedkar, the dominant castes worked out a humorous rhyming slogan: '*Gharat nahi pith kashala maagtai vidyapeeth*' (you don't have bread in your house why ask for university). Such rhymes often accompanied the public desecration of Ambedkar images or statues. Post-*namantar* (the movement to rename the University), much conflict between Marathas and Dalits has been over the SC/ST Atrocities act. Shalinitai Patil, who is known for her crass language in public and her anti-Ambedkar/Dalit/Reservation sentiments, regularly mocks Dalit discomfort at being called by their caste names.

While Maratha disgust against Dalits cannot be voiced using caste slang anymore. Dalit political gatherings are, thus, a source of anger or discomfort for Marathas. At one Dalit village festival, I joined one of the Marathas who was looking on and mocking Dalit leaders and their inability to deliver 'proper' speeches. He also made fun of Dalit symbolism.

> These are all *antus pantus* (insignificant) leaders […] This fellow cannot speak […] As the Republican Party of India (RPI) leader completed his speech with *Jaibhim Jaibharat*, the Maratha youth commented again *ithe hyo chukla bagha* (fellow made a mistake here). He should have said *Jai Hind, Jai Maharashtra* instead. (fieldnotes, 2008)

The Maratha man mocked the incongruence of the Dalit gathering, which for him was not in sync with mainstream symbols, ideas and politics. Everything in the speech of the RPI leader seemed humorous as a result. The Ambedkarism of the Dalits is an aberration in the popular social practices of caste and nationalism, more particularly as they engage in the mainstreaming Dalit concerns.

The increasing use of sophisticated and hostile humour against Dalits reflects the anxieties of the privileged and dominant castes over their eroding control of ex-untouchables. Such humour is simultaneously pan-Indian and localised, regional and increasingly virtual. The growing use of the Internet and virtual politics also serves as a space for anonymity where caste Hindus can mask themselves and resort to disparagement humour against Dalits. For instance, a user named Stranger Jat (a dominant caste in some parts of north India) has hosted a recorded telephonic conversation on youtube named *Chamari Di Seal Todi Jatt Ne*[12] (a Jat man took a Chamar woman's virginity) which is supposed to entertain Jats. This video is a kind of collective sexualised attack on Chamars and so far has had 2,689,213 views. The potency of this celebration of Jat virility is highlighted in a rise of 'honour crimes' against cross-caste couples and the vehemence of dominant caste reactions when Dalits marry someone from their caste. The intention here, clearly, is to present Dalits as lesser citizens who are still prey to Jat whims.

Not all such anti-Dalit sentiment is masked either. There are facebook groups like: *We hate Reservations* which circulate cartoons showing fat SC/STs sucking blood out of 'general' and 'meritorious' castes. Other sites include 'We hate Mayawati and BSP', and 'We hate Ambedkar'. These are rather sophisticated versions that mock incongruity of 'Dalit-ness'. There has been an increase in disparagement humour targeting Dalits couched under criticism of reservations and the celebration of merit. Such humour targeting reserved categories helps strengthen the bonds amongst the caste-privileged and 'meritorious' Hindus while avoiding action under the PoA Act because they are criticising government policies and categories rather than particular castes. The very constitutional categories (SC and ST) of welfare and justice that were created to institutionalise anti-caste sentiment are turned into tools of disparagement and humour. In 2006, following the call for OBC reservations in higher education—*The Times of India* recycled an old cartoon by R.K. Laxman. This cartoon showed a tribal man who is recruited as an officer under the 'reservation-scheme' sitting on a table instead of a chair. In another instance, the Mumbai Mirror in 2006 carried an article titled Shoaib (Pakistani fast bowler) can't bowl too fast to the quota boys. It was a satire on reservations and imagined what would happen if reservations were implemented in cricket.

Hostile humour against Dalits has a considerable role in consolidating elite disgust toward Dalits under newly changed modern conditions. It facilitates the satisfaction of hostile instincts and masks destructive ones (Freud 1959 [1911]). Hostile instinct dressed as humour, thus, is a form of aggression performed politely. In this context, it is critical to clarify what is *modern* about anti-untouchable humour. The key point is that hostility against ex-untouchables needs moderation due to the institutionalisation of untouchables as equal Hindus/citizens. Further measures such as PCR and the SC/ST (Prohibition of Atrocities) Act have banned the use of derogatory words/abuses that could demean or humiliate SCs. Hostility against Dalits, thus, has to be suppressed and humour (of incongruity) serves as the best means of being modern, meritorious *and* anti-Dalit. The earlier crass and direct caste abuses are not exactly out, but they are declining in overt usage.

Dalits, for their part, find the mainstream humour that demeans them a matter of *unlaughter*. In 2012, for instance Dalits protested against the inclusion of a cartoon in the national school textbook depicting Ambedkar sitting on a slowly moving snail (the Constitution), whilst Nehru goads them on with a whip. Ashis Nandy best summed up the mainstream responses to the Dalit protest and reaction, terming them 'absurd' and speaking of a 'new found political tool to score points and nothing to do with Ambedkar' (TNN, 12 May 2012). Ashis Nandy, however, made matters worse—and underpinned his lack of sensitivity—by stating that SCs, STs and OBCs were most corrupt at the Jaipur Literary Festival in January 2013. His defenders called for detractors to understand the humour in his statement, whereas some Dalits resorted to the use of the SC/ST (PoA) Act against Nandy. This clash of privileged as analytical vs. Dalit as affective positions was best summarised by Satyanarayana:

> The running theme of the Nandy defence team is that the public (especially the marginalised) has neither skills of reasoning nor a sense of humour to appreciate Mr. Nandy's words in context. In fact, the campaign to produce Mr. Nandy as a victim as well as a great man constructs SC, ST and OBCs as fools and criminals. Satyanarayana (2013)

The protesting Dalits are generally seen in the mainstream media as reactionaries who lack reason and a sense of humour, as opposed to caste Hindus who could get the humour in the cartoon and Nandy's statement rather easily. The summary—Privileged castes got the humour and Dalits misunderstood it.

The privileged castes, in other words, are sophisticated and modern, whereas Dalits remain trapped within a low-caste mindset. The same people and castes that can laugh in these instances, however, suffer a humour bypass when it comes to their response to Dalit political humour. What makes Dalit political humour contentious is not merely the elite reaction of *unlaughter*, but also the middle caste (OBCs) intolerance of Dalit radicalism. Humour in Dalit movements and politics, however, is less about disparagement of caste Hindus and more about poking fun at the irrationalities of caste and its embedding in Hindu religion. Such oppositional Dalit humour mocks the incongruities of elite Hinduism, and includes self-deprecation of brahmanism amongst Dalits. Though mostly a hidden transcripts, such humour also involves saying aloud what in mixed caste space is usually forbidden.

Beyond Accommodation: Political Humour in Dalit Movements

Though the Constitution imposed anti-caste sentiment as a modern Hindu sentiment of citizenship, Ambedkar himself was wary of the utility of such institutionalised and legalised morality. Post-constitution, he became more concerned about the situation of Dalits and the limited protection provided to them, following which he did not fail to criticise the Constitution that he helped to draft. He emphasised that Dalits were a minority needing protection and were not part of the Hindu order:

> People always keep on saying to me. 'Oh you are the maker of the Constitution.' My answer to them is I was a hack. What I was asked to do, I did much against my will…. My friends tell me that I made the Constitution. But I am quite prepared to say that I shall be first person to burn it…. Remember there are majorities and minorities; and they simply cannot ignore the minorities by saying: 'Oh no, to recognise you is to harm democracy.' (Keer 2005: 450)

Towards the end of his life, Ambedkar took two major political steps. First was the formation of the Republican Party of India—which put securing political power at the heart of Dalit struggles. Second was his conversion to Buddhism, thereby separating untouchables from Hindu *doxa*. For Ambedkar, the constitutional achievement and establishment of legal and governmental protection for the advancement of the Untouchables conflicted with another major goal, the ideological transformation of the Untouchables (Gokhale 1986). This could only be achieved by moving out of Hinduism which for him lacked the moral sentiments of liberty and equality (Ambedkar 1936). Ambedkar, upon conversion, declared that he felt as if he had walked away from hell (Gokhale 1986).

The caste ideology of hierarchy privileges *purity* and normalises incivilities, it disciplines both caste subjects and modern technologies of governance so as to create a universe of pure citizens under conditions of liberal democracy. Ambedkar seems to have foreseen the power of caste purity and the dynamism of Hinduism which could overwhelm the disciplining abilities of the modern liberal state. The co-option of untouchables into Hindu doxa had, therefore, to be ideologically subverted. Ambedkar's politics have had a long-lasting impact on Dalits; politically this has meant continuance of Dalit struggles to move beyond Congress patronage and Hindu morals.

Humour serves as an important medium within Dalit movements to communicate and perform Ambedkarism. I will elucidate this through my ethnography of Dalit politics. My fieldwork focused on two movements in Marathwada, one is *Manavi Hakk Abhiyan* (Human Rights Campaign, MHA hereon), which is a Mang-Ambedkarite Organisation with some INGO support and the other is the Bahujan Samaj Party (BSP—Majority People's Party), a national Dalit political party. The political humour in Dalit movements is distinct from the mainstream standard humour that does not critically engage with caste dispositions. In the following sections, I will present political humour in informal conversations and speeches of Dalit activists and participants of Dalit movements. Such humour has significant potential as political protest, and is aimed at questioning beliefs of caste purity and their effect on society and state institutions. It is also through humour that Dalits transgress the ideas and institutions that normalise Dalit exclusion. I will begin with Dalit humour around temples, religions and gods, followed by humour around food and caste.

Temples, Gods and Religion

In Dalit movements, the 'village' temple is framed as an institution that normalises Dalit exclusion. Critique and humour of/around temples and Hindu gods, therefore, have long been part of Dalit politics. Ambedkar's

Challenging Normalised Exclusion 165

book *Riddles of Hinduism* that outraged the Shiv Sena can be seen as a satire on the incongruence and irrationality of some Hindu texts and practices. The Dalit Panthers practiced a radical version of Ambedkarism that involved mocking Hindu Gods and Goddesses, the way they looked, and what they stood for. This in turn led to violence against Dalits in rural locales. Present humour around Hinduism and Hindu Gods in Dalit movements is toned down as a consequence, but still exists. While Ram Gopal Verma shocked the mainstream by mocking Ganesh, such humour is commonplace in Dalit cultural and political performances:

> Eknath Awad, the president of MHA, while addressing Dalit activists on effective use of SC/ST (PoA) Act would suggest ways of identifying villages that oppressed Dalits. This included observing the *size* of the temple in the village; 'the bigger the temple the more the chances of untouchability being practiced, watch out for big temples'. (fieldnotes, 2009)

Cultural performances that are generally hosted during Ambedkar Jayanti celebrations across Maharashtra are frequent sites of Dalit satire. Yerekar is amongst the best-known performers of *bhim-sangeet* (Ambedkar music) in Dalit gatherings across Maharashtra. He regularly mocks Hindu Gods and texts like Ramayana and Mahabharata. Through his music and performances, he reiterates Ambedkar's argument that Hinduism is synonymous with caste and critiques Hindu morals that are antithetical to equality. Such humorous criticism includes criticism of Hindu texts for lack of science and reason. Some anecdotes of humour from his performances are as follows:

> They say Brahman was born from Brahmas Mouth, Kshatriya from Shoulder, Vaishya from Stomach and Shudra from his feet. I wish I was there when Brahma was in labour, I would have asked him where all he was getting contractions? What exactly is the centre of contractions? Ok accepted that Brahma was pregnant and delivered the four varnas, but tell me with whom did you get pregnant?

> They say Kumbhakara was so big that animals used to enter his nose, graze inside and come out. Not sure who was the shameless person who wrote this. Was it his nose or tunnel of khandala?[13]

Such assertion and humour by Dalits is meant to produce laughter on the incongruence and irrationality of Hindu beliefs that construct caste and untouchability. These performances are mostly seen in Dalit rallies and are not aimed at aggressive non-Dalit castes. However, the material of such speeches and performances is not inaccessible for non-Dalits, so it does not remain as a 'hidden transcript'. Next, I share the field notes from Savitribai Phule Jayanti (anniversary) in a village where a Dalit gathering had to extend beyond Dalits. This village belongs to a political lord from the Teli caste of Beed and any political or religious gathering in the village has to have some member of this family. The MHA workers had, thus, invited a woman member of this family who was also sarpanch here. Manisha, MHA activist was to address this gathering and the woman sarpanch from Teli caste was invited to act as *adhyaksha* (chair/president).

The group of women and MHA activists waited for the woman sarpanch who arrived in a white ambassador car. The sarpanch was in her mid-1950s, slightly stout compared to all Dalit women. She was sweating profusely as the meeting was organised under the asbestos in front of a Dalit community hall. After garlanding the framed picture of Savitribai Phule, she addressed the assembled landless Dalit women. As opposed to ritual salutations made to Ambedkar, Phule and others in Dalit gatherings, she quickly focussed on the importance of *Japa*[14] and urged Dalit women to attend a forthcoming gathering of Jalgaon Maharaj (a local godman). She also distributed some pamphlets about this event. Some portions of her speech, which focussed on *japa* and how it would solve problems of Dalit women are as follows:

> We need to do *japa* of Ram's name [...] Don't say Ram Ram loudly, just do it through your lips. [Shows through example]. All the sins we have done, [...] *japa* helps digest. [...] You should do *japa* for one hour in the morning, one in the afternoon and one hour at night. If you do it for some more time its better. If you do this it will open *dwaar* (doors) within your body. [...] see all our body aches, back ache does not allow us to sit at times. If you do *ram ram* only that will solve all your problems....
>
> The guru maharaja from Jalgaon will come. He will explain this to you better than me and you will realise the difference within six months [...] doors will open. [...]If you do it 4–5 days for 8 days you will experience the change. Seven generation's ahead of you will benefit from your *japa* [...] These are the pamphlets about the programme. Don't throw this down [to earth] they are from the *paramaatma* (God). For this puja there are no MC (menstrual cycle) requirements, or to burn incense sticks, but we have to do it with our lips.

If the chair was hoping to subvert the Dalit meeting to her own ends, she was to be frustrated. Manisha (36) has been an activist in MHA since 1995 and is now the president of its women's wing. She is not from SC but from *yelam* caste identified as OBC in Maharashtra, she is, however, admired by most Dalit women (she interacts with) for her fiery speeches and activism and is also appreciated in other Dalit movements. She is married to Ashok (a Mahar convert to Buddhism) another MHA activist, a marriage which was also political as it happened on 14 April to mark their protest against endogamous marriages. Manisha, however, was not her fiery self in this village meeting as it would have meant some trouble for the Dalit women present there; she, therefore, called the women to stay away from God and godmen in a slightly polite and humorous speech.

> When we ask people if they know Savitri, they tell us yes they know the Savitri of Satyanarayana.[15]
>
> But now the world has moved far ahead, so far that, how life is lost can be explained. It is not because of Yama that people die but failure of body mechanisms [yantra] [Laughter]. [...]
>
> What does the sanskriti (culture) here say? Women have no right to education. If women access education it was said that invited a curse [...]
>
> You [Dalit women] are told that the *devi* possesses your body [...] If your body had God then you would have reached places, you would been very close to Sonia Gandhi's position [laughter].

In her generally charged speeches, Manisha radically criticises the temple's space, 'dogs go and pee on the stone statues in your temple, but Dalits are not allowed inside'. Manisha, however, spoke more about science in this gathering which around 40 women from Mang and Mahar caste were attending. In doing so, she also mobilised Dalit women in favour of Savitribai Phule and asked them to distance themselves from Savitri of Satyanarayan. She also distinguished [Dalit] Gods that enter Dalit women's bodies in her critique, creating a community within Dalit women. In a thinly veiled mockery of the earlier speech she appealed to Dalit women to adhere to 'scientific' reasoning instead of Baba and Parmatma for solving their problems.

If we can say that Manisha had the last laugh here, Dalit political humour that pokes fun at Hindu Gods can result in violence or threat of violence for Dalit activists or those participating in such meetings. Dalit workers of MHA poked fun at God Hanuman in X village in one of their gatherings as Dalits are not allowed to enter the Hanuman temple here. Tukaram, a Dalit worker of MHA, was threatened by the local Marathas for poking fun at the Monkey God and the irrationality that prohibited temple entry for Dalits. One Maratha told Tukaram:

> Your workers spoke against Hanuman and you tuck your shirt in and go around the village. You should not tuck your shirt in the village and once you enter the village you should remove your tucked shirt. You encroached upon the *gaairan* [common grazing land], did we say anything? No. Then why should you speak against our Gods and religion. You think you are President (of India) after tucking your shirt in (Interview with Tukaram, 5 December 2008).

The discomfort of the Maratha just discussed was not merely with Tukaram's criticism of gods and religion but also with his non-docile existence as symbolised by his clothing that challenged the previous caste codes and dominance. Use of humour in Dalit movements is not confined to Gods, however, but also criticises caste Hindu obsessions with vegetarianism and their labelling of non-vegetarians particularly beefeaters as low and untouchable.

On Food and Caste: Celebrating the Impure

Caste ideology and hierarchy encompasses several spheres including food. Ideologically speaking, in caste hierarchy, the classification of food is essentially related to the classification of people and to the relationship between human groups (Dumont 1980). The interplay between food and associated ideas of purity and pollution continues to be a site of intense contestation. In July 2014, for example, the Government of India announced a 5 billion Rupee ($82 million) mission to breed [indigenous] cows and house stray cows. In brahmanic tradition, the cow signifies an ultimate form of purity in its urine, milk, ghee, curd and dung [*panchgavya*]. As heinous a crime as brahmanicide is bovicide, and situated at the opposite end of this social continuum is dog and *Svapaca* [dog eater caste—fifth caste that is not a caste, therefore untouchable] (White 1992). There are no state schemes or missions to this tune for the protection of stray indigenous dogs. While forced sterilisation and savage killing of dogs are common stories (Srinivasan and Nagaraj 2007), the privilege of the pure cow continues. In 2014, the newly elected BJP government in Maharashtra banned consumption and possession of beef—which could attract up to five years of imprisonment. While a ban on cow slaughter already existed in Maharashtra, this was extended to other cattle as well. Attributing the contemporary purity politics of the cow to Hindutva or Hindu nationalism would be misleading, however. Cow purity found recognition in the Constitution of India (Directive Principles of State Policy) through the lobbying by members of the Nehruvian Congress. The regulations on cow slaughter proceed on a fundamental constitutive elision of the religious aspects of cow slaughter, which legitimise the dominant caste Hindu ethic (Chittageri 2011). Where the caste Hindus worship the cow, however, Dalits have long eaten beef and they counter the impurities attached to their food preferences through humour. Amongst activists and Dalit movement participants, humour and discussion around food, their preference for non-vegetarian meals, particularly beef is common place. Informal exchanges on *vajadi* (beef stomach), *par* (intestines) and *khure* (paya) which are otherwise considered filthy in mainstream culture, serve as an instant ice breaker. A kind of caste bond was worked out immediately, especially between Mang and Mahar activists, while engaging in discussion around beef.

> During lunch in a meeting on land reforms, one of the Mahar participants asked Eknath Awad why he was eating so little. To this Awad responded, *Aagodar Aakha Bail Khala Aahe Aaata Mhanun Kami Khaycha* (I have eaten a whole ox before so have to eat less now), and both instantly broke into laughter. (fieldnotes, 2009)

However Dalits are not all assertive and aggressive about beef consumption due to the stigma attached to eating bigger animals. Madhukar Londe is the District president of MHA in Beed. Awad and some of his followers in MHA converted to Buddhism as a protest against Hinduism in 2006. Madhukar was part of this group, but he follows Ambedkarism selectively and has not opted to fully move into Buddhism. Any song for instance of Sai Baba (famous spiritualist and Guru) playing gets Madhukar spiritual but this does not in any way make him sympathetic to the mainstream caste Hindu concerns. His passionate commitment remains towards Mangs. He appreciates Ambedkarism, but is wary of Mahars who for him have dominated every field of life—even MHA.

Madhukar, despite his Ambedkarism, is not a vegetarian as some Mahar Buddhists would insist. He is particularly fond of Beef biryani but does not like to be seen in front of the beef restaurants. Due to the caste stigma attached to beef eating amongst the mainstream, Madhukar mostly tries to hide this from upper caste government officers and leaders with whom he engages frequently. When with Dalit activists, however, he would make fun of those who did not like the idea of eating beef and cow meat.

> When a Brahmin member of Goa Raksha Samity in Beed had climbed on a tree in front of collector's office threatening suicide against cow killings, Madhukar saw this as entertainment and asked me and other activists to enjoy the scene despite us being late for another important meeting. (fieldnotes, 2009)

Further given are some notes of Madhukar's observations on and liking for beef, which were mostly hidden and not overtly performed in the presence of privileged castes:

> True to his word he took me to a Beef [Muslim] eating joint where one gets beef. He also introduced me to the owner of this restaurant where he used to work as a waiter earlier. By now he had started introducing me as a friend from Bombay. While having food at the restaurant one could well sense his familiarity with the Muslim waiter. He introduced me to him as his 'special' guest and requested him for the food to be 'special' too. He kept on appreciating the food and its quality in that eatery very much. [...]
>
> As we ate he said, 'Sir, a few Brahmins and Marathas come and eat here'. I shook my head in disagreement. He called the waiter (Mamu for him) and asked him to clarify. The waiter said, '*Saab, tumhare humare aad main woh log kha ke ja rahe hain*' (Saab, these people eat while using us as cover). Madhukar continued, 'Sir, this is pure cow'. I had my doubts again. He continued, 'people from various talukas and villages come to eat here'. He again called Mamu to confirm. He said, 'Yes, we do not slaughter anything else.' Madhukar said, 'Why should anyone not eat this. You can have all the 36 crore gods in your stomach at once. Moreover, mutton has become ₹150 per kg. Who would not like to have a decent meal here for just Rs. 60 or buy 1 kg for Rs. 60?' (May 2007).

While Dalits are not ashamed of beef eating and in fact relish it, they are made to feel ashamed of their food when they encounter caste Hindus, whose social norms prohibit beef consumption (Gundimeda 2009). Madhukar keeps his wit on beef informal, and it constitutes a hidden transcript in his politics against caste, testifying to the power of the Hindu caste *doxa*. Other Dalit leaders, however, raise the Dalit liking for beef regularly in public meetings to cause laughter. At times, such humour is out of place but still remains humorous for Dalit participants. Ramdas Athawale is a leader for RPI who regularly uses *reda, bail* and *mutton* in his speeches irrespective of the content he is addressing.

> At a *gaairan* rally meant for demanding gaairan land for Dalit cultivators that was attended by some Congress ministers including the revenue minister Narayan Rane, Athawale in his usual humorous and poetic style demanded that lands encroached till 2010 should be regularised in advance. He also added that, 'let us [Mahars and Mangs] be farmers too, though bullocks do not stay with us and most will be taken there [slaughter-house]. (fieldnotes, 2008)

Athawale's comments drew instant laughter amongst the participants. However such humour is a source of contempt and matter of *unlaughter* in Hindu culture. Commenting on Dalit assertion around beef in a different context, Gundimeda (2009) notes that such Dalit assertion democratises the public sphere by fracturing the hegemony of Hindu culture, creating space for the representation of marginalised cultures. More importantly, it challenges the banal purity rituals attached to food by celebrating consumption of highly impure beef—both publicly and in private.

Caste in Anti-caste Humour

As discussed earlier, using untouchable caste names with derogatory intentions has become difficult due to the institutionalisation of anti-caste sentiment and Dalit protest against such humiliations. This does not mean that Dalits have stopped using caste names altogether despite the ideal of conversion to Buddhism. There are at least three forms of caste name usage amongst Dalit movement actors: One is the sanskritised form of older caste titles—Charmakar for Chambar, Matang for Mang. Secondly, the older forms—Mang, Mahar and Chambar—persist alongside these more honorific labels. Thirdly, there is the invocation of an imagined broader political community like Dalit, Bahujan, Buddhist and Mulnivasi.

Though in legal terms, it is a criminal offense for privileged castes to call people by their untouchable caste names, Dalit activists often joked by calling each other in caste slang forms. For instance, in BSP gathering, in jest, a Mahar worker would often call his Mang friend, *ai Manga* [slang used by upper castes to intentionally humiliate], the Mang worker immediately shot back, *ai Mahara* [for some orthodox Ambedkarites the use of word Mahar itself is derogatory, they claim to have lost their Mahar identity after conversion to Buddhism], with both laughing after these exchanges.

Amongst the Mahars there is no sanskritised version of Mahar unless one considers Harijan which is at times used. Most call themselves Bauddha. Some Mahars/Buddhists insist on giving up the Mahar title altogether to emphasise their new identity of Buddhist. This flight between Buddhist and Mahar is a vexed one and also a source of humour for Dalit activists. Athawale once mocked a 'Buddhist Professor' in one of the social gatherings, which was attended by Dalit activists across parties. The Professor had suggested that conversions have not undone caste amongst Mahars who continue to use 'Mahar' in caste certificates. Athawale clarified:

> Professor just said that we write Hindu Mahar [...] just for the records. We are original Ambedkarite, we are Buddhists. Even if we call ourselves Mahar people call us Buddhists (implied out of fear, laughter). Looking at all of you [Professors] I too think of doing a PhD. If I get elected this time good or else I too will do a Phd [laughter]
>
> There are people like Eknath Awad here, you are matang, you are *ambuj*, we are *bhukare* [in Farashi which mostly Mangs speak]. My wife is a Brahmin but she has become a Buddhist now. Babasaheb Ambedkar had said that there should be inter-caste marriages. All should do inter-caste marriages marry a Brahmin woman, marry a Maratha woman. Please tell the Mangs we [Mahars] are ready to give our girls in marriage and we are ready to marry your girls in marriage [Laughter].

Humour around caste names and identities in Dalit politics has different connotations as compared to the mainstream variants. Such humour lacks derogatory intent/content and aims at mobilisation towards transgressing caste and articulating anti-caste ideas and ideology. Such mocking and self-deprecation of Hindu-ness and docility amongst Dalits is used towards forming a new assertive and autonomous Dalit subject.

Challenging Normalised Exclusion 173

Similarly, in the mobilisation of the BSP, ex-untouchable caste names were taken overtly, humoured and mobilised towards forming a bahujan collective. Rahul Anvikar is an important BSP artist whose music inspires many BSP workers. How he engaged the caste in humour is given as follows:

> He asked the participants, 'Are there any Mangs here?' Some of the Mang participants raised their hands. He asked the Mangs to be bold and not shy, 'I too am a Mang, do not be shy'. This evoked laughter from the audience and also resulted in more Mangs raising their hands. He followed this up by emphasising that he was a Mang of Baba, Shahu and Phule and also added that *Matang* meant 'elephant' in Pali resembling not just the symbol of BSP but also the power and strength of Mangs. He then sang a song on Annabhau and his role in making the life of Bahujans golden.
>
> He later moved to the Charmakars and asked, 'Are there any Chambars here?' Fewer hands compared to Mangs went up, but he added again, 'Do not be shy I too am a Chambar', causing laughter in the audience. Rahul however treated Chambars differently, 'the Chambars of Maharashtra have to be gathered in one place and bombed to death. How come you do not have *akkal* [brains]. The daughter of a Chamar [referring to Mayawati] is going to be the PM of India'. As laughter prevailed Rahul went on to sing a song in praise of Ravidas and his anti-caste philosophy.

In MHA the focus is on mobilising and politicising Mangs in a nonsanskritic way. Awad would jokingly refer to Mangs as *thanda raktache prani* (not hot blooded) to explain lack of politicisation amongst Mangs. Further, Mahars are not framed as permanent enemies as some of the other Mang organisations do. Activists of MHA suggest to Mangs that Mahars are doing better because they follow Ambedkar. Humour comes in handy here as well.

> It is my humble request to the Mangs, at least learn from the Mahars we have been saying this for so long [claps]. Look at this Ojgare [local Mahar leader] he has become so fat and got his children educated, please take this strength become like him. (laughter and claps). (Eknath Awad; Speech 23 August 2008)
>
> Activists also tease Mangs who use symbols like those of Marathas for forgetting their Mang identity. In another small meeting of Mangs in Kaij Taluka, in his speech Madhukar poked fun at the saffron dressing of one of the male participants who was wearing a saffron towel with a *tika* on forehead. He reminded him of his Mang identity, 'If you wear *bhagwa* [saffron], you are not going to be *Chatrapati* [implied Maratha], you are a Mang. If you put a *gandha cha tikala* [a saffron mark on forehead], no one is going to call you *Chatrapati*, you will still be Mang or Mahar' (fieldnotes, 2008).

While the disparagement humour of privileged castes aims to denigrate Dalits. Dalits too mocked Maratha superiority and the performance of their kingly-hood in public spaces. Such mocking of Maratha superiority did not always appear in collective political gatherings and was mostly toned down. Most criticism of Maratha dominance, their symbols and perceived arrogance happened in private and constituted an anti-caste hidden transcript that informed the wider struggles against caste.

Beyond Hindu *Unlaughter:* Humour and Hopeful Rationality in Dalit Politics

Accommodative policies targeting Dalits are based on logics of integration that consolidate caste *doxa*. Anti-caste sentiment in a Hindu form has thus ended up normalising Dalit exclusion. It has modernised anti-Dalit sentiments which are now moderated and humour is increasingly an important means of performing disgust against Dalits. The study of anti-Dalit humour and the use of anti-caste humour in Dalit movements help us understand the surge of Hindu modernity and the coupled normality of caste exclusion. Humour exposes the limits of accommodative policies in challenging the social practice of prejudice and discrimination. Humour at the margins, as pursued by Dalits, also challenges the notions of *unlaughter* in Hindu modernity.

The mainstream notions of humour and tolerance in India closely resemble Dryzek's (2000) insistence on moving beyond public reason, whereas the burden of defending the power of reason seems to reside with Dalits. The humour in Dalit movements challenges Hindu prejudice and unsettles the coherence of the modern Hindu universe. Humour also serves as critical voice that alters dispositions of caste *doxa*. Caste dispositions operate within imaginary limits of caste privilege, any violation triggers popular violence or state action against the exception. The vernacular Hindu modern is, thus, illiberal and lacks civility as far as Dalits are concerned (Waghmore 2013).

Against such incivility, Dalit political humour engages in a kind of hopeful rationality that seeks to reform ideas of humour in general and caste humour in particular. Humour and laughter in Dalit movements, thus, are less intended to cause disparagement and are largely about

Challenging Normalised Exclusion 175

setting up new standards in which a critique of popular culture and ideas of purity and pollution is possible. While challenging the normality of caste violence, Dalit political humour also expands the ideas of tolerance and self-critique in the popular culture of Marathwada. Such humour and rationality, however, is still at the margins and speaks to the continued marginalisation of Dalits in contemporary India.

Notes

1. An earlier version of this chapter was presented on 11 May 2015 at the CeMIS colloquium in the summer semester 2015. Comments and questions from participants have helped improve this chapter.
2. See *Times of India*, http://timesofindia.indiatimes.com/tech/social/Ram-Gopal-Varma-creates-a-furore-with-controversial-tweets-on-Ganesha/articleshow/41231034.cms (accessed 30 August 2014).
3. See *Indian Express*, http://indianexpress.com/article/india/india-others/pm-takes-leaf-from-batra-book-mahabharat-genetics-lord-ganesha-surgery/ (accessed 28 October 2014).
4. https://www.youtube.com/watch?v=NeIWu1NLuzE&spfreload=10 (accessed 4 April 2015).
5. http://indianexpress.com/article/india/india-others/history-congress-takes-dig-at-pm-dont-distort-past/ (accessed 31 December 2014).
6. http://ibnlive.in.com/news/prime-minister-narendra-modi-actress-rekha-named-indias-hottest-vegetarian-celebs-by-peta/520448-8-66.html (accessed 20 April 2015).
7. 'A display of not laughing when laughter might otherwise be expected, hoped for or demanded' (Billig 2005: 192).
8. *Sab ka Saath, Sab ka Vikas* (Together with all, Development for all), see also Swenden (this volume).
9. Mosse (2010) has provided a critical reading of adverse accommodation of Dalits. He suggests that adverse incorporation and social exclusion are not competing concepts and could well help us understand the durable inequalities facing Dalits (and Adivasis).
10. The AIB and Comedy Nights with Kapil are good examples, see (Vohra 2014).
11. As opposed to general slang, this is considered worse for forcing of a Mahar man over a non-Mahar woman.
12. http://www.youtube.com/watch?v=uvqFAXjwBKE (accessed 22 April 2015).
13. http://www.youtube.com/watch?v=kumVIa0eVHo (accessed 5 March 2015).
14. *Japa* is a Sanskrit word which refers to a kind of meditation where name of god is continuously repeated.
15. A story in Hindu mythology where Savitri, wife of a hermit named Satyavana reclaims the soul of her dead husband from Yama (lord of death). Most government offices organised Satyanarayan Pooja in Maharashtra making it governmental technology with popular support.

References

Ambedkar, B.R. 1936. *Annihilation of Caste, Social Justice and Political Safeguards for Depressed Classes*. New Delhi: Shree Publishing House.
Bajpai, Rochana. 2000. 'Constituent Assembly Debates and Minority Rights', *Economic and Political Weekly* 35(21/22): 1837–1845.
Billig, Michael. 2005. *Laughter and Ridicule: Towards a Social Critique of Humour*. London: SAGE.
Bourdieu, Pierre. 1977. *Outline of a Theory of Practice*. Cambridge: Cambridge University Press.
Chiriyankandath, James. 2000. '"Creating a Secular State in a Religious Country": The Debate in the Indian Constituent Assembly', *Commonwealth and Comparative Politics* 38(2): 1–24.
Chittageri, Shraddha. 2011. 'Negotiating the "Sacred" Cow: Cow Slaughter and the Regulation of Difference in India', in Monica Mookerjee (ed.), *Democracy, Religious Pluralism and the Liberal Dilemma of Accommodation* (pp. 137–159). Netherlands: Springer.
Davis, Murray S. 1995. 'The Sociology of Humor: A Stillborn Field?' *Sociological Forum* 10(2): 327–339.
Dryzek, John. 2000. *Deliberative Democracy and Beyond*. Series edited by Will Kymlica, David Miller and Alan Ryan, *Oxford Political Theory*. Oxford: Oxford University Press.
Dumont, Louis. 1980. *Homo hierarchicus*. Chicago: University of Chicago Press.
Elst, Koenraad. 2011. 'Humour in Hinduism', in H. Geybels and W. Van Herck (eds), *Humour and Religion: Challenges and Ambiguities* (pp. 35–53). Newyork: Continuum.
Freud, Sigmund. 1959 [1911]. *Jokes and their Relation to the Unconscious*. New York: Norton.
Galanter, Marc. 1963. 'Law and Caste in Modern India', *Asian Survey* 3(11): 544–559.
Gokhale, Jayashree. 1986. 'The Sociopolitical Effects of Ideological Change: The Buddhist Conversion of Maharashtrian Untouchables', *The Journal of Asian Studies* 45(2): 269–292.
Gundimeda, Sambaiah. 2009. 'Democratisation of the Public Sphere: The Beef Stall Case in Hyderabad's Sukoon Festival', *South Asia Research* 29(2): 127–149.
Jaffrelot, Christophe. 2005. *Dr Ambedkar and Untouchability: Analysing and Fighting Caste*. London: Hurst.
Kaviraj, Sudipta. 1984. 'On the Crisis of Political Institutions in India', *Contributions to Indian Sociology* 18(2): 223–243.
Keer, Dhanajay. 2005. *Dr Ambedkar: Life and Mission*. Mumbai: Popular Prakashan.
Lockyer, S. and M. Pickering. 2008. 'You must be Joking: The Sociological Critique of Humour and Comic Media', *Sociology Compass* 2: 808–820.
Madan, T.N. 1997. *Modern Myths, Locked Minds: Secularism and Fundamentalism in India*. Delhi: Oxford University Press.
McGhee, Paul E. 1979. *Humor, Its Origin and Development*. San Francisco: W.H. Freeman.
Mendelsohn, Oliver and Vicziani, Marika. 1998. 'The Untouchables: Subordination, Poverty and the State in India', in Jan Breman, G.P. Hawthorn, Ayesha Jalal, Patricia Jeffrey, Atul Kohli and Dharma Kumar (eds), *Contemporary South Asia*. Cambridge: Cambridge University Press.
Mosse, David. 2010. 'A Relational Approach to Durable Poverty, Inequality and Power', *The Journal of Development Studies* 46(7): 1156–1178.
Mulkay, Michael. 1988. *On Humor*. New York: Basil Blackwell.

Pandey, Gyanendra. 2013. *A History of Prejudice: Race, Caste and Difference in India and United States*. New Delhi: Cambridge University Press.

Satyanarayana, K. 2013. 'The Question of Casteism still Remains', *The Hindu*, 6 February 2013.

Singh, Pritam. 2005. 'Hindu Bias in India's "Secular" Constitution: Probing Flaws in the Instruments of Governance', *Third World Quarterly* 26(6): 909–926.

Srinivasan, Krithika and Nagaraj, Vijay K. 2007. 'Deconstructing the Human Gaze', *Economic and Political Weekly* XLII (13): 1085–1086.

Tsakona, V. and Popa, D.E. 2011. *Studies in Political Humour: In Between Political Critique and Public Entertainment*. Amsterdam and Philadelphia: John Benjamins Publishing Company.

Vohra, P. 2014. *Give us a Good Laugh, Not a Stupid One*. Mid-day, 30 November 2014.

Waghmore, S. 2013. *Civility Against Caste: Dalit Politics and Citizenship in Western India*. New Delhi: SAGE Publications.

White, David Gordon. 1992. 'You are What you Eat: The Anomalous Status of Dog-cookers in Hindu Mythology', in Ravindra Khare (ed.), *The Eternal Food: Gastronomic Ideas and Experiences of Hindus and Buddhists* (pp. 53–94). NY: SUNY.

8
Contentious Spaces: Guru Pujas as Public Performances and the Production of Political Community

D. Karthikeyan

We understand that contemporary politics in India has increasingly involved competition over symbolism and the strategic location of cultural signifiers—a competition over style and performance even over what constitutes a public space. (Zavos et al. 2004: 3)

Introduction

Guru pujas are public processions and commemorative events to mark and celebrate the birth anniversaries of prominent leaders or figures in India. In the context of Tamil Nadu, these annual pujas have enabled locally dominant castes such as Thevars[1] to showcase their community's strength and power through the appropriation of public space and the organisation of mass rallies, flag hoisting ceremonies and related events. In recent years, however, historically marginalised castes have replicated the public performances, which have hitherto been integral to the public production and consolidation of the dominant caste as a political community, in celebration of their own leaders and to give voice to their demands for equal status in, and access to, public space.

Caste status and power is played out through these performances in multiple ways. They serve not only to demonstrate power but to create boundaries and reinforce group identities. As previously marginalised groups have asserted themselves, these shows of strength and status have increasingly been contested. On 30 October 2012 during Thevar guru puja, thus, a group of young Thevars in a van who entered a Pallar Dalit[2] (ex-untouchable) dominated village—despite a police ban on such movement—was brutally attacked by an irate mob and one of them was killed. On the same day, in another incident, motorcycle-borne young Thevar men were waylaid and beaten to death by Dalits. As the news spread, the Thevars started to retaliate, and, two Dalit men were fatally hacked. At 9 PM later that night, approximately 70 kilometres away in Madurai, a petrol bomb was hurled at an SUV full of Thevar youth who were on their way back from guru puja. All 20 passengers were injured and seven died in that attack.

The context for this extraordinary manifestation of Dalit violence lies in the previous year when, on 11 September 2011, police opened fire on Dalits who had amassed to celebrate the anniversary (guru puja) of their leader Immanuel Sekaran, at Paramakudi in Ramanathapuram, a highly caste-sensitive region in southern Tamil Nadu. Six Dalits were killed, two died on the spot and another two were allegedly caught alive and beaten to death. The continuing marginalisation of Dalits was seen in the immediate exoneration of the police for this action despite countless eyewitness and independent accounts accusing the police of being heavy-handed.

These performances, thus, provide a micro-lens to understand caste dynamics and how local power is generated and made visible through a politics inscribed in space. The 11th of September and 30th October have become occasions to assert relative status through the occupation of public space, thereby reactivating the enmity that characterises interactions between the Dalits and Thevars. For the locals in southern districts Septembers and Octobers pass in fearful anticipation of disruption and violence.

These events form the background of my chapter, which aims to interrogate guru pujas as public performances and their utility in the construction of new forms of group solidarity and political community and as potential avenues for the habituation of violence and hatred. This chapter draws on participant observation, interviews and journalistic accounts to highlight the changing nature of caste in Tamil Nadu, south India. There is a long history of Dalit protests in the state, but there has been an upsurge since 1990 as Dalit movements challenged the ability of the dominant Dravidian parties to represent their interests. This chapter begins with an overview of the literature on space, place and public performances—setting out the complex and contested ways in which social space is constructed, it then briefly considers the interplay between caste and space before turning to the example of the guru pujas that are the focus of the chapter. We conclude with a discussion that brings the literature into conversation with the data and considers the implications.

Space, Place and Power

The concepts of space, place and mobilisation (to show dissent or resistance) have become central to the understanding of social movements, and space and place are not merely seen as providing a physical background for mobilisation but as mutually constitutive of social movement agency (Martin and Miller 2003). Perspectives on space explain the possible connections and relations between everyday life experiences and the much more general socio-political and economic processes. This helps us understand the constitution of space and its context in terms of how it influences and shapes collective action. Space, according to Lefebvre, is produced through social relations and structures, the notion of space as socially produced rests on an acknowledgement that space is an integral part of all social life, both affecting and affected by social action (Lefebvre 1991: 14–16, 280–283).

Lefebvre (1991: 38) defined the representations of space as abstractions inherited through the ideologies and epistemologies of 'scientists, planners, urbanists, technocratic subdividers and social engineers'. He distinguished these abstract representations with what he called lived or representational spaces. Lived space takes into account a person's actual experience of space in the everyday life. 'It overlays physical space, making symbolic use of its objects.' Social relations and lived space, thus, unite together in everyday life (Lefebvre 1991: 39; Martin and Miller 2003).

In other words, lived spaces are spaces that characterise quotidian lives and histories. Lefebvre sees these lived spaces as oppositional to dominant modes of representation and production of spaces. Thus, in terms of the production of spatial practices, the representations of space are significant to understand its production, but quotidian forms of life also shape space and its modes of representation. Mitchell highlights the processes by which one form of spatial order may give way to another:

> ...public space often though not always, originates as a representation of space, as for example, a courthouse square, monumental plaza, public park or pedestrian shopping district. But when the public uses these spaces, they also become representational spaces, appropriated in use. Public space is thus socially produced through its utility aspects as public space. If public spaces arise out of dialectic between representations of space and representational spaces, between the ordered and the appropriated, then they are also very importantly spaces of representation. (Mitchell 1995: 128)

This notion of a dialectical relationship in terms of spatial meaning is important in highlighting processes of agency and cultural contestation. The discussion of everyday practices renders Lefebvre's work useful in understanding the complexities of marginalisation in public spaces. The struggle to gain command and control over social space, he argues, has become a central element of everyday life, and this has indeed created a situation where the spatial aspects of everyday power relations have become more tangible, thereby resulting in more frequent incidences of sociopolitical contestation (Lefebvre 1991: 416).

Performing Power and Protest

Visual spectacles or public performances to highlight a political agenda or to mark the presence of a community or group are common forms of such contestation. Processions, marches and parades are different forms of public performance where the community displays their loyalties or attachments which could be religious, ideological, national or cultural (Diamond 1996: 1–12). However, the question here is to see if these performances act as markers of a categorical state or as conditions which could help in the formation of newer categories. Indeed, Schechner (1993: 5–22) argues that the most critical part of performance is the transformation of the subject. He notes the 'startling ability of human beings to create themselves, to change, to become what they ordinarily are not'.

There is, thus, a strong political element in performances which serve as a mode of communication between the performer and the audience.

Hansen (2004: 21), consequently argues that performances in public spaces—from central squares to the street corners in the slum, from speeches to images—must move to the centre of our attention since they are generative political movements in which historical imageries, the state and notions of community and society become visible and effective. Performances are not simply directed outward, however. In analysing political performances, I draw upon Butler (1993: 2) who has defined performativity as the conformed replication of acts, a simulation or representation of the dominant conventions. Whilst 'performance presupposes a preexisting subject', for Butler (1993: 33), 'performativity contests the very notion of the subject'.

Following Butler, we can comprehend the ways in which political performances not only serve as vehicles for the communication of messages, but also act to constitute new subjects in the process. As Hansen (2004: 23) puts it: 'Political Performativity could be defined as a body comprising acts that characterize the construction of images, spectacles, forms of speech, dress and public behaviour that endorses the identity of an organisation, party or movement, defines its members and promotes its cause or worldview'.

Marches, processions and parades, thus, can be seen as a form of political communication and identity formation which have spatial meanings attached. These performances in public space can be seen as expressions of power relations within the social order of a particular society (Davis 1986; Marston 2002). Processions include expressions of state or elite power (Nazi Germany and Soviet Union), as well as efforts to convey a dissident message, for instance, processions enacted by those excluded from larger public spaces on economic, social, or cultural grounds: 'Pride Rainbow Marches of Lesbian and Gay Communities' across the globe are an example (Goheen 1993).

T. Davis (1995: 297) captures the importance of public performance for identity in noting that 'for some neighborhoods and identity-based social movements, the creation of "communities" has been integral to their histories, and parades have served as a method of self-expression and as well as a method of representation of the self to society as a whole'. Likewise, in Harlem, Kugelmass (1994: 23) found that the spectacle of the 'Bamba Day' parade has brought the Murids (Sufi practitioners of Islam) onto the urban stage and brought them into the public gaze of others.

Contentious Spaces 183

More importantly, the parade allows these Sufi practitioners to publicly perform what it means to be marginalised as Black, African and Muslim in a predominantly white city of New York.

Since my relative focus is on how a marginalised community uses public performances to showcase assertion and perform newer meanings of identity-based assertion, it is significant to look at the fine distinctions of such performances. Parades and processions whether political or religious attach a performative spatial component to cultural identities which is more visible in relation to the marginalised communities. The routes that these processions take are often in themselves symbolic acts to invade the spaces which were hitherto unavailable for them. Processions can be seen here as constructive of particular spaces and identities and the participants, by performing a visual exhibition on streets and making claims to those public spaces. During such performances, bodies in motion, by taking up space, 'perform the streets' since the space that they are in belongs to those marching.

Public performances have been important to dramatise all sorts of group concerns and issues related to religious and political convictions. These public performances, thus, offer insights into the nature of the social system or cultural edifices and enhance our understanding of the meanings of political and religious behaviour. One of the major sources of identity formation in terms of religiosity in South Asia is the popular practice like congregation during festivals and religious processions. The latter have been seen as a major source in the expression of a collective identity (Gooptu 2001).

In terms of the guru pujas discussed here—it becomes critical to examine the process of solidification in terms of a larger identity on the one hand and the countervailing ruptures that challenge those processes. Dalit or Thevar assertion in terms of guru puja, this reminds us, does not happen in isolation. They entail the coming together of different sub-castes within the fold and the intricacies and implications remain crucial to our understanding of the larger picture. Gooptu's (2001) work explores the process of assimilation of Shudras[3] into the formal Hindu fold and reveals that the process is marked by conscious efforts on the part of Shudras to contest their own marginality. However, these efforts have larger ramifications as they slip into intense visual modes of communication and a process of othering. Processions play a critical role in these events.

Freitag argues that religious processions define the sacred space of the community. This attribute becomes conducive for violence in certain contexts, since when one group's space is overlapped with another's, then those circumstances can prompt riots (Freitag 1989: 134–135). The control and protection of sacred spaces has historically been an important symbol around which religious conflicts are organised and it holds true even to the present times, and it is not only sacred spaces but also spaces in general which have significant symbolic values and remain potential causes for communal conflicts (see Das 1990; Freitag 1989; Gooptu 2001; Jaffrelot 1998; Pandey 1990).

The conflicts thus generated may, in turn, lead to the reinforcement or construction of particular identities. 'Riots and rituals', as Van der Veer argues, 'both appear to play a significant role in the construction of social identities' (1996: 154–176). He suggests that rituals and riots derive their meaning from the way they relate identities to public space. 'The ritual nature of riots and the riotous nature of rituals are thus connected through discursive traditions on the nature of "self" and "other"' (van der Veer 1996: 155). Public space here not only shapes ideas of community but is itself, to an important extent, constructed through ritual and rioting. The spatial factor is as much a result as a basis of conception of community. In terms of production of space, public spaces derive their meanings in relation to the specific contextualised repertoire, which is in itself a process where different players are involved in the shaping, reshaping, structuring, restructuring and challenging through spatial practices.

My argument here is that rituals are double-binding in nature; as a process, they integrate individuals into a community of participants, but they set that group apart from those who do not participate. Moreover in many cases, they tend to portray 'the other' as 'threatening' and 'impure', such conceptualisation can imply ritual action to exorcise, subjugate or conquer the alien presence. Through these rituals, a sort of legitimacy is applied towards the appropriation of public spaces. Rituals, through various modes of deification on one hand and marked spatial boundaries on the other, lead to a situation where such invasions of these spaces become a political affair.

Any form of desecration, desacralisation and invasion of community spaces may, thus, spark violence. These processions highlight the contested nature of spatial zones and provide the much needed fillip to lay claim to a large territory and pave way for assertion where it becomes possible for the respective community in processions to infringe on other community's space. The contestation over these spaces is twofold in nature: for the dominant sections, the focus is on maintaining those spaces as 'spaces of privilege', and for the weak, the goal is to attain equality through access to these spaces.

While echoing the previously mentioned authors in many ways, one further point is central to my analysis. Colonial modernity paved way for discussions on caste and religion. The colonial government found culture to be an explicit category where social and ascriptive identities like religion and caste became sites of political conflicts and contestations. Prior to that in the Tamil context, there was an effort to naturalise caste and invalidate its presence as a category both in the public sphere and politics. The presence of modernity did not eventually bring in caste as a valid category as one can see from the work of Pandian (2002). He notes how caste both in the colonial and postcolonial eras was seen as representing the pre-modern. By default, therefore, the modern quintessentially became upper caste in its orientation and caste (as an 'other' to the modern) became associated with lower castes.

Pandian (2002: 1739) then explains through Dalit autobiographies what the Indian modern offers to the Dalits, 'it demands and enforces that caste can live only secret lives outside the public sphere'. It is within this context that the construction of public sphere becomes important where lower caste groups have started to assert themselves to claim their rights to access it. Though widely recorded in South Asian literature in the North Indian context (Freitag 1989; Gooptu 2001) where it discusses about the Hindu–Muslim question, it becomes pertinent to understand the construction of public sphere in the South in terms of caste-based assertion and performance.[4] It is to the contested construction of this caste space that we now turn.

Caste and Space

Drawing upon the earlier discussed theoretical concepts, let's now turn our attention to the South Indian context, to understand the production of space through embodied practices, where the existence of caste becomes the decisive factor in the mobility of bodies. Dalit bodies operate within the premise of a spatial coding in terms of caste-based practices which functions in the production and maintenance of abstract, exclusionary public spaces. These spatial practices are not constrained only to the physical but transcend every aspect of life and play a role in constituting the identity of Dalits. In the following pages, we will look at the spatial aspects of guru puja, but the symbolic significance of these events only makes sense in the context of caste structures in South India.

In Tamil Nadu, representational/lived spaces are carefully designated according to social hierarchies and the most prominent amongst those is the spatial demarcation[5] on the basis of caste. The historical separation of Oor (village proper) and Cheri (untouchable inhabitation) is a common demarcation in Tamil society. This form of separation was practiced across India, and different terms were used to explain those habitations based on regional languages. The latter are seen as the stigmatised neighbourhoods where the untouchable (impure) people dwell. These lived spaces, or representational spaces as termed by Lefebvre, give us an idea of how social relations determine spatial meanings, and explain that the hierarchical nature of social relationships in a given society (read Hindu) has profound spatial meanings. The demarcation has its meaning not only in social terms but also in economic terms where the untouchables as agricultural labourers are made to live in low-lying areas (Ramaiah 2007: 1–13).

Caste-based restrictions on interaction affect the mobility of Dalits who are denied access to certain public spaces where the social control over their mobility rests with dominant castes. The complexities of social relationships within the caste context in the rural setting are highlighted in numerous village studies (for example, see Beteille 1969; Gough 1981; Moffatt 1979). Though there are clearly demarcated spaces that operate within the rural/village setting, how important a space is in terms of understanding social meanings within an urban context becomes pertinent. One of the most prominent themes in the study of urban spaces in South Asia is the role of public spaces in local politics, in which the neighbourhood as a site of everyday class, gender and caste relations takes a central place (De Neve and Donner 2006: 12).

Unlike the rural set-up, the tangibility of caste in the everyday urban life is complex. Though there are distinct caste estates or ghettoes or Dalit neighbourhoods, it does not operate in same terms as we witness in villages. There are clear markers and convoluted ways in which caste operates in urban spaces. An examination of the lives of Dalits reveals that they rarely escape the oppressive impact of spatial planning irrespective of the rural or urban contexts or the public and private contexts in everyday life. Space is pivotal to the ongoing process of subordination and social exclusion of Dalits (Loynd 2009). As Gorringe (2010) points out:

> For the Dalits, the notion of space formed the central social idiom of their struggle. Dalits in urban areas continue to live predominantly in slums or particular enclaves. Urban space in this sense is still marked by caste; people seeking homes for rent are often asked about their caste or are asked to get references from upper caste people before being offered a place.

Though caste-based social relations determine the spatial ordering, space, as an idiom of identities, becomes the very premise on which marginality is contested. Public space operates within the ideology of inclusion/exclusion framework, people belonging to certain sections of the society are excluded from the space and this exclusion happens at different levels. A specific kind of spatial form is being produced in these instances of exclusion. Here, the spatial form derives meaning from the body, which becomes a significant marker determining one's access to these spaces. Mitchell's definition, thus, becomes crucial in our understanding of these public spaces as embodied spaces.

In order to understand and explain the contested nature of public space in a caste context, we now turn to the guru pujas marking the anniversaries of Immanuel Sekaran[6] (leader of the Pallar sub-caste of Dalits) and Muthuramalinga Thevar[7] (a prominent Thevar leader and a Member of Parliament of the All India Forward Bloc[8]). Caste tensions and an underlying culture of violence become palpable through these public performances, which lay claim to particular public spaces. It becomes pertinent for our analysis to see whether these public performances could offer us a platform to study the changing socio-spatial relations amongst Dalits (Pallars) and Thevars.

Thevar Guru Puja

Thevar Jayanthi (birthday) as a performance includes festivities surrounding the birth and death anniversary of Muthuramalinga Thevar (1908–1963). This event provides space for the Thevar community to showcase its strength and political power. Pandian (2000) has argued that escalating caste conflicts between the backward castes and the Dalits distinctly marked the political biography of Tamil Nadu during the 1990s. A new form of caste politics simultaneously marked the Dalit assertion that took place in the 1980s. In this context, the Thevars regrouped themselves as a strong political community influencing state politics through various modes (Pandian 2000). Thevar guru puja in the early 1990s provided a visible platform for the Thevars to showcase their community's presence and political strength.

For our understanding, it is crucial to unpack the spatial meanings attached to Thevar Jayanthi as an event. The event, which was initially celebrated in a simple manner was announced as a state function in 1993. Becoming a state-sponsored event accords legitimacy to the event and means that police protection is assured, roads are blocked and traffic redirected to facilitate the procession of Thevars bearing flowers with which to garland the statue of their leader. 'Indeed the city of Madurai is atypically shut down for the celebration of Thevar Jayanthi' (Karthikeyan et al. 2012).

Different Thevar caste associations and political outfits, to display their strength and caste pride in public, started utilising the occasion of Thevar guru puja. The institutionalised nature of Thevar Jayanthi, through consciously created myths surrounding Muthuramalinga Thevar, his iconisation, canonisation and the construction of a social identity provides a point of entry to study the process of how political power is ritually constructed through public ceremony.

The event could be seen as an exercise to visually represent Thevar authority and power over the public space in general, but since there is a history of animosity between the Thevars and Dalits, it becomes more of a contestation between these two castes over the dominance and occupation of the public space. The Thevars carry a self-image of being former rulers of the Tamil land, and they announce through all available modes of communication that they are the real descendants of the ancient Tamil Monarchs. The state recognition accorded to the event enables them to dominate public spaces on the occasion of Thevar puja and claims to superiority are bolstered by films focusing on their caste, which reinforce their sense of dominance (Anand 2005).

Political performativity in other words comprises the construction of images and spectacles, forms of speech, dress and public behaviour that promotes the identity of a movement or party, which defines its members and promotes its cause or worldview. Interestingly in the case of Thevars, moustache and sickle-shaped machete are seen as cultural signifiers (personal communication from senior police officers). The 1990s guru puja related performative tradition or culture opened the floodgates for unseen levels of glorification of caste pride of the Thevars, it was more of a politics of presence and they who were never part of the non-Brahmin collective wielded much power, irrespective of which party came to power since the 1990s (Pandian 2000).

The production of authority is a central strategy of Thevar mobilisation, their dominance in all forms of the public sphere is almost complete and interestingly occurs in the film world too. Thevar sub-culture has strong visual idioms or markers and violent masculine performances are integral to their style. Nethaji Subhas Chandra Bose[9] is a permanent figure in their visual signifiers and discourse. On Thevar Jayanthi, Thevars put up flex boards and posters asserting: 'We are the rulers who controlled the land, people and resources, don't confront us.' Whilst the event started off as an extremely localised affair, confined to the village level, it was converted into a mass event entering the larger public spheres of the southern districts of Tamil Nadu and also to Chennai, the capital of Tamil Nadu. Thevar guru puja became an institutionalised civic affair; sanctioned, supported and policed by district administrations and state governments. Thevar dominance, by this means, was institutionalised into sociopolitical rituals in the state.

Thevar Guru puja attracts throngs of devotees (caste people) clad in the Thevars' chosen yellow and red who march in unison, singing and chanting forcefully as they descend on the temple dedicated to Muthuramalinga Thevar. They make their way to his temple both in vehicles and on foot, during which they make jarring public assertions most of which are either self-glorification of their caste pride (*Indha Mukkulathu Padai Podhuma Innum Konja Venuma*—Is this force of Mukkulathors enough or do you need more?) or shouted insults directed at Immanuel and at Dalit communities writ large as they complete their occupation of the Pasumpon area. Most of the slogans refer to the deified Thevar as an immortal who cannot be compared to mere mortals. For example, in a lyrical and metaphorical turn of phrase, one slogan says: *Panai Marathula Vavvalu Deivathukke Savala* (Can a bat hanging on the palm tree, offer a challenge to the God (Thevar)).

In addition to assertions of masculinity through competitive denigration, mock performances of martial arts like *silambam*, sword fighting and torch relays form part of the event. An interesting feature in Thevar Guru puja are the bloody performances of Thevar *attam*, an ecstatic dance in which men's sides are pierced with small spears for the duration of the performance, which helps to integrate masculine violence into the process. Indeed, Thevar *attam*, danced to the beats of drums, may be the most eloquent analogy for the habituation of violence at the guru puja. Men gyrate for hours to the cheers of spectators, suppressing their grimaces as blood pours down their sides.

As Pandian demonstrates, a type of rogue, aggressive hyper-masculinity has long been envisioned as inextricably linked to the inherent character of certain sections of the Thevar community (Pandian 2007). Banners, posters and slogans prominently display martial imagery, and the stature of Thevar is further protected by attacking any who are seen to insult or belittle their leader (Jaishankar and Karthikeyan 2011). In this sense, the public space becomes both the site and object of a power struggle, wherein the Thevars through marches, banners and flags assert their dominance with respect to other communities and through their occupation of such space during these celebrations. The dominant Thevar population is not always willing to cede control of the 'public' space of the street. In fact, the event has become a sort of an exercise to visually represent Thevar authority and power over the public space to the Dalits.

The Thevar Guru puja, during the last two decades has emerged as a strong signifier of Thevar assertion and community's political strength. However, as a significant counter-cultural event, the Immanuel Sekaran Guru puja has drawn much attention in the last decade, the Dalit movements and Pallar organisations have turned this event into a more visible platform of counter mobilisation and through this, the Dalit movements showcase their political presence and present their demands. The emergence of Immanuel Guru puja and its political and cultural implications will be discussed next.

Immanuel Sekaran Guru puja as a Symbol of Dalit Assertion?

Immanuel Sekaran Guru puja, which is held every year on 11 September, at Paramakudi, is an event of the recent past, though a small function was held in 1958 to remember his contributions to the fight against caste discrimination, it was never continued due to the pressure from the Thevars. It was during 1989, after the establishment of Tiyagi Immanuel Peravai

(TIP—Martyr Immanuel Forum) that they started celebrating it again and it was only during the mid-2000s that the event drew the attention of the media (interview with P. Chandrabose, founder, TIP). The annual Immanuel Sekaran Guru puja as the single most important site both in terms of visual and political presence of contemporary Dalit caste identity politics, amounts to a visual occupation of the given landscape, which is progressively mounted in the days leading up to the event. Dense and intense Dalit visual signifiers including flex boards, cutouts and flags are erected or hung three days ahead of the event. National Dalit icon Ambedkar's images can be seen everywhere, apart from that, posters of Dalit leaders, icons, historical figures and film stars supposedly from the Pallar caste can be seen in various sizes. Immanuel Sekaran's images in various sizes occupy the landscape and the flex boards include a line or two about the great sacrifice of Immanuel. Power, pride and masculine aggression are loudly broadcast from images of Immanuel Sekaran holding a machine gun in a military garb or a juxtaposed image of Liberation Tigers of Tamil Eelam (LTTE)'s Prabhakaran. LTTE stands as an important cultural signifier of masculinity in the Tamil imagination and Prabhakaran has already been immortalised in the political fiefdom.

The aesthetic in terms of its political manifestation within the Tamil political space is largely influenced by DMK's cultural aesthetics and visual culture, no political party is an exception to this rule and neither are the Dalits (Rajadurai and Geetha 1996). In this connection, I see the influence of Dravidian visual culture here, the aesthetic, in terms of both its symptomatic meaning towards sense perception and feeling and as a mundane method to understand art, taste and the beautiful is critical to understand the agency of the visual as the aesthetic here provides value to the movements and moments of Dalit mobilisation. As members of a historically oppressed community, the sense of being unheard and unseen is writ large and these feelings about politicised aesthetics, about having a sense of visibility and presence, were incendiary at the Immanuel Guru puja. The revenue and police authorities well ahead of time would conduct meetings proposing spaces for the erection of flex boards and discuss roadblocks to divert the flow of Dalits away from villages dominated by Thevars and vice versa on Thevar Guru puja.

On the day of guru puja, in front of Immanuel Sekaran's gravesite, the masses of tightly packed bodies donning their colours of green and red push forward to pay their respects to the anti-caste martyr. For the Pallars, Immanuel occupies a position parallel to that occupied by Pasumpon Muthuramalingam for the Thevars. He is remembered as a heroic martyr signifying the strength and valour of the community, who sacrificed his life resisting dominance. As the boundaries between the sacred and the political are porous, Immanuel Sekaran through various forms of ritual stands as a potential figure to be deified more on the lines of Muthuramalinga Thevar.

Following Gooptu's (2001) analysis of religious processions, we can see how the guru pujas operate as key venues for showcasing masculine power. During Immanuel's Guru puja, thousands of men pour into Paramakudi from around Tamil Nadu. They march in groups, occupying the public space (street) and once they enter the memorial they form a line shouting slogans about the courage of their leader. *Veera Vanakkam, Veera Vanakkam, Tiyagi Immanuelukku Veera Vanakkam* (Brave salutes to our hero the martyr Immanuel) is rhythmically chanted as they make their way to the gravesite of their late leader. Swarms of bodies push against rows of police in a show of masculine power.

The potential for violence may build in this collective act of memorialising murder,[10] riots and fallen heroes. Pallar men, who enact the daring heroism, associate themselves with Immanuel and in turn attribute it to their community and overwhelmingly dominate the guru puja. Moreover, their assertion of their masculinity stands in contrast to their attempts to emasculate[11] the Thevars. Much to the embarrassment of the Thevar community, Pallars often assert that Muthuramalinga Thevar was a transgendered person, or eunuch. The Pallars, furthermore, imitate the Thevars in their assertion of violent masculinity and rituals as a defining feature of their caste identity, which they perform in the stylised actions of the guru puja.

The Pallar's through the guru pujas are alleged of crudely imitating the Thevars, and this act could then imply that they accept the very system that oppresses them (Moffatt 1979). However, this is not as simple as it seems, as Deliege (1992) argues, replication does not necessarily indicate consensus on the part of Dalits, but instead can be seen as a mode of resistance. If Pallars can easily match the Thevars in their hypermasculine aggression, the Thevars are then reduced to become just an example amongst many. The why and how of inter-caste rivalry and violence are troubling to say the least. They may have to do with ruptures in construction of a golden past, with acts of habituating violence, and/or with increasingly possible modes of imitation.

In a comparative perspective, the celebration of Immanuel Guru puja is more of a political mobilisation for equality. The event through the occupation of public spaces seems to claim access to symbolic equality and to guarantee that public spaces are common and easily accessible to one and all; in that sense, one can claim that the event highlights through its performative aspects the question of equality. This aspect of political action needs to be read against the background of history where age-old caste practices of disciplining, constraining and regulating Dalit bodies by denying them space in the public exist.

Transformation of the Guru Puja

On an important note, the act of replication does not stop there in terms of its implications as seen in the case of Gooptu's (2001) work where the Shudra Hindu assertion towards its own upward mobility had unforeseen consequences in terms of its slippage towards becoming an anti-Muslim assertion, there are similar sorts of slippages. Though there are elements of replication and possible modes of imitation, the act of memorialising Immanuel Sekaran's sacrifice as part of anti-caste struggle has its own fixation as an act of counter-performance which has a deep social-psychological meaning towards questioning modes of dominance where the oppressed speak the language of the oppressor to counter such forms of oppression. These modes of replication do not stop there, they have certain forms of implication, which could then turn inimical to the cause of a united struggle against the oppressor. The deification process has led to a situation where attempts are being made to reduce Immanuel, the leader, who stood for anti-caste struggles to a caste-icon (Devendra icon), exclusively for the sanskritisation process of the educated middle class amongst Pallars who want to shed their Scheduled Caste tag and get rid of the caste name of Pallar.

Termed or addressed as Thiyagi (martyr) Puratchialar (rebel) Immanuel Sekaran, he is now called Immanuel Devendra. Chandrabose of TIP reiterates that Immanuel Memorial Day was originally observed as Veera Vanakka Naal, a day to remember/salute the martyr and was also called as Saathi Olippu Maaveerar Naal (Caste Annihilation Hero's Day). However in 2007, the educated Pallars appropriated the event and termed it as the 'guru puja' likening it to that of the Thevars. An event, which was seen as the symbol of Dalit assertion inviting Dalit leaders from as far as Punjab and Delhi is now reduced to an event to glorify the caste pride of Devendras. The visual signifiers, which had a strong presence of Dr Ambedkar's imagery, are on the wane, instead kings and historical figures from the past much like that of Thevars occupy the landscape. The event that usually attracted enthusiastic crowds from the other Dalit sub-castes of Adi-Dravidars and Arunthathiyars is no more the case.

The recent transformation and the propagation of sanskritised versions of caste history stating that we were of royal lineage by choosing such terms as Devendra/Mallars is conceptually nothing but a brainchild of Hindutva influence, says Chandrabose. Only the elite amongst the Pallars, who would not even form 10 per cent of the total population, receive it. Their rhetoric is not based on Ambedkar's concept of annihilation of caste but glorification of caste pride claiming that Devendras are actually twice born and erstwhile rulers of this land. They more than anything wish to project that they are not like Adi-dravidars and Arunthathiyars. This is indeed inimical to the Dalit cause and the practice of emancipatory politics.

Understanding Caste Performance?

The Immanuel Guru puja with its visual signifiers and highly gendered performance replicating contested forms of masculinity needs to be understood against the background of marginality. The feeling that they belong to an oppressed section and a yearning to move upward in the social ladder defines the performance.

In terms of understanding the occupation of public space, both physically and visually, we need to look at Ranciere (2004)'s work where he argues that the aesthetic is, in some sense, always political. Contextually speaking, however, I hope to suggest that in Dalit movements in particular, the political itself becomes primarily aesthetic. For Ranciere, who attends more pointedly to the fine arts than to the arts of political mobilisation, the 'distribution of the sensible' illuminates the complex relationships between politics and aesthetics. He calls the 'distribution of the sensible the system of self-evident facts of sense perception that simultaneously discloses the existence of something in common and the delimitations that define the respective parts and positions within it' (Ranciere 2004: 12). As Jain (2014: 150) clarifies: 'The distribution of sensible is intimately tied to the political, through the institution within specific structures of power of divisions between sayable and the unsayable, the visible and the invisible, the audible and inaudible.'

The distribution of the sensible reveals who can have a share in what is common to the community, based on what they do and where and when they do it (Jain 2014: 150). While for Ranciere, this temporally and spatially delimited action is one's occupation, roughly analogous to class, in the Tamil context, caste weighs heavily on sense perception. The distribution of who feels what in terms of a range of experiences, including but not limited to food consumption, the occupation of particular spaces, the enjoyment of particular clothing and jewellery, and the sight, smell and sound of deities and modes of worship, is oftentimes determined by caste. As a foil to these modes of deprivation, Dalit mobilisation is characterised by sensory intensity and even extravagance.

These rituals function as re-enactments of the past and acts of memory, but they are also attempts to refashion interpretations of the past, to shape memory and thus to construct social identity. They are in every sense collective representations. The occupation of space in the guru pujas, thus, not only constructs identities but also the possibilities of reproducing social differences through a metastasis of class, caste and spatial positions. 'If the policies of space allow for the disconnecting of locality and community', as De Neve (2006: 21) argues, 'it could allow as much for the reconnecting of identities and localities under particular circumstances'. The guru puja in the latter context could be seen as functioning as an important space that offers a challenge to local forms of dominance and seeks to contest the meanings and symbols attached to traditional forms of power exercised by Thevars.

In an effort to define how contestations over the appropriation of public space are played out, we can draw a parallel in the Western context to the transformation in the nature of public space through spectacles of inversion. In the European context, large public spaces were used by royalty to display their sovereign power through periodic spectacles; however, European history saw the transformation of these spaces through the increasing mobilisation of the urban poor (Kaviraj 1997: 95). Popular forces gradually came to use the spaces, which were used for spectacles of the state's authority and coercive power through military marches, assemblies and religious ceremonies in their own ways (Kaviraj 1997: 95). However, these public spaces for the subaltern classes who were on the other side of spectacles of power, started to hold marches and rallies of their own. These 'spectacles of inversion' showcased the power of the vulnerable, the victimised and the excluded. Taking this 'Spectacle of Inversion' concept, I argue that the annual Dalit mobilisation that happens as guru puja could be seen as inverting social dominance by replicating the very social idiom of caste and using it as a tool of political moblilisation to challenge established codes.

Talking about the political aspects of public space, Mitchell (1995: 115–116) says: 'Public space is a place within which a political movement can stake out the space that allows it to be seen.' This then enables social and political movements to represent themselves to the wider public. Thus, by claiming/reclaiming space in public and by creating public spaces, the social groups themselves become public. In the case of Thevar Guru puja, as a government-sponsored and recognised event, it becomes a legitimate space for the Thevars to display their domination and appropriation of public space. Immanuel's Guru puja is yet to be recognised by the state as a government-sponsored event; however, Dalits use the countercultural performance in public space as a 'representational' space to defy norms and take over the roads and public thoroughfares. Temporarily, at least, they install huge flex banners and various forms of imagery depicting their caste pride and leaders, which becomes crucial. Does such appropriation of public spaces provide us an understanding of how the established codes of dominance are being challenged? Does the event provide Dalits the space to represent their needs and desires to the state?

The logic of representation in guru pujas becomes critical in my project as a key argument as it remains significant both in terms of collective and individual actors as rights claiming entities to make their voices heard and indicate what their needs and desires are to both the state and also to other competitive groups. This aspect of historical struggle to claim equal rights over public spaces as a form of representation, therefore, is critical to our understanding of public space in terms of contestations between the castes, and the research project intends to look at those struggles and forms of representation. In this struggle, the development or often the radical claiming of a 'space of representation', a place in which groups and individuals can make themselves visible, becomes crucial. This then leads us to see whether the occupation of public space by Dalits could be seen as a representational one or not.

These forms of self-expression of the Dalits could be seen as a combination of both—defiance and complicity. Thus—as the key festival of the Pallars—Immanuel Sekaran Guru puja enables participants to occupy public spaces openly on the basis of their caste identities and cultural markers. As such, the event points towards a shift from the upper-caste hegemony over the streets in the public. Simultaneously, however, we have seen how an exclusionary emphasis has resulted in an erosion of an anti-caste Dalit identity in favour of more specific and Sanskritised caste identities. If Immanuel Guru puja becomes the vehicle for a hypermasculine performance of a particularist Pallar identity, then its capacity to challenge the dominant norms of caste society will be diluted. This then leaves us with a question of how even such attempts to challenge established codes of dominance result not only in reductionist tendencies, but also with the emergence of another form of dominance.

Notes

1. The term 'Thevar' is a caste title of the Mukkulathor caste in Tamil Nadu, constituting three distinct sub-castes of Kallar, Maravar and Agamudaiyars. Thevar is the popular reference term used to denote these castes. A Government Order to announce these sub-castes under the umbrella term of Thevars is pending since 1995.
2. Dalits are the members of the former untouchable castes. The Constitution refers to Scheduled Castes referring to those former-untouchable castes that are on a list of castes entitled to affirmative action. SC, however, excludes those who have converted out of Hinduism but otherwise experience discrimination. I use the term Dalit as it is more inclusive.
3. Shudras are the members of service providers belonging to the fourth category of the fourfold Varna division of the Hindu hierarchy which includes Brahmins (Priestly), Kshatriyas (Royal), Vaishyas (Trading). Shudras serve these castes.
4. I am grateful to the anonymous reviewer for this point.
5. In terms of caste-based demarcation, distancing between caste groups was a meticulously planned practice to avoid pollution. Practiced everywhere in India but crudest in Kerala where the number of paces had to be maintained between castes, and prohibition to enter village, roads leading to the temples and entering the temples (see Hutton 1963; Jeffrey 1974).
6. Immanuel Sekaran was a Pallar Dalit leader who fought against caste discrimination and dominance and was murdered in 1957.
7. Pasumpon Muthuramalinga Thevar was a prominent Tamil politician and Indian nationalist who is best known for mobilizing Thevars in Tamil Nadu – particularly in opposition to the Criminal Tribes Act – and for supporting Subhas Chandra Bose's Forward Bloc. He was Tamil state President of the All India Forward Bloc from 1948

when it became an independent party until his death. His mobilization of Thevars placed him in opposition to Immanuel Sekharan and he was arrested following Immanuel's murder but was later acquitted.
8. The All India Forward Bloc (AIFB) emerged in the late 1930s as a faction within the Indian National Congress led by Subhas Chandra Bose. It emerged as a recognized party after the Second World War with a loosely socialist programme and has contested elections since that point. In Tamil Nadu the party is largely associated with the Thevar caste.
9. Subhas Chandra Bose, fondly referred as Nethaji, was a national leader who formed the Indian National Army and believed in militarily fighting the British as against Mohandas Gandhi's approach of non-violence. He founded Forward Bloc, a political party, after resigning from Congress. Muthuramalinga Thevar was his lieutant in south India. The Thevars in Tamil Nadu use his image widely both for political and cultural purposes.
10. Memorialising as a social ritual forms an integral part of the political practice of Dalits in Tamil Nadu, the brutal murder of 44 Dalits mostly women and children in Keezhvenmani, Thanjavur, and murder of six Dalits in Melavalavu are remembered through erection of memorials and annual events. These form symbolic measures to remember anti-caste struggles. The erection of herostones as an ancient culture of Tamils could also be seen as a precursor.
11. Two days before the 2011 Immanuel Guru puja, a 16-year-old boy was murdered in a village called Pallapacheri alleging that he insulted Muthuramalinga Thevar through a graffitti depicting that he was a eunuch, the allegation was denied by the Pallars.

References

Anand, S. 2005. 'Politics, Tamil Cinema Eshtyle', *Outlook*, 30 May 2005. http://www.outlookindia.com/article.aspx?227523 (accessed 30 September 2013).
Beteille A. 1969. *Caste, Class and Power: Changing Patterns of Stratification in a Tanjore Village*. Delhi: Oxford University Press.
———. 1996. 'Caste in Contemporary India', in C.J. Fuller (ed.), *Caste Today* (pp. 150–179). Delhi: Oxford University Press.
Butler, Judith. 1993. *Bodies that Matter. On the Discursive Limits of Sex*. London and New York: Routledge.
Das, V. (ed.). 1990. 'Introduction', in *Mirrors of Violence: Communities, Riots and Survivors in South Asia* (pp. 1–37). Delhi: Oxford University Press.
Davis, S.G. 1986. *Parades and Power: Street Theatre in Nineteenth-Century Philadelphia*. Philadelphia: Temple University Press.
Davis, T. 1995. 'The Diversity of Queer Politics and the Redefinition of Sexual Identity and Community in Urban Spaces', in D. Bell and G. Valentine (eds), *Mapping Desire: Geographies of Sexualities* (pp. 284–303). New York and London: Routledge.
Deliege, R. 1992. 'Replication and Consensus: Untouchability, Caste and Ideology in India', *Man*, 27(1): 155–173.
De Neve, G. and Donner, H. (eds) 2006. 'Introduction', in *The Meaning of the Local: The Urban Neighbourhood in India* (pp. 1–21). London: Routledge.

Diamond, E. (ed.). 1996. 'Introduction', in *Performance and Cultural Politics* (pp. 1–12). New York: Routledge.

Freitag, S.B. 1989. *Collective Action and Community: Public Arenas and the Emergence of Communalism in North India*. Berkeley: University of California Press.

Goheen, P. 1993. 'The Ritual of the Streets in Mid-19th Century Toronto', *Environment and Planning: Society and Space* 11(1): 127–145.

Gooptu, N. 2001. *The Politics of the Urban Poor in Early Twentieth Century India*. Cambridge: Cambridge University Press.

Gorringe, H. 2010. 'Dalit Unity is Undermined', interview in *Frontline* 27(5), 27 February–27 March 2012.

Gough, K. 1981. *Rural Society in South East India*. Cambridge: Cambridge University Press.

Hansen, T.B. 2004. 'Politics as Permanent Performance: The Production of Political Authority in the Locality', in J. Zavos, A. Wyatt and V. Hewitt (eds), *The Politics of Cultural Mobilization in India* (pp. 19–36). New Delhi Oxford: Oxford University Press.

Hutton, J.H. 1963. *Caste in India: Its Nature, Function and Origins*. Bombay: Oxford University Press.

Jaffrelot, C. 1998. 'The Politics of Processions and Hindu Muslim Riots', in A. Basu and A. Kohli (eds), *Community Conflicts and the State in India*, pp. 58–92. Delhi: Oxford University Press.

Jain, K. 2014. 'The Handbag that Exploded', in P. Chatterjee, Tapati Guha Thakurta and Bodhisattva Kar (eds), *New Cultural Histories of India: Materiality and Practices* (pp. 139–179). Delhi: Oxford University Press.

Jaishankar, S. and Karthikeyan, D. 2011. 'Five Killed in Police Firing at Paramakudi', *The Hindu*, 12 September 2011. http://www.thehindu.com/news/national/tamil-nadu/five-killed-in-police-firing-at-paramakudi/article2444651.ece (accessed 21 August 2014).

Jeffery, R. 1974. 'The Social Origins of a Caste Association, 1875–1905: The Founding of the S.N.D.P. Yogam', *South Asia* 1(4): 39–59.

Karthikeyan, D., Rajangam, S. and Gorringe, H. 2012. 'Dalit Political Imagination and Replication in Contemporary Tamil Nadu', *Economic and Political Weekly* XLVII(36): 30–34.

Kaviraj, S. 1997. 'Filth and the Public Sphere: Concepts and Practices about Space in Calcutta', *Public Culture* 10(1): 83–113.

Kugelmass, J. 1994. *Masked Culture: The Greenwich Village Halloween Parade*. New York: Columbia University Press.

Lefebvre, H. 1991 [1974]. *The Production of Space*, translated by Donald Nicholson-Smith. Oxford: Blackwell.

Loynd, M. 2009. 'Understanding the Bahujan Samaj Prerna Kendra: Space, Place and Political Mobilisation', *Asian Studies Review* 33(4): 469–482.

Marston, S.A. 2002. 'Making Difference: Conflict over Irish Identity in the New York City St. Patrick's Day Parade', *Political Geography* 21(1): 373–392.

Martin, D.G. and Miller, B. 2003. 'Space and Contentious Politics', *Mobilization* 8(2): 143–156.

Mitchell, D. 1995. 'The End of Public Space? People's Park, Definitions of Public, and Democracy', *Annals of the Association of American Geographers* 85(1): 108–133.

Moffatt, M. 1979. *An Untouchable Community in South India: Structure and Consensus*. Princeton, NJ: Princeton University Press.

Pandey, G. 1990. *The Construction of Communalism in Colonial North India*. Delhi: Oxford University Press.

Pandian, M.S.S. 2000. 'Dalit Assertion in Tamil Nadu: An Explanatory note', *Journal of Indian School of Political Economy* 12(3 and 4): 501–517.
———. 2002. 'One Step Outside Modernity', *Economic and Political Weekly* 37(8): 1735–1741.
Pandian, A. 2007. *Crooked Stalks: Cultivating Virtue in South India*. Durham NC: Duke University Press.
Rajadurai, S.V. and Geetha, V. 1996. 'DMK Hegemony: The Cultural Limits to Political Consensus', in T.V. Satyamurthy (ed.), *Social Change and Political Discourse in India* (pp. 550–586). New Delhi: Oxford University Press.
Ramaiah, A. 2007. 'Untouchability and Inter-caste Relations in Rural India: The Case of Southern Tamil Villages', *Journal of Religious Culture* 70 (2004): 1–13.
Ranciere, J. 2004. *The Politics of Aesthetics: The Distribution of the Sensible*, edited and translated by Gabriel Rockhill. London and New York: Continuum.
Schechner, R. 1993. *The Future of Ritual: Writings on Culture and Performance*. London: Routledge.
van der Veer, P. 1996. 'Riots and Rituals: The Construction of Violence and Public Space in Hindu Nationalism', in Paul R. Brass (ed.), *Riots and Pogroms* (pp. 154–176). New York/London: Macmillan Press.
Zavos J., Wyatt, A. and Hewitt, V. 2004. 'Deconstructing the Nation: Politics and Cultural Mobilization in India', in J. Zavos, A. Wyatt and V. Hewitt (eds), *The Politics of Cultural Mobilization in India* (pp. 197–215). New Delhi, Oxford: Oxford University Press.

9

Institutionalising Peace? Mohalla Committees in Contemporary Mumbai[1]

Qudsiya Contractor

Introduction

As we sat in a corner of a local non-governmental organisation (NGO) office in Shivaji Nagar, a predominantly Muslim *basti* locality in suburban Mumbai, Naeem[2] narrated his memories of experiencing the communal violence after the Babri Masjid was demolished in Ayodhya on 6 December 1992. Shivaji Nagar was reportedly one of the major sites of violence in the city following the demolition of the mosque.[3] It was one of the few areas which witnessed acts of Muslim aggression, where groups of protesting Muslims attacked state property as well as the police force. The local police engaged in the destruction of property—numerous homes, a local mosque, businesses and vehicles owned by Muslims were set on fire and they open fired on anyone trying to put out the fire or rescue trapped individuals ([Justice] Srikrishna 1998, Engineer 1995). Muslim men and youth were especially targeted and picked up by the police on the slightest pretext with family members left uninformed about their whereabouts. Naeem is a member of the local *mohalla* (neighbourhood or locality) committee, a quasi-state institution set up all across Mumbai city after the bomb blasts on 12 March 1993 following months of communal violence in December 1992 and January 1993. These were set up to serve as an interface between the city's police and members of the public in an attempt to foster communal harmony, engage in conflict management and promote tolerance through peaceful coexistence. The daily activities at the office continued in the background as we spoke as though oblivious of the interview in session. Naeem, however, was careful to speak softly especially when he expressed his disillusionment with the state's discourse of peace and communal harmony at a time when events such as the 1992–1993 communal violence welled up feelings of intense hatred. He elucidated,

> People were barging into our homes, throwing stones at us, setting our homes on fire. In the midst of all this, instead of just getting killed it is better to fight back and then die. [...] When there is no such thing like peace, what is the point of going around teaching people let's maintain peace, let's maintain peace,

Although well-accustomed to the peace 'jargon' of NGOs, he still expresses his misgivings about how effective this discourse is in actual situations of violence. Despite his active membership in the local mohalla committee, he is critical of the state's effectiveness in maintaining peace and more importantly delivering justice to Muslims, who are left to protect themselves during violent conflicts.[4]

In this chapter, I engage with the mainstream notions of reconciliation as a way of healing the ruptured social fabric of Mumbai city (then referred to as Bombay) manifested in its segregated landscape after the communal violence that followed the demolition of the Babri Masjid in 1992–1993. The maintenance of peace and communal harmony was perceived as one of the main outcomes of such reconciliation, especially in the wake of the bomb blasts that shook the city in March 1993 allegedly masterminded by Dawood Ibrahim, a noted member of Mumbai's notorious underworld to avenge the violent aftermath of the Ayodhya-based mosque demolition by Hindu extremists. The Srikrishna Commission (1998) report indicted several police officers across the ranks of either actively participating in anti-Muslim violence or not taking the desired action to save Muslim lives. The city's police force on its part faced public criticism from the media and the city's intelligentsia for its partisan (anti-Muslim) conduct during the violence that ravaged the city. Mohalla committees were formed through a concerted effort towards a collaboration between concerned individuals, sensitive police leadership and local representatives with the aim to forge

Institutionalising Peace? 203

an amicable relationship between the local police establishment and neighbourhoods they considered 'sensitive' post-1992–1993 from a 'law and order' point of view. These committees have widely been understood as sites of inclusion in the larger interest of maintaining peace and communal harmony (Mehta and Chatterji 2007; Sharma 2000; Thakkar 2004). These were envisaged to act as effective problem-solving channels that would enable the law enforcers to garner the cooperation of local neighbourhood representatives in addressing a situation of conflict through negotiation and dialogue rather than the use of force and violence. This chapter explores the workings of mohalla committees instituted post-riots, as an associational engagement between the state (through the police force), non-governmental organisations (NGOs) and the city's 'Muslim public'. By focusing on mohalla committees as sites for a state-societal interface, this chapter seeks to understand how institutionalised efforts at negotiating everyday peace are experienced by Muslims at a neighbourhood level. The production and maintenance of peace though local interaction is not insulated from national events or circumstances, very much like violence in local contexts is not entirely local but has to be understood within the larger sociopolitical context.[5] Through its everyday functioning in Shivaji Nagar, a predominantly Muslim *basti*, or locality, situated in suburban Mumbai, this chapter explores how mohalla committees as an effort towards institutionalising peace stand today. How do local Muslims experience this process of institutionalisation? As instruments of the state, mohalla committees have been likened to state commissions of inquiry into the aftermath of the demolition, based on which the state engaged in the production of legitimacy by engaging in public spectacles meant to reinstate the sublime dimensions of the state—fairness, reasonableness, tolerance and justice to its preferred audience—the educated middle class (Hansen 2001b). In other contexts, such as that of civil strife, it has been observed that grievances that drive such conflicts are altered rather than substantially transformed through elite-negotiated transitions (Stokke 2009). This chapter explores the workings of the mohalla committee in Shivaji Nagar to highlight that the labour in maintaining everyday peace is mainly the burden of local Muslim representatives that may or may not effectively diffuse communal tensions. I argue that these efforts offer a façade of inclusion in a societal context where communal politics and the mainstream disgust against Muslims continues unabated, reinforcing representations of 'Muslim' areas like Shivaji Nagar as culturally deviant (at times anti-national) urban 'disorders' that need to be comprehended and dealt with by the state.

In the following four sections, the chapter critically engages with key perspectives on the dynamics of violence and peace-making in the Indian context. It then traces the evolution of Mumbai's mohalla committees, describing their functioning and philosophy in the present context. In the third section, the chapter illustrates the workings of the mohalla committee in Shivaji Nagar and the challenges it faces in negotiating non-violence. In the concluding section, it critically examines the politics of peace-making since mohalla committees seem to function more as sites for negotiating non-violence for the city's Muslims rather than sites of inclusion.

Between Violence and Fragile Peace

The existing work on Hindu–Muslim violence has long emphasised the role that political processes play in creating communal tensions and provoking violence (Brass 2003; Engineer 1995; Hansen 2001a; Tambiah 1996). Brass's (2003) study explains that Hindu–Muslim violence can hardly be attributed to spontaneity, rather their persistence can be attributed to 'institutionalised riot-systems' that have a close association to electoral competition. Brass (2003: 378) argues that dramatic productions of violence that seem spontaneous can only occur 'because the scene has been prepared with numerous rehearsals marked by tension, rumours and provocations in which the signals that an outbreak is about to occur and that the time for participation has arrived have been made clear'. Wilkinson (2004), in a similar vein, argues that electoral incentives at two levels—the local constituency level and the level of government that controls the police—interact to determine both where and when ethnic violence against minorities will occur, and, more important, whether the state will choose to intervene to stop it.

Recent research highlights that riot politics is an integral part of a larger game of capturing (state) resources and developing the capacity to facilitate the interaction between state institutions and citizens. In an insightful ethnography of riot hit Ahmedabad in 2002, Berenschot

(2011: 36) demonstrates how in order to understand recurring outbursts of communal violence, attention needs to be paid not only to the shifting relations between communities, but also to how the pattern of interactions between the political elites, their supporters and local residents of a single community change over time taking into account the development of state institutions, economic shifts and political developments. Others have pointed out that the relationship between infra-power and urban vulnerability in a context of inadequate provision of security by the state is such that it incentivises physical perpetration of violence—seen as an urban survival strategy for the more vulnerable sections of society (Gupte 2012; Sen 2008). As ethnographies of everyday mediation of political actors between state and society (Berenschot 2011), political mobilisation (Brass 2003; Hansen 2001a; Sen 2008) and neighbourhood level urban vulnerability (Gupte 2012) contribute to our understanding of communal violence, there still is hardly any exploration into how everyday peace and reconciliation is negotiated.

A significant contribution to our understanding of how some Indian cities manage to remain free from violence even in instances of seemingly powerful external shocks is Varshney's (2002) study of six violent and relatively non-violent cities. He argues that violence is less likely in cities with strong and active inter-ethnic associations than in those with little civic engagement. He makes a distinction between associational and quotidian (or everyday) forms of civic engagements, maintaining that both 'if robust, promote peace' and the absence (or weakness) of these 'open up a space for communal violence', adding that the presence of the former is sturdier than everyday engagements. Furthermore, inter-ethnic engagement in which Hindus and Muslims cooperate, he argues, can prevent communal violence by preventing 'exogenous shocks' from creating local tensions, hence, maintaining 'communal peace'. Varshney's (2002) study brings attention to the role of civil society institutions making a distinction between those that are non-state as opposed to those that are anti-state, where the presence of the former plays a significant role in maintaining peace. Where Varshney limits his analysis to civic engagement leaving out the political context, in creating an environment for maintaining peace, or encouraging violence, Brass (2003) and Wilkinson (2004) attribute Hindu–Muslim violence to an institutionalised by-product of the political system seemingly static and, hence, endemic. If one were to consider the existence of inter-ethnic engagements as a sign of a more active cultural integration of marginalised minorities into the mainstream public sphere, Varshney's thesis makes a significant contribution towards our understanding of how peace can be maintained in a multicultural yet deeply hierarchical society such as ours. However, the distinction Varshney makes between ethnic conflicts, which he posits as natural in multicultural societies as opposed to ethnic violence, that he urges us to address as a matter of concern, seem far too simplistic.

World over, there have been several attempts at making peace in the aftermath of highly politicised and intense civic strife such as in Nepal, Sri Lanka, South Africa and Ireland, to name a few. The experiences through these attempts continue to highlight the complexity of reconciliation and peace-making and how it is deeply embedded in the same societal processes that throw up situations of violent conflict, involving ethnic, racial, linguistic and religious groups. In the case of post-apartheid South Africa, the Truth and Reconciliation Commission (TRC) resulted in the setting up of peace committees in several cities with an objective to enhance access to justice and safety. Roche (2002) argues that these peace committees display the core elements of restorative justice derived from the TRC and are largely effective owing to their independence from the formal criminal justice system, their handling of a wide range of offences (from apparently trivial disturbances through to the most serious crimes) and their attempts to address the structural conditions that underlie offending. Others have, however, observed that the TRC's restorative justice approach to healing the nation had little effect on popular ideas of justice as retribution and rather individualised victims of apartheid, failing to move beyond a formal acknowledgement of apartheid as a 'crime against humanity' against entire communities for ethnic and racial policing and cleansing (Mamdani 2002; Wilson 2001). Closer to home, conflicts in Nepal and Sri Lanka have been largely represented either as challenges to urban security or global security threats seeking justification for elitist interventions through localised institutions (Gupte and Bogati 2014; Odendaal and Olivier 2008; Stokke 2009). Such a representation finds resonance in the Indian state's response to violent attacks claimed by Islamic militant groups justifying the need to address these within a framework of a threat to national security, linking it to global security threats rather than addressing issues of deprivation and exclusion within.

City-based comparisons, such as those made by Varshney (2002), thus, fail to give us a nuanced picture of how the dynamism of local contexts contributes not just to the endemic nature of Hindu-Muslim conflict but also to routine negotiations between the two communities. Williams (2013) warns us against a tendency for mainstream discourses to imagine situations of peace as unchanging and as the aftermath or absence of violence, stressing the need to understand peace as a process and deeply embedded within political contexts. Through the ethnography of Hindu–Muslim relations in the silk sari industry of Varanasi, she brings focus to the interactive work of discourse and action in the construction and continuation of everyday peace. More significantly, her study shows how within a Hindu-dominated economic and political milieu, coercion and consent often bound Muslims into economic relationships with more powerful traders. Hence, notions of everyday peace, as Williams (2013) argues, are ultimately contingent on maintaining distinctions, reproducing boundaries and knowing one's place.

A focus on the local can provide us key insights into how peace for Muslims is not just fragile but also subversive, turning them into tamed subjects. As a microcosm site, state-NGO collaborations like mohalla committees help us understand why the accommodation of Muslim voices in achieving justice and everyday peace post-violence remains a challenge.

The next section traces the genesis of mohalla committees as an attempt at reconciliation in Mumbai post-1992–1993. Mohalla committees can be seen as a site for the inclusion of the city's Muslim voice through an institutional response to addressing communal violence. The section also describes the functioning, activities and challenges facing mohalla committees and their limitations for Muslims.

Mumbai's Mohalla Committees

Genesis

The *Ram Janmabhoomi* agitation spearheaded by the BJP and the subsequent demolition of the Babri Masjid in Ayodhya, Uttar Pradesh by *karsevaks*[6] in December 1992 remains a landmark in the communalisation of politics in India. Soon after the demolition, Muslim protestors took to the streets across the country. In Bombay (as it was known then), angry Muslims engaged in public protests that turned violent targeting state transport and in certain areas temples too. The city burned in a violent communal frenzy that was fuelled by the Shiv Sena, a regional ethno-nationalist party. While the police shot at and arrested Muslim demonstrators, the Shiv Sena was allowed to conduct large public celebrations of the demolition.[7] The party continued with their political demonstrations across the city by organising mass prayers and *maha aartis* as a show of strength against Muslims and to boost the confidence of Hindus (Hansen 2001a). The state government ruled by the Congress party remained mere onlookers and took no action, supposedly fearing a Hindu backlash. The city's police force participated in the violence, openly assaulting Muslims alongside the rioting Shiv *sainiks*. Though there are several estimations of the number of deaths by the media, activist groups, inquiry commissions and the state (which provided the most conservative figures), the toll could have been around a thousand and many more injured. Nearly 150,000 Muslims left the city and another 100,000 took shelter in refugee camps set up in Muslim areas across the city (Indian People's Human Rights Tribunal 1994, Engineer 1995, Srikrishna Commission Report 1998).

F.T. Khorakiwala, a Muslim businessman who was appointed the Sheriff of Mumbai towards the end of December 1992, with a team of volunteers visited Bhiwandi[8] to study 'why the town with a background in communal riots had remained peaceful and not gone up in flames while Mumbai burned' (Barve 2003: 169). The team studied Bhiwandi's mohalla samitis, an experiment started by the Deputy Commissioner of Police, Suresh Khopade, during his tenure. Bhiwandi had seen one of the worst incidents of communal violence in 1984.[9] In his three-year term since June 1988, Khopade worked towards building bridges between Hindus and Muslims motivating committed individuals from both communities to work together on common issues of concern in their neighbourhoods. This was done through the involvement of the police in mohalla samitis which continue to function even after Khopade completed his tenure. This played a significant role in transforming Bhiwandi from a town whose capacity for rioting had become legendary to one that could meticulously work for and keep communal peace, even in the worst times as between 1988 and 1993 (Varshney 2002).

In the light of the severe criticism that the Congress government had faced due to the gross misconduct of the police during the 1992–1993 communal violence and its inability to bring the perpetrators to justice, the then Governor of Maharashtra, P.C. Alexander invited the city's prominent citizens to appoint a peace committee that included F.T. Khorakiwala and Sushobha Barve, a social worker involved in post-violence relief work. The Governor's peace committee was meant to be a think-tank to address the fear amongst citizens of another bout of violence and to restore the city's everyday routines, but unfortunately survived only one meeting. During the meeting, there were some key suggestions made by those present to address the situation at hand, and Khorakiwala spoke of the need to set up mohalla committees in Mumbai, on the pattern of Bhiwandi town. He informed the group that a team had prepared such a plan for Mumbai (Barve 2003). Despite the untimely demise of the Governor's peace committee, individuals at the meeting like many others across the city undertook their own efforts at finding solutions for reconciliation.

Immediately afterwards, on 12 March 1993, a series of 13 bomb blasts shook the city within a span of two hours claiming 250 lives and leaving 700 injured. These blasts took place in hotels, banks and office buildings in the predominantly Hindu business localities of the city as well as other significant landmarks such as the Bombay Stock Exchange building, the regional passport office and Air-India building. In the face of rising violence, F.T. Khorakiwala and his team were fairly convinced that an initiative such as that in Bhiwandi could be adapted well in Mumbai, and with a nod from the Chief Minister, mohalla committees were launched in four police stations of the city to begin with, in consultation with the then police commissioner of Mumbai—Jogeshwari, Mahim, Ghatkopar and Colaba. Within six months, before Khorakiwala's term was over, mohalla committees were started throughout the city (Barve 2003). It was around this time that F.T. Khorakiwala happened to meet Julio Ribeiro, the former director-general of police in Punjab who had just returned from Romania completing his term as India's ambassador at a social event and requested him to join this effort. Mr. Ribeiro, who was at the time on the lookout for some voluntary engagement with the police force, was happy to take this up. The very next day, Julio Ribeiro was invited to a meeting by Kekoo Gandhy, an eminent Parsi art gallery owner and art connoisseur, where Sushobha Barve, was also present.

> I was asked if I could get associated so that the police connection would be there because they said without a police connection it is difficult to get the police involved and without police involvement this work of getting the communities together will be lost. So I agreed immediately and then it was decided [...] that Sushobha [Barve] and I should both go and meet the present police commissioner Satish Sahney. [...] When we went he was most enthusiastic. (Interview with Julio Ribeiro, Chairman Mohalla Committee Movement Trust, 10 June 2014)

According to Barve (2003), though there was an attempt to follow the Bhiwandi model, the significant difference was that in Bhiwandi, the intervention took place several years after the incident had taken place, which gave people the time to recover. In Mumbai, the intervention had begun almost immediately and the recent bomb blasts had added another dimension to an already tense situation. Barve who was involved in relief work after the violence in various parts of the city was of the opinion that an initiative of this nature would only work if there could be an effort at reconciliation to build trust and confidence through a dialogue between the city's Muslims and the police. With Ribeiro and Barve having first hand experiences with the 1984 anti-Sikh riots and its aftermath, they were more concerned about the parallels that event had with the 1992–1993 violence, especially the issues of terrorism and separatism and how to mitigate them (Barve 2003). The groundwork for the mohalla committee first began in Mahim, where those accused of the bomb blasts were arrested after a series of combing operations and preventive arrests by the police. Mahim was identified by the team as an ideal place to begin the process of reconciliation through several visits and meetings with local Muslims to convince them of a need for a platform for regular dialogue with the local police to diffuse communal tensions in the area and prevent incidences of large-scale violence in the future. Several individuals the team met were suspicious of the agenda of the police and did not wish to be associated with any effort that involved the police. There were also others who were convinced and helped the team to convince more individuals to join in.

Institutionalising Peace? 211

Post-1992–1993, one of the main preoccupations of the state was to engage in the policing of Muslim localities, especially in the light of the bomb blasts that took place in March 1993 that were allegedly carried out by Dawood Ibrahim, don of a Mumbai-based international crime syndicate as a response to the toll on the city's Muslims. There was a perception that the 1992–1993 violence severed the relationship of the city's police force with its Muslim 'informers', which it had nurtured all these years in order to keep a close watch on the city's much fabled criminal underbelly situated in its Muslim working class neighbourhoods. As Satish Sahney took over as Commissioner of Police, the first anniversary of the riots was approaching and his priority was to do everything possible to not just prevent a recurrence of the communal flare-up but also prove that the police could control a violent situation without any human rights violations. Hence, what also ensured the participation of the police force was the involvement of the leadership at the time that was concerned about improving the image of the city's police force and its functioning, mainly assuring the middle and upper classes so that an incident like the bomb blasts could be prevented. Furthermore, to ascertain that a truce could be achieved through closer contact with the Muslim 'public' through a formalised channel of communication with the police.

> The atmosphere of the city was completely vitiated. Now in a city of the size of Mumbai if one community doesn't trust the other community, which is sizeable in number...the Muslim population in Mumbai is considerable. If the two major communities do not trust each other and both do not trust the law enforcement agency then it is a very bad situation. That was the situation I inherited on 16th November 1993. [...] Both Hindus and Muslims had lost their faith in police not just the Muslims. Hence it was a greater concern. But an even greater concern was you cannot always establish peace through force...if you want to have peace by generating a sense of fear then you declare Marshall law. Then your human rights and everything goes down the drain. (Interview with Satish Sahney, Retired Mumbai Police Commissioner, 2 June 2014)

Another challenge was involving the lower echelons of the police force in a process of dialogue, which certainly exposed them to sharp criticisms from the Muslim middle class with whom they eventually interacted during the initial meetings. Once Satish Sahney readily agreed to be part of the initiative, the rest of the force had no choice but to follow suit.

> With the police it is a very simple story...if the commissioner of police is interested and involved and commissioner is himself going to those places...each mohalla committee he goes himself and he goes openly in his uniform and his official car and sits in a school or a *chawdi* and listens to the people the message goes down right to the constable. (Interview with Satish Sahney, Retired Mumbai Police Commissioner, 2 June 2014)

The formal involvement of the police began through a meeting at a neutral location in Mahim, between Sahney and an invited group of a dozen of the city's Muslim intelligentsia and middle class, including doctors, journalists, teachers, businessmen and human rights activists who spoke of human rights violations during the 1992–1993 violence and bomb blast investigations with concrete evidence, expressing their resentment, anger and hurt (Barve 2003).

> One of the main grievances of women which was discussed was that whenever there was a communal tension, the police indiscriminately picked up only young Muslim men from the age group of 15–25. They were brought to the police station kept there...no cases were made out, no registering was done, nothing. So the police in return said that this will not happen and it stopped immediately. Unless there is evidence or the person is a known criminal don't touch every young man because he is a Muslim. (Interview with Satish Sahney, Retired Mumbai Police Commissioner, 2 June 2014)

Sushobha Barve was largely involved in garnering neighbourhood support and identifying possible individuals who were willing to volunteer to be on the mohalla committees. Satish Sahney and Julio Ribeiro were present at several of the initial meetings that were held at neutral locations such as schools and *dargahs*, where a safe environment could be created for an open dialogue between the police and local residents. These meetings were attended only by Muslims, where they narrated incidences of violence and police misconduct in great detail. These meetings went on for hours and in certain cases for two days with more people joining in. A few of those who had been arrested on suspicion of the serial bomb blasts and were later released were also present in the meetings. In certain cases, the local police were kept out of these meetings since the hostility against them ran very high (Barve 2003). Though most of those directly affected by the violence belonged to the poorer sections of the Muslim community, they remained largely excluded from these initial processes of dialogue. The discussions in the meetings were centred on police excesses during

Institutionalising Peace? 213

the violence and its conduct during the investigations of the bomb blasts. There was an obvious gap in the way the police and the city's Muslims perceived the situation. The speakers wanted justice. They wanted to know what was being done about those who had committed serious criminal acts. The police had shown their bias against the community by putting 200 Muslims under TADA in the bomb blasts case but had failed to show similar zeal in the riot cases, they said:

> At one stage Sahney tried to explain the difference between acts of violence during a riot and a serial blasts conspiracy that was hatched along with outside forces. The latter act was clearly anti-national. At this there was pandemonium in the room. [...] One man standing in the last row stood up and asked Sahney, 'Sir, you explained to us why the serial bomb blasts were an anti-national act and a conspiracy. I accept it. But please tell us if the demolition of the Babri Masjid was an anti-national act and a conspiracy that was planned, rehearsed and executed. What is the police doing about this?' (Sushobha Barve, in *Healing Streams* [Barve 2003: 179])

Meetings with Hindus were also attempted separately in Mahim and Dongri where they were in minority. Unlike the meeting with Hindus in Dongri that went fairly smoothly and was even attended by local politicians, the meeting in Mahim did not materialise since the pressures of moving on to other areas took priority and, hence, the team never succeeded in creating a strong local team that facilitated greater interaction amongst Mahim's diverse communities (Barve 2003).

The initial plan was to set up mohalla committees in each police station of Mumbai city and a beat committee for each of the beat posts assigned to a police station. The team planned to select 10 to 15 people representing the diversity in each locality for each beat committee. The aim was to get as many people as possible to volunteer for this effort. Initiating mohalla committees in Mahim and Dongri proved to be most challenging for the team, while the others followed suit quite smoothly. When the committees were set up, they mainly recruited members from the Muslim middle classes. Many of the members were the people who were highly respected in the locality and the individuals who were often involved in volunteer work and accustomed to being in close contact with state institutions. Between 1994 and 1995, 22 mohalla committees were set-up in most predominantly Muslim suburbs in the city (Barve 2003).

Present Form

After Shiv Sena's electoral victory in 1995, R.D. Tyagi, was appointed as the city's new police commissioner to succeed Satish Sahney. Tyagi, a former joint commissioner, was indicted in the Suleman Usman Bakery killings on 9 January 1993 by the Srikrishna Commission. He instituted a parallel mohalla committee with a mandatory police presence in its functioning and also included local politicians. In order to safeguard the original mohalla committee's independent and non-sectarian functioning, the Mohalla Committee Movement Trust (MCMT) was formed in 1996. Its purpose was to give these mohalla committees an identity independent from the police administration and also to bring in funding to enable the smooth functioning of the committees that had been formed across the city. The MCMT is now a registered charitable trust with its stated objectives to 'promote communal harmony, national integration, unity and peace amongst citizens of India and more particularly in greater Mumbai [...] and the advancement of national integration and patriotism'[10]. The trustee membership has undergone several changes over the years and the present office bearers comprise mainly retired government officials, mostly religious minorities.[11] As of today, with a total of 93 police stations across the city, only 24, that is, nearly one-third have active mohalla committees, most of which happen to be in Muslim localities. The committees comprise individual volunteers who are respected in the neighbourhood and those who can offer their time and have the courage to help in situations of crisis. Members must also have no affiliations to political parties or a criminal record. Each committee has a facilitator who is expected to be 'vigilant for signs of communal tension'[12] and acts as a link between the local police station, the neighbourhood and other facilitators across the city. The facilitator convenes a meeting of all other members within the neighbourhood. Local police officers are at times invited to attend these meetings. Each mohalla committee facilitator is expected to attend a monthly meeting organised by the MCMT coordinator and attended by the chairman. The trustees and chairman play advisory roles and mainly provide assistance for a smooth collaboration with the police force. The mohalla committees function entirely on the spirit of volunteerism on part of the citizen members. The committees do not have a formalised mode of day-to-day functioning or conflict resolution. The nature of its work heavily depends upon the citizen members involved, especially the facilitators.

Facilitators and members are from diverse religious backgrounds and are mainly professionals such as lawyers, doctors, social workers, school teachers, and also small businessmen, auto rickshaw drivers and housewives. Today, several facilitators with the mohalla committees have been involved with it right from its inception. Several of them were already involved in some voluntary work in their respective neighbourhoods, especially in the relief camps post 1992–1993 and found mohalla committees a relevant platform to take this work further as well as connect with others doing similar work in other parts of the city. For some, the 1992–1993 violence was a realisation that the social worlds of the city's Hindus and Muslims were deeply segregated and they used mohalla committees as a platform to bridge this gap by observing religio-cultural festivals together, recreating a historiography of local communal harmony and creating visual media on communal amity.[13] Through the work of mohalla committees, facilitators have been able to address communal tensions within their neighbourhoods and localise them, preventing them from spreading to other areas. The involvement and cooperation of the police in their work keeps changing based on the equation each facilitator has with the police personnel stationed there. In recent times, incidences involving the celebration of religious festivals, conflicts between supporters of political rivals or intra-religious sects or factions, desecration of religious symbols, conflict over space for places of worship, inter-religious love and marriage have been addressed and resolved by mohalla committee facilitators within their neighbourhoods.

Over the years, the activities of the MCMT have been considerably diversified to initiating community-based programmes on women's empowerment (such as women's grievance redressal cells addressing domestic violence) to subsidised vocational training (such as tailoring and computer training classes) and addressing civic issues such as sanitation and garbage disposal, especially in Muslim localities. The MCMT organises several activities annually to foster the message of communal harmony such as inter-community celebration of religious festivals, annual poster and essay competitions for school children and the 'Cricket for Peace' tournament, which has gained substantial popularity. The 'Cricket for Peace' tournament is an annual event organised by the mohalla committees for young men (below 21 years of age) and policemen at the neighbourhood level all across the city since 1995. The Mumbai police force makes an official announcement of the tournament annually and subsequently teams are formed based on the jurisdiction of each police station where mohalla committees exist from which players are selected by local policemen and mohalla committee members. Each team has to adhere to guidelines set by the MCMT to qualify for the tournament—out of the 16 players, four must belong to any religious minority community but should preferably be Muslims. In the playing 11, the team should include at least two players from minority communities and one player must be a policeman from the local police station. Once the teams have been selected, they are briefed about the history, objectives and functioning of mohalla committees. Matches are conducted in open spaces and grounds within the neighborhoods, which ensure that local audiences are exposed to the work and ideology of the mohalla committees. In reality, these neighbourhood events hardly attract much of an audience apart from a few curious onlookers and passers-by. The winning team of the tournament receives a trophy and prize money from the commissioner of police or a local celebrity at an event organised by the MCMT. Police officers participate with enthusiasm and find this annual tournament a de-stressing exercise often personally financing prizes for individual players. Through the 'Cricket for Peace' tournament, the MCMT aims to create a space for a non-threatening, friendly interaction with local policemen and the involvement of young men in peace-making. Though there have been a few instances where these young cricketers have been involved in defusing communal tensions in their neighborhoods, there is a need to study how such initiatives impact the attitude of the police force towards Muslim localities in particular and religious minorities in general, especially in a scenario where the social distance between the two is as wide as ever.[14] As a state-NGO collaboration, mohalla committees must tread the delicate balance of an ideological allegiance to the state's commitment to justice and fairness as well as maintaining 'order'. Their emphasis on communal harmony rather than retributive justice is visible in one of their most popular poster campaigns. This shows four young boys dressed as a Hindu Brahmin, a Muslim (in a sherwani and topi), a Sikh (in a turban and a festive looking *kurta*) and a Christian (wearing a cross) with a caption that reads 'we are one' (*hum sab ek hain*). Through masculine public rituals like 'cricket for peace', mohalla committees engage in the construction of state benevolence in which creating an image of the police as a trustworthy neighbourhood watch-dog as opposed to its anti-Muslim image plays a central role. On the other hand, their near exclusive presence in Muslim localities demonstrates that Muslim localities tend to be understood and culturally represented in a manner that renders them susceptible to irrationality and communal passions that need stringent policing and surveillance. The next section explores the workings of the mohalla committees at the neighbourhood level in Shivaji Nagar to highlight that the labour in maintaining everyday peace is mainly the burden of local Muslim representatives that may or may not effectively defuse communal tensions.

Fragile Peace and Local Negotiations for Non-violence

Shivaji Nagar is located in an industrial suburb at the outskirts of the island city of Mumbai. It is situated on the city's oldest and largest garbage dumping ground subjecting it to the worst living conditions. It has a population of approximately 600,000 of which Muslims constitute more than two-thirds, while the rest comprise Dalits, Christians and migrants from out of Maharashtra.[15] The city's poorest reside here and the area lacks even the most basic civic amenities such as water supply and sanitation.[16] Shivaji Nagar was also one of the most gruesome examples of police repression in the city during the 1992–1993 violence.[17] Several Muslim residents of Shivaji Nagar recounted details of the initial days of violent conflict, narrating personal stories of loss and describing the experience of living in fear. Nearly all recollections by Muslims described the inaction and apathy of the state. Like most affected areas in the city, most of the violence occurred here in the first few days following the demolition. According to the Srikrishna Commission's findings unlike in other areas such as Nagpada, Pydhoni and Dharavi, the 'acts of Muslim aggression' here were a spontaneous disorganised reaction, which commenced as peaceful protest, but soon degenerated into riots. During the second phase of violence in 1993, Shivaji Nagar remained relatively calm. Local residents remember this as a conflict between the police and Muslims rather than Hindus and Muslims. The evidence presented before the Srikrishna Commission (1998) pointed towards a nexus between the local police and the Shiv Sena. The fact that the city's police force was overwhelmingly Hindu also became obvious after the 1992–1993 violence. Furthermore, it has been noted that its ranks are recruited from the social groups and caste communities from which the Shiv Sena's masculine Hindu chauvinism has also emerged (Hansen 2001a).

In Shivaji Nagar, Naeem (introduced earlier in this chapter) and his family were amongst those who suffered huge losses during the 1992–1993 violence. His maternal uncle, who is married to a Hindu woman, was specifically targeted during the violence. His house and workshop were looted and set ablaze. His uncle's family lost all their belongings and narrowly escaped death when the mob attacked. Naeem's younger brother who was 17 years old at the time was one of the many Muslim boys and men who were arrested by the police while he was pelting stones at the attackers. His brother was in jail for the next six months till his case proceeded in a fast-track court owing to his juvenile status. He was charged under IPC section 295A a non-bailable offence meant for 'deliberate and malicious acts, intended to outrage religious feelings or any class by insulting its religion or religious beliefs' which is punishable with 'imprisonment of up to three years or a fine or both'. He was eventually released on the payment of a fine that was paid by a local *jamaat*.

The state engaged in the systematic erasure of brutalities faced by Muslims during the violence. Several cases have been classified as 'A summary' citing insufficient evidence in spite of witnesses for several such cases and many others were not even registered by the police.[18] In the memorandum of action taken by the Shiv Sena–BJP government in 1995 to the report of the Srikrishna Commission, they denied the police having made any excesses or specifically targeting Muslims and maintained that the police was largely secular and impartial.[19] Police action was justified in the name of self-protection and security in an area that was labelled by the mainstream media as notoriously criminal. After the 1992–1993 violence, the policing machinery in Muslim localities all across the city expanded considerably in the next four to five years as was also the case in Shivaji Nagar. At the time of violence, Shivaji Nagar was under the jurisdiction of the Deonar police station that was located at quite a distance from it.

There was neither a police station nor a police beat in the vicinity. After the violence, a police station was built right at the entrance of Shivaji Nagar. Five police beat *chowkies* or outposts were constructed within the area. Despite their ominous presence, most of these remain closed today though a police van with 6–8 police constables constantly patrols the area. There are police outposts located in public spaces like market places either in close proximity to Hindu temples or have been named after them. One of the police outposts situated on the main access road into Shivaji Nagar is located right in front of the local Shiv Sena *shakha*.[20]

As was seen in other Muslim localities of the city, the state engaged in greater policing and surveillance in Shivaji Nagar but played a minimal role in relief or reconciliation. Nearly all of the organised relief and rehabilitation work post-violence was carried out by non-state actors in the area. Local *jamaats* and mosques set up relief camps in the area. Apart from their own efforts at providing food and temporary shelter, they also served as networks for the distribution of relief material from Muslim groups across the city. The city's Muslim elite including businessmen, film actors and politicians visited Shivaji Nagar and distributed relief materials. Several local NGOs (headed by progressive middle-class Hindus) were also involved in relief and rehabilitation work in the area. Some of these, who had been working with the *basti* dwellers in the past, took their activities to the interiors of Shivaji Nagar and much closer to the dumping ground. Majority of those living in these areas were daily wage earners working in various parts of the city whose livelihoods had been severely affected due the violence. The violence had worsened the living conditions there, and with no access to food or water the residents of these neighbourhoods were dependent on relief for survival. However, building trust in a state of intense vulnerability during a communally charged environment was challenging for both local Muslims and progressive Hindus who were engaged in organised relief work. It took some convincing by local community leaders on their behalf for them to gain acceptance and start the provision of elementary health services in the area. However, a major part of the immediate relief operations was undertaken by local youth and Naeem was one of them. He was a teenager when the violence in 1992–1993 broke out and had been involved in voluntary community work, what he describes as the 'social field', through his involvement in a local group of youth volunteers facilitated by a local non-governmental organisation

(NGO), NF which he is now employed by. During the 1992–1993 violence, Naeem along with his group of youth volunteers were involved in distributing relief material and arranging makeshift shelter for those who had lost their homes. A local community centre was turned into a relief camp not just for local residents, but it also provided a refuge for Muslims who had fled from neighbouring areas in search of safety.

Naeem who is in his mid-30s has been living in Lotus Colony since he was 4 years old. Being the eldest of his siblings, at a young age, he took to assisting at his father's cap manufacturing workshop that produces traditional embroidered cotton caps, worn by Muslim men, on the mezzanine floor above their tenement. Naeem was always interested in helping people and often involved himself in local community activities as a young adult. In 1997, Naeem joined NF as part-time staff on a community welfare programme and since 2001 started working full-time as part of their sport programme for local youth and children. He is presently an active member of the mohalla committee of Govandi area that covers eight police stations. He was inducted after the death of a friend who was an active community volunteer and had been nominated by NF to be a facilitator in the committee. According to Naeem, who has taken over as a facilitator since the last 5 years, one of the main tasks of the mohalla committee is to promote *aman* (Hindi/Urdu: peace) through 'aman-kaam' (peace work) which include cultural programmes organised all across the city such as those just discussed. The committee has also been able to defuse tension between communities by dialogue and negotiation locally. One such situation was related to altercations between Samajwadi Party (SP) and Maharashtra Navnirman Sena (MNS) supporters in Shivaji Nagar when MNS MLAs slapped SP legislator Abu Azmi inside the state assembly since he chose to take oath in Hindi instead of Marathi at the swearing-in ceremony.[21] A group of SP supporters was gathered in a public protest against the assault by MNS MLAs, which soon turned violent with the pelting of stones. The incident resulted in 79 people being arrested, of whom 35 were charged under section 151 of the IPC for 'knowingly joining or continuing in assembly of five or more persons after it has been commanded to disperse' and released within 24 hours. Others including 21 of those charged under IPC section 295 and some even under section 395 for dacoity were released only after 15 days.[22]

The citizen members of the mohalla committee were able to negotiate the release of a few, one of them was a local medical practitioner who was only closing the shutter of his clinic before he was arrested. According to Naeem, it was the 'public' who was arrested not those leaders who were actually involved in the altercation at the state assembly. Several of those arrested in Shivaji Nagar (Abu Azmi's constituency) were not even part of the protest but were probably onlookers or just passing by.

One of the responsibilities of Naeem, as a Muslim citizen on the mohalla committee, is to prevent what he terms as 'one-side', 'the police harasses Muslims a lot, it is always one-side'. 'One-side' refers to the acts of violence on, or harassment of, Muslims by the police, which include wrongful arrests, fabricated charges and even torture in police custody. Despite the lack of funds or infrastructure, there are also opportunities to address critical issues not necessarily linked to peace work, where there is a need to collaborate with the police such as addressing the peddling of narcotics, which is rampant in the area or the issue of extortion that the police itself is involved in. Being part of the mohalla committee has enabled Naeem access to and familiarity with the police system and if need be even with the top brass such as in situations of conflict mentioned previously, which has been crucial in preventing outbreaks of violence. Despite Naeem's experience of an anti-Muslim bias in the police force, he maintained that many policemen are 'very good', naming few who are sincere and committed to the cause of justice. Naeem sees himself as a representative of local Muslims on the mohalla committee to see that a good impression (*accha* message) is made on their behalf to resolve a conflict or address a 'one-sided' situation. Naeem reminisced about the time when the police used to invoke such fear that he could not enter a police station. This has changed now due to his involvement in the 'social field' through his late friend and his membership in the mohalla committee.

One the other hand, the presence of Muslim voices in the mohalla committees do not necessarily ensure a successful negotiation either for non-violence or an impartial investigation as was the case with Faiz Usmani, a resident of Shivaji Nagar who was arrested in connection with the three bomb blasts that took place at different locations in Mumbai—Zaveri Bazaar, Opera House and Dadar (west)—on 13 July 2011 killing 26 and injuring 126 people. The police allegedly suspected the Indian

Mujahideen, a designated terrorist group by the state, and Faiz happened to be the elder brother of Afzal Usmani who is currently in Sabarmati jail for his alleged role in the serial bombings in Ahmedabad on 26 July 2008 as a suspected member of the group. Faiz Usmani died only hours after his arrest by policemen in plain clothes from the Chembur crime branch of a brain haemorrhage.[23] The Chembur crime branch was apparently not part of the probe team investigating the Mumbai blasts and was making enquiries independently.[24] A CID probe had been ordered into the death after Usmani's family members alleged he died of police torture. The police consistently denied the possibility of torture and took no responsibility for his death. This brought Muslim NGOs, activists as well as Muslim political leaders from the Samajwadi Party together to demand an impartial inquiry in the Mumbai blast case as well as a judicial probe into the custodial death of Faiz Usmani.[25] The MNS defended the police investigation and accused north Indians and migrants for the blasts attributing all the other criminal activities in the city to them.[26]

In the case of Shivaji Nagar, everyday experiences of negotiations with the police reflect how the labour of maintaining everyday peace is a burden of local Muslim representatives in the mohalla committee who respond through strategies grounded in pragmatism, acceptance and resilience (Heitmeyer 2009; Williams 2013). Memories of past violence are never erased for those who live in constant fear of renewed violence but are in fact often re-lived in the present through newer incidents or threats of potential violence. For the Muslim poor, the concerns that emerge in the light of such events go beyond notions of insecurity but rather highlight the complex and tenacious process of substantiating formal citizenship. With its inability to reduce communal enmity, mohalla committees have become limited to sites for negotiating fair treatment to Muslims in situations of everyday conflict.

Institutionalising Peace?

As a state-societal interface, Mumbai's mohalla committees have been able to make a breakthrough by institutionalising a space for Muslim voices in negotiating non-violence and opening up possibilities of seeking justice. Mohalla committees face day-to-day challenges in sustaining their work that involves bridging the gap between the police force and Muslim neighbourhoods due to several reasons. First, mohalla committees have had to often deal with insensitive police leadership that have either tried to sabotage its efforts or been non-cooperative. The MCMT on their part continue to maintain their distinct identity and they both continue to function fairly independent of each other. However, the work of the MCMT mohalla committees still runs the risk of being co-opted within the fold of the police administered committees that might result in an interface governed by patronage rather than the pursuit of justice for the marginalised.

Second, the lack of volunteers willing to join this effort has resulted in a select few being involved in its work. Most of those involved have been associated with mohalla committees right from its inception and the number has not increased substantially. Furthermore, though mohalla committees are most successful in mixed localities, they remain concentrated in Muslim-dominated neighbourhoods of the city and involving predominantly Hindu localities continues to pose a challenge. Third, the facilitators themselves often finance most of the work of the MCMT mohalla committees. Though it has diversified its activities to address local needs of education and employment generation, it still has to hustle to make its place in the landscape of funded NGOs with an agenda of peace-making that is often not a priority for funders, especially in seemingly 'peace times'. Anxieties of the police force in addressing newer security risks have found a new relevance for mohalla committees as modes of community surveillance into areas that seem unintelligible to the state.

> Relevance has not changed. If you believe in the principle of democracy and if you say that the best government is that which governs the least and leaves to people to govern themselves then this concept of mohalla committees is most relevant to a democracy that a group of people living in a mohalla decide what is good for our mohalla. It's like a local self-government. (Interview with Satish Sahney, Retired Mumbai Police Commissioner, 2 June 2014)
>
> How do we meet the strength of this *jehadi* type of terrorism putting these explosives here and there? Who is going to tell you? Hindus are going to tell you? Hindus don't know these people. And they are not going to stay in the Hindu locality. Which locality are they going to stay in? They are going to stay in a Muslim locality and who is going to give you that

information? Only Muslims. But Muslims will give it to you if you treat them with dignity, treat them with respect, you treat them as equal citizens, you trust them. Like what we are trying to do in the mohalla committee. Then they will give you. But if you go on like a police with that bias and all that, they are not going to. Earlier they used to give all this information to the police, but now they don't give. (Interview with Julio Ribeiro, Chairman Mohalla Committee Movement Trust, 10 June 2014)

Gupte (2012) argues that an environment where credible channels of legally provided security are easily accessible breaks down the incentive structures for the physical perpetration of communal violence, thereby dismantling the riot-production system reducing the reliance of urban folk on extralegal channels, together with the promotion of inter-communal civic engagement which would form a more holistic and sustainable strategy to counter trends in urban communal violence. The recent debates regarding the drafting of a bill that would operationalise the prevention of communal violence through the creation of a bureaucracy devoted only to this purpose has raised several questions regarding the efficacy of such measures. One of the key concerns regards the unabated involvement of police officers and state administrators in the perpetration of communal violence (Desai, 2011; Anand, 2011). The setting up of more institutions for addressing communal violence may have very little impact unless Muslim voices are institutionalised. Their alienation and absence from state institutions including the everyday state structures of policing and governance such as the police, municipal corporation and judiciary are intrinsically linked to accessibility and seem to raise larger questions of representation as a means to maintain checks and balances for the rights of minorities.

> Today, the percentage of Muslims in any (government) department is very low. Everybody knows this. The police department is no different. We should get at least some positions, something based on our numbers. Only if we have our share in the police force, only if we have our share in the other (government) departments there will never be any fights. [...] This has been the case for years...from Lokmanya Tilak's time, he did not want Muslims in government posts. I'm not afraid to say this. [...] There is no one to speak for Muslims. There was Maulana Azad but no one after him. Not that the person should only be a Muslim. Just take the recent bomb blasts in the train, those who saved people's lives, gave water to people were Muslims. This is how it is...it is the Muslims who work hard but it is the

Muslims who end up in jail. These political parties hold *iftaar* parties, have they ever asked Muslims what they want? (Naeem, 23 November 2009)

At one level, inter-community associations might seem like an opportunity for negotiating peace during communal tensions, but they hardly address the larger sociopolitical context that contributes, creates and maintains such situations. The absence of legal provisions that address communal violence and an institutionalisation of Muslims that defines them as citizens, and not just as a minority group with specific religio-cultural needs, calls for non-institutional means to press for representation. Though it may be unfair to expect mohalla committees to address larger issues looming over minority communities, they do play a role in reducing communal tensions locally. However, they offer a veneer of inclusion against a backdrop in which communal politics continues unabated. The inability of extending the work of the mohalla committees beyond Muslim majority areas has localised communal tensions and conflict to the city's Muslim neighbourhoods reinforcing the need for greater surveillance and policing of Muslim neighbourhoods. This seems to contribute to representations of 'Muslim' areas like Shivaji Nagar as culturally deviant (at times anti-national) urban 'disorders' that need to be comprehended and dealt with by the state. The burden of maintaining peace remains on the city's minorities in the absence of state mechanisms to address their security concerns. This is evident in the fact that sustaining the work of initiatives such as Mumbai's mohalla committees is a continuous struggle not just with the state administration but also society at large.

Notes

1. This chapter is based on ethnographic fieldwork conducted from June 2009 to May 2010 and May–June 2014 in Shivaji Nagar and other locations across Mumbai. I would like to thank Julio Riberio, Satish Sahney, Arif Sayed, Maria Ishwaran and Yasmin Sheikh for their valuable insights and time. Comments from Roger Jeffrey and Hugo Gorringe on an earlier version helped improving the chapter. Any faults remain my own.
2. This is a pseudonym.
3. According to the Srikrishna Commission Report (1998), 50 individuals (44 Muslims and 6 Hindus) were killed, 1,673 establishments (1,006 Muslim and 665 Hindu) were subjected to damage and looting and 140 arrests (129 Muslims and 11 Hindus) were made.
4. Interview with Naeem, 23rd November 2009.

5. See, for instance, Basu 1995, Heitmeyer 2009 and Berenschot 2011.
6. A volunteer to a religious cause, popularised by the Sangh Parvivar to refer to volunteers at the destruction of the Babri mosque in Ayodhya.
7. Nearly 200 demonstrators mostly Muslims had been killed and hundreds wounded. See Hansen 2001a.
8. Bhiwandi is a city known for its textile industry located to the north-east of Mumbai and part of the greater Mumbai metropolitan agglomeration.
9. See Engineer 1984.
10. Mohalla Committee Brochure, (undated).
11. The current trustees of MCMT are former police commissioners Julio Ribeiro, Satish Sahney, R.H. Mendonca, former Attorney General of India Goolam Vahanvati and K.M Aarif.
12. Mohalla Committee Brochure, (undated).
13. See *Naata* (Jayshankar and Monteiro 2003), a documentary on the working of mohalla committees in Dharavi.
14. Maharashtra follows the national trend, being one of the worst states with very low representation of Muslims in the police force. The number in the IPS was four out of 203 officers in 2011, the sanction cadre for Maharashtra being 302 (Patel 2013). On the other hand, Muslims have a significant presence amongst prison inmates in Maharashtra where they comprise 32.4 per cent of the prison population, higher than the national average. For those incarcerated on terms of less than a year, the figure rises: 42 per cent of prisoners on short-term sentences in the state are Muslims (Raghavan and Nair 2011). With their socio-economic vulnerabilities, several of them find it difficult to access legal assistance Shaban 2008.
15. This is an unofficial estimate based on those of local NGOs and elected representatives in the area. Official sources do not give segregated data based on religion and language.
16. Shivaji Nagar is situated in M (east) ward of Mumbai, which according to the Mumbai Human Development Report (2009), has the lowest Human Development Index at 0.05, much lower than the city's average of 0.56. For a detailed account on the history of Shivaji Nagar and its living conditions, see Contractor (2011).
17. Behrampada in Bandra (east) was another *basti* locality that saw a blatant bias of the police, which functioned in tandem with local Shiv Sena goons in killing, looting and damaging property. For a detailed account, see Agnes (1993).
18. 'Nearly 20 years on, no justice for parents of Mumbai riots victim', *The Hindu*. http://www.thehindu.com/todays-paper/tp-national/nearly-20-years-on-no-justice-for-parents-of-mumbai-riots-victim/article4145369.ece (accessed 8 September 2013).
19. Accessed from http://www.sabrang.com/srikrish/atr.htm (accessed 15 May 2013).
20. Also the presence of Hindu temples inside police stations and their premises or the prominent display of Hindu deities has been noted in Muslim localities located in other parts of the city. See Hansen (2001a).
21. 'Abu Azmi slapped by MNS MLA for taking oath in Hindi', *Indian Express*, 9 November 2009.
22. According to this section, 'whoever commits dacoity shall be punished with imprisonment for life, or with rigorous imprisonment for a term which may extend to ten years, and shall also be liable to fine'. The IPC also describes the role of witnesses in this section,

> there the presence of informant and other witnesses at the time and place of incident was established and their positive evidence regarding the way in

which the dacoity was committed found reliable having no previous enmity with accused, no case of false implication established therefore, conviction of accused under section 395 was just and proper. Chhedu vs. State of Uttar Pradesh, 2000 Cr LJ 78 (All).

23. 'Mumbai blast suspect dies'. http://twocircles.net/2011jul17/mumbai_blast_suspect_dies.html (accessed 8 September 2013).
24. 'Suspected IM has feared for his life'. http://articles.timesofindia.indiatimes.com/2011-08-20/mumbai/29909203_1_crime-branch-faiz-bomb-blast (accessed 8 September 2013).
25. 'NGOs denounce Mumbai blasts investigations for its "predetermined line"'. http://twocircles.net/2011jul21/ngos_denounce_mumbai_blasts_investigations_its_%E2%80%98predetermined_line%E2%80%99.html#.VdbX8vmqqko (accessed 21 August 2015) and 'Samajwadi Party demands judicial probe of Faiz Usmani's death' accessed from http://twocircles.net/2011jul20/samajwadi_party_demands_judicial_probe_faiz_usmani's_death.html (accessed 8 September 2013).
26. MNS chief Raj Thackeray more specifically targeted the Samajwadi Party for protesting against the custodial death. See 'Raj Thackeray again attacks north Indian migrants' accessed from http://twocircles.net/2011jul18/raj_thackeray_again_attacks_north_indian_migrants.html#.VdbZQvmqqko (accessed 21 August 2015).

References

Agnes, F. 1993. 'Two Riots and after: A Fact Finding Report on Bandra (East)', *Economic and Political Weekly* 28(7): 265–268.
Barve, S. 2003. *Healing Streams: Bringing Back Hope in the Aftermath of Violence*. New Delhi: Penguin Books.
Basu, A. 1995. 'Why Local Riots are not Simply Local: Colective Violence and the Sate in Bijnor, India 1988–1993', *Theory and Society* 24(1): 35–78.
Berenschot, W. 2011. *Riot Politics: Hindu–Muslim Violence and the Indian State*. New Delhi: Rainlight.
Brass, P.R. 2003. *The Production of Hindu–Muslim Violence in Contemporary India*. New Delhi: Oxford University Press.
Contractor, Q. 2011. '"Unwanted in My City": The Making of a "Muslim slum" in Mumbai', in L. Gayer and C. Jaffrelot (eds), *Muslims in Indian Cities—Trajectories of Marginalisation* (pp. 23–42). London: Columbia University Press.
Desai, M. 2011. The Communal and Targetted Violence Bill. *Economic and Political Weekly* 46(31): 12–16.
Engineer, A.A. 1984. 'Bombay-Bhiwandi in National Political Perspective', *Economic and Political Weekly* 19(29): 1134–1136.
———. 1995. *Lifting the Veil: Communal Violence and Communal Harmony in Contemporary India*. Hyderabad: Sangam Books.
Gupte, J. 2012. 'Linking Urban Vulnerability, Extra Legal Security and Civil Violence', in R. Desai and R. Sanyal (eds), *Urbanizing Citizenship: Contested Spaces in Indian Cities* (pp. 190–211). New Delhi: SAGE.
Gupte, J. and Bogati, S. 2014. *Key Challenges of Security Provision in Rapidly Urbanising Contexts: Evidence from Katmandu Valley and Tarai Regions of Nepal*. London: Institute of Development Studies.

Hansen, T.B. 2001a. *Violence in Urban India—Identity Politics, Mumbai and the Post-colonial City*. New Delhi: Permanent Black.
———. 2001b. 'Governance and State Mythologies in Mumbai', in T.B. Hansen and F. Stepputat, *States of Imagination: Ethnographic Explorations of the Postcolonial State* (pp. 221–256). Durham: Duke University Press.
Heitmeyer, C. 2009. '"There is Peace Here": Managing Communal Relations in a Town in Central Gujarat', *Journal of South Asian Development* 4(1): 103–120.
Indian People's Human Rights Tribunal. 1994. *The People's Verdict: An Enquiry into the December '92 and January '93 Riots in Bombay*. Bombay: Indian People's Human Rights Comission.
Jayshankar, K.P. and Monteiro, A. (Directors). 2003. *Naata (The Bond)* [Motion Picture]. Mumbai.
Mamdani, M. 2002. 'Amnesty or Impunity? A Preliminary Critique of the Report of the Truth and Reconciliation Commission of South Africa (TRC)', *Diacritics* 32(3–4): 33–59.
Mehta, D. and Chatterji, R. 2007. *Living with Violence: An Anthropology of Events and Everyday Life*. New Delhi: Routledge.
Odendaal, A. and Olivier, R. 2008. *Local Peace Committees: Some Reflections and Lessons Learned*. Kathmandu: Academy for Education Development/USAID.
Patel, V. 2013. 'Socio-economic Profile of Muslims in Maharashtra', *Economic and Political Weekly* 48(36): 68–73.
Raghavan, V. and Nair, R. 2011. *A Study of the Socio Economic Profile and Rehabilitation Needs of Muslim Community in Prisons in Maharashtra*. Tata Institute of Social Sciences, Centre for Criminology and Justice, School of Social Work. Mumbai: Tata Institute of Social Sciences.
Roche, D. 2002. 'Restorative Justice and the Regulatory State in South African Townships', *British Journal of Criminology* 42(3): 514–533.
Sachar, R. 2006. *Social, Economic and Educational Status of the Muslim Community*. Government of India, Prime Minister's High Level Committee. New Delhi: Government of India.
Sen, A. 2008. *Shiv Sena Women—Violence and Communalism in a Bombay Slum*. New Delhi: Zubaan.
Shaban, A. 2008. 'Ghettoisation, Crime and Punishment in Mumbai', *Economic and Political Weekly* 43(33): 68–73.
Sharma, K. 2000. *Rediscovering Dharavi: Stories from Asia's Largest Slum*. New Delhi: Penguin.
Srikrishna, B.N. 1998. *Report of the Srikrishna Commission: An Inquiry into the Riots at Mumbai during December 1992 and January 1993*. Mumbai: High Court.
Stokke, K. 2009. 'Crafting Liberal Peace? International Peace Promotion and the Contexual Politics of Peace in Sri Lanka', *Annal of the Association of American Geographers* 99(5): 932–939.
Tambiah, S. 1996. *Leveling Crowds: Ethnonationalist Conflicts and Collective Violence in South Asia*. New Delhi: Vistaar Publications.
Thakkar, U. 2004. 'Mohalla Committees of Mumbai: Candles in Omnious Darkness', *Economic and Political Weekly* 39(6): 580–586.
Varshney, A. 2002. *Ethnic Conflict and Civic Life*. New Delhi: Oxford University Press.
Wilkinson, S. 2004. *Votes and Violence: Electoral Competition and Ethnic Riots in India*. Cambridge: Cambridge University Press.
Williams, P. 2013. 'Reproducing Everyday Peace in North India: Process, Politics and Power', *Annuals of Association of American Geographers* 103(1): 230–250.
Wilson, R. 2001. *The Politics of Truth and Reconciliation in South Africa: Legitimising the Post-apartheid State*. Cambridge: Cambridge University Press.

10
Institutionalising Informal Socialities: Dalit Urban Poor in Dharavi

Martin Fuchs

Interacting with people in India whom we call marginalised, especially Dalits and the urban poor, two basic aspects have always stood out for me. On the one hand, what impressed me in particular was the faculty of many—certainly not all—marginal actors to organise their lives and their environments informally in ways that actually work. I have called this 'informal sociality' and 'informal governance', applying the notion of informality originally coined with regard to those kinds of economic structure that elude the conventional economic organisational models to the wider social and political field. Those who invent informal modes of self-governance are, however, to a large extent also involved in certain types of informal economy. On the other hand, and this concerns the second of the aspects that I have found striking, I became intensely aware of the precariousness of many of the economic and social achievements of marginal actors, and this affects their attempts at institutionalisation. Even in cases of seemingly successful development, such as improvements of living conditions and economic prospects, marginalised people continue to be faced with ever-new threats that might endanger what they have so far achieved through their efforts and struggles. In addition to neglect and exclusion as major factors explaining their dismal condition, there is also the factor of avarice, the attempt to divert and appropriate even those few resources that marginalised people have created for themselves, for the benefit of some stronger, dominant, financial, economic or social powers. Thus, the institutionalisation of social and economic positionalities does not seem a stable achievement for actors as long as they remain in a marginal position. There is a permanent danger of rollbacks.

But there is one more aspect to consider when we talk about marginalised actors in the Indian context. It is the *compartmentalisation* of social issues and, thus, of social struggles that in my view constitutes a major factor explaining why marginal actors have difficulties in overcoming the situation they are caught in, which hampers institutionalising them as a major social and/or political force. That social actors are often divided along caste and religion as well as linguistic lines is a fact all too well-known to Indian scholars. Societal division along identity markers—as a shorthand one might call them 'primary', even if we know that these are also contingent and constructed (and only believed to be primary)—represents a major handicap of the political and economic struggles of the disadvantaged sections of Indian society. Casteism, especially, matters much more for those at the lower end of the social scale than for those at the top end. Crossing caste boundaries, especially through inter-caste marriage, is often (not always, however) easier amongst urban sections of the so-called upper castes than amongst lower castes, and this often has direct effects on the chances of collaboration amongst them. Even worse, the failure to overcome caste divisions regularly leads to an 'ethnicisation' of struggles, identity politics replacing, or pushing to the background, immediate social concerns like livelihood or human rights issues.

But equally important, or so I would argue, is the multiplicity and multi-directionality of the concerns and struggles of marginal people. This not only with regard to the sheer range of modes of discrimination they are subjected to, or what one could call the *over-determination* of discrimination. Even more importantly, this multiplicity of discrimination has the effect of focal distraction and of scattering and, thus, *disintegrating* (the unity of) people's struggles. In the case of the urban marginalised, the problems they are faced with include issues of humiliation and demands for social recognition, securing one's livelihood, housing rights, civic amenities (water supply, sanitation, medical provisions and so on) and educational opportunities, the issues of implementation of human rights and attempts to vanquish the discrimination of women, just to name the most obvious aspects, each of which involves the question of self-determination and political agency. All of these issues are of relevance at the same time, but each entails a different agenda of struggle and is addressed to a different target group. We are used to analyse and arrange or categorise the various life concerns of people separately. We have learnt to distinguish, and for certain reasons cannot avoid distinguishing—reasons that would have to be discussed in detail elsewhere—different social issues, and for us it seems almost natural that these issues should be dealt with in separation, both analytically as well as politically. For the people affected, however, these issues are all interconnected or even derivative of their basic condition of stigmatisation, exclusion and disdain. Taking the angle of institutionalisation, pursuing each of the issues separately can only mean reinforcing and hardening the fragmentation of concerns and struggles of the marginalised. What complicates things further is the fact that each issue requires a different strategy and different format of institutionalisation. Institutionalization of social struggles, thus, is a double-edged sword not only, as social movement literature has pointed out, because it removes the critical sting from the struggle. It is a double-edged sword also because of its disintegrative effect on struggles, and it can mean hampering the very prospects of development for the marginalised.

What I discuss here is primarily based on viewpoints and experiences of Dalits (and some members of other marginalised groups) in Dharavi (Mumbai) of various regional, linguistic and social backgrounds, with whom I interacted and engaged during several research stints between 1999 and 2005, and short visits afterwards. In addition, I met the members of several NGOs and one community-based organisation (CBO) as well as concerned individuals, journalists and town planners. Reports and other documentation on Dharavi, which I consulted, proved only partially reliable. My approach is, thus, primarily 'from the bottom up', starting from the local level and the everyday experiences as well as the perspectives of marginalised people, even though 'local' in my case means one million people, squeezed into little more than 2 square kilometers.[1]

In the following, I will especially look into the modalities and forms of the institutionalisation of marginal actor activities in Dharavi and will stress the diversity of these modes as well as the frictions between them and their limitations. When discussing such issues, one also has to reflect on the type of social processes that we refer to when we speak of 'institutionalising marginal actors'. Does institutionalisation of marginalised actors primarily refer to the processes of *consolidation* of social movements in the form of political parties, NGOs or other organisational forms supposedly representing the concerns of the marginalised within the overall (or mainstream) social and political set-up? Or, alternatively, does one refer to the establishment of separate social spaces for the disadvantaged, and of networks of their own, *outside* of, and *parallel* to, the mainstream organisations or the institutions representing the dominant actors? Or does institutionalisation of marginalised groups suggest a process of *integration* and *participation* of these groups, as collectives, or of each of their members as individuals, within the mainstream of social life and civil society? Or finally, considering the Indian context in particular, does institutionalisation refer to the consolidation of *primary* groups and primary group *identities* as collective political actors?

Regarding the first three options mentioned, the social and political actors—the social movements and NGOs—those who get institutionalised are largely issue-oriented, bringing together people who try to address the same or at least similar problems and want to initialise *structural* change. The actors to be institutionalised in the last instance (castes, communities), however, are those who already share some kind of identity, based on the identities they have shared earlier, and fight for a larger stake for their group in the public goods and in the public arena. While the first options are inclusive, insofar as they in principle would allow taking all marginalised people in a locality or region on board, the last mentioned possibility is fundamentally exclusive and further ruptures solidarity amongst Dalits and even more so the marginalised in general.

***

By a very rough estimate the number of Dalits in Dharavi amount to around 60 per cent of its population, perhaps 25 per cent are Muslims, and a few per cent of the members of Dharavi belong to the so-called Denotified Tribes.[2] But these people are not just Dalits, Muslims or Tribals. They are also slum dwellers, actors in the informal as well as formal economy and people with infrastructural needs. They are marginalised in various respects and are involved in struggles separately geared to each of the dimensions. Taking the entire range of citizen rights as well as human rights as a foil, they organise struggles, or are involved in struggles organised by others, that tend to focus on one aspect at a time. Considering the rural background of most

Dharavi residents—everyone in Dharavi being a migrant or descendant of migrants mainly hailing from rural areas—it would seem apposite to relate all the different forms of marginalisation and discrimination back to the basic dimension of status discrimination, stigmatisation, ritual exclusion and spatial segregation already experienced in the villages. Slums prolong or redouble the experience of social exclusion found in rural contexts. However, this is not the way slums are discussed in public or academic discourse.

One could argue that the way slums are approached in these discourses, as primarily a problem of poverty or illegality and development or rehabilitation, respectively, obfuscates the fact that the vast majority of slum dwellers in India are inevitably from Dalit, Tribal, Denotified and Muslim, and elsewhere also Adivasi, backgrounds. In these discourses, slums are defined as problems of social policy and social engineering, to be tackled by town planners, thus blanking out a continuing fundamental defect of a society set to follow a path to modernity. What one can though state is that slums add a new dimension of exclusion to the existing ones and introduce new modes of discrimination. The struggles led by and on behalf of slum residents then follow agendas that bracket the Dalit question, or that of other marginalised groups, keeping the original sources of stigmatisation in the background. Whatever the demographic as well as economic, physical and legal changes during its history have been—and they have been huge—Dharavi has remained a site of marginalised groups.

Dharavi has experienced large changes since the late nineteenth century. During its formative period (that is, between the late nineteenth century into the 1950s or 1960s), Dharavi grew into a multicultural site, providing space for Dalits, Muslims and members of Denotified Tribes, plus a few members of intermediate castes, from all over India, with the exception only of the eastern and the north-eastern regions. Often only certain sub-regions of a state are represented though, as also certain regional (Dalit) castes tend to be more prominent numerically, for contingent historical reasons, than others. Amongst the numerically prominent ones are Adi Dravidas; various Chamar subgroups from UP and Bihar; Chambars, Dhors and Mahars from different sections of Maharashtra; Madigas from certain districts of Andhra Pradesh and Karnataka; Valmikis, originally from the undivided Punjab and Rajasthan; as well as Nadars from Tirunelveli, Kumbhars (potters) originating from Gujarat and the Koli fisher-people as the original inhabitants of Dharavi. The most prominent amongst the Denotified Tribes in Dharavi are the Kunchikorve, who have come from southern Maharashtra and northern Karnataka (Shinde 2011). Dharavi has been a hub of economic production activities since the late nineteenth century, starting with large tanneries, now largely defunct, and including today, amongst others, the production of leather goods for national and international markets, of clothes, food items and pottery, as well as a diversified recycling industry. Only about a third of Dharavi's working population works outside the area. It has been estimated that Dharavi's annual turnover ran at around 500 million Euros by the mid-2000s. Unemployment in Dharavi is extremely low. Through their struggles, since the end of the 1970s, Dharavi residents accomplished the stepwise rehabilitation of wards ('chawls', today administratively called 'cooperative societies') in the form of new high rises, in which families, who can prove earlier residence (see also further), are being provided with small flats. Many Dharavi residents invest in the education of their children.

I would like to argue for the development of an integrated approach, which tries to focus on the linkages between the various issues, at least on the analytical or research level. Discussing the question of institutionalisation with respect to marginalised actors cannot, or should not, mean that we mainly consider identity politics. We would then ourselves be captive of essentialist thinking. If we take what we know seriously, it is the reproduction of discrimination in all spheres of life and on all levels that should be of primary concern. The picture that we then get of institutionalisation is a very diverse and discrepant one. Not only do different spheres of life follow different trajectories and different dynamics, the ways discrimination works and is being reproduced in each area is also very different.

In the economic sphere, certain sectors, especially the leather business, are being protected by corporate arrangements (associations and syndicates), the stigmatisation of certain occupations has been converted into a resource to be protected. However, this works to some extent only. Muslims have also started expanding their presence in this industry, being confronted with opposition from some of the established Chambhar leather shop owners. The most defamed kind of occupation, that of scavenging and sanitation work, has likewise been treated as a resource to be protected (now under threat because of the Municipality's shift to contract labour in this occupational field). Competitors in this field come from various caste groups, including especially Valmikis and Kunchikorve. In few cases only, occupational specialisations get translated into formal cooperative associations, primarily regarding parts of the leather industry, and this also only on the level of shop-owners, not the one of the workers. Such associations, however, are usually limited to the members of one caste and follow a policy that affirms and even deepens caste differences, as has been the case especially with the associations of Maharashtrian Chambhars (or Charmakars, as they prefer labelling themselves in this attempt of formal institutionalisation) (Saglio-Yatzimirsky 2013). In general, the sectors of menial and of informal labour, practically by definition, provide little opportunity for institutionalisation outside caste networks and allow for mobilisation only when this suits political interests (as in the case of Shiv Sena support for the Chambhars in the 1990s and to a much smaller extent in the case of *safai* workers, whose associations are translocal, remain weak and do not get down to the level of the actual workers).

With respect to the political sphere too, the institutionalisation of the marginalised has remained very limited in the case of Dharavi. What seems striking here is that the concentration of a large number of Dalits and members of other marginalised groups in one place and the commonalities they otherwise share (I will come to that a little later) has not boosted Dalit unity, or Dalit-bahujan unity for that matter, or the fight for a common agenda. Also, considering institutionalisation as just discussed, Dalit parties have made few efforts to establish a support base in Dharavi. The Republican Party, or its various factions, respectively, as well as the Bahujan Samaj Party, have remained rather weak, both organisationally and electorally. While Namdeo Dhasal had links with Dharavi during the time in which he supported the Shiv Sena, and Ramdas Athawale paid visits to some of the Mahar groups in Dharavi, no sustained efforts have been undertaken in Dharavi by any national or regional Dalit association to address the issues of discrimination. Even less in the public limelight is the situation of the marginalised Denotified Tribes, who are still largely confined to working within their respective tribal or caste set-ups. The dominant party for most of the time has been the Congress, with the Shiv Sena as second major player. Shiv Sena, however, gained more strength in recent years (Congress lost the 2012 municipal elections in Dharavi, but managed to hold the Dharavi seat in the 2014 assembly elections). These two parties, however, mobilise locally with slum development agendas and show very little concern for the specific issues of discrimination of

Dalits, Muslims and, least of all, for those of the Denotified Tribes. At the most, as mentioned, one comes across attempts to support the corporate interests of one caste group.

Nor do we encounter other strong initiatives that would try to bring Dalits or Bahujans of different caste or community affiliations closer to each other—on the contrary. While in general, residents of Dharavi have managed to get along with each other relatively smoothly, with the exception of the two pogroms incited from the outside (the anti-Tamilian riots in the 1960s, the riots after the destruction of the Babri Masjid in Ayodhya in 1992–1993, both by Shiv Sena activists), several communities congregate physically in separate pockets and occupy specific occupational niches. But even the fact that other sectors of Dharavi actually have a religiously and caste-wise mixed population and that an increasing number of residents enter new (and, to some extent, increasingly skilled) occupational fields has not led to a high increase in cross-caste engagements and inter-caste marriages. Nearly every person of Dalit background I talked to put the demand for respect and social recognition at the top of their agendas, even above poverty eradication or slum development, and nearly all of them, even many of those who support Hindutva forces, showed high regard for Ambedkar. However, little collaborative effort can be observed.

It is the field of slum rehabilitation and slum development that gained the largest organisational attention. It is here that we can actually speak of new processes of institutionalisation, processes of a particular kind. Dharavi has been the target of demolition and later gentrification drives. The greater part of what now is being called 'Dharavi' developed, starting in the late nineteenth century, as an 'illegal' settlement on the earlier dumping grounds of the Bombay Municipality and on self-reclaimed land, gained from mangrove swamps around little islands inhabited by Koli fisher-people. At a time when the threats of demolition were mounting, in the early 1980s, Dharavi residents got the help of an external NGO that, following a model they had applied in the Philippines, helped them set up a CBO and organise road blocks and demonstrations and activate public opinion through the print media. It was a time at which the attitudes towards slum dwellers started changing internationally as well as nationally. Becoming the showcase of slum rehabilitation, based on the perception of it being 'the largest slum of Asia', and being able to involve the then Prime Minister, Rajiv Gandhi, Dharavi residents in the mid-1980s managed to obtain a guarantee of residence, corroborated through the payment of a monthly fine in place of rent, as well as the first large improvement funds, mainly used to develop a road infrastructure. Over the following two decades further struggles led, on the one hand, to improvements in the fields of water supply, sanitation, electricity supply, on the other hand to the introduction of a series of housing schemes. The basic idea here is to supply each Dharavi family with a flat in a high-rise, originally of 220 square feet each, including bathroom and kitchen facilities. A considerable number of such high rises have meanwhile been erected, and the regulations of the schemes, developed through negotiations with Dharavi residents and their CBOs/NGOs, secured their involvement at each stage of this transition process. This way, it was largely ensured that those eligible for a new flat would actually get one.

A continuous problem, however, has been the lack of provision for the industrial activities in Dharavi, which give employment to roughly two-thirds of its working population. Slum redevelopment is geared to the idea of primarily providing dormitory residences, following the suburban middle-class model, and refuses to acknowledge that people with informal sector employment have to use their residential places as work sites. This shows in a striking manner how survival issues—the one regarding (tolerable) housing, the other regarding gaining one's livelihood—have reached a point where these are at loggerheads with each other and tend to make the continuity of existence in Dharavi for many residents difficult, if not impossible.

The plans to finally rehabilitate the whole slum reached their apex in 2004, when the Central Government under the then Prime Minister Vajpayee announced the new Dharavi Redevelopment Project. Under this scheme big consortia, combining national and international building companies, were to be brought in not only to raise new residential high rises, but also build up an infrastructure of schools, colleges, parks, and so on. However, this was linked to the stipulation that the participatory rights of the respective local residents, available in the earlier redevelopment schemes, would be scrapped. Like the earlier schemes, the new one too intends to provide additional flats at market prices for middle-class people from outside Dharavi. The Dharavi Redevelopment Project has as yet (mid-2015), however, not really taken off. Procedures have again and again been stalled. Difficulties occurred on the government and administrative side, involving especially the Government of Maharashtra and its subsidiaries, which culminated in the critique of the main consultant (Mukesh Mehta), whom the administration had originally brought in. Also several of the building consortia withdrew from the scheme following the world financial crisis of 2008. More importantly, however, was that the scheme repeatedly faced opposition from within Dharavi. The Indian media have throughout closely covered the protests. One hassle again concerns the defective provisions for industrial units—the underlying concept being still that of a purely residential, 'dormitory' suburb—others concern the cut-off date for eligibility for a flat, the size of the new flats, the lack of provisions for those who live in Dharavi on rent (about one-third of Dharavi residents), and of course the proviso that the locals should no longer have a say regarding the plans that are to affect their future. While the scheme, in threatening to disrupt the socio-economic structures that the locals have created, exhibits the precariousness of slum existence and of the achievements once gained, the symbolic as well as actual power of Dharavi and the continuous mobilisation of sections of its population (their composition, to a certain extent, changing), have so far saved Dharavi.

However, institutionally, no sustainable counter-structures have developed, and this itself is an expression of that very precariousness. Adapting to policy changes on the one hand, depending on the discrepant stratagems of the various NGOs on the other, the longest lasting institutional arrangement of this struggle was that established by one CBO, People's Responsible Organisation of United Dharavi (PROUD), with sectional representatives, issue-related committees and ward ('chawl') assemblies. This CBO played a dominant role over 20 or 25 years but lost the hold it had had over protest activities in Dharavi by the mid-2000s. Partially, this was due to its involvement with the new government scheme, which caught PROUD in between the interests of the Dharavi residents and the government plans which they largely supported. The adjustment of their position was partially the consequence of the drying up of funding from European funding agencies, but partly also the result of PROUD's very successes in its earlier struggles. The younger generation takes the achievements of slum development for granted and sees little meaning in mobilisation, they rather focus on their own personal advancement. Other NGOs involved in Dharavi include Society for Promotion of Area Resource Centres (SPARC), which however is not a Dharavi organisation, nor is it an organisation of slum dwellers. The more recent struggles have been largely led by new action groups like Dharavi Bachao Andolan and have intermittently got support from the then opposition parties, especially the Shiv Sena. Still, all these remain precarious arrangements, and it is less the institutional consolidation of Dharavi residents that has saved them from the large-scale disruption of their self-developed structures, than their numbers, their voting power, their economic importance, and Dharavi's symbolic significance as India's most outstanding 'slum'.

***

While my field-wise scan of institutionalisation in Dharavi has shown imperfect results, we can also look at the question of institutionalisation from a different angle. What strikes one, once one has been exploring Dharavi for some time, is the way it has been functioning as a township or suburb of its own without an administrative centre and for a long time with little direct state involvement. State agencies for a long time had little knowledge about what was going on in Dharavi, and even most conflicts were settled internally without involving official law enforcement agencies. Ostracised by the outside, defended as their own space by the residents, Dharavi developed its own modes of informal governance. I just point out the two most prominent features, network structures and structures of mediation. Aside from the CBOs and NGOs just mentioned, one encounters numerous short- and medium-term social action groups, informal self-help groups, discussion circles and community associations, their numbers and intensity fluctuating over time. In a sense, these alternative civil society groups have revived modalities of internal caste self-governance, something which, obviously, also still plays a significant role in Dharavi.

On the other hand, one finds a number of different mediators, brokers, arbiters or social entrepreneurs, mostly, but not exclusively men, who act as counsellors of smaller or larger neighbourhoods or for some other restricted clientele within Dharavi. These people, called 'social workers' by the locals, manage a wide range of conflicts. Interestingly, and representing an ironic recognition of these informal modes of self-governance, those political parties that have successfully operated in Dharavi—and Dharavi because of its population size has always been important for political parties—are the ones that adapted best to those informal structures or replicate them in their organisations. The Congress for a long time worked with the social worker or broker model, while the Shiv Sena with its *shakhas*, which recently gained a stronger foothold in Dharavi, can be seen as replicating the network model.

The informality of these models is decisive, and sociologically speaking I would see this also as a mode of institutionalisation. Being informal, this mode depends a lot on the individuals who get themselves involved, and on the ways in which they engage with others. The precariousness of this arrangement becomes visible, when we look at the development of relations with the outside world. The new strategy of the Central Government as well as the State Government intends a wholesale refurbishment of Dharavi, the replacement of all slum houses and hutments by residential high rises, and the induction of additional, and in this case middle class and higher caste, inhabitants to this place, which already has one of the highest population densities in the world. This is connected with the revocation of participatory rights Dharavi residents had until now, as this policy also largely disregards the needs of local producers as well as of those who live on rent. The danger of this development plan is that it will destroy the sensitive informal networks of slum people, which are indispensable for their social and economic survival, and that many residents at the end will be forced to vacate the place and start afresh in new and upcoming slums. It is such reasons that lead locals to oppose the government plans.

To sum this up: urbanised marginalised people do manage to set up their own institutional arrangements, but these are largely informal in character. While these provide a good basis for reproduction and survival under contemporary conditions and for the individual development of residents, this form of institutionalisation in and of itself does not provide a satisfactory perspective for the future advancement of the urban poor. However, designating a space of self-determination, the modes of informal institutionalisation provide an important starting base and a cornerstone of an alternative institutional modality, and the first requirement should be that this be protected and nurtured.

What I have been calling a mode of informal self-governance emphasises a still underexposed mode of governmentality. The marginalised have developed their own constructive ways of governance. While aspects of this are alluded to by Partha Chatterjee in his discussion of what he calls 'political society' (Chatterjee 2004), the specificity and significance of this mode of governmentality tends to disappear behind the stretched canvas of the very notion of political society. One might perhaps ponder to what extent such forms of informal social self-governance not only are the effect of segregation and non-recognition, but are also a *necessary condition* for non-recognition and segregation to continue. Moreover, it seems that informal self-governance also is a pre-condition of the informal economy, or at least the form of informal economy largely practised in urban India. If the state wants to bring slums under full control and develop them into lower middle-class residential spaces, the only other options would be to either include the urban poor—that is, Dalits and other marginalised sections who reside there—as full equals, and this also economically by including them into the formal economy, *or* to regress to authoritarian forms of control to check and break the informal modes of governance.

***

My concluding remarks have to remain tentative. The attempt to describe what has been happening in the most prominent place in India at which marginalised people congregate, does not give a uniform idea of processes of, or even perspectives for, institutionalisation. The best I can do here, therefore, is to spell out certain observations and to try to take some steps towards an overall picture. But the picture remains patchy, and perhaps has to remain patchy, considering the diversity of Dharavi and the multiplicity of discrimination and the resulting multifarious struggles against it.

The success model of Dharavi (up to now!) is that of limited integration with the wider society and the wider institutional set-up, keeping as much control over internal processes as possible; a basically informal mode of these processes of self-organisation; and the penchant for, and ability of, negotiation across communal (including caste) boundaries, negotiation, that is, of specific problems, and not primarily about abrogating these boundaries; and, finally, the support role of the national and international media and publics. To a large extent Dharavi developed according to self-set agendas and its occupants' own considerations (and disputes). Outside actors (and this includes many developmental state agencies besides NGOs), who wanted to cooperate and coordinate their agendas with those of the locals, were successful only when they managed to link in with the self-governance structures of Dharavi (that is, networks and social workers as well as neighbourhood representatives) and refrained from imposing their agendas wholesale on the locals (this includes the earlier ward-wise reconstruction and rehabilitation schemes).[3]

To put it harshly: Of the two formal pathways towards institutionalisation that I could distinguish in Dharavi, the one communal, that is via mobilisation of communities, the other issue-oriented, only the last one shows potential. Regarding the communal pathway, that is, the cases in which local caste and religious groups form associations and run their own organisations, this has helped individual members as well as leaders to pursue their individual projects of improvement (like getting better education and getting into better, even white-collar jobs). However, it has not helped create a new potency of (political) self-assertion of these marginalised groups.

Regarding the orientation to social issues, few Dalits in Dharavi have pursued a formal agenda of social recognition and political contention beyond the slum redevelopment issue. Those who did to a limited extent tried to pursue this through affiliation to Dalit parties or Ambedkarite organisations based outside Dharavi, or, alternatively—and this may sound paradoxical at first view—through affiliation to Hindutva organisations. This last strategy, through which some Dalits sought to achieve equality and equal opportunity by impressing higher caste leaders of their loyalty to the Hindu cause, largely failed, until at least the mid-2000s, because of its inner contradictions. It did not gain them the recognition they were looking for. Moreover, all strategies of working through political affiliations basically mean that the local Dalits would be anchored in organisations based outside Dharavi and controlled by outsiders. They have so far had only limited meaning for the daily-life perspectives of larger sections of Dalits in the township.

Mobilisation on larger scales happened, and was often successful, only in cases of joint struggle concerning overarching developmental issues of Dalit residents, facing the outside in the forms both of state agencies and the wider public. The downside of this is that these struggles remained limited, focussing each issue separately, and sometimes running into contradictions, as with regard to the terms for housing rehabilitation that clash with the livelihood requirements of many of the residents. On the other hand, these struggles could only materialise because they remained issue-focussed. It is the specification and, thus, fragmentation of struggles that opens up some chances for the urban poor and urban Dalits, but these struggles do not allow for them to change their situation overall. Moreover, issue-related struggles can be sustained only for the short and sometimes medium term. Different from these, communal or community-oriented forms of institutionalisation are more sustainable, but remain caught in their identitarian logic and do not help to build bridges across communal divides.

Notes

1. This includes people who do not have their own hutment, but live on rent.
2. In 1871, the British Government passed The Criminal Tribes Act which categorised or 'notified' certain communities as being inherently criminal. This Act was repealed in 1952, following Independence, and the Tribes in question became known as Denotified Tribes. Despite denotification, these tribes continue to face stigmatisation and have been subject to new ordinances such as the Habitual Offenders Act. For more details see the Human Rights summary here: http://www.countercurrents.org/hr-hrf090704.htm (accessed 28 August 2015).
3. While Dharavi receives an identity both from inside and from outside, an identity that has undergone some changes for the better, larger numbers of its inhabitants have acted and fought together as a larger group in special situations only. Still, being a resident of Dharavi provides a sense of belonging, even a symbol of pride (captured in the frequently heard slogan of Dharavi as a 'mini-India'), and many struggles happen with reference to Dharavi as a whole: to develop the place, to defend the place. People are well aware of their status as doubly marginalised, and also take advantage of the situation of relative exclusion. We also have to be aware, especially with respect to the theme of institutionalisation that Dharavi appears as an entity from a synchronic perspective only. In actual fact, sections of the population of Dharavi keep fluctuating and rotating, people moving in and out.

References

Chatterjee, Partha. 2004. *The Politics of the Governed: Reflections on Popular Politics in Most of the World*. Delhi: Permanent Black.

Chatterji, Roma and Mehta, Deepak. 2007. *Living with Violence: An Anthropology of Events and Everyday Life*. New Delhi: Routledge.

Fuchs, Martin. 2003. 'Dalit Struggle for Recognition: Reflections from Dharavi', in P.G. Jogdand and S.M. Michael (eds), *Globalization and Social Movements: Struggle for a Humane Society* (pp. 128–149). Jaipur: Rawat.

Fuchs, Martin. 2005. 'Slum as Achievement. Governmentality and the Agency of Slum Dwellers', in Eveline Hust and Michael Mann (eds), *Urbanization and Governance in India* (pp. 103–123). New Delhi: Manohar/Centre de Sciences Humaines/South Asia Institute.

———. 2006. 'Slum als Projekt: Dharavi und die Falle der Marginalisierung [Slum as Project: Dharavi and the Marginalization Trap]', in Ravi Ahuja and Christiane Brosius (eds), *Mumbai–Delhi–Kolkata. Annäherungen an die Megastädte Indiens* (pp. 47–63). Heidelberg: Draupadi.

———. 2007. 'Slum als Projekt? Dharavi zwischen Fremdbestimmung und Selbstregierung [Slum as project? Dharavi between Heteronomy and Self-Governance]', in *Archplus* 185, November 2007: 77–80.

———. 2014. 'Slum als Lebenswelt [Slum as Lifeworld]', in Karlheinz Sonntag (ed.), *Arm und Reich*, Sammelband der Vorträge des Studium Generale der Ruprecht-Karls-Universität Heidelberg im Wintersemester 2012/2013 (pp. 129–155). Heidelberg: Universitätsverlag Winter.

Saglio-Yatzimirsky, Marie-Caroline. 2002. *Intouchable Bombay. Le bidonville des travailleurs du cuir*. Paris: CNRS Éditions.

———. 2013. *Dharavi. From Mega-Slum to Urban Paradigm*. London: Routledge.

Sharma, Kalpana. 2000. *Rediscovering Dharavi: Stories from Asia's Largest Slum*. New Delhi: Penguin.

Shinde, Pradeep. 2011. *Kunchikorve Worlds of Work*, PhD Thesis, London School of Economics.

11
India and the Management of Ethnic Diversity: The Unfinished Business of Accommodation

Wilfried Swenden

Introduction

For comparative political scientists, the holding together of India as a democracy presents a puzzle (Norris 2008). This is so because of India's demographic scale; its high degree of ethnic and cultural fragmentation (Alesina et al. 2003, Fearon 2003) combined with low (albeit rising) levels of economic development (ADB 2007). Where low levels of economic development coincide with high levels of ethnic or cultural fractionalisation, conflict is more likely and the chances for democracies to consolidate are much lower (Collier 2008).

The reasons for the relative success of India's democracy—in these comparatively adverse conditions—are manifold and cannot be explored in full in this chapter (for a good summative coverage, see Oldenburg 2010 and Tudor 2013). Yet, I argue that *one* of the contributory factors concerns the way in which the Indian state has accommodated its widespread ethnic diversity (on this point in particular also see Stepan et al. 2011).[1] By and large, the Indian state has deployed 'accommodative strategies' more often than 'control' or 'assimilative' strategies, although there are important temporal and spatial exceptions. Furthermore, in *time,* such accommodative practices have become more and not less widespread. The overall gist of this chapter is, therefore, one of relative optimism. This optimism arrives from adopting a *longue durée* approach and from briefly comparing India with neighbouring Pakistan and Sri Lanka. At the same time, this author shares many of the concerns that are voiced by other contributors to this volume. For one, accommodative policies are not without contestation and they are often criticised on normative grounds (as illiberal or as not based on principles of social justice). Furthermore, critics take issue with the design of some of these schemes, their lack of implementation on the ground and their limited contribution to alleviating the social conditions of the subaltern. Finally, accommodative schemes sit uneasily with the dominant ideology of the Bharatiya Janata Party (BJP) that won an overall majority in the 2014 general elections.

In this chapter, I document these normative, empirical and party political objections to these accommodative schemes with reference to quotas or reservations benefiting the Backward Castes (but similar arguments have been made with regard to territorial or linguistic accommodation). While sharing some of these criticisms (especially those that condemn how these schemes operate in practice), I argue that in the current Indian context, quotas are a necessary but insufficient mechanism to alleviate the political and material exclusion of the Backward Castes. They should operate in tandem—and not be replaced—with broader welfare schemes of a redistributive nature.

The chapter is structured in two main parts. The first part situates India within the comparative literature on 'governing divided societies'. It demonstrates and explains the accommodative trajectory of Indian democracy since independence and briefly contrasts this trajectory with that of two approximate and multiethnic neighbours: Sri Lanka and Pakistan. The second section highlights the contested nature of accommodation by exploring the normative, empirical and party political objections to accommodation with reference to quotas benefiting the Backward Castes. The conclusion provides a qualified assessment of accommodation in India up to date and cautiously looks ahead.

Managing Ethnic Diversity: India in Comparative and Longitudinal Perspective

The Accommodation of Ethnic Diversity: A Framework

Following Chandra (2012: 11), the term ethnicity here is understood as 'ethnic structure', that is, referring to 'nominal *descent*-based attributes that characterise individuals or populations' (my emphasis). In the Indian context, therefore, ethnic diversity relates not only to attributes like caste, tribe and territory (sons of the soil), but also to language and religion. Although caste identity is 'more fixed' than, say, linguistic and even religious identity which can be acquired (or lost), one is still born into a family with a specific religious or linguistic background. Not all of these ethnic attributes are activated all of the time, and the extent to which they are is often a function of political agency. As Paul Brass (1973) showed decades ago, in India, the same political entrepreneurs may have activated *different* ethnic categories when and where these best suited their interests (for instance, shifting from Sikh (religion) to Punjabi (language) to obtain a Punjabi (and Sikh) dominated state.

The broader framework for situating India in the management of ethnic diversity derives from the 'governing divided societies' literature (Choudry 2008 for a review). Broadly speaking, there are three possible ways in which a state can address ethnic diversity. The first of these is not normally an option in a procedural democracy in which all citizens have the right to vote and are equal in the view of the law. It is what Lustick (1979) referred to as a 'control strategy' in which one or a few ethnic groups capture state power and repress minority rights and even regulate and limit the expression of cultural difference in the private sphere. Such control strategies applied, for instance, to South Africa during the Apartheid regime, or they apply to contemporary Malaysia whose Indian and Chinese citizens only obtain political rights on their acceptance of privileges or reservations benefiting the Malay demographic majority (Bhattacharyya 2010). It is a strategy which we also associate with much of the history of post-independence Pakistan and Sri Lanka (see further).

The second and third strategies, however, place the institutional and policy choices that divided societies face on a continuum from integrationist to accommodationist (McGarry et al. 2008: 41–90). The key difference between integrationist and accommodationist policies is that the former tolerate the privatisation of societal divisions on ethnic grounds, but argue *against* their *public* (state) recognition. By advocating equal citizenship rights, integrationists emphasise the ties that bind and they condemn group-based practices such as affirmative action, quotas, asymmetric territorial autonomy or multicultural policy as causes of political instability. Conversely, accommodationist policies start from the belief that ethnic, religious, social, cultural, linguistic differences should be recognised in public through group-specific rights and policies.

In terms of where India is positioned on the integration–accommodation continuum, I propose to focus on three dimensions.[2]

The first dimension relates to what Anne Phillips labelled as a 'politics of presence' (Phillips 1994), that is, the extent to which public institutions allow for the *representation* of different ethnic groups. An integrative approach starts from the assumption that access to core political and public institutions should be entirely based on merit and considers quotas or reservations as an unnecessary distortion. An accommodative approach accepts that such quota's may be required in order to guarantee a minimum level of representation for minority linguistic, religious, caste, tribe, aboriginal, territorial or other groups in the core institutions of the *trias politica* (legislative, judiciary and executive including public services such as the police force, military, diplomacy and the educational sector). This dimension also concerns the nexus between voters and political representation through the electoral system, that is, the mechanism used to translate votes into political representation and the choice between a presidential and parliamentary regime. The need for legislative quotas (or 'reservations' as they are called in India) may be less clear in a system of proportional representation because smaller ethnic groups that are territorially dispersed should stand a better chance of being directly represented (Lijphart 1999). Similarly, a parliamentary system opens up more possibilities for multiethnic representation than a presidential one due to the prevalence of cabinet government in the former and the 'winner-takes-all' principle which normally undergirds the election of a president.

The second dimension concerns *territorial pluralism*. As an ideal type, territorial pluralism implies that states not only recognise a right to *self-rule* for territorially concentrated ethnic groups, but combine this with a degree of *shared rule* for these groups in the governance of the centre. Therefore, territorial pluralism not only assumes a type of federal arrangement or at the very least devolution (Swenden 2013); it also embraces a territorial structure that uses ethnicity as the basis for the delineation of the territorial units in the state (provinces, states and cantons), and sanctions asymmetric arrangements of self-rule to reflect the different aspirations of the sub-state nations within the multi-level polity. This contrasts with the US experience where state boundaries were drawn explicitly to prevent aboriginal minorities from constituting territorial or state majorities (Kymlicka 1995). Territorial pluralism assumes that strengthening the voice of these ethnic units in the political system will squelch their appetite for secession or exit. Integrationists do not oppose federalism, but unlike territorial pluralists, they favour a federal design in which ethnic minorities do not constitute majorities at the regional level. In their view, territorial pluralism is a recipe for instability and puts the said majorities on a slippery slope towards secession (Erk and Anderson 2009; Roeder 2007).

The third dimension is in some sense linked to the first two and concerns the dominant *'narrative' of the state and the recognition* that may be given to different ethnic groups within (on this issue see also Keating 2004). Is the state primarily conceived along the lines of the Republican French *état-nation* in which different ethnic groups melt into a 'common identity' under the guise of the 'one and indivisible Republic' *or* do the symbols of the state (flag, anthem and constitutional preamble) portray the state as plurinational or multiethnic and make this diversity a part of their historiography and practice? In multilingual societies, is there an attempt to make the language of a majority the official or national language, or does the state support the multi-lingual nature of the state through the official recognition of minority languages? Are citizens of the state subject to one Bill of Rights, applicable to all, or, does the state recognise differential citizenship rights based on ethnicity? (In case of the latter a minimum threshold should apply to all, that is, ethnicity cannot be used as a ground to exclude certain groups from political rights such as the right to vote or freely express themselves—as this would amount to a control strategy—but the state could create possibilities for differentiating cultural or social rights).

Situating and Explaining India's Trajectory Across Time

The Integrationist Turn at Independence

On at least two of the three dimensions just discussed (the politics of presence and territorial pluralism), India has moved away from a relatively integrationist path at independence to a more accommodative position today. However, India's trajectory is less clear on the third dimension (understandings of the Indian nation) because of the rise of Hindu nationalism since the 1980s.

The relative 'integrationist path' which India adopted at independence can be attributed to Partition; a critical juncture with a dramatic impact on the shape of Indian nationalism and the prevailing state strategies for governing diversity. India's founders insisted on the indestructability of the Indian state and sought to apply this notion to its entire territory, notwithstanding the rather artificial nature of the new state's north-western and north-eastern borders. As Talbot and Singh (2009: 133) assert, in popular imagery this affection for territorial integrity was expressed through the image of 'Bharat Mata' (Mother India); 'borders became coterminious with the body politic; the new metaphor for the nation that had suffered "vivesection", "division" and "amputation"'. Clearly, in the wake of Partition, a Hinduist control strategy was a possibility: Vallabhbhai Patel, Deputy PM until his death in 1950, called for the dismissal of all Muslim state officials after Partition and argued against the protection of Muslim citizens by the army (Khilnani 1997: 31). Partition, therefore, pushed India into an integrationist direction on each of the three dimensions.

In terms of the *politics of representation,* the Constituent Assembly abolished separate electorates and reserved seats for Muslims, Christians and Sikhs (Jayal 2006: 48), and it reluctantly agreed to retain reserved seats for Scheduled Castes (SCs) and Scheduled Tribes (STs).[3] The founding fathers also relinquished religion-based quotas in government jobs (Stuligross and Varshney 2002: 442). Although several states of India practiced a reservation policy for the so-called 'Other Backward Castes' (OBCs—initially referred to as 'Classes'), the Congress Party, which dominated the Constituent Assembly only gave heed to setting up a Commission (the so-called Kalekar Commission) to look into the economically and socially backward *classes* in addition to the STs and Castes. When the Commission finally reported in 1955 and recommended 25 to 40 per cent reservations of vacant positions in the civil service for these OBCs, Congress simply ignored it.

Dalit legislative reservations were retained, but their link with Dalit voters was weakened. Under the Poona Pact (1932), Dalits were required to organise primaries and the broader electorate would subsequently select one of four shortlisted candidates. The Constituent Assembly dropped the principle of separate primaries and candidates—while still having to originate from the SC group—were more often than not nominated by a predominantly non-Dalit selectorate (Heath, Glouharova and Heath, 2008: 140). Next to reservations for SC (15 per cent), the Constituent Assembly also agreed to extend reservations benefiting the STs (7.5 per cent). As for SC, these reservations cover not only representation in legislative (elected by all voters within a ST designated constituency) but also representation in the civil service and higher education. The Constituent Assembly expressed continuity with British India insofar as it continued to rely on the 'first past the post' (FPTP) electoral system—a system that is generally not well-suited to accommodate minority interests due to its 'winner-takes-all' format—to lower house elections (Lok Sabha) of the union parliament (Jayal 2006: 93; Sridharan 2006).

With regard to the second dimension, territorial pluralism, the Constituent Assembly insisted on the construction of an 'indestructible union' (Austin 1966: 193, Talbot and Singh 2009: 132). Plans to establish a weak federal centre in a united India with powers in foreign policy, defence and communications alone or Gandhi's even more 'eccentric' plan for radical decentralisation built around 700,000 villages or panchayats (Sáez 2002: 24–26) were dropped. The Congress reverted to the more centralised state format of the 1935 Government of India Act (Saxena 2006: 105), but without the power-sharing incentives at the centre to accommodate the large Muslim minority which the Muslim League came to defend. The Constituent Assembly 'centred' the nation around territorial civicness (Adeney 2002: 21), by defending a 'union' at the centre and the states at the periphery (Sáez 2002: 30). According to Ambedkar, the strength of the constitution was its flexibility. It could be *'both unitary as well as federal, according to the requirements of time and circumstances'* (cited in Sáez 2002: 33). This 'centralised imprint' was reflected in the recognition of Indian citizenship alone; the creation of an integrated judiciary, civil service and police services, a system of universal rights and the ability of the Supreme Court to supervise it, limited fiscal autonomy of the states with all major tax revenues set and raised at the central level, a relatively weak second chamber of the union parliament in which state representation would be more or less proportionate to their relative demographic weight in the union (thus departing from the principle of equal state representation that applies to the US, Swiss or Australian second chambers). Centralised planning, through the enactment of Five Year economic plans by the para-constitutional Planning Commission further added to the centralisation of the Indian state. Perhaps most importantly, the 'union' government could extend its control of the states through the appointment of state governors and the redrawing of state boundaries without their (formal) explicit consent. By invoking 'Emergency powers', it could assume full legislative and administrative control in the states. Furthermore, the union parliament (through Article 226) could legislate on exclusively provincial subjects in normal times if they became a matter of national concern. The founding fathers did not engage in a significant 'restructuring' of the states in the Indian union, save the forceful incorporation of the princely states that were located at the Indian side of the border (with the exception of Kashmir, for which an eventual referendum and a much more extensive degree of self-rule, including a separate Kashmiri constitution was promised).

Finally, in terms of the *recognition of ethnic pluralism and the metanarratives of the nation*, the Constituent Assembly—seeking to dismiss the 'two-nation theory' which justified the birth of Pakistan—favoured the image of India as a 'composite' state. This image was built on the metaphor of a 'family' in which all religions and ethnic groups have an equal place and none would dominate the functioning of the state, but it had been challenged from the outset by a more assimilationist or controlling narrative which considers Hinduism as the defining characteristic of the Indian Nation (Bajpai 2012; Stuligross and Varshney 2002: 434–435). In its purest form, this Hindu nationalist view calls for a close link between Hindi (language)—Hindu (religion) and Hindustan (India as its homeland). The adoption of secularism was more than just an integrative device: it was also accommodative to the extent that the Indian version of secularism does not require a 'strict' separation of state and religion but assumes 'an equidistant approach' of the state in relation to the various religious communities (Bhargava 2008). Therefore, the state can interfere in religious matters, for instance, through supporting the establishment and administration of religious educational institutions but in so doing 'the state shall not discriminate against any educational institution (Article 340 of the Constitution). Furthermore, separate personal laws (marriage, divorce and inheritance) for Muslims and smaller religious minorities, some of which predated Independence, were carried forward after India gained Independence (Lijphart 2007: 28). Although many members of the Constituent Assembly (not only Hindu nationalists) defended the issuing of a 'Universal Civil Code', the inclusion thereof as a 'directive principle' under the Indian constitution precluded its judicial enforceability (Lerner 2012), and thus secured the continuation of distinctive relational personal law regimes in practice. The choice of national anthem and Indian flag also project an accommodative notion of Indian citizenship. The Constituent Assembly chose the more inclusive *Jana Gana Mana* to the *Vande Mataram* as national anthem because the latter, more widely known hymn, contained references to the Hindu goddesses of Durga and Kali (symbolising India's knowledge, power, greatness and glory). Similarly, the Chakra wheel (a symbol of Buddhist Emperor Ashoka) at the centre of India's flag expresses tolerance, while the Green band is said to refer to the presence of a large Muslim community.

Of further importance in terms of accommodating diversity is the Constituent Assembly's decision to reconsider its decision to make Hindi the national language of India after it was approved with the smallest of margins (78 against 77 votes). Due to this extremely narrow majority in favour of upgrading Hindi (and downgrading English), the Assembly postponed the implementation of the measure until 1965, but also established language commissions to oversee the phasing out of English and supervise the progress of Hindi as the official language (Chandhoke 2007). In other words, the Constituent Assembly was committed to a more integrative linguistic policy in the future. There was also no concession to reorganise the states along linguistic lines, even though it would have been in keeping with tradition insofar as the Congress Party itself, following a number of organisational reforms, was rearranged in 1920 through the creation of 21 vernacular units in the form of Provincial Congress Committees (Chandhoke 2007: 121). Especially Nehru feared that to accept linguistic federalism was to open up more divisions in a country that had already been divided in the name of religion.

An Accommodationist Path Since Independence?

Extension of Reservation Policy to Other Backward Castes

Since Independence, reservations to SCs and STs have not only become entrenched but administrative and educational reservations have been extended to the large group of OBCs. Congress' refusal to incorporate OBCs in reservation policy was first successfully challenged by the Socialist party in the 1960s under the leadership of Ram Manohar Lohia. He maintained that 'caste and not class was the basic unit of Indian society and that Nehru's version of socialism would not be enough to combat inequalities' (Jaffrelot 2004: 4). No major change occurred nonetheless until the 1977 national elections, after which the Socialists participated in the Janata Party coalition and commissioned a 'second Backward Classes Commission' (the so-called 'Mandal Commission') which apart from identifying 3,743 castes as 'backward' also recommended 27 per cent administrative reservations for 'OBCs' *beyond* the 22 per cent which already applied to SCs (Dalits) and STs. Congress, however, which returned to power in 1980, still refused to implement its recommendations. It was left to the Janata Party (headed by V.P. Singh, at one point a prominent Congress leader) to do so in 1990, that is, almost immediately after Congress was ousted from power and coalition government at the centre became the order of the day. The implementation of Mandal in 1991 and the extension of OBC reservations to higher level graduate education in 2006 by a Congress-led coalition government (so-called Mandal II) had firmly entrenched caste accommodative policies. Since then, non-caste-based parties (such as

Congress or the BJP) have accepted that they must field OBC candidates in order to secure votes. For instance, in the 2014 general elections, Narendra Modi clearly played out his 'OBC' background as a vote-seeking strategy. As Wilkinson puts it, 'the political arithmetic in favour of reservations is so overwhelming that no major politician will come out openly against them' (Wilkinson 2010: 266).

The implementation of the Mandal Commission report in 1991 initially reinforced and unified OBC identities, especially because upper caste Hindus campaigned heavily against its implementation. In time however, the OBC category itself had become too heterogeneous and the number of groups that was eligible for reservations outstripped the supply of civil service positions that could be filled up (Wilkinson 2010: 266). In a landmark ruling, the Indian Supreme Court warned of a 'creamy layer' of dominant OBC castes across various states that shut out other OBCs in the promotion of reservations or government benefits. Furthermore, it 'limited' the application of OBC reservations to 27 per cent so that in total not more than half of the Indian population could benefit from reservation policy.

State Reorganisation as a Precondition for the Manifestation of Political Federalism

Changes in centre–state relations were at least in part contingent upon accommodative policies with regard to linguistic policy, a component of the third of our dimensions. The temporary status of English as a connecting language became de facto permanent after 1965. Reflecting pressure from below (see further), Congress through the Official Languages Amendment Act (1967) eventually sanctioned a multilingual India and recognised the right of states to use regional languages in communication with their citizens. Hence, every state may adopt by law any language in use in the state (that is, the regional majority language, possibly in addition to any other language) *or* Hindi. However, all proceedings of the Supreme and High Courts, or all bills and acts passed in the central parliament *and* state legislatures, and all orders, rules and regulations *must* be in English. Therefore, English retained its role as a connecting language, also at the state level. This change helped to accommodate the speakers of minority languages (such as Tamil) at the centre or in the states (such as Hindi in Tamil Nadu). In parallel with the acceptance of a linguistic regime that applied to India as a whole, political leaders endorsed 'linguistic federalism' as a basis for state reorganisation. In 1951, there were 27 States in the Indian federation. In 1952, the process of state-reorganisation started with the carving out of the predominantly Telugu speaking state of Andhra from the state of Madras. Four years later, the States Reorganisation Act brought into being Karnataka and Kerala and major changes were made to the boundaries of Punjab, Madhya Pradesh and Bombay. The latter was divided into Maharashtra and Gujarat, after a regionalist party, the Maja Gujarat Parishad made significant inroads into the electoral support for Congress. Punjab was split into Punjab and (predominantly Hindi-speaking) Haryana in 1966. The States Reorganisation Act (1956) initially *reduced* the number of States to 14, but that number increased again to 28 (and 7 Union Territories) by 2003, and, since the formation of Telengana in 2014 to 29 states (Majeed 2003: 84). Chandhoke (2007: 125) notes that these successive state reorganisations have come much closer to the objective of linguistic homogenisation, in that districts in which the predominant language is different from that of the state or union territory in which the district is located make up less than 10 per cent of India's territory and represent less than 3 per cent of its overall population. States created since 1966 may have done so by invoking an identity that is not language-based. Tribal movements and/or the expression of socio-economic grievances in a context of a transforming Indian party system with the gradual rise of OBC-parties and the BJP played a role in the formation of Chhattisgarh, Uttaranchal, Jharkhand and most recently, Telangana (Tillin 2013).

Although the constitutional architecture of Indian federalism has undergone little change since independence (except for the size and nature of the federal units themselves as described previously), states have become much more successful in defending their political autonomy. The creation of ethnically more homogenous units played a role in shifting voter allegiances to the states and (as I will discuss later), state-based parties, but the 'revival' of Indian federalism cannot be seen in isolation from the transformation of the Indian party system from a one-party dominant to a fragmented multi-level party system.

Explaining the Shift Towards More Accommodative Policies in Practice

How can we explain the accommodative shift towards OBC reservations and the practice of a more decentralised federation based on the creation of more homogenous ethnic units? Accommodative shifts cannot be seen in isolation of social or democratic pressures. The pan-Indian elections of 1952 were the first general elections to be held on the basis of universal suffrage. Provincial (state) elections in 1946 were still held on a limited franchise in which two-thirds of the Indian electorate were shut out of the electoral process (notwithstanding reserved seats for the SC and the ST). Even so, the extension of the franchise did not immediately empower the Dalits, tribes or OBCs in Indian Politics. The Congress Party, the dominant party in Indian politics until 1989 had built its 'vote-banks' by working out a system of patronage in the countryside into which 'traditional institutions of kin and caste were gradually drawn and involved and a structure of processes and compromises was developed' (Kothari 1964: 1163). By making the party dependent on the support of local notables, often landowning or dominant castes, Congress became invested with a socially conservative bias which hampered the implementation of pro-poor policies (that is, support for the weakest, eradication of caste discrimination) which it proclaimed. That it took until 1967 before Congress (and dominant caste) hegemony in (North) Indian elections was seriously challenged can be attributed to the leadership capacities of Prime Minister Nehru; the 'multiplier' effect of first-past-the-post, returning handsome Congress legislative majorities notwithstanding minority electoral support; Congress' association with the national liberation movement (Spieß 2010) and its internal operation as a 'Congress system' (Kothari 1964: 1161–1173). The latter was not only reflected in the comparatively strong organisation of the party on the ground, but also in its ability to 'accommodate "parties of pressure" at the margins' so long as they did not fundamentally undermine its key principles of secularism, socialism (or rather planned economic development), democracy and non-alignment. However, Congress did not operate as an internally consociational system (Adeney 2007; Wilkinson 2000). At best, it had the attributes of a vertically integrated *federal* party, not a '*consocational*' one, and thus it was limited in the extent to which it gave ethnic minorities (Muslims, SC and ST) a veto-right (Brass 1994:73).

Using a historical-institutionalist perspective, one could argue that growing subaltern protest against the tokenist policies of Congress was inevitable (see Pierson 2004: 92 for the applicable notion of 'cumulative effects' in this context). Universal suffrage was to provoke a 'silent revolution' (Jaffrelot 2003) which in time made the emergence of parties that address subaltern grievances and propose their direct political representation inevitable. The inability of Congress to transform its internal organisation and programme to allow for more direct representation of these groups facilitated their recourse to group-specific movements and parties. Conversely, some of the policies which Congress *did* implement after independence; most notably the spread of primary education (which gradually pushed illiteracy rates down), the Green Revolution (introduction of new fertiliser techniques since the 1960s) and the abolition of large (absentee) landlordism in North India empowered the OBCs in particular. The latter two policies enriched some of the small land-owing agricultural labourers, gradually transforming them into 'bullock capitalists' (Rudolph and Rudolph 1987). Frequently, these constituted the dominant *jatis* amongst the so-called OBCs (for example, the Jats, Yadavs or Kurmi's). Their empowerment also instilled a growing group awareness and identity amongst the Dalits.

Grass-roots mobilisation also underpinned the acceptance of linguistic federalism (in fact, the centre caved into demands for a separate Telugu-speaking state of Andhra Pradesh after the fast-unto-death of a Congress activist there). As indicated previously, linguistic federalism contributed to make the states the prime arena of voter identification. Indira Gandhi's decision to uncouple national and state elections in 1971 (a short-term strategy meant to rein in the Syndicate; a rivalry faction of state party leaders and branches which split from the Congress Party in 1969) also strengthened state political autonomy in the longer run: state election campaigns were no longer overshadowed by national campaigns and turnout in state elections started to exceed turnout in national elections (Yadav and Palshikar 2009). Furthermore, the centralised nature of Indian federalism notwithstanding, the *provision* of health, education, food (agriculture) and power is controlled by the states. Thus, while *legislative* authority in these fields often rests with the union government, their *implementation* requires state consent. For voters then, states (and since their direct election also panchayats) have become the strongest frame of reference. As such, parties challenging the Congress Party in this context often failed to adopt a nation-wide following. The Janata Party and more recently the Janata Dal quickly disintegrated into various state parties. Few backward caste parties also transcend state boundaries (although the Bahujan Samaj and Samajwadi Parties aspire to a nation-wide following, their stronghold is unquestionably in Uttar Pradesh). Thus far, even the Hindu nationalist BJP has formed only one South Indian state government (Karnataka between 2008 and 2013).

In the aggregate, the transformation of the Indian party system from a one party dominant into a multi-party system in which states are dominated by different party constellations has produced a more accommodative political system. The rise of state-based parties cemented support for federalism in two ways. First, one party government at the centre became impossible. Between 1989 and 2014, all Indian governments were coalition and/or minority governments. As such the brokerage power of state parties, either as part of a coalition government or as parties supporting the union government from outside led to a stronger (if sometimes selective) awareness of state interests at the centre. Second, state political autonomy and state self-rule were more easily accepted. The frequency and average duration of President's Rule (the imposition of central rule in the states) has substantially decreased since the 1990s, as shown by Table 11.1. The relative decrease is attributable not only to the participation of regional parties in a federal coalition government, but also to the more interventionist actions of the Indian Supreme Court, which since its *Bommai* ruling

Table 11.1

The incidence and frequency of the President's Rule (1950–2012)

Time period	Frequency	Average days lasted
1950–1960	6	234 days
1960–1970	14	239 days
1970–1980	47	197 days + Emergency
1980–1990	23	251 days (2,109 days Punjab)
1990–2000	22	165 days
2000–2012	6	125 days

Source: Calculated from Adeney (2007: 185–189); for figures up to 2005; PR between 2005 and 2012 was only applied to Nagaland and Meghalaya for relatively limited periods of time. (See http://www.worldstatesmen.org/India_states.html)

(1994) restricted the use of President's Rule for party political purposes by specifying guidelines for its legitimate use (Sathe 2008). Yet, party fragmentation created the conditions in which the Supreme Court could more easily deliver such a verdict.

Furthermore, there is evidence to suggest that by being more tolerant of party incongruence in the composition of central and state governments, India has also become more accommodative of ethno-territorial diversity. Since the 1990s, procedural democracy has been restored in the Punjab, Assam and (since 1998 also in) Kashmir. Regionalist parties from each of these states have participated in national coalition governments (the Akali Dal as part of the BJP-led NDA, and the Assam Gana Parishad and Jammu and Kashmir National Conference as part of the Congress-led UPA). Yet, although Indian federalism has become more accommodative, it has not transformed into a form of territorial pluralism. As Tillin (2006: 47) argues, the special constitutional status that was accorded to Jammu and Kashmir in 1950 and the specific arrangements that apply to some of India's North-Eastern states and tribal areas has given an 'asymmetrical *appearance*' to the Indian federation. Their significance should not be exaggerated. Jointly they only affect a small share of the Indian population, and the special provisions for Kashmir (according to which the Indian Parliament could only legislate in foreign affairs, defence and communications) have been entirely hollowed out (Bose 2013; Tillin 2006: 52). The North-Eastern states can lay claim to a disproportionate entitlement to central government grants and some states can delegate law-making powers to tribal district councils. However, their ethnic distinctiveness is such that perhaps a case for more and not less asymmetry could have been made. Continuing ethnic insurgencies (especially in Nagaland) also led to a high securitisation of the area, including the application of central and state anti-terror laws, which has distorted the operation of democracy on the ground.[4]

Situating India in Comparative Perspective

In India, the control strategies of the central (and sometimes also state) governments in some parts of the North-East, some districts affected by Naxalite rebellion and Kashmir are an exception, not the rule. Yet, India's accommodative trajectory is rather unusual in the region as the following brief comparison with neighbouring Pakistan and Sri Lanka demonstrates.

Although Pakistan and India started off with the same interim constitution (Government of India Act 1935), following Partition, they chose different paths in terms of ethnic management. As Pakistan sprang from the 'two nation theory', the Pakistani constitution of 1956 declared Pakistan as an *Islamic* Republic. Even though members of minority religions (prior to the secession of Bangladesh in 1971, especially Hindus) were constitutionally protected and allowed to practice their personal law regimes, the President of Pakistan had to be a Muslim and the Muslim League, the pre-eminent Pakistani party at independence was only open to Muslim members (Adeney 2007: 96–99). Similarly, by initially adopting Urdu as its state language (only spoken as a first language by 3 per cent of the people), Pakistan alienated the large Bengali speaking majority in East Pakistan and the Sindhi speaking community of West Pakistan (this was less detrimental to Punjabi, Pashtu and Baluchi speakers because these languages were more widely used in speech than in writing). Although Bengali was eventually recognised as a national language in 1954, the Pakistani state soon after entrenched the political dominance of West Pakistan by enacting the One Unit Plan (Adeney, 2007: 137–162). This 'plan' amalgamated all the western provinces into 'one unit' with the same voting weight in the national legislature as the demographically preponderant East Pakistani unit. East Pakistanis were heavily underrepresented in the top civil service and army, whereas Pakistan as a whole was primarily governed by the 'Muhajirs' (Muslim settlers from North India and the bedrock of Muslim League support) and the Punjabis (through their control of the military, and with the Muhajirs, much of the administration). Formally speaking provincial autonomy in West Pakistan was restored after the secession of Bangladesh and the provinces were allowed to promote their regional majority languages. However, in practice, central incursions into provincial politics have remained much more common than in India post-1991 and peripheral but resource rich provinces (such as Baluchistan) have witnessed important insurgency movements against the Punjabi controlled state (Jaffrelot, 2015: 127–194). Even under the current civilian government and the prospect of restoring a degree of provincial self-rule, resentment of the peripheral provinces towards the central government remains large (Talbot 2012).

Similarly, whereas the secessionist aspirations of Tamil Nadu were successfully accommodated through self-rule and the recognition of Tamil as a regional majority language in India, in neighbouring Sri Lanka, the Tamil-speaking majority was quickly alienated after independence. The Sri Lankan Government first weakened the Tamil community by disenfranchising the 'Up-Country Tamils' who settled from India to work in the Sri Lankan tea plantations in the nineteenth century and for that reason were not considered as part of the Ceylonese nation. In 1956, less than 10 years after independence, the Sri Lankan Government (under the influence of ethnic outbidding between two Sinhalese parties) also declared Sinhala the only official language of Ceylon and this was followed in 1978 by declaring Buddhism as the state religion and entrusting the Sri Lankan state with 'the duty to protect and foster the Buddha Sasana' (Stepan et al. 2011: 156). Therefore, within 30 years, the Sinhala controlled government succeeded in excluding and alienating most of the Tamil minority. The Sinhalese 'control' policies fuelled a radicalisation amongst the Tamil community who became increasingly beholden to the influence of the authoritarian and militaristic Tamil Tigers.

The Limits to Accommodation

Despite the increasingly accommodative trajectory of India since Independence and its more accommodative stance compared with Pakistan and Sri Lanka, accommodation is not without its critics. These criticisms can be clustered in three groups. The first group puts forward normative grounds for questioning accommodative policies and is voiced by left- and right-wing ideologues alike. The second—and often connected—reason for dismissing accommodative policies, especially quotas is more empirical in nature as it links reservations to social outcomes: have reservations served their purpose, and if not, might other devices have been more appropriate to alleviate the social conditions of the subaltern. The third and final criticisms (which build on normative and empirical arguments) find their expression in the ideology of the Hindu nationalist BJP and more in particular in the threat of its Hindutva ideology for the longer-term survival of accommodation in India. In what follows I turn to each of these aspects in turn.

The Normative Critique

The normative grounds for contesting accommodation have been voiced by influential political thinkers from the left and right. Reflecting his defence of classical liberalism, Brian Barry has argued that social justice requires the direct redistribution from those who have to those who have not, and that multicultural policies which base discrimination on identity, ethnicity or culture detract from the essentially material conditions that underpin social injustice (Barry 2001, for an extensive critique on multiculturalism). Put differently, the voice of the subaltern should not be strengthened other than through the ballot box. Universal suffrage guarantees that the elected will express a multitude of voices and beliefs, irrespective of their ethnic, gender or linguistic background. Reservations, or indeed, also territorial autonomy to some groups who consider themselves as sub-state nations or ethnic minority groups but not to others within the state, are potentially illiberal to the extent that they privilege some groups (lower castes, minority nations or ethnic groups) over others. There are good reasons to support the need for general welfare schemes in India. Indeed, as Drèze and Sen (2013: 107–212) have demonstrated, India spends comparatively little on education and health compared with other countries at similar levels of economic development. Yet, the case for accommodation through welfare schemes alone misses the point insofar as not only materialist but often and sometimes especially cultural reasons underpin widespread discrimination against lower caste groups (such as the SCs) or religious or ethnic minorities. For instance, the material upliftment of some Dalits does not necessarily terminate their marginalisation in politics or social life more generally. Without clear policies in place that increase the direct representation of the subaltern in politics, not merely as electors but especially as legislators, discrimination on the basis of cultural background and identity are less likely to be taken seriously. As Anne Phillips puts it:

> …[W]hen the politics of ideas is taken in isolation from the politics of presence, it does not deal adequately with the experiences of those social groups who by virtue of their race or ethnicity or religion or gender have felt themselves excluded from the political process.... If the range of ideas has been curtailed by orthodoxies that rendered alternatives invisible [by under-representing marginalised groups], there will be no satisfactory solution short of changing the people who represent and develop the ideas. (Phillips 1994: 78)

Similarly, democratic equality cannot exist without the recognition of equal worth and the latter cannot be adequately explored let alone realised without proper representation (Phillips 1994: 79). Since liberals expect an open debate or contestation between all possible arguments within the polity, quotas can be warranted where—other things being equal—they provide a stronger guarantee that marginalised groups will be heard. For the same reason, territorial asymmetry in combination with some degree of shared rule at the centre may commit the loyalty of minority nations to the state. Neither reservations nor territorial asymmetry are illiberal or undemocratic as they build towards the development of compound and multiple identities in a culturally and ethnically diverse polity.

The Empirical Grounds for Contesting Accommodation

Those who oppose accommodation on normative grounds often take recourse to the (mal)functioning of accommodative policies on the ground to support their arguments. Even so, the operation of accommodative policies in practice can be criticised on its own grounds. There are four possible points of critique. I will illustrate these here with reference to reservations benefiting the backward castes. However, it is possible to make similar arguments with regard to territorial accommodation (which in India has been criticised especially in relation to the asymmetric constitutional status of Kashmir).

The first criticism points at the potentially counterproductive effects of positive discrimination measures on the attitudes of its intended recipients and the erstwhile elites. The latter may resent political reservations and the group-based benefits which they invoke (from which they feel excluded); whereas, the recipients of these policies could use them as mechanisms of retribution to punish the (erstwhile) leading castes or classes, for instance by questioning the suitability of government or civil service appointments, pubic contracts or educational admissions even where these were allocated based on merit. Yet, in this regard, Varshney (2013: 36) takes comfort from developments in South India, where the anti-Brahmin agitations of the 1950s eventually gave way to more inclusive understandings of citizenship and social justice. Conversely, erstwhile dominant castes have quickly learned to play the game, for instance, by joining lower caste parties or at least cooperating with them in the pursuit of political power. In this sense, while in the short-term group-based policies can lead to verbal (and sometimes physical) aggression and retributive policies, in the long-term, they should enhance inclusiveness and equality.

The second criticism points at the haphazard implementation of lower caste reservations or other policies targeting the Backward Castes and the STs. Senior law and police officers often refuse to implement anti-discrimination legislation or enforce quota-legislation. In an earlier study assessing why states scored so poorly in enforcing the Untouchability Offences Act, Marc Galanter (1968) pointed his finger at the underlying mechanisms preventing their implementation:

> …[A]nti-disabilities prosecutions depend on the initiative of the local police and the sympathy of local magistrates, both of whom have obvious reason to be disinclined to antagonize the dominant elements of the local community. If they are not themselves members of the latter, they are heavily dependent upon their cooperation in order to do their jobs and gain promotions.

Unfortunately, more than 40 years after Gallanter's assessment, discrimination against lower castes remains widespread (Gorringe 2005, 2013). Dalit children are more likely to drop out of school, in part because they are subject to illegal but overt discrimination; for instance, by having to drink water from separate pots (Shah et al. 2006). Lower educational attainment subsequently hinders access to reserved positions in the public sector for which minimum educational standards must be met (especially category A and B jobs). Although Dalits fill up the reserved places in public sector jobs of category D and C, they remain underrepresented especially in category A jobs (11.84 per cent in 2003; Jodhka 2012: 136–137).

Similarly. Corbridge et al. (2013: 208) pointed at the inadequate implementation of the STs and Other Traditional Forest Dwellers (Recognition of Forest Rights) by the central and state governments across India. The act vested (tribal) forest dwellers with inheritable and non-transferable rights in land. But too much is at stake here for business and political elites in India: millions of STs have already been displaced as a result of the appropriation of forest land for mining, forestry or economic development (the so-called Special Economic Zones)—or sometimes even wildlife conservation (all without adequate monetary compensation). This forced migration and appropriation of land has played a key role in the resurgence of Maoist rebellion in a large number of districts, especially across the east and south-east of India.

However, a failure to implement anti-discrimination laws or forest rights protection legislation should not in itself be seen as a sufficient reason to oppose accommodative schemes of this nature. If at all, it shows that caste and tribe remain a 'sociological institution' or a 'habitus' (Bourdieu): 'an embodied system of dispositions durably inscribed in people's reflexes, movements and desires' (Corbridge et al. 2013: 255). In the short- to medium-term quotas and general welfare schemes benefiting the lower castes such as land reform, cheap credit or housing and livestock subsidies—can only accomplish so much.

The third criticism is a variant of the former in which it criticises a different aspect of how these schemes are implemented, namely the arbitrary and often discriminatory way in which the beneficiaries of the said policies are defined. Earlier, I already pointed at the struggle to delineate the 'OBCs' and indeed to ensure that quotas trickle down to all the *jatis* of that caste cohort, and not just to the higher status 'creamy layer', who, in material terms least need them. Here, I point at the discrepancy between accommodative policies vis-à-vis OBC, SC and ST in terms of reservations and the near absence thereof in relation to Muslims. As a religious minority, Muslims have their *cultural and religious rights* protected, enabling them to express their religious identity (for example, the right to use and write Urdu in a distinctive script and the right to establish and administer educational institutions), but few policies promote their political representation and social inclusion. Yet, as Hasan (2009: 49) asserts, 'when it comes to education and employment, the average Muslim is at the bottom of the heap and trailing behind SC and OBCs on many indicators of social development.' This differential treatment of Muslims is difficult to justify in view of their socio-economic position. Unlike reservations and centrally sponsored schemes that specifically target the lower castes and STs; until recently, there was very little in the way of welfare schemes benefiting the Muslims. The findings of the Sachar Committee (2006) led to the establishment of a Ministry of Minority

Affairs, a National Commission for Religious and Linguistic Minorities and a National Commission for Minority Educational Institutions; but the Eleventh Plan (2007–2012) which followed shortly after the publication of its report did little in the way of devising special plan outlays for the socio-economic betterment of the minorities (Hasan 2009: 52–53). The inclusion of a minority sub-plan was feared to 'fuel the communal propaganda of minority appeasement' (Hasan 2009: 55). Similarly, the government of Andhra Pradesh's attempt in 2004 to reserve 5 per cent of administrative and educational reservations for Muslims was struck down by the state High Court on the grounds that reservations cannot be granted on the basis of religion and the total quantum of reservations cannot exceed 50 per cent (Hasan 2009: 178). Even so, Muslims (and other religious minorities) could be included in reservation policy on account of their 'backward *class*' affiliation (effectively defined in caste terms). Yet, although 40 per cent of Muslims are OBC and Muslims comprise 15.7 per cent of OBCs, Muslim OBC reservations only account for about 3 per cent of all OBC reservations (Hasan 2009: 178). Furthermore, Dalit Muslims and Dalit Christians (unlike Sikhs and Buddhists) have not been incorporated into the SC category and, thus, cannot benefit from the SC reservations. Hasan invokes the socio-economic deprivation of Muslims as a ground to include them in reservation policy, but from a multicultural perspective, the case *for* their inclusion can be based on the fact that the caste system is a general feature of social life in India which even affects the so-called 'egalitarian' religions. Furthermore, it is difficult to justify why SC reservations can apply to Sikhs and Buddhists but not to Muslims and Christians. Possibly, this is the case because extending reservations to Muslim Dalits *without* enlarging the overall pool of places to which SC can lay claim would strengthen competition amongst the Dalit constituents.

A fourth set of criticisms attempts a more direct link between reservations or caste-specific welfare schemes and social outcomes. Despite decades of reservations and anti-discrimination policy, SCs and Tribes are still worse off in terms of material wealth and well-being. Indeed, in a recent overview, Heyer and Gopal Jayal (2009: 19–55) demonstrate that the SCs remain disproportionately poor across urban and rural India; still have much lower land holdings and non-land asset holdings than the population as a whole and remain over-represented amongst poor agricultural and non-agricultural wage labourers. SCs also have considerably lower educational attainment than other population groups and, where they succeed educationally, they fail to find employment that matches their level of education.

In part, the disappointing social outcomes can be attributed to the faults with these schemes that were identified previously: their non-implementation altogether or the difficulty with allocating these schemes to the most deserving beneficiaries. It is also important to put the limited reach of these schemes into perspective: The liberalisation of the Indian economy has shrunk the size of the public sector and with it the relevance of reserved public jobs as a source of employment overall. Private employers cannot be forced to recruit Dalits and OBCs. Studies have shown that recruitment agencies rarely assess the suitability of a candidate on the basis of merit and job experience alone. Private employers frequently take into consideration family background and the ability to speak English as well. On both accounts, locality and caste background (which in turn influences quality and levels of schooling) are important criteria (study by Jodkha and Newman, reported in Jodhka 2012: 166). Next to 'cultural capital', 'social capital' affects recruitment decisions and in this respect too upper caste members are at an advantage because they are better networked.

Despite these shortcomings, it is worth emphasising what has been achieved already by attempting a longitudinal and not just a cross-sectional comparison of data. For instance, there is evidence to support a narrowing literacy and educational attainment gap between Dalits and members of the other castes *across time*. In 1961, non-Dalits were more than twice as likely to be literate than Dalits (literacy rates of 24.02 per cent versus 10.27 per cent). By 2001, that gap had narrowed significantly (64.8 versus 54.7 per cent). In 1965, Dalits were adequately represented in the lowest type of public sector jobs (so-called level D), but only made up about 8, 3 and 1.6 per cent of level C, B and A positions, respectively. By 2003, Dalit underrepresentation remained significant in level A jobs only (about 12 per cent of positions filled against a reservation of 15 per cent), but was almost negligible in level B positions (14.3 per cent). Dalit representation was on a par with their reserved quota for level C and D jobs (Jodhka 2012). These more encouraging outcomes may not be directly attributable to reservation policy or specific welfare schemes *alone* (just as the limited progression on other indicators is not necessarily sufficient evidence of their failure), but most likely have contributed to it.

A variant of the fourth criticism focuses specifically on legislative reservations (that is, guaranteed representation in the federal legislature or state assemblies) and laments the inability of subaltern legislators to speak on behalf of the subaltern. Too often, the few SCs or STs who make it to parliament may appear to be SC stooges who put party, constituency or self-interest above caste, ethnicity or religion. Prominent Dalit leaders have been criticised for paying too much attention to Dalit symbolism when in office. For instance, former Chief Minister of Uttar Pradesh, Mayawati has been widely criticised for erecting numerous statues of Ambedkar or Kanshi Ram instead of focusing on setting up schemes to improve the material conditions of the Dalits and the poor more generally within her state. Arguably, the disproportionate attention to symbolism is a normal feature of groups who for long remained systematically shut out of the political process. It may be a passing phase; the 2014 general elections demonstrated that voters do not automatically sanction 'a politics of presence without a politics of substance' as significant shares of Dalit and OBC voters across India were swayed by the 'developmental' promises of the BJP. At the same time, this should not be seen as an argument to dismiss reservations altogether. It is likely that with no reserved presentation of the subaltern in politics, the civil service, the police, the judiciary and education, anti-discrimination legislation may have received even lower implementation records and even fewer welfare schemes may have benefited the poor, of whom a disproportionate amount belong to the SCs, Tribes and some sections of the OBCs (and the Muslims). Furthermore, in non-reserved or open constituencies, parties are still much more likely to field upper caste or OBC candidates than Dalit candidates, underscoring the need for reserved seats for Dalits. Admittedly, one can question reservations as the best possible institutional strategy to achieve larger representation in politics. Elections by proportional representation would have reduced the need for legislative reservations as Dalit or Muslim specific parties would have faced much lower barriers to enter Parliament and even 'non-ethnic parties' may have placed more Dalit candidates on their party lists. Yet, in the current Indian context, a change in electoral system is very unlikely and does not appear to have much political or even public support. In the absence of electoral change, reservations appear to be the best channel through which the Backward Castes and Tribes can enter parliament.

None of the above downplays the current faults of the reservation system or the specific policies targeting the subaltern. But their partial failure should not be seen as a sufficient reason to support their replacement with redistributive policies alone. For one, in India, the connection between poverty and ethnic identity is strong. More importantly, general welfare schemes that can bring about more redistribution of land and capital should *complement* and not substitute reservation policies. Factoring in social deprivation when determining who within each cohort (ST, SC, Muslims or other religious groups) may be entitled to reservations or targeted welfare can ensure that these policies benefit those who most need them.

In sum, the road to sociopolitical inclusion and substantive representation is still long. This will require not only the eradication of upper caste prejudice, but also a more effective mobilisation amongst the lower strata (who are divided by intra-group rivalry and geography). It will require a need to match demands for dignity (status and identity) with the delivery of substantive policy outputs of a more redistributive nature.

Hindu Nationalism and the Threat to Accommodation

Notwithstanding the more accommodative stance of India compared with Sri Lanka and Pakistan, there are limits to the accommodative trajectory which India traversed since independence. The alternative meta-narrative of the 'Hindu-Rashtra' which was there from the outset but suppressed by Nehruvian secularism has gained more traction since the 1970s. In *theory*, the Indian state is still secular and continues to recognise the right of the most important religious minorities to practice their own set of personal laws. However, in practice, the rise of Hindu nationalism has provoked at the very least a more widespread dissatisfaction with the 'secularist' narrative of the Indian state, or at its worst, a more widespread discrimination of the Muslim minority. The Hindu nationalist BJP openly opposes cow slaughter and it strives for a Uniform Civil Code that is applicable to all religions. Hindu nationalists also take issue with the 'three language formula' (Hindi should be given a more prominent role in relation to English and the regional languages) and with the special constitutional status for India's only Muslim-dominated state, Kashmir.

The mobilisation on religious issues for political ends has been a widespread practice across India for decades. For instance, since the 1970s, the Congress Party took a rather opportunistic view in this regard, sometimes playing the Hindu nationalist card, sometimes standing up for its Muslim vote bank.[5] Yet, against Congress' opportunism (though the party has come out more strongly in support of secularism under the leadership of Sonia and Rahul Gandhi) stands the BJP's programmatic projection of Hindutva and the mainstreaming or 'banalisation' of Hindu nationalism in Indian society at large (Corbridge et al. 2013: 177–196; Hansen 1997). The rise of Hindu nationalism since the 1980s is linked to caste because the growing Dalit and OBC caste mobilisation posed a much greater threat to the interests of upper caste Hindus than Congress' tokenist policies in relation to lower castes. The Sangh Parivar has been implicated in instigating Hindu–Muslim violence (Brass 2003; Wilkinson 2004) for electoral gain.

When in national office between 1998 and 2004, the BJP has worked effectively to implement several Hindutva policies. Through its control of key posts in the NDA federal coalition government, it replaced the heads of the National Council of Educational Research and Training, the Indian Council of Social Science Research and the Indian Council of Historical Research with individuals who were sympathetic to the Hindu nationalist cause. As such India's post-independence history as taught at secondary schools and universities was rewritten in a more Hindu-favourable light (Ogden 2012). In 2001, The BJP-led central government also refused to impose President's rule in Gujarat in spite of the BJP-ruled state government's alleged involvement in the massacre of more than 1,000 (mainly Muslim) citizens following the killing of 50 Hindu volunteers (*kar sevaks*) upon their return from a Hindu pilgrimage to Ayodhya. The BJP at the centre defended its inaction by invoking the federal nature of India and the responsibility of the state level for 'law and order' (Singh and Verney 2003: 18). That the Gujarati-BJP led by the then Chief Minister Narendra Modi extended its lead in subsequent Gujarati assembly elections, especially in those constituencies that were most widely exposed to communal violence, seemed to suggest that communal polarisation and violence generated electoral payoffs (Corbridge et al. 2013: 186).

Modi's communal tactics during his first years in power as Chief Minister raised legitimate doubts about his intentions amongst the Muslim minority even though his recent Prime Ministerial campaign placed a much stronger emphasis on his 'developmental achievements' in Gujarat. The unanticipated overall majority for the BJP in the 2014 general elections (and the subsequent elevation of Narendra Modi and Amit Shah to the posts of Prime Minister and BJP president, respectively) have not alleviated those fears. Shah masterminded the BJP's electoral campaign in Uttar Pradesh and used communal tactics to lure voters away from the BSP and SP. Although Modi recently spoke out in favour of 'India first' (ahead of communal interests), elements of the Sangh Parivar have pursued more radical Hindutva policies. For long, the BJP implicitly tolerated anti-conversion initiatives such as 'love jihad' (the condemnation of the conversion to Islam of young Hindu girls through marriage with Muslim men) and *ghar wapsi* (mass religious conversions into Hinduism). Rising international pressure (especially in the wake of President Obama's visit to India in January 2015) and a major electoral defeat in the Delhi Legislative Assembly elections (February 2015) forced Modi to distance himself more explicitly from these policies.

However, the extent to which the BJP's hold on the centre will jeopardise the accommodative nature of Indian federalism remains to be seen. For one, the BJP victory in 2014 should be placed into context. The 'Modi-wave' still left much of South and North East India without significant BJP support. Though it holds a national parliamentary majority on its own (but with scarcely 31 per cent of the general vote), the BJP's seat share would have been lower without the cooperation of a range of regional and 'secular' parties such as the TDP and BJD. These parties may no longer lend their support to the BJP in future state and general elections through seat sharing arrangements or post-election coalition deals if the BJP were to push through its more radical Hindutva agenda. Much will also depend on how the party fares at the state level, given that accommodative policies (for instance, who belongs to the OBC community) are often shaped there. The BJP may have won an impressive array of state elections in the second half of 2014, but in the case of Jammu and Kashmir, for instance, it entered into a power sharing coalition with the PDP, a party catering to a largely Muslim electorate. Consequently, the party's intention to scrap the special autonomy arrangement of the state under Article 370 of the Indian constitution has been kicked into the long grass (Akhzar 2014). Although the party's 2014 general election manifesto lamented the tokenism and identity politics associated with reservations, it did not call for their abolition, but proposed a stronger focus on 'social justice and harmony' instead (BJP 2014 general election manifesto, 15–17). Given that the BJP now has a substantive following amongst the SC, ST and OBC, it is not likely to reduce the accommodative policies that are in place in relation to these groups. However, it may focus on the linguistic and religious elements of its Hindutva ideology instead. Indeed, since entering into office, the BJP encouraged the more widespread use of Hindi (to the detriment of English) in public announcements via social media (Gahlot 2014) and several BJP ruled states have banned cow slaughter. Although the BJP may keep an open mind to further state reorganisation, it is only likely to sanction such steps where they do not undermine the integrative notion of the state and possibly, through the creation of smaller states, increase their dependence on the centre.

Conclusion: From Integration to Cautious Accommodation?

In this chapter, I have situated India within the comparative literature on governing divided societies and explained its trajectory on an integrationist–accommodationist continuum since independence. I showed how the vibrancy of multilevel party competition and the long-term consequence of implanting universal suffrage onto a highly unequal society pushed India from a relatively integrationist blueprint after Partition into a more accommodative direction. This accommodative shift occurred on at least two of three dimensions: the politics of representation and the dynamics of centre-state relations. Insofar as the linguistic plurality of India has become firmly entrenched (and underpinned the implementation of linguistic federalism during much of the 1950s and 1960s), some accommodation was also achieved on the third dimension: the constitutional and legal acceptance of India as a linguistically composite state.

By heading into a more accommodationist direction, India went against the trend of nearby Pakistan and Sri Lanka in which Punjabi–Muhajir and Sinhalese control strategies were gradually established. Yet, as I have shown, India's accommodative stance is incomplete. India certainly does not come near the 'power-sharing' or 'territorial pluralist' institutions which scholars of governing divided societies have identified as the institutional 'ideal types' of accommodation even though it has moved somewhat closer to these types since independence. Indeed, this chapter demonstrated that reservation policies, while extended to OBCs, do not normally apply to India's most important religious minority. Similarly, centre-relations remain open to strong central oversight and the absence of strong territorial shared rule mechanisms at the centre make the influence of the states more dependent on party political circumstances (in particular the participation of regional parties in central coalition governments). In Kashmir and the North-East, self-rule operates under the shadow of a strong military presence and central political oversight. Finally, proposals to increase minority accommodationist policies are challenged by appeals to reconfigure India as a Hindu *Rashtra*. With its absolute parliamentary majority at the centre, the BJP is in a position to negotiate some of its proposed 'integrative' or even 'assimiliationst' reforms in the years to come.

This leads me to two final questions: one normative, the other prospective. The normative question asks if more accommodationist policies are desirable; the prospective question assesses the sustainability of the present status quo. I would argue that the shift towards accommodation has provided a better fit for the highly segmented and stratified nature of Indian society than the integrative blueprint at independence. At the same time, Indian policy makers will continue to assess the implications of decentralised federalism or the granting of ethnically based group rights against their capacity to speak or act for India as a whole. In my view, this is defensible to the extent that growing territorial and inter-personal inequalities (both of which have increased since the 1990s) without some commitment to inter-territorial or inter-personal solidarity could jeopardise the stability of the Indian *state*-nation (Stepan et al. 2011) just as much as community blind policies might have done shortly after independence. For instance, group-based policies targeting the SC, ST and OBC do not provide a panacea for the betterment of the subaltern, especially since they do not extend to the non-state sector. In India, there is also widespread and justified dissatisfaction with the design and implementation of some of these schemes. Yet, notwithstanding these shortcomings, I would argue that they are an insufficient, yet necessary step towards substantive representation. Furthermore, accommodative and integrative policies do not necessarily stand in a zero-sum relationship; for instance, group-specific and general welfare schemes can complement each other.

The prospective question addresses the fragile consensus underpinning the current levels of accommodation. By seeking to unite the Indian Hindus behind a 'meta-narrative' of 'development' (more so than Hindu nationalism), the BJP will attempt to 're-centre' the Indian nation. Although the BJP is not likely to abolish the reservation policies benefiting the OBCs and Dalits, the party may put less emphasis on pro-poor welfare schemes targeting these groups, emphasising 'development' over 'inclusive growth'. By accelerating the process of (domestic) liberalisation, the party could entrench the dominance of upper castes in the private sector. Above all, the BJP would seek to put in place more assimilationist policies with regard to the—at present—at best culturally, but neither politically nor economically accommodated Muslim minority. Under the guise of improving efficiency, it could also promote the further division of some of India's states and in the process strengthen its grip on state politics. This said, the dominance (at least in vote share) of secular parties across India and the institutional and constitutional checks and balances (from federalism, to the Supreme Court and at present non-BJP controlled federal second chamber) in a politically still decentralised India will constrain the BJP's ability to implement such policies to the full. Insofar as accommodative policies especially in relation to religious but more widely also ethnic minorities may have passed their peak when said minorities remain very much second class citizens within their own state, this could be a significant step backwards.

Notes

1. Other reasons that are not explored in this chapter are: (1) the gradual introduction of democratic practices during the colonial regime, most notably at the provincial and local levels (2) the presence of a strong argumentative tradition which Amartya Sen (2005) perceives as part of India's cultural and religious (especially Hindu) heritage; (3) the widespread legitimacy of a national independence movement under the form of the Congress Party which in turn helped to secure the primacy of politics in relation to the military and civil service (unlike in neighbouring Pakistan but see Jayal 1995 for a more critical note on India) (4) the mitigating effect of cross-cutting instead of coincident social cleavages within Indian society.
2. Multicultural policies related to immigrant communities or refugees are often portrayed as a fourth dimension but I exclude them from the analysis here as this chapter focuses on cleavages that apply to minority groups of an indigenous nature. India counts at least 6 million refugees or immigrants (the real number is likely much higher than this official estimate) who range from political refugees (primarily from Tibet, Sri Lanka or

Myanmar) to economic refugees (primarily from Bangladesh and Nepal). Arguably, one could anticipate a link between the accommodation of domestic minority groups and the accommodation of immigrants, refugees as well as non-resident Indians (for a discussion of the link between both, see Adeney and Lall (2005) and Gopal Jayal (2013)).

3. Furthermore, in determining the 'eligibility' to SC and ST status and the share to which they can lay claim, policy-makers have continued to rely on the census of 1931; until 2011, the most recent for which caste was recorded (Glazier 2007: 152). One of the reasons for this may have been the expectation that reservations for SC would no longer be required after the first ten years of independence as it was assumed that SC and ST would have successfully integrated by then. Liberal clauses in the constitution, proclaiming non-discrimination on the basis of caste (but also religion, sex, place of birth or race) or equality of opportunity were thought to generate lower caste integration.

4. Although not contributing to more accommodative policies per se, the process of economic liberalization which set in during the 1980s, but deepened substantially since 1991 increased the autonomy—but potentially also vulnerability—of state chief ministers and governments in economic management. Central deregulation, the reduced visibility of central economic planning through the retrenchment of federal grants and the role of states and state-agencies in attracting Foreign Direct Investment provide evidence of this. At the same time, economic liberalization is said to have increased inter-state inequalities, in part because the pattern of (pre-) and post-independence industrialization did not create an equal level playing field.

5. The Hindu nationalist stance was made apparent by its dealings with Sikh dominated Punjab in the 1970s and 1980s or by the 1983 state electoral campaign in Jammu and Kashmir in which Congress deployed an anti-Muslim electoral rhetoric to court the Hindu vote in Jammu (as a possible 'test-strategy' for the anticipated national elections in 1984; Bose 2013). Furthermore, by turning a blind eye to the Ram Mandir agitation of the Sangh Parivar, Congress could be held *indirectly* responsible for the destruction of the Babri Masjid in December 1992 (Hasan, 2012; The Congress central government did not impose President's Rule against the BJP-led ruled government of Uttar Pradesh). In contrast, satisfying its Muslim vote bank, Congress enacted legislation to overrule the Supreme Court's *Shah Bano* judgment; supporting the (male and conservative) Muslim Personal Board in its view that Muslim women divorcees should not be entitled to financial compensation. The judgement caused wide resentment amongst leading Muslim female activists and the Hindu majority alike (see Gopal Jayal 2006: 51–52; Rudolph and Rudolph 2008: 303).

References

ADB (Asian Development Bank). 2009. *Key Indicators for Asia and the Pacific 2009, 40th Edition*. Manilla: Asian Development Bank. http://www.adb.org/Documents/Books/Key_Indicators/2009/pdf/Key-Indicators-2009.pdf (accessed 28 July 2015).

Adeney, Katharine. 2002. 'Constitutional Centring: Nation Formation and Consociational Federalism in India and Pakistan', *Commonwealth and Comparative Politics* 40(3): 8–33.

———. 2007. *Federalism and Ethnic Conflict Regulation in India and Pakistan*. Basingstoke: Palgrave-Macmillan.

Adeney, K. and Lall, M. 2005. 'Institutional Attempts to Build a National Identity in India: Internal and Extneral Dimensions', *India Review* 4(3–4): 258–286.

Akhzar, A. 2014. 'Minister's Kashmir Autonomy Comment Sparks Criticism—Leaders in Jammu and Kashmir Sharply Divided over Union Minister's Comments about Eliminating the State's Special Status', *Khabar South Asia*. http://khabarsouthasia.com/en_GB/articles/apwi/articles/features/2014/07/09/feature-01 (accessed 18 August 2014).

Alesina, Alberto, Easterley, William, Kurlat, Sergio and Wacziarg, Romain. 2003. 'Fractionalization', *Journal of Economic Growth* 8: 155–194.

Austin, G. 1966. *The Indian Constitution: Cornerstone of a Nation*. New Delhi: Oxford University Press.

Bajpai, R. 2012. *Debating Difference: Group Rights and Liberal Democracy in India*. New Delhi: Oxford University Press.

Barry, B. 2001. *Culture and Equality. An Egalitarian Critique of Multiculturalism*. Cambridge: Polity.

Bharatiya Janata Party. 2014. '"Ek Bharat, Shrestha Bharat" Election Manifesto 2014'. http://bjpelectionmanifesto.com/pdf/manifesto2014.pdf (accessed 18 August 2014).

Bhargava, R. 2008. 'Outline of a Political Theory of the Indian Constitution', in R. Bhargava (ed.), *Politics and Ethics of the Indian Constitution* (pp. 1–42). New Delhi: Oxford University Press.

Bhattacharyya, H. 2010. *Federalism in Asia*. London: Routledge.

Bose, S. 2013. *Transforming India: Challenges to the World's Largest Democracy*. Cambridge, MA: Harvard University Press.

Brass, Paul R. 1973. *Language, Religion and Politics in North India*. Cambridge: Cambridge University Press.

———. 1994. *The Politics of India since Independence*, 2nd ed. Cambridge: Cambridge University Press.

———. 2003. *The Production of Hindu–Muslim Violence in Contemporary India*. Delhi: Oxford University Press.

Chandhoke Neera. 2007. 'Negotiating Linguistic Diversity: A Comparative Study of India and the United States', in K. Shankar Bajpai (ed.), *Democracy and Diversity: India and the American Experience* (pp. 107–143). New Delhi: Oxford University Press.

Chandra, K. 2012. 'Introduction', in K. Chandra (ed.), *Constructivist Theories of Ethnic Politics* (pp. 1–50). Oxford: Oxford University Press.

Choudry, Sujit (ed.). 2008. *Constitutional Design for Divided Societies: Integration or Accommodation?* (pp. 41–90). Oxford: Oxford University Press.

Collier, P. 2008. *The Bottom Billion: Why the Poorest Countries are Falling and What Can be Done about It*. Oxford: Oxford University Press.

Corbridge, S., Harris, J. and Jeffery, C. (eds). 2013. *India Today. Economics, Politics and Society*. Cambridge: Polity Press.

Drèze J. and Sen, A. 2013. *An Uncertain Glory: India and Its Contradictions*. London: Penguin Books.

Erk, J. and Anderson, L. 2009. 'The Paradox of Federalism. Does Self-rule Accommodate or Exacerbate Ethnic Divisions?' *Regional and Federal Studies* 19(2): 191–202.

Fearon, James. D. 2003. 'Ethnic and Cultural Diversity by Country', *Journal of Economic Growth* 8: 195–222.

Gahlot, M. 2014. 'India PM Modi Demands Hindi, not English for Social Media', NBC news. http://www.nbcnews.com/news/asian-america/india-pm-modi-demands-hindi-not-english-social-media-n172421 (accessed 18 August 2014).

Galanter, M. 1968. 'Changing Legal Conceptions of Caste', in M.B. Singer and B.S. Cohn (eds), *Structure and Change in Indian Society* (pp. 299–338). London: Transaction Books. http://marcgalanter.net/Documents/papers/scannedpdf/changinglegalconceptionsofcaste.pdf (accessed 28 August 2015).

Gorringe, H. 2005. *Untouchable Citizens. Dalit Movements and Democratiziation in India* (pp. 119–128). New Delhi: SAGE.

———. 2013. 'Dalit Politics: Untouchability, Identity and Assertion', in A. Kohli and P. Singh (eds), *Routledge Handbook of Indian Politics* (pp. 119–128). New York: Routledge.

Hansen, T.B. 1997. *The Saffron Wave: Democracy and Hindu Nationalism in Modern India*. Princeton: Princeton University Press.

Hasan, Zoya. 2009. *Congress after Indira. Policy, Power, Political Change (1984–2009)*. New Delhi: Oxford University Press.

Heath, Anthony, Glouharova, Siana and Heath, Oliver. 2008. 'India: Two Party Contests within a Multiparty System', in Gallagher Michael and Paul Mitchell (eds), *The Politics of Electoral Systems*, (pp. 137–156). Oxford: Oxford University Press.

Heyer, J. and Jayal, N. Gopal. 2009. 'The Challenge of Positive Discrimination in India', *CRISE (Centre for Research on Inequality, Human Security and Ethnicity) Working Paper* No. 55, University of Oxford, Queen Elizabeth House.

Jaffrelot, Christophe. 2003. *India's Silent Revolution: The Rise of Lower Castes in North India*. London: Hurst.

———. 2004. 'Composite Culture is not Multiculturalism: A Study of the Indian Constituent Assembly Debates', in Ashutosh Varshney, *India and the Politics of Developing Countries. Essays in Memory of Myron Weiner* (pp. 126–149). New Delhi: SAGE.

———. 2015. *The Pakistan Paradox: Instability and Resilience*. London: Hurst.

Jayal, N. Gopal. 2006. *Representing India: Ethnic Diversity and the Governance of Public Institutions*. Basingstoke: Palgrave-Macmillan.

———. 2009. *Citizenship and its Discontents. An Indian History*. Cambridge: MA, Harvard University Press.

Jodhka, S.S. 2012. *Caste: Oxford India Short Introductions*. Delhi: Oxford University Press.

Keating, Michael. 2004. *Plurinational Democracy: Stateless Nations in a Post-Sovereignty Era*. Oxford: Oxford University Press.

Kothari, Rajni. 1964. 'The Congress System in India', *South Asian Survey* 4(12): 1161–1173.

Khilnani, S. 1997. *The Idea of India*. London: Penguin Books.

Kymlicka, W. 1995. *Multicultural Citizenship. A Liberal Theory of Minority Rights*. Oxford: Oxford University Press.

Lerner, H. 2012. *Making Constitutions in Deeply Divided Societies*. Cambridge: Cambridge University Press.

Lijphart, Arend. 1999. *Patterns of Democracy. Government Forms and Performance in Thirty-Six Countries*. New Haven: Yale University Press.

———. 2007. 'Democratic Institutions and Ethnic/Religious Pluralism: Can India and the United States Learn from Each Other – and from Smaller Democracies', in K. Shankar Bajpai (ed.), *Democracy and Diversity: India and the American Experience* (pp. 14–49). New Delhi: Oxford University Press.

Lloyd I, Rudolph and Hoeber Rudolph, Susanne. 2008. 'Living with Difference in India; Legal Pluralism and Legal Universalism in Historical Context', in Rudolph Lloyd I and Susanne Hoeber Rudolph (eds), *Explaining Indian Democracy. A Fifty Year Perspective,*

1956–2006 Volume 1, The Realm of Ideas. Inquiry and Theory (pp. 281–307). New Delhi: Oxford University Press.

Lustick, I. 1979. 'Stability in Deeply Divided Societies. Consociationalism versus Control', World Politics, 3(April): 325–344.

Majeed, Akhtar. 2003. 'The Changing Politics of States' Reorganization', Publius: The Journal of Federalism 33(4): 83–98.

McGarry, John, O'Leary, Brendan and Simeon, Richard. 2008. 'Integration or Accommodation? The Enduring Debate in Conflict Regulation', in Sujit Choudry (ed), Constitutional Design for Divided Societies. Integration or Accommodation? (pp. 41–90). Oxford: Oxford University Press.

Norris, Pippa. 2008. Driving Democracy. Do Power-Sharing Institutions Work? Cambridge: Cambridge University Press.

Ogden, C. 2012. 'A Lasting Legacy: The BJP-led National Democratic Alliance and India's Politics', Journal of Contemporary Asia 42(1): 22–38.

Oldenburg, P. 2010. India, Pakistan and Democracy. Solving the Puzzle of Divergent Paths. London: Routledge.

Pierson, P. 2004. Politics in Time. History, Institutions and Social Analysis. Princeton: Princeton University Press.

Phillips, Anne. 1994. 'Dealing with Difference: A Politics of Ideas or a Politics of Presence?' Constellations 1(1): 74–91.

Roeder, P. 2007. Where Nation-states Come from: Institutional Change in the Age of Nationalism. Princeton: Princeton University Press.

Sáez, Lawrence. 2002. Federalism Without a Centre: The Impact of Political and Economic Reform on India's Federal System. New Delhi: SAGE.

Sathe, S.P. 2008. Judicial Activism in India: Transgressing Borders and Enforcing Limits, 2nd ed. New Delhi: Oxford University Press.

Saxena, Rekha. 2006. Situating Federalism. Mechanisms of Intergovernmental Relations in Canada and India. Delhi: Monahar.

Shah, G., Harsh, M., Sukhadeao, T. and Satish, D. (eds). 2006. Untouchability in Rural India. New Delhi: SAGE.

Singh, Mahendra P. and Douglas V. Verney. 2003. 'Challenges to India's Centralized Parliamentary Federalism', Publius: The Journal of Federalism 33(4): 1–20.

Spieß, C. 2010. One Party Dominance in Changing Societies: The ANC and INC in Comparative Perspective. London: Routledge.

Sridharan, E. 2005. 'The Origins of the Electoral System: Rules, Representation and Power-sharing in India's Democracy', in Hasan Zoya, E. Sridharan and R. Sudarshan (eds), India's Living Constitution. Ideas, Practices, Controversies (pp. 344–369). London: Anthem Press.

Stepan, A., Linz, J.J. and Yadav, Y. (eds). 2011. Crafting State-nations. India and Other Multinational Democracies. Baltimore: The Johns Hopkins University.

Stuligross, David and Varshney, Ashutosh. 2002. 'Ethnic Diversities, Constitutional Designs and Public Policies in India', in Andrew Reynolds (ed.), The Architecture of Democracy. Constitutional Design, Conflict Management and Democracy (pp. 429–458). Oxford: Oxford University Press.

Swenden, W. 2013. 'Territorial Strategies for Managing Plurinational States', in J. Loughlin, J. Kincaid and W. Swenden (eds), Routledge Handbook of Regionalism and Federalism (pp. 61–75). London: Routledge.

Talbot, I. and Singh, G. 2009. *The Partition of India*. Cambridge: Cambridge University Press.
Talbot, I. 2012. *Paksitan: A New History*. London: Hurst.
Tillin, Louise. 2006. 'United in Diversity? Asymmetry in Indian Federalism', *Publius: The Journal of Federalism* 37(1): 45–67.
———. 2013. *Remapping India. New States and Their Political Origins*. London: Hurst.
Tudor, M. 2013. *The Promise of Power. The Origins of Democracy in India and Autocracy in Pakistan*. Cambridge: Cambridge University Press.
Varshney, A. 2013. *Battles Half Won, India's Improbable Democracy*. Gurgaon: Penguin India.
Wilkinson, S. 2000. 'India, Consociational Theory and Ethnic Violence', *Asian Survey*, 40(5): 767–791.
———. 2004. *Votes and Violence: Electoral Competition and Ethnic Riots in India*. Cambridge: Cambridge University Press.
———. 2010. 'Communal and Caste Politics and Conflicts in India', in R. Paul Brass (ed), *Routledge Handbook of South Asian Politics* (pp. 262–274). Abingdon: Routledge.
Yadav, Y. and Palshikar, S. 2009. 'Between Fortuna and Virtu: Explaining the Congress' Ambiguous Victory in 2009', *Economic and Political Weekly* 44(39): 33–46.

Glossary and Abbreviations

ABAVP	Akhil Bharatiya Adivasi Bikash Parishad (All India Committee for Development of Adivasis)
Adivasi	literally 'original dweller', it is used to translate 'indigenous'; in the Indian context, it is treated as equivalent to Scheduled Tribe
AIADMK	the All India Anna Dravida Munnetra Kazhagam, Tamil political party founded in 1972 by M.G. Ramachandran and now led by J. Jayalalitha
Ambedkar, Dr	1891–1956. Known as 'Babasaheb', he was the leader of India's Dalits. As India's first law minister, he chaired the constitution-drafting committee. Believing that Hinduism could not be reformed, he led his followers into Buddhism in 1956 shortly before his death at a mass ceremony in Nagpur
Bajrang Dal	the (male) youth branch of *Vishva Hindu Parishad* ('World Hindu Council'), Hindu nationalist organisation
BC	Backward Classes; see OBC
Birsa Munda	Indian freedom fighter and folk hero who belonged to the Munda tribe. In the late nineteenth century, he spearheaded the Millenarian movement that rose in the tribal belt of the present day Bihar and Jharkhand.
BJP	Bharatiya Janata Party, founded in 1980 as a successor to the Bharatiya Sangh Party; the BJP led coalition governments and provided the PM from 1998 to 2004. The party won an outright majority in the 2014 national elections which saw Narendra Modi become the Prime Minister.
BSP	Bahujan Samaj Party, founded in 1984 by Kanshiram. It is a Dalit-led party seeking to unite Dalits, Adivasis and OBCs

cheri	the Tamil name for the traditional Dalit settlements on the outskirts of a village
Chhetri	the Nepali spelling of *ksatriya*, it refers in particular to the largest of the Parbatiya castes, comprising approximately 13 per cent of the total Nepali population
CID	Crime Investigation Department
CPI (ML)	Communist Party of India (Marxist Leninist)
Dalit	modern, politically correct term for ex-Untouchables, the lowest category in the caste system, outside and below the four *varnas*; literally 'the oppressed' and adopted by politically active members of the Scheduled Castes.
DPI	Dalit Panther Movement (Iyakkam—Tamil Nadu), originated in 1982 as the Tamil branch of the Dalit Panthers of India. Initially it was led by Malaichamy but Thirumavalavan became leader in 1990 and renamed the movement the Liberation Panthers (Viduthalai Ciruthaigal) in 1999. Since entering electoral competition in 1999, they have become known as the Liberation Panther Party (VCK).
Gorkhali	literally 'from Gorkha', hence used for the dominant group in post-1769 Nepal, the Bahun and Chhetri Parbatiyas; also used as an epithet of the state, as seen from a subordinate perspective
gram panchayat	village council (India)
guru puja	Traditionally, this refers to a ceremony which honours one's teachers or spiritual leaders. In current parlance, it also refers to annual ceremonies honouring, and celebration of, past community leaders.
Hindutva	literally 'Hindu-ness', a term coined by V.D. Sarvarkar in 1923; it now refers to the ideology of Hindu nationalism animating the BJP and Sangh Pariwar
IPC	Indian Penal Code
JAM	Jharkhandi Adhikar Mancha (Platform for the Rights of Jharkhandis)
Janajati	originally Hindi neologism coined to translate 'tribe' in the 1930s, it was adopted in Nepali at the very end of the 1980s and it gained currency after 1990 to refer

	to tribal groups in Nepal; often translated as 'ethnic group' in English, the preferred translation of NEFIN is 'nationality'
jati	caste, literally 'birth' or genus.
jungli	uncultured, literally wild
MCMT	Mohalla Committee Movement Trust
MLA	Member of Legislative Assembly
MNS	Maharashtra Navnirman Sena, founded in 2006, is a nativist, anti-immigrant offshoot of the Shiv Sena
mohalla	ward, neighbourhood
NEFIN	Nepal Federation of Indigenous Nationalities (Nepal Janajati Adivasi Mahasangh), a federal body with one representative body for each Janajati group in Nepal (see nefin.org.np) (previously known as NEFEN, the Nepal Federation of Nationalities, the term 'indigenous' was added in 2003)
NGO	Non-governmental Organisation
OBC	Other Backward Class (an Indian official term for those low castes who are neither Dalits nor Tribals but suffer from educational and economic backwardness). In different contexts, there are also references to BCs (Backward Classes) and MBCs (Most Backward Classes)
panchayati raj	literally 'rule by panchayats', it is the term used for the Indian local government with elected bodies (panchayats) at the levels of village (*gram*), block (*kshetra*) and district (*zilla*)
PMK	Paatali Makkal Katchi or 'Toiler's Party', supported predominantly by Vanniyars in Tamil Nadu. Founded by S. Ramdoss in July 1989 as the political organisation of the Vanniyar Union
RSS	Rashtriya Swayamsevak Sangh or National Volunteers Association, founded in 1925 by K.B. Hedgewar as a national movement of Hindus for social welfare; RSS members were involved in the murder of Gandhi and the RSS was banned for a year thereafter
sainik	member of Shiv Sena
sangh	association

Sangh Pariwar	association of Hindu nationalist organisations, including the RSS, BJP, VHP, Bajrang Dal, and so on
Scheduled Castes	(SC) official Indian term for those formerly belonging to untouchable castes placed 'on the schedule' for receipt of 'reservations', that is, positive discrimination
Scheduled Tribes	(ST) official Indian bureaucratic term for those tribal groups placed on the 'schedule' for receipt of 'reservations', that is, positive discrimination
Shiv Sena	literally 'the army of Shiva (that is, Shivaji)': a political party founded by Bal Thackeray in 1966, it has ruled Mumbai for the last 20 years on a Mumbai for Maharashtrians platform; it is often in alliance with the BJP
Sidhu-Kanu	Sidhu Murmu and Kanhu Murmu were Santhal leaders. They led the Santhal rebellion against the British soldiers and the corrupt upper caste landlords.
SP	Samajwadi Party, founded in 1992. Based in Uttar Pradesh and seen as the party of Yadavs.
Tarai (Terai)	strip of Gangetic plains territory belonging to Nepal and bordering India, now home to half the Nepalese population
Tilka Majhi	First Adivasi leader to take up arms against the British. He organised the Adivasis to form a liberation group to fight against resource grabbing and exploitation.
VHP	Vishwa Hindu Parishad or World Hindu Council, founded in 1964, with the involvement of the RSS; ostensibly non-political its aim is 'to promote Hindu values'; it pressurises the BJP and acts in concert with the RSS (for example, over the Ramjanam Bhumi/Ayodhya mosque issue) and campaigns for the 'reconversion' of Muslims and Christians
ward panch	neighbourhood representative on town council (India)

About the Editors and Contributors

Editors

Hugo Gorringe is a Senior Lecturer in Sociology at The University of Edinburgh. His research in India focuses on the sociopolitical mobilisation of Dalits and their struggle to achieve equality and deepen Indian democracy. He is the author of *Untouchable Citizens* (SAGE 2005) and multiple articles on caste, Dalit politics and violence.

Roger Jeffery is a Professor of Sociology of South Asia at The University of Edinburgh. His research has covered public health policy, social demography and pharmaceuticals regulation. He is the University's Dean International (India), Director of the India Institute and President of the European Association of South Asian Studies. He has recently edited (with Craig Jeffrey and Jens Lerche) *Development Failure and Identity Politics in Uttar Pradesh* (SAGE 2014) and (with Oliver Heath) *Change and Diversity: Economics, Politics and Society in Contemporary India* (OUP 2010). He is the author and co-author of numerous books including most recently *Education, Masculinities and Unemployment in North India* (with Craig Jeffrey and Patricia Jeffery, Social Science Press 2010).

Suryakant Waghmore is Associate Professor and Chairperson at the Centre for Social Justice and Governance, TISS, Mumbai. He is author of *Civility Against Caste* (SAGE 2013). His current research focuses on changing forms of caste etiquette in modern India.

Contributors

Supurna Banerjee completed her PhD in Sociology from The University of Edinburgh. She is presently working as Assistant Professor in the Institute of Development Studies, Kolkata.

Qudsiya Contractor is an Assistant Professor at the Centre for Study of Social Exclusion and Inclusive Policies, TISS, Mumbai. She completed her PhD in 2014 as a Max Planck Institute Doctoral Fellow at the School of Development Studies, TISS. She has previously worked in the development sector on issues of displacement, human rights and urbanisation. Her research interests include the anthropology of cities and development, social identities and communal politics. Her work has been published in peer-reviewed journals and a volume edited by Laurent Gayer and Christophe Jaffrelot (2012) titled 'Muslims in Indian Cities—Trajectories of Marginalisation' published by Hurst & Co.

Karthikeyan Damodraran is a doctoral candidate at The University of Edinburgh. His research focuses on caste processions and commemorations in Tamil Nadu. He previously worked as a special correspondent for *The Hindu* newspaper. He has written numerous newspaper articles and has co-authored work for *Economic and Political Weekly*.

Martin Fuchs is an anthropologist and sociologist. He currently holds the Professorship for Indian Religious History at the Max Weber Center for Advanced Cultural and Social Studies in Erfurt. His areas of interest include social and cultural theory, social and religious movements, Dalit studies, urban anthropology and religious individualisation.

Valerian Rodrigues is a Professor at the Centre for Political Studies, School of Social Sciences, Jawaharlal Nehru University, Delhi. He works on issues in political philosophy and political institutions in India and has researched political ideas in Modern India, and the issues and concerns of the marginalised. He is the author of numerous books including *B.R. Ambedkar: Essential Writings* (OUP 2002), articles and reports. He has recently edited (with B.L. Shankar) *The Indian Parliament: A Democracy at Work* (OUP 2011).

Abdul Shaban is Professor (Centre for Public Policy, Habitat and Human Development, School of Development Studies) and Deputy Director, TISS, Mumbai. He is also currently Deputy Director TISS, Tuljapur campus. He is the author of *Mumbai: Political Economy of Crime and Space* (Orient Blackswan 2010) and the editor of *Lives of Muslims in India: Politics, Exclusion and Violence* (Routledge 2012) and *Muslims in Urban India: Development and Exclusion* (Concept Publishing 2013). He has published several papers on the development and deprivation in India, and the production of ethnic spaces in cities. He was a member of the Study Group appointed by the Government of Maharashtra to assess the 'Social, Economic and Educational Status of Muslims in Maharashtra' (2012–2013), and the member of the 'Post-Sachar Evaluation Committee' appointed by the Ministry of Minority Affairs, Government of India, to assess the implementation of the programmes for development of Muslims and other religious minorities. He has been Visiting Professor at Erasmus School of History, Culture and Communication, Erasmus University, The Netherlands; Department of Geography, University of Paris, Paris, France; Department of Environmental Studies, Masaryk University, Brno, Czech Republic; International Development Studies, Palacky University, Olomouc, Czech Republic. He was visiting fellow at London School of Economic and Political Science (LSE) in 2008–2009 (at Department of Geography and Environment), and 2011–2012 (at Cities Programme).

Jeevan Sharma is a Lecturer in South Asia and Development at The University of Edinburgh. He worked as a Senior Researcher and Assistant Professor at Feinstein International Center at Tufts University (Boston) where he conducted extensive fieldwork on the Maoist insurgency, labour migration and social change in western Nepal, and taught graduate courses at Fletcher School of Law and Diplomacy and Friedman School of Nutrition Science and Policy. He is currently a visiting professor of anthropology at Nepal School of Social Sciences and Humanities (Kathmandu). He is the author of articles on gender, migration and development and of several key research reports on similar themes.

Wilfried Swenden is a Senior Lecturer in Politics at The University of Edinburgh with a background in comparative federal and regional studies and comparative democracy in divided societies. He has a particular interest in India, more in particular in the dynamics of centre–state relations and territorial party politics. He coordinates a Leverhulme International Network on Continuity and Change in Indian Federalism with three Indian and three UK partners and since August 2015 has been a Co-Director of the Centre for South Asian Studies at The University of Edinburgh.

Index

2001 census, urban and rural SC population proportion Tamil Nadu and Uttar Pradesh for, 109t
acceptable allies, 137
caste arithmetic suggestion, 139–140
electoral terms in, 138
just a Dalit party, 139
PMK and VCK, differences between, 140–141
Third Front, 139
VCK supporters, 138
accommodating Dalits
accommodative politics and, 157
Ambedkar's politics, outcomes of, 157
anti-caste sentiment in, imposition of, 157–158
Dalit exclusion, persistence of, 158
state policies, aim of, 157
Adivasi Janajati movement
formal politics, 99
CPN-UML, 100
Federal Socialist Party (FSP), 100
Social Democratic Pluri-national Party (SDP), 101
ILO, role of, 102
institutional politics, 102
institutionalisation of, 96–99
Gender and Social Exclusion Assessment (GSEA), 95
Janajati Empowerment Project (JEP), 95
Nepal's Maoist insurgency (1996–2005), 94
Nepal's, as pet country, 95
NFDIN Act, 93
institutionalisation, process of, 88
issues emerged, 102
leaders, decision of, 89
Nepal's political interregnum
exclusionary state, 89
inclusive politics of, 88
kot parba, 90
Rana period, 90–91
rise of, 87
politics of, 102–103
rise of, 91–93
United Nations (UN), role of, 102
anti-caste humour, caste in
caste name
humour around, 172–174
three forms of, 171–172

caste and space, 185
caste-based restrictions, 186
caste-based social relations, 187
public space, nature of, 187
Tamil Nadu, 186
tangibility of caste, 186–187
caste slang to disparagement
anti-Dalit humour lacks, 160
anti-Dalit sentiment, 161
hostile humour against Dalits, 162
mainstream humour, 158–159
Marathas, 160
privileged castes, 163
citizenship
meaning of, 1
Muslims in India, 2
notions of, 2
Communist Party of Nepal [Unified Marxist-Leninist] (CPN-UML), 100

Dalit politics
   humour and hopeful rationality in, 174–175
   Tamil Nadu, in
      allies, acceptance of, 137–141
      cost of connections, 145–148
      Frontline, 131
      institutionalising contentious politics, 133–136
      institutionalising rebellion, 136–137
      insurgency, 131
      optimistic accounts of, 132
      rebels in power, 141–145
      rise of, 131–132
      Viduthalai Chiruthaigal Katchi (VCK-Liberation Panther Party), 131
Dalit urban poor in Dharavi
   institutionalising informal socialites, 229
      competitors, 234–235
      discussion about, 231
      economic sphere in, 234
      institutionalisation, field-wise scan of, 235, 239
      Kunchikorve, 233–234
      large changes, 233
      marginalised actors, 230
      mobilisation on larger scales, 243–244
      NGOs, 232
      provision for industrial activities, lack of, 237
      rural background of, 232–233
      slum rehabilitation and slum development, 236
      social and political actors, 232
      social issues, orientation to, 243
      social movements, 232
      societal division, 230
      Society for Promotion of Area Resource Centres (SPARC), 238–239
      success model of Dharavi, 241–242

food and caste
   Athawale's comments, 170
   caste ideology and hierarchy, 168
   cow purity, 169
   cow slaughter, regulations on, 169
   Madhukar's observations, 170
fragile peace and local negotiations
   non-violence, for, 217–222

guru puja
   caste performance, 194–197
      distribution of sensible, 194–195
      occupation of public space, 194
      rituals function, 195
   transformation of
      act of replication, 193
      Immanuel Devendra, 193–194

humour and hopeful rationality in Dalit politics
   challenging normalised exclusion, 153–156
   critical voices, 155
   Ganesha's head-replacement surgery, 154
   robust theory of humour, 153–154
   vernacular modernity, 155–156

identity
   communal riots in India 1900–2013, 12f
   exclusion from development and, 8–10
   Hindu-Muslim riots in India
      1900–1946, 13f
      1900–1946, causalities in, 15f
      1900–1946, persons injured and killed, 18t
      1947–2013, 14f
      1947–2013, causalities in, 16f
      1947–2013, persons injured and killed, 19t
   minoritisation and
      intensification and sharpening of divisions, 6–7
      Muslims, 7
      religious schism, 8
      stereotyping and communal violence, 10–19
      ten communally most violent cities in India, 17t

Index

ten communally most violent cities in India, 17t
Immanuel Sekaran Guru Puja, 190
  Gooptu's (2001) analysis, 192
  Liberation Tigers of Tamil Eelam (LTTE), 191
  political mobilisation for equality, 193
  potential for violence, 192
incarceration of Muslims, 24–25
India and management of ethnic diversity
  India's democracy, success of
    reasons for, 245–246
  insights from Dalit electoral data
    institutionalising marginal actors
      adverse incorporation, 106
      Dalit revolution, 106–108
      disadvantaged groups of, 105
      reserved constituencies and, 105
      Tamil Nadu and Uttar Pradesh in, 104–110
      voting, 104
      voting patterns, 108–109
  institutionalising contentious politics
    academic commentator, 148
    corollary process, 134
    definition of, 133
    electoral contestation, 136
    insurgency, 148
    Jordan and Maloney argument on, 134
    Meyer and Tarrow argument on, 133
    non-Dravidian challengers, emergence of, 135
    protest cycle, 133
    Racine notes, 135
    VCK, 148
  institutionalising informal socialities (socialites)
    Dalit urban poor in Dharavi, 229
      competitors, 234–235
      discussion about, 231
      economic sphere in, 234
      institutionalisation, field-wise scan of, 235, 239
      Kunchikorve, 233–234
      large changes, 233
      marginalised actors, 230
      mobilisation on larger scales, 243–244
      NGOs, 232
      provision for industrial activities, lack of, 237
      rural background of, 232–233
      slum rehabilitation and slum development, 236
      social and political actors, 232
      social issues, orientation to, 243
      social movements, 232
      societal division, 230
      Society for Promotion of Area Resource Centres (SPARC), 238–239
      success model of Dharavi, 241–242
  institutionalising marginalities
    introduction, 63–64
    methodology
      aims of social movements, 68–69
      Aminzade's claims, 72–73
      co-option process, 69
      Coy and Hedeen argument, 74
      Gorringe's opinion, 71–72
      government announcement, 74–75
      identity of, 82
      language and identity, 65–68
      Nabhitha's opinion, 70–71
      process of, 83
  institutionalising rebellion
    first-past-the-post electoral system, 136
    neutralisation, 137
    radical mobilisation phase, 136
    VCK activists and leaders, 137

language movement, 81–82
  trajectory of, 83

managing ethnic diversity
  accommodation of
    accommodative approach, 248
    caste identity, 247
    control strategy, 247
    derives from, 247
    ethnic structure, 247
    first dimension, 248–249
    legislative quotas, 248
    second dimension, 249
    strategies, 247–248
    third dimension, 249–250

accommodation, limits to
  empirical grounds for, 264–270
  Hindu Nationalism and threat to, 270–273
  integration to cautious accommodation, 273–275
  normative critique, 263–264
accommodative shift towards, 257–260
  incidence and frequency of the President's Rule (1950–2012), 259t
  comparative perspective, situating India in, 260–262
  India's trajectory across time
    accommodationist path, 254–256
    independence, integrationist turn at, 250–254
modern democratic
  nations, 1
  quintessential element of, 1
mohalla committees in contemporary Mumbai, 201–204
Mumbai's mohalla committees
  genesis, 207–213
  institutionalising peace, 222–225
  present form, 214–217

National Foundation for Development of Indigenous Nationalities Act (NFDIN), 93
Nepal's political interregnum
  Adivasi Janajati movement, 88
  first Constituent Assembly (CA), 89
  parliamentary democracy in 1990, 88
  social movement, 87
NGO formation
  JAM, 82
  margins, agency at, 75–81
  social movements development, 75–76

percentage share of Muslims in jail, 26–27
performing power and protest
  conflicts, 184
  Freitag argument, 184
  marches/processions and parades, 182
  Pandian view, 185
  political element in, 181–182
  processions, role of, 183
  public performances, 183
  T. Davis, role of, 182–183
  visual spectacles/public performances, 181
political humour in Dalit movements
  caste ideology of hierarchy, 164
  humour, role of, 164
  post-constitution, 163–164
political power and democratic enablement
  assumptions and prior claims
    axis of power, caste as, 33–36
    Depressed Classes (DCs), 38
    Praja Mitra Mandali, 36
    regional context of Karnataka, caste relations in, 36–40
  lower caste mobilisation, 31–32
  Urs intervention, 40
    assembly elections 1978 and 1983, performance of social groups in, 42t
    backward castes, reservation to, 44–47
    caste/communities, representation of, 52f
    caste/community background of TDB presidents, 43t
    categories of enumeration, shift in, 47–51
    land reforms, 53–55
    Mysore Legislative Assembly 1952–1972, social composition of, 41t
    policy on backwardness, impact of, 51–53
    political power, shift in, 41–44
Praja Mitra Mandali, 36
predicament of Muslims
  brands of nationalism, 4
  centralised planning, failure of, 5
  condition of Muslims, 6
  definition of, 4
  ethno-nationalist discourses, 3–4, 5
  historical legacies and tensions, 4
public processions
  caste status and power, 178–180
  guru pujas as, 178

Index **293**

rebels in power
  Dhanapal, 144–145
  emergent challengers, 141
  intervention, 142–143
  Madurai District secretary, 144
  marathamizhar.blog.com, 142
  police firing, 141–142
  political institutions, 142
  Tamil politics, 144
    informal and mediated nature, 145

space, place and power
  concepts of, 180
  dialectical relationship, notion of, 181
  Lefebvre definition of, 180
  perspectives on, 180
success model of Dharavi, 241–242

Tamil Nadu
  Lok Sabha and Legislative Assembly elections
    Dalit voting proportions by party/alliance 2001 to 2011, 114t
    voting patterns, 2001–2012, changes in, 113–114
    Dalit voting preferences, 114
temples, gods and religion
  cultural performances, 165
  Dalit movements, 166
  Dalit politics, 164–165
  Manisha, an activist in MHA, 167–168
terrorism and fake encounters
  bomb blasts, 21
  fake encounter cases, registered at National Human Rights Commission (NHRC), 23
  Muslims' citizenship rights, encroachment of, 22
  number of cases, 22–24
  religious fanaticism, rise in, 19
  right-wing Hindu outfits, role of, 20
Thevar Guru puja, 187
  bloody performances, 190
  central strategy of, 189
  competitive denigration, 189
  devotees, throngs of, 189
  political performativity, 188–189

Urs intervention, 40
  backward castes, reservation to, 44–47
  caste/communities
    representation of, 52f
  categories of enumeration, shift in, 47–51
    policy markers, 51
  land reforms, 53–55
  limits and limitations of, 55–58
  Mysore Legislative Assembly 1952–1972, social composition of, 41t
  policy on backwardness, impact of, 51–53
    caste/communities, representation of, 52
  political power, shift in, 41–44
Uttar Pradesh
  Lok Sabha and Vidhan Sabha elections
    Dalit voting proportions by party/alliance 2002 to 2012, 115t
    voting patterns, 2001–2012, changes in Lok Sabha and Vidhan Sabha elections, 115t

violence and fragile peace, between, 204–207
  Hindu-Muslim violence, role in, 204
voting and non-voting, by Dalits
  early assumptions, 110
  National Elections Surveys (NES), 112
  state-level variations in, 112
    ordinary voter, 113
    Yadav's assertion, 113
  uncertainty about, 111
voting patterns, 2001–2012, changes in
  Tamil Nadu, 113–114
    Lok Sabha and Legislative Assembly elections, 114t
  Uttar Pradesh, 114–115
    Lok Sabha and Vidhan Sabha elections, 115t
voting patterns, within SC populations
  features of, 123–124
  institutionalisation of marginalisation, relationships between, 121
  simple conclusions, 122–123
  political institutionalisation, 124
  possible issues, 116

Tamil Nadu
  caste, 116–117, 125t
  education, 118–119
  educational differences, 2001–2011 in, 118t
  gender, 117–118
  gender differences, 2001–2011 in, 117t
  Lok Sabha elections, 2004, post-poll survey, 116–117, 125t
  voting intentions, 2006, pre-poll survey, 126t

Uttar Pradesh
  caste, 119
  education, 120–121
  educational differences, 2002–2012 in, 121t
  gender, 119–120
  gender differences, 2002–2012 in, 120t